Comparative ethnic and race relations

European immigration policy

Comparative ethnic and race relations series

Published for the ESRC Research Unit on Ethnic Relations at the University of Aston in Birmingham
Edited by
Professor John Rex *Director*
Dr Robin Ward *Deputy Director*
Mr Malcolm Cross *Deputy Director*

This series has been formed to publish works of original theory and empirical research on the problems of racially mixed societies. It is based on the work of the ESRC Research Unit for Ethnic Relations at Aston University – the main centre for the study of race relations in Britain.

The first book in the series is a textbook on *Racial and ethnic competition* by Professor Michael Banton – a leading British sociologist of race relations and the former Director of the Unit. Future titles will be on such issues as the forms of contact between majority and minority groups, housing, the problems faced by young people, employment, ethnic identity and ethnicity, and will concentrate on race and employment, race and the inner city, and ethnicity and education.

The books will appeal to an international readership of scholars, students and professionals concerned with racial issues, across a wide range of disciplines (such as sociology, anthropology, social policy, politics, economics, education and law), as well as among professional social administrators, teachers, government officials, health service workers and others.

Other books in this series:

Michael Banton: *Racial and ethnic competition* (issued in hardcover and as a paperback).
Frank Reeves: *British racial discourse*.
Robin Ward and Richard Jenkins (eds.): *Ethnic communities in business*.

European immigration policy

A comparative study

Edited by

TOMAS HAMMAR

Stockholm University, Center for Research in International Migration and Ethnicity

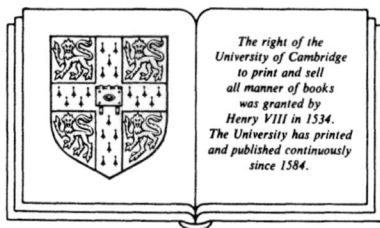

The right of the
University of Cambridge
to print and sell
all manner of books
was granted by
Henry VIII in 1534.
The University has printed
and published continuously
since 1584.

CAMBRIDGE UNIVERSITY PRESS

Cambridge

London   New York   New Rochelle

Melbourne   Sydney

CAMBRIDGE UNIVERSITY PRESS
Cambridge, New York, Melbourne, Madrid, Cape Town, Singapore,
São Paulo, Delhi, Dubai, Tokyo

Cambridge University Press
The Edinburgh Building, Cambridge CB2 8RU, UK

Published in the United States of America by Cambridge University Press, New York

www.cambridge.org
Information on this title: www.cambridge.org/9780521124379

First published 1985
This digitally printed version 2009

A catalogue record for this publication is available from the British Library

Library of Congress Catalogue Card Number: 84–17477

ISBN 978-0-521-26326-9 Hardback
ISBN 978-0-521-12437-9 Paperback

Contents

Contributors

HAN ENTZINGER
Studied sociology with economics in Leiden, Rotterdam and Strasbourg and received his PhD at the University of Leiden, for a thesis on immigration policy.

He worked for the Netherlands Ministry of Cultural Affairs, Recreation and Social Welfare as well as for the International Labor Office in Geneva. Since 1978 he has been the secretary to the Advisory Commission for Research on Immigrant Minorities (ACOM), an independent commission of experts set up by the Netherlands government. The secretariat of ACOM has been attached to the Center for the Study of Social Conflict in Leiden. Most of his publications deal with international migration and its social effects on receiving countries and with various aspects of policy oriented research.

HARTMUT ESSER
Professor of Methods in Social Science at the University of Duisburg, 1978–82. Professor of Empirical Social Science Research at the University of Essen since 1982. Studied sociology and economics in Cologne, PhD in Bochum. His recent publications include works on interview surveys (1975), theory of social science (1977), labor migration and integration of immigrants (1979), and the sociology of migration (1980).

TOMAS HAMMAR
Associate Professor of Political Science at the University of Stockholm and Director of the Center for Research in International Migration and Ethnicity. In 1978– 83 head of the office of the Swedish Commission on Immigration Research. Research interests include: political socialization of immigrants, both adults (resocialization) and young people; political behavior and participation and political rights of aliens (especially studies of voting and of party sympathies of foreign citizens who have been granted voting rights in local elections); national identity, dual nationality and minority rights; immigration policy.

HANS-JOACHIM HOFFMANN-NOWOTNY
Professor of Sociology at the University of Zurich, he received his MA from Cologne University (1966) and his PhD from the University of Zurich (1969). His research interests include studies on migration and problems of immigrant minorities, studies on the sociocultural determinants and consequences of demographic developments, and on systems of social indicators. Professor Hoffmann-Nowotny has also worked intensively on a general sociological theory, the Theory of Structure and Culture. Further fields of interest are philosophy of science, research techniques, sociology of the family and sociology of knowledge. His research has resulted in more than 100 publications, among them several books.

Professor Hoffmann-Nowotny is President of the Swiss Sociological Association, President of the Research Committee on Migration of the International Sociological Association, and a member of the Council of the German Sociological Association.

HERMANN KORTE
Professor of Sociology at the Ruhr University in Bochum since 1974. After his dissertation, "Multifunctional city planning and the political public", he worked at the Center for Interdisciplinary Research at the University of Bielefeld. His main publications include works on urban sociology, demography and migration. He is at present engaged in research on social problems of computer technology. Co-director of the Norbert Elias Foundation.

ZIG LAYTON-HENRY
Lecturer in politics at the University of Warwick, where he teaches courses in Comparative Race Relations, British Government, Political Sociology, and Research Methods. In 1979–80 he was a visiting research fellow at the Research Unit for Ethnic Relations at the University of Aston. His major research interests are in immigration and race relations policies in Britain, the political participation of ethnic minorities in Western Europe, and policymaking in British political parties. He is a regular contributor to *New Community*, the journal of the Commission for Racial Equality. He is author of the *Politics of Race in Britain* (1984), and editor of *Conservative Party Politics* (1980) and *Conservative Politics in Western Europe* (1982).

GILLES VERBUNT
Professor of Sociology. Teaches Social Sciences in Créteil (University of Paris XII), having presented his dissertation on "Integration by autonomy" at the University of Strasbourg. Born in the Netherlands, he moved to France in 1959, was active in social work and organizations dealing with migrant issues, and spent one year studying the problems of the integration of Porto-Ricans (at Fordham University, New York). In 1975 published three volumes on methods for basic training on migrant issues for social workers (*Immigrés en France*). Numerous articles since 1968, and together with Françoise Briot *Immigrés dans la crise* (Paris, 1981).

Preface

This book presents a comparative analysis of immigration policy in six countries: Sweden, the Netherlands, Great Britain, France, Switzerland and the Federal Republic of Germany (hereafter called "Germany"). These six countries, referred to as the "immigration countries" or the "project countries", have all experienced large-scale postwar immigration, and they exemplify a range of different policy responses. They provide examples of rotation or guestworker systems as well as of policies aiming at permanent settlement. They include substantial post-colonial immigration as well as recruitment of foreign labor and consequent family immigration.

This study has been organized around a series of conferences, in which the seven authors have taken part. Six countries are compared, and each author has written one chapter about his own country's immigration policy. In the case of Germany, two authors have collaborated. All the authors met first to discuss the design and content of the study and to agree on a format for each chapter. The second conference was devoted to a discussion of the first drafts of these chapters which, of course, led to discussion of each country's immigration policy as well. The third and fourth conferences concentrated on the comparative analysis presented in the second part of the book.

Although the chapters dealing with each country are based on a common outline and generally address the same questions, each author has also included a discussion of what is unique to his country. Thus, the chapters differ in length and emphasis.

Each country chapter begins with a short discussion of the size and composition of recent immigration and also surveys the terminology used to refer to immigration and immigrants. After this introductory material, there is a section on the "general preconditions" to the immigration in each country. This discussion includes discussion of geographical, demographic, economic, social, and domestic and international political factors which place immigration and immigration policies in their proper context.

The next two sections discuss the two principal ways in which policy towards immigrants is formulated: the actual regulation and control of immigration and policy formulations which influence the condition of immigrants.

The final section in each chapter on the individual countries examines the policymaking process. It attempts to relate immigration policy to the country's political system and also to perceptions of both decision-makers and the general public. This section also discusses the organization and administration of immigration policy.

The second part of the book, chapters 8–12, presents an analysis of the preceding material. Four chapters summarize and compare the most important aspects of the individual country analysis. The common background to immigration of the six countries is discussed in chapter 8. This is followed by chapters about immigration regulation and aliens control, immigrant policy, and the policymaking process. The final and concluding chapter includes both a summary of the previous comparative analysis and a discussion of a number of trends in immigration policy in Western Europe.

The project leading to this book has been financed by the Swedish Ministry of Labor and coordinated by the Swedish Commission on Immigration Research (EIFO) and the Center for Research on International Migration and Ethnicity at the University of Stockholm. The latter is a research organization for applied policy-related studies. The project is part of a major evaluation of the long-term effects of immigration in Sweden. The other two parts are entitled "Immigrants on the Swedish labor market" and "The social situation of second-generation immigrants in Sweden". One purpose of this third part, "Comparative European immigration policy", is to provide documentation on which to assess Swedish immigration policy.

A comparative policy project must both attempt to describe and analyze each country's immigration policy and to compare the different policies. The tendency to judge the immigration policies of other countries from an ethnocentric and, therefore, slanted point of view always exists in a project such as this. Yet, I hope that our extensive project discussions have helped us to raise our level of objectivity.

I would like to express my thanks to the other authors. They have generously given of their time and interest and without this effort this project would of course not have been possible. A great number of people with expertise in this field have made valuable suggestions on our book. Yet, in acknowledging this, each author remains responsible for his chapter.

However, there is one person I would like to thank explicitly. Thomas Curtis has been my editorial assistant throughout this project. His main task has been to achieve a uniformity of style and a correctness of grammar in a book, most of which has been written by authors whose first language is not English. Thomas Curtis has also participated actively in several project discussions and contributed substantially to the structuring of our analysis. He has been a most valuable assistant editor.

Finally, I would like to thank Dr Halina Vigerson for compiling an index, Mr Wojciech Luterek for drawing figures, and Ms Gunilla Pagés, Ms Britha Svensson and Ms Rose-Marie Lind for typing the several versions of this book.

Stockholm, July 1984   TOMAS HAMMAR

1

Introduction

The six immigration countries studied in this book have experienced a
period of large-scale immigration caused mainly by similar factors. None
of these countries had planned or even foreseen an international
migration of the size that actually occurred. Their reaction to this
migration has been strikingly similar and at the same time decisively
different, but in the long run immigration control has become more strict
everywhere and active labor recruitment has been stopped; at the same
time, there have been a number of improvements in the social and cultural
situation of immigrants.

Selecting six countries

The project countries have been chosen partly because of their size and
their large immigrant populations and partly because they offer a high
degree of variation in the regulation of immigration and in immigrant
policy. Germany, France and Britain were included from the outset
because of their sizeable immigrant populations, and Switzerland because
of its high proportion of foreigners. In addition these four countries
provide examples of very different sorts of international migration as well
as different immigration policies. Sweden could not be left out, partly
because the initiative and financing of this study was Swedish, but more
important it deserves a place as the Scandinavian country which has both
admitted the most immigrants and developed first a specific immigration
policy. The Netherlands was included as the sixth country because of its
mixture of post-colonial and Mediterranean labor immigration, and also
because of its traditional emphasis on cultural pluralism and its influence
on current "ethnic minorities" policy.

The selection of countries was also made with the idea that the two
major ways of regulating immigration should be represented: the

1

"guestworker" or rotation system (Germany and Switzerland), and the policy of permanent immigration (Britain and Sweden). The post-colonial immigration that prevails in Britain and has played a major role in France and in the Netherlands is included as well as immigration to countries with no such colonial ties, represented by Sweden, Germany, and Switzerland. We further hoped that our selection would give examples of various types of immigrant policy, based on different welfare ideologies and on the different social and political organizations of the societies represented.

Other immigration countries, of course, could have been included as well, had the project resources not required that the number of selected countries be limited. Norway and Denmark have both admitted immigrants from, among other countries, Turkey and Pakistan, and they offer interesting cases for policy comparison. Yet immigration to these two countries has been relatively small, and if only one Scandinavian country can be included, Sweden is the logical choice. Belgium had a large immigrant population of some 900,000 in 1980. The number of foreign citizens residing in Austria at the same time was estimated to be about 250,000. Although both countries have adopted policies directed towards the temporary employment of foreign workers, they have found that their immigrants tend to stay permanently. They would offer excellent additional studies, but their exclusion does not significantly reduce the breadth of our study.

Since we study changes over several decades in immigration and immigrant policy, we may claim that we cover more than six cases. We are able to present data for each country emanating from different time periods. The comparison of six national cases will improve our knowledge about the preconditions of immigration policy, about the interrelations between regulation of immigration and immigrant policy, and in general about the dynamics of international migration and national policymaking.

Migratory paths

Postwar migration to and within Europe has been characterized as a movement from south to north, although such postwar migration would be better characterized as a movement from the periphery to the center. Migration from Italy reached considerable proportions in the 1950s and was joined during the 1960s by an even larger migration from Spain and Portugal in the southwest and from Yugoslavia, Greece, and later Turkey in the southeast. African migration has gone mainly to France, while the bulk of transoceanic migration from the West Indies, Pakistan, and India has gone to Britain. The Netherlands has had immigration from Indonesia and Latin America as well as from Morocco and Turkey.

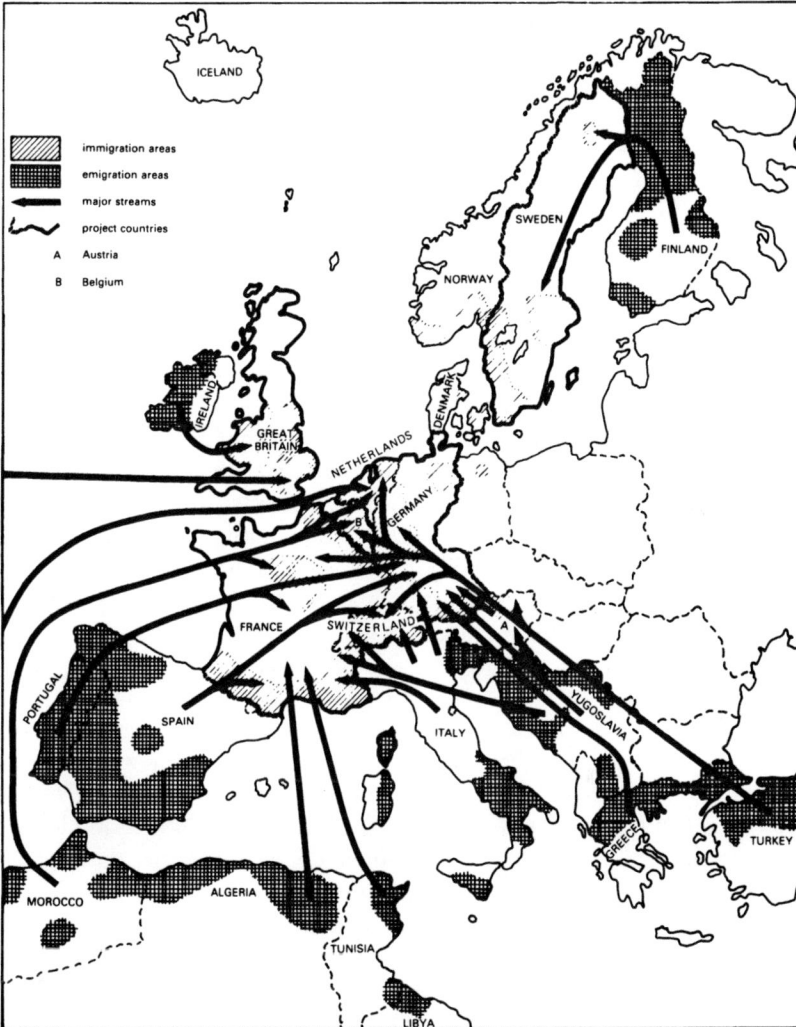

Figure 1.1. Postwar migration to Europe

On the map (Figure 1.1) two additional arrows from Ireland to Britain and from Finland to Sweden reinforce the impression of a movement from periphery to center. Nevertheless, although both arrows show a movement across national boundaries, one is reluctant to say that they represent "international migration" in the same sense as do the other arrows. Irish immigrants have always been allowed to enter Britain and seek employment without restriction. Until at least 1948 they were regarded as full British citizens. Finnish immigrants have a similarly privileged position because of the common Nordic labor market and their country's traditional ties to Sweden. In contrast to the Irish, however, a large number of Finnish immigrants have considerable language difficulties after arrival, and in this respect they resemble the immigrant groups in Sweden that have more distant origins.

Eastern Europe is blank on the map, not because it has no migration or exchanges of labor, but because we lack information about it. The sizeable immigration to West Germany from East Germany and from Poland is discussed in the chapter on Germany, but it would also be interesting to have had examples of migration within Eastern Europe. We probably would have found surprising similarities and enormous differences from the immigration phenomenon in Western Europe. For example, the German Democratic Republic has signed an agreement with Algeria that provides for the transfer of workers with relatively stringent provisions which might be compared with similar agreements in the West. In the countries of Eastern Europe, however, state planning and control of the economy, including labor mobility, predominates, which means that the background for immigration and immigration policy is completely different there. Thus, we leave this part of the map blank, mainly because a thorough study of migration in Eastern Europe requires a separate research project.

More than three fourths of the foreign citizens in the immigration countries live in France, Germany, and Britain. Each of these countries has approximately four million resident immigrants, although the statistics are difficult to compare and in some cases are rather unreliable. Except for Liechtenstein and Luxemburg, Switzerland has the highest percentage of foreign citizens in its population (14.5 percent in 1982). If one compares statistics on the percentage of foreign workers in the project countries, they are about the same as the percentage of foreign residents (see Table 1.1).

These figures do not reveal that immigrants in Western Europe represent a great number of different nationalities, nor do they show how immigrants with the same nationality often settle in the same country and even the same region. Spanish and Portuguese immigrants have gone mainly to France, and to a lesser extent to Switzerland. Yugoslavs and Turks have gone mainly to Germany. Italians are an older immigrant group and have settled primarily in Switzerland and to a lesser extent in Germany and France. Immigrants from North Africa have gone to France and later to the Netherlands as well, although the bulk of immigration to the latter country has come from its former colonies in Asia and Latin America. The same is true for Britain, where almost all postwar

Table 1.1. *Foreign citizens residing in the European project countries in 1983*
(thousands)

	All residents		Labor force	
	Foreign citizens	Percent of total	Foreign citizens	Percent of total
Sweden	405.5	4.9	227.7	5.2
Netherlands*	543.6	3.7	208.4	3.7
France*	4,459.0	7.2	1,436.4	6.3
Great Britain†	1,705.0	3.1	931.0	3.8
West Germany	4,666.9	7.6	2,037.6	9.2
Switzerland‡	925.8	14.5	647.9	21.9

Source: OECD, *Continuous Reporting System on Migration*, SOPEMI 1983, for all
countries except Great Britain.
Notes:
* Data from 1982, and for labor force in France 1981. Based on number of
residence and work permits, and therefore an overestimate of the size of the
foreign population.
† Data from 1981, Labour Force Survey.
‡ Yearly average. Seasonal workers (13,400) and frontier workers (108,400) are
included.

immigration has come from former colonies in the West Indies and from
India and Pakistan. The majority of immigration to Sweden has come
from Finland and from the other Nordic countries, although there has
also been a significant inflow of immigrants from Yugoslavia, Greece, and
Turkey.

There are a number of possible explanations for the distribution of
nationalities among the receiving countries. In many cases bilateral agreements and recruitment practices based on such agreements have led to
concentrations of certain nationalities, for example, Turks and Yugoslavs
in Germany or Moroccans in the Netherlands. Geographical proximity
between sending and receiving countries has often had a similar effect,
particularly when accompanied by a history of close relations. Geographical distance has sometimes reduced the potential for certain kinds of
immigration. Since Britain and Sweden are located somewhat on the
periphery of continental European migration, they have not received as
many immigrants from Southern Europe and Turkey. Ex-colonies and
countries with whom they have historically had close contact have provided much of the immigration to France, the Netherlands, and especially
Britain. Finally, the distribution of immigrants by nationality can also be
explained by "chain migration", which occurs when an initial group of
immigrants settles in a country and then, by encouraging others in their

home country or by providing a model for them, attract others of the same nationality to a particular receiving country.

The sources of migration to Europe have progressively moved to areas farther and farther away. While immigration from Southern Europe, initially quite extensive, has decreased in recent years, immigration from Africa, Asia, and especially the Near East has increased. The change in the sources of immigration has meant that many of the new minority groups are more highly visible, as they differ more in culture and tradition from indigenous European population than did the so-called "traditional" immigrant groups of the past. There are indications that this newer long-distance immigration will continue and increase in the future.

An important change in immigration policy occurred during the period from 1970 to 1974. For economic and other reasons the immigration countries of Western Europe heavily restricted or usually stopped recruiting foreign labor, and since then only refugees and the relatives of resident aliens are admitted. Policymakers have now come to realize, to their surprise, that many foreign workers are likely to remain as permanent residents.

This change in immigration policy, which we will call the "turning point", was the first clear break with the relatively open and unrestricted policies of the previous two decades. The change was declared in Switzerland (1970), Sweden (1972), Germany (1973), and France (1974). Though it was made with the consent of each national government, it was made without open political debate and without any formal, official decisions. It is important to note that this turning point should be thought of as a policy change towards stricter regulation but not necessarily as a "stop" for labor migration.

In Britain and the Netherlands, where most immigrants came from colonies or former colonies and usually held the citizenship of the mother country, the turning point in immigration policy did not occur at a specific time but came gradually. In Britain this process has involved the gradual elimination of the immigration rights of colonial citizens. Though this process began there in 1962 and has not yet ended, one can nevertheless say that the passage of the 1971 Immigration Act was perhaps the most significant legislation in this area. In the Netherlands there was a major reevaluation of immigration policy at the end of the 1970s. The number of new work permits issued fell sharply in 1973, but labor immigration was never formally "stopped". Not until 1980 did the government impose serious restrictions on post-colonial immigration and begin to develop a new immigrant policy.

Immigration to the six European project countries has changed during the past decade in other ways as well. While the number of single, male immigrants has decreased, mainly because of the policy change that occurred at the turning point, the immigration of refugees and the dependants of resident aliens has increased. In other words, the total amount of immigration to the project countries has not decreased substantially as a result of the "stop" in labor recruitment, but has remained constant or in some cases has actually increased. Thus, there is a relationship between the imposition of the "stop" and the change in the composition of immigrant population. This relationship is discussed in more detail in the comparative analysis presented in Part II.

Immigration policy

There are many definitions of immigration policy. They vary even within a single country. Yet when we compare a number of countries, we need a working definition that is relevant to all these countries. Thus, under our scheme, "immigration policy" will consist of two parts which are interrelated, yet distinct: (a) regulation of flows of immigration and control of aliens, and (b) immigrant policy.

Immigration regulation and aliens control

Regulation of immigration is the oldest, the most obvious, and according to some people the only aspect of immigration policy. Immigration regulation refers to the rules and procedures governing the selection and admission of foreign citizens. It also includes such regulations which control foreign citizens (aliens) once they visit or take residence in the receiving country, including control of their employment. Deportation also falls under these regulations. Employers may be allowed to recruit foreign labor on their own, or labor transfer agreements may be entered into by the state and official information and recruitment bureaux be opened abroad. All this, of course, is a part of immigration regulation and must be included along with measures taken to restrict immigration or to stop it completely. The free movements of peoples, such as occur in the common labor markets of the EEC and Nordic areas, are also an aspect of immigration regulation; even though in these two cases policymakers have decided that certain kinds of immigration should *not* be regulated.

In general, all sovereign states reserve the right to determine whether foreign citizens will be permitted to enter their territory and reside there, and in all the project countries this power of the state is found in law or in administrative regulations. Most changes in immigration policy, for example the changes at what we call the "turning point", have been made by changing the application of existing aliens laws and not by changing the laws. Such laws were applied in a liberal way as long as immigration was encouraged, but later, when the goal was to limit the volume of immigration, discourage potential immigrants, and reduce the total number of foreigners in the country, the application of the same aliens laws became more strict. At the same time, however, immigration regulation was abandoned for certain groups of foreigners who were admitted without restrictions. Examples of this are, as already mentioned, the free circulation of labor in the EEC and the Nordic area and the acceptance on a permanent basis of political refugees.

Immigration regulation implies that foreign citizens remain under some kind of aliens control until they become naturalized citizens. The conditions that foreign citizens are subject to during this period of "controlled" residence vary greatly from country to country. Some countries at an early stage guarantee their foreign residents the right to remain permanently. Other countries keep them in a position of legal insecurity and uncertainty for many years. Some countries admit foreign workers for seasonal employment and require them to leave when the season ends, although they are often permitted to return again the following season. Some countries organize so-called "rotation" systems under which foreign workers are allowed to stay in the country only a maximum number of months or years, after which (in theory at least) they must depart to make room for new workers. In this way these countries hope to avoid the establishment of any new, permanent population groups whose needs and demands would be considerably greater than those of temporary "guestworkers".

Even in countries that do not apply seasonal employment or rotation systems, however, it often takes many years before foreign citizens are guaranteed that they will not be forced to leave the country against their will. By delaying "permanent status", immigration countries retain the legal right to repatriate foreign workers when desired, even those with many years of residence. The conditions attached to permanent status can thus function as a means of controlling the size or composition of immigration and must therefore also be included as a part of immigration regulation.

Compulsory repatriation of large groups of immigrants is rare. Nevertheless, it has long been a possibility which hangs over the heads of many of the foreign workers employed in Western Europe. Though seldom utilized, it nonetheless influences their living conditions and their attitudes towards residence in the host country.

Thus, the very existence of the possibility of compulsory repatriation is a factor in a country's immigrant policy. Immigration regulation may be said to foster a considerable degree of legal insecurity because decisions concerning permanent status are made by administrative authorities who have much discretion in interpreting such regulations. Such legal insecurity is made worse when foreign citizens have no right to appeal against the decisions of administrative authorities.

Immigrant policy

Immigrant policy is the other part of immigration policy and refers to the conditions provided to resident immigrants. It comprises all issues that influence the condition of immigrants; for example, work and housing conditions, social benefits and social services, educational opportunities and language instruction, cultural amenities, leisure activities, voluntary associations, and opportunities to participate in trade union and political affairs. Immigrant policy may be either direct or indirect.

Immigrants have a number of special needs to begin with because they are different from the host population. They often speak a foreign language and represent a different culture. Immigrants also have special economic interests and ambitions for the future. All of this may sometimes prompt a country of immigration to devise special measures to improve the situation of its immigrants. Since these measures do not usually apply to the non-immigrant population, we will call them "direct" immigrant policy.

Like the non-immigrant population, immigrants are also affected by a country's general public policy, which involves economic, social, political, and other measures. These measures are not designed with only immigrants in mind; instead, they are intended to apply to all inhabitants of a country whether citizens or not. Yet they may not be applied to all inhabitants in the same way, i.e. there may be discrimination, both positive and negative, in the allocation of resources and opportunities. When general public policy affects immigrants substantially, we will talk about "indirect" immigrant policy.

Indirect immigrant policy can be termed "inequitable" or "discriminatory" when immigrants receive significantly less than others, and when they are denied opportunities to participate in society. Even when the distribution of benefits is perfectly equal, however, immigrants can still remain in an inferior position, primarily because they have recently made a new start in the host country and experience less favorable circumstances than the rest of the population. This situation can be ameliorated if immigrants are given greater benefits than other people, e.g. special language instruction, special cultural support, and so on. These measures are the tools of direct immigrant policy.

To summarize in outline form, immigration policy comprises:

1. Immigration regulation and aliens control
    (a) "strict" or "liberal" control of the admission and residence of foreign citizens
    (b) guarantees of "permanent status"; legal security versus vulnerability to arbitrary expulsion

2. Immigrant policy
    (a) indirect: immigrants' inclusion in the general allocation of bene-
         fits; "equal" versus "discriminatory" distribution
    (b) direct: special measures on behalf of immigrants; "affirmative
         action" and the removal of legal discrimination

Although we will in our analysis distinguish between these two parts of
immigration policy, they are of course in practice at work simultaneously.
What is very often not understood is the profound effect that they can
have on one another. A system of rotation might, for example, leave most
immigrants in a very weak legal position as residents. This may in turn
impede integration and the full enjoyment of social and civil rights – both
areas of concern to immigrant policy. Another example of the mutual
influence between immigration regulation and immigrant policy would be
when a country uses instruments of immigrant policy (e.g. housing applications, school registers, and so on) to identify and expel illegal immigrants, thus accomplishing a task of immigration regulation.

General preconditions

Immigration policy should be analyzed in the context of a country's
history, economy, geography, population, international relations, etc., for
these are factors that affect immigration to a country, both quantitatively
and qualitatively. Valid comparisons between the project countries are
possible only when the general preconditions for the countries' immigration policies are analyzed.

Policymakers in each country may have tried to shape immigration
policy on the basis of their own experience and their particular national
needs, but the policies of all the project countries nevertheless have numerous features in common. Periods of passport exemption, rigid immigration control, and active recruitment of foreign workers have come at the
same or almost the same time in every country. Thus, it seems that the
shaping of immigration policy is determined in part by conditions beyond
the control of policymakers in the individual countries. For example, two
world wars have disrupted long-standing patterns of habitation and have
forced people to flee their home countries. Economic disruptions, resulting either from the wars or from other causes, have been possibly even
more unsettling than the wars themselves. The Great Depression in the
1930s affected the entire industrialized world and resulted in the widespread traumatic belief that future economic crises had to be avoided at
all costs. During the following decades, Keynesian economic theory gradually provided new policy options, starting with active budget policies,
which were applied to counter depressions.

Of course, all countries have not been affected by war and economic crisis to the same degree, and partly because of this, there are significant differences in the immigration policies of the project countries. One might say that although they came from different parts, they are all sailing on the same heaving ocean, all exposed to the same fluctuations in weather, winds, and currents. Yet because they each set a different course and sail in a different kind of vessel, no two voyages are ever exactly alike. Similarly, no two countries' immigration policies are ever exactly alike, even though all countries are affected by and must contend with the same external conditions.

"General preconditions", as the term will be used here, are background conditions which, on the whole, remain stable for a considerable period of time and are not easily influenced or altered in the short term. For the general as well as attentive public, and also for policymakers, these conditions act as constraints on the possibilities for state action; in other words, they form a factual, concrete framework for immigration policy over a relatively long period of time.

Terminology

Two of the key concepts in this comparative study are immigrant and immigration. The term "immigrant" is sometimes used in the very broad sense of its root-word "migrant", a person who moves from one country to another. In common usage, however, the term "immigrant" has acquired the narrower meaning of "a person who migrates to a country with the intention of taking up permanent residence", something akin to the term "settler". The definition of immigrant that will be used in this book lies somewhere in between the broad sense of "migrant" and the narrow sense of "settler":

> "Immigrant" is a person who migrates to a country and then actually resides there longer than a short period of time, i.e. for more than three months.

> "Immigration" refers to the physical entrance of immigrants as here defined, either singly or as a group, into a country.

This definition thus excludes people that pay only a short visit to a country; for example, those who come on vacation or to visit relatives, or those who come on business trips or to do some specific job (a mechanic to install machinery for instance, or artists to give a performance), as long as their stay is for less than three months. On the other hand, "immigrant" does not only refer to those who plan from the beginning to stay permanently in a country. Thus, students, scholars, artists, and others who spend longer than three months as "guests" in a country are considered immigrants although they do not plan to stay permanently.

The decisive criterion is the actual length of time that a person resides in the country of immigration. People that intend to remain permanently, i.e. "settler" immigrants, are *not* included in the definition if they return home after only a couple of months; on the other hand, people that intend to remain only a couple of months but later change their mind and stay for several years are included. Obviously, the length of residence necessary for a person to be included in our definition of "immigrant" cannot be determined in any but an arbitrary fashion. Each project country allows most foreign citizens to take up residence for a limited period of time, usually three to six months, without requiring visas or residence permits, and for this reason we have set the residence criterion in our definition at three months.

Foreign citizens that remain in a country for longer than three months must usually obtain a residence permit; therefore, any foreign citizen who has such a permit is likely to become an immigrant, and is therefore considered such under our definition. But the definition also includes people who do not have residence permits, in particular illegal or "undocumented" aliens. In general, it is difficult to say with certainty that people are or are not immigrants when they arrive, although those who have applied for residence permits in advance are of course more likely to stay longer than those who have not. Under our definition, the criterion determining whether or not a foreign citizen should be considered an immigrant is if he or she stays in the country for longer than three months.

The terms "immigrant" and "immigration" are applied in a different manner in each project country, and their meanings have changed over time. The definition used here will for this reason cause more difficulties in some project countries than in others. As the following chapters will show, there is an obvious relation between a country's immigration policy and its terminology. In Germany and Switzerland immigrants are "foreign workers" (*ausländische Arbeitnehmer* in Germany and *Fremdarbeiter* in Switzerland) and they are controlled by "aliens bureaux" (*Ausländerbehörde*, or in Switzerland *Fremdenpolizei*). France has always used the terms *les immigrés* and *l'immigration*, and Sweden used similar terms (*invandrare* and *invandring*) in the 1960s when its new immigrant policy was launched. In Britain the term "immigrant" has been applied particularly to colored people, while in the Netherlands the new policy envisioned for immigrants is called a "minorities" policy.

The technical language used in each country is adjusted so that it best describes and explains the country's policy. Terminology also influences the way in which immigration policy is conceived and understood in each country; terms that should be instruments of description gradually become fixed concepts that limit flexibility and creativity. For this reason it is important that our comparative discussions use terms that are well defined. The above definitions of "immigrant" and "immigration" will be used in a strict sense in the comparative chapters and will also serve as the general frame of reference in the country chapters, although each author has naturally chosen to use the terminology of his particular country by way of illustration.

PART I

Six nations

2

Sweden

TOMAS HAMMAR

1. Immigration and immigration policy

In the nineteenth century, Sweden was a country of emigration, and as late as 1930 the number of persons leaving the country exceeded the number entering. Not until after the Second World War were large numbers of foreign citizens employed in Sweden, and immigration did not assume major proportions until the end of the 1960s.

Sweden is today one of the world's "rich" nations, but only a century ago it occupied a position similar to that of some of the more advanced of today's "developing" countries. Industrialization started later than in continental Europe and the economy was characterized by a heavy reliance on agriculture, with people living primarily in rural areas. This was the background to the great migration to America.

The first emigrants to America included those who in the 1840s opposed the religious control of the Swedish state church. The economically motivated migration, which began in the 1890s and continued with varying degrees of intensity until the 1920s, far surpassed the more limited movements of earlier times. Approximately one million people emigrated from a total population of only around five million. Perhaps an even greater number of persons would have left had they been able to do so. Nearly everyone had relatives or friends who had emigrated, and letters to travel agents in Gothenburg show that the general interest in emigration was very strong. It is reasonable to assume that at some point most people considered leaving.

Though its immigration was small and had not caused major problems, Sweden applied similar restrictive policies that other European countries used during the First World War. The first Deportation Act of 1914 only allowed the government to adopt a system of visas, residence permits, and work permits in cases of emergency. During this period of free-trade ideology Sweden was reluctant to impose controls on immigration: people, it was thought, like goods, ought to move freely between nations. Of course, there had been some exceptions to this laissez-faire attitude. Near the end of the nineteenth century several groups, among them small trades-men who sought protection from foreign competition, had demanded that the government take a more restrictive position on immigration. In the early 1900s some companies and large farms had recruited foreign strike-breakers to fight against unionization, and so the growing labor movement became interested in some form of immigration control.

Regulation did not define the size of immigration. Instead, a policy of *selection* was used. Sweden accepted those persons or groups who were either needed or wanted and kept out the rest. Periods of high unemploy-ment and recession were common in the interwar years and there was little desire to accept immigrants then. After the Second World War, on the other hand, when the economy needed labor, a relatively liberal immigra-tion policy was instituted. An agreement in 1954 between Sweden, Norway, Denmark, and Finland created a common Nordic labor market, which first of all led to an expanded influx of Finnish labor. The demand for foreign labor increased throughout the 1960s, and in 1969 and 1970 immigration reached its highest level. Two years later, in 1972, recruit-ment of foreign workers was stopped, which did not mean, however, that immigration came to an end (see Figure 2.1).

Total annual immigration to Sweden during the early 1980s has been approximately 32,000 persons. Total emigration during the same period has been approximately 16,000 persons, leaving a net balance of some 16,000 immigrants. As shown in Table 2.1, the immigration of workers from non-Nordic countries has been of little significance. In 1980, 5 percent of the Swedish labor force (250,000 persons) were foreign citizens. To this number must be added an almost equal number of other persons who are foreign born and have become Swedish citizens through naturalization.

Sweden has never had a system of immigration similar to the "guest-worker" programs of other European countries. Although direct recruit-ment by Swedish industry has taken place over the years, labor immigra-tion has never been planned on a large scale and has never been actively used as a remedy, short-term or long-term, for the problems of the econ-omy. Sweden has accepted foreign workers and their families as *individ-uals* insofar as this did not harm the country's interests. While in 1972 it limited the number of foreign workers allowed entry, Sweden retained its belief that immigration policy should not separate the right to work from the right of residence. In part this belief is a recognition of the virtually secure legal position of foreigners in Sweden, who enjoy the same social rights as Swedish citizens. Principally, however, this belief demonstrates a

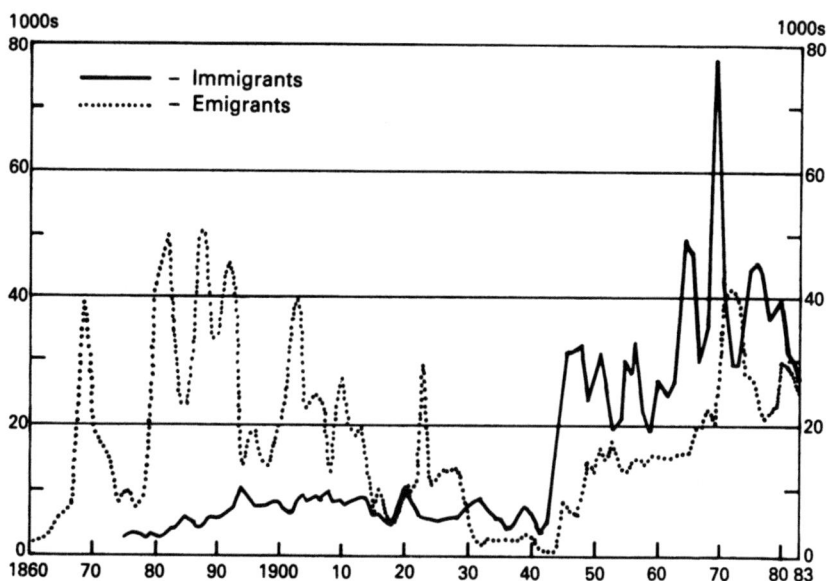

Figure 2.1. Immigration and emigration in Sweden, 1860–1983

Table 2.1. *Immigration to Sweden in 1980*

Type of immigration	Number	Percent
Non-Nordic immigration		
Adopted children	1,600	5
Refugees and quasi-refugees	5,500	16
Family reunion and immigrants		
married to Swedes	7,800	23
Labor immigration	700	2
Re-immigrants and others	1,800	5
Guest students	800	2
Total outside Nordic area	18,200	53
Immigration from Nordic countries	16,200	47
Total	34,400	100

desire to treat resident foreigners and their families as *immigrants* rather than simply as manpower.

This emphasis on immigration has gained strength over the past two decades and is reflected in changes in official terminology. In the 1960s the word *utlänning* (alien), which had come to have a negative connotation, was replaced with the word *invandrare* (immigrant). For example, the national agency for immigration control was called "Statens *utlännings-* kommission" (Aliens Commission) until 1969; its successor was named "Statens *invandrar*verk" (Swedish Immigration Board). But after a while even the word "immigrant" lost part of its positive ring. Moreover, it has a very broad meaning, and there is in fact no official definition of the term. It includes all foreign citizens, even political refugees, as well as all Swedish citizens born abroad, though it is sometimes even used to refer to the children of the latter group who are born in Sweden. One consequence of this terminology is that people who have no intention of remaining in Sweden often find themselves designated as "immigrants". As a result, Swedes tend to believe that every resident foreign citizen plans to stay for good.

2. General preconditions

We will limit our discussion to the six areas that constitute the set of identifying characteristics that form the context within which immigration occurs and Swedish immigration policy is made: geography and population, culture, economic development, the educational system, society and polity, and international relations.

Geography and population

Sweden is the fourth largest country in Europe, roughly twice the size of the United Kingdom, and has a land area of nearly 450,000 square kilometers. Its length is approximately the same distance as from its southernmost point to Rome (1,500 kilometers). Over half the land area is covered with forest and only 10 percent is cultivated. To outsiders Sweden conjures up an image of vast, frozen expanses, but the climate is actually relatively moderate, thanks largely to the proximity of the Gulf Stream. In 1982 Sweden had more than 8,300,000 inhabitants, of which 7.7 million were native born while around 600,000 were not. The population is concentrated in the southern region; two areas, one centered around Stockholm in the east and the other around Gothenburg in the west, account for nearly one half of the total population. Thus, while the average population density is 20 inhabitants per square kilometer, more than 70 percent of the country's land area has a population density of only six inhabitants or less per square kilometer.

It might appear that with such a low population density Sweden could find room for a large immigrant population, provided of course that new towns and industries were established in regions currently consisting of forests or scattered farms, and provided that the products of these new areas could be exported to pay for the imports that the new and larger population would require. It is important to emphasize, however, that such speculation should not be taken seriously. Swedes have for many years been forced to move to industries in southern Sweden, where job opportunities are much better. Northern Sweden continues to suffer from internal outmigration despite its important sources of raw materials.

A low birthrate and slowly increasing average age have combined to reduce the rate of natural growth in the Swedish population. The percentage of working-age persons has declined from 71 percent in 1940 to 63 percent in 1980. During the latter part of the 1960s an increasing number of women entered the labor market. In 1980, 65 percent of all Swedish women belonged to the labor force; the figure for men was 78 percent. Immigration has helped to remedy many of these demographic conditions, but it would not be correct to say that these conditions have themselves caused immigration.

Homogeneous culture

The population of Sweden in the nineteenth century was remarkably homogeneous in culture and ethnic background. In part this homogeneity was the result of Sweden's geographical isolation from most of the major paths of European migration. Until large-scale immigration began there were only two major "native" minorities, the Lapps and the Finns in northern Sweden, particularly the Tornedal Finns. In addition, small numbers of Jews have settled in Sweden since first being allowed to do so in 1780. Through immigration during and after the Second World War their number has almost doubled.

In particular the past several decades have been trying for the Lapps, primarily because of difficulty in maintaining their reindeer herds in the northern regions. Their grazing lands are limited when highways, power dams, military facilities, and tourist sites are developed. Increasing numbers of Lapps have moved south to other occupations and other ways of life. At the same time, however, in recent years the Lapps have become increasingly aware of their ethnic identity, and there has been a growing interest in maintaining the Lapp culture and protecting the minority's common rights. A great – but mostly unsuccessful – legal struggle was waged against the Swedish state throughout the 1970s to force the recognition of historic ownership to grazing lands.

The Tornedal Finns live in the northern part of Sweden along the Finnish border. From a cultural or ethnic point of view this border was drawn arbitrarily when Sweden and Finland were separated in 1809 and some areas that were predominantly Finnish were included in Sweden. From the 1890s on, Sweden sought to assimilate the population of these

Table 2.2. *Approximate evaluation of Swedish minorities*

Minority	Estimate
Original	
Finnish-speaking (Tornedalen and North Sweden)	30,000
Lapps (*samer*)	10,000
Jews	16,000
Gypsies	3,000
Immigrant (language)	
Finnish	250,000
Serbo-Croatian	34,000
Greek	19,000
Turkish	9,000

areas. The measures taken in educational policy during the 1930s to achieve that goal have since received – with justification – very severe criticism. Today the Finnish-speaking minority in the northern region has benefited from the gains of the larger Finnish community in Sweden created by migration from Finland in the 1950s and 1960s.

But apart from these two relatively small, native minorities and a small number of Jews and Gypsies, one can say that at least until twenty years ago the Swedish people spoke a single language, belonged to the same religion (the Lutheran state church), and shared a long and common history. The society had no divisions based on race, ethnicity, or religion. Though there were some cultural differences between provinces, these differences, unlike in Norway, were relatively small and progressively tended to disappear under the influence of national schools, radio, and television.

Because of this traditional cultural homogeneity, economic and social differences have constituted the major divisions in Swedish political life. Starting after the Second World War, an attempt has been made to even out socioeconomic or class differences through more egalitarian educational policies and other social reforms. The salient point is that before the beginning of large-scale immigration Swedes had very little experience with cultures and ethnic groups other than their own.

Economic development
Economic progress was rapid during most of the postwar period. The Gross National Product grew in the 1950s and 1960s at an average annual rate of 3.6 percent, although it slowed down considerably in the

1970s (to around 1.8 percent), and came to a halt in the early 1980s. Sweden is still mainly dependent on its traditional industries (forestry and mining), but more emphasis is now being placed on advanced technological industries, e.g. motor vehicles, aircraft, electronics and electrical equipment, and chemicals. Employment patterns in Sweden have changed; there is now a greater emphasis on service-sector occupations. The Swedish economy is highly dependent on foreign trade, with imports and exports accounting for approximately 30 percent of total GNP.

The Swedish economy, which had not been subject to the ravages of the Second World War, developed rapidly and brought about a high standard of living. GNP per capita has been among the highest in Western Europe. By any index that is used to measure the standard of living – per capita measurements of passenger cars, television sets, telephones, newsprint consumption – Sweden ranks near the top.

Since about 1975, however, the Swedish economy has faced increasing problems. While industrial growth has slowed down, the public sector has continued to expand, reaching a point where taxes can hardly be raised further. International loans have been taken to cover higher oil prices as well as other consumption. The unemployment rate is still low, about 3 percent in 1983, but this is partly because so many jobseekers are placed in retraining courses. Young people, and especially young immigrants, have a higher unemployment rate (5 percent and 10 percent), and those among them who have little education are often unable to find a job. Rapid inflation, about 8 percent annually, accompanies unemployment. Full employment and price stability, the traditional goals of the Swedish economy, have not been attained in recent years.

These problems are explained in several ways. Some say that wages have reached too high a level in comparison with international standards, or that the public sector has grown too much. Others point out that several industries have fallen behind, failed to modernize, and are being forced out of business. This indicates that a comprehensive reorganization of Sweden's economic structure is under way – a painful process. Furthermore, industrial companies have had to pay rather high production taxes and at the same time have had to adjust to new legislation protecting the environment.

Education

The past several decades have witnessed a rapid expansion and democratization of education, led by government reforms designed to remove economic, social, and geographic obstacles to equal opportunity. The period of obligatory schooling has been increased to nine years, and the percentage of students going on to the three-year high school has increased. But higher education is no longer – as it once was – an automatic ticket to a good position. Students who put extra time and effort into advanced studies often find that they cannot get the kind of job traditionally associated with their education. This problem is made more difficult by the generally high expectations that most young Swedes have concerning both their careers and the quality of their working environments. These expectations are often not satisfied.

Immigrants often have to accept jobs that many Swedes will not take. Even if they are overqualified for a position by virtue of education received in their country of origin, poor ability in Swedish may exclude them from positions that correspond to their backgrounds. In addition, when immigrants compare their situation in Sweden with the one they left in their home country, many conclude that they can put up with the relatively much better Swedish situation – at least for a while.

Society and polity

The emphasis in Sweden has been on the establishment of a stable and secure society. From 1932 to 1976 and again from 1982 Sweden has had governments controlled by the Social Democratic Party. During the six years when the Social Democrats were out of power, governments were formed by combinations of the three non-socialist parties on the basis of the majority they received in the general elections of 1976 and 1979. Despite the long control of the Social Democrats, nationalization of the economy has not taken place. On the other hand, the recent period of non-socialist governments did not lead to any major shift in policies. This reflects a general consensus of opinion and a readiness to cooperate and compromise.

Some foreign observers believe that Sweden is a "socialist" country. This is wrong, both politically and economically. In fact, the economic power has remained concentrated mainly in private hands, although extensive social reforms have occurred. Most large corporations in Sweden are privately owned and corporation tax is relatively low. The Swedish electorate has for a long time been divided into two blocs of about equal size, the divisive issue in the early 1980s being economic power. The Social Democrats have promised to give wage-earners influence in the big corporations' economic decisions, while the non-socialist parties claim that this implies a threat to the market economy. At the same time all parties accept a large measure of state intervention in the economy to ensure full employment and the equal distribution of income. Since the 1930s the state has engaged in long-term economic planning, influencing corporations with legislation and with the selective application of taxes and credits. During the 1970s the state took, through public corporations, an increasingly active part in, for example, energy production and the steel industry.

The stable political system and the existence of a consensus on the main goals of Swedish society have had important consequences for immigration and immigration policy. Immigrants arrive in a society with a very explicitly expressed responsibility for the welfare of each individual. No longer are they expected to turn to family and friends for help when sick, aged, or in trouble. Instead, they are encouraged to turn to a social agency which is administered by the state or the local community. The service they receive is good, regardless of their income. In principle, all members of society are entitled to equal treatment, and this includes immigrants as well. Immigration policy is strongly affected by this ideology and, as will be shown, it aims at ensuring that immigrants live and work as equals with Swedish citizens, even though these aims are not always fully achieved.

A small Nordic nation

Small nations often emphasize international law more than great powers do, and this has been especially true of Sweden because of its neutrality during the two world wars. The basic principle of today's Swedish foreign policy is non-alliance in peacetime in order to stay neutral in event of war. In full accordance with this principle Sweden strives to strengthen international law and to support peace efforts. Swedish immigration policy includes participation in international efforts to prevent situations in which people have to leave their countries as refugees. When this nevertheless occurs, Sweden helps with its share of the problems. The law grants asylum to political refugees, who are transferred annually to Sweden from international camps.

Sweden is located on a peninsula between the two great power blocs but outside the direct confrontation and division of continental Europe. Since neighboring Norway and Denmark belong to NATO and Finland has a defense treaty with the USSR, a Nordic defense system is inconceivable. But many other forms of close Nordic cooperation have been developed, one of the most important being the common labor market.

Finland and Sweden constituted one state from the twelfth century to 1809. When Sweden was a major European power in the seventeenth century, Finnish and Swedish regiments fought together and both Swedish and Finnish were spoken in the Riksdag. The same legal and administrative traditions are still followed in Sweden and Finland. Furthermore, there is a Swedish-speaking minority in Finland comprising some 6–7 percent of the population.

Emigrants from Finland to Sweden are about 80 percent Finnish-speaking and 20 percent Swedish-speaking. In 1983, the Finnish-speaking immigrants living in Sweden were more numerous than the Swedish-speaking native minority in Finland. Obviously, the history of Finnish–Swedish relations plays a major role for Finnish emigration to Sweden as well as for Swedish immigration policy.

3. Immigration regulation and control

Swedish immigration regulation and control is characterized by two traditions: a well-developed legal tradition that insures the civil rights of immigrants and guarantees the appeal of their cases to the highest administrative and political bodies, and a tradition of placing Swedish national interests first when deciding how large immigration should be (the number of persons admitted can vary, but the system of regulation should be the same).

The first law concerning immigration, the so-called Deportation Act of 1914 (*utvisningslagen*), gave the government the right to impose a regulatory system in emergency situations. This is exactly what happened when in 1917 a decree was issued requiring passports and visas in order to enter the country. Shortly thereafter, for the same reasons of emergency, the government decided to require work and residence permits for resident foreigners. Immigration regulation became somewhat more permanent in 1927 when the Deportation Act was replaced with the Aliens Act (*utlänningslagen*). Rules concerning the deportation of foreigners were then integrated with rules concerning work and residence permits. Originally valid for only five years, this law was extended several times and in 1954 was finally adopted as a permanent statute.

The Deportation Act of 1914 set forth the conditions under which a foreign citizen visiting or residing in Sweden could be expelled. A series of arbitrary expulsions, including an expulsion of Jews who had resided in Sweden for a long time, induced a group of lawyers to draw up a set of guarantees for the rights of non-Swedish citizens. With the passage of these guarantees as law in 1914, Sweden developed at this early stage a legal precedent in immigration regulation and control. This precedent has two fundamental aspects: first, no foreign citizen can be removed from Sweden on grounds other than those specified by law; second, decisions regarding removal can be taken to a higher authority on appeal.

This legal precedent was never fully implemented; it was weakened somewhat by a 1918 ordinance which said that a non-Swedish citizen wishing to reside in Sweden had to obtain a residence permit. Lack of a residence permit was made grounds for expulsion. Since the issuance of residence and work permits became the province of an administrative body, and since it could arbitrarily reject applications for permits, thereby forcing the expulsion of a foreign citizen, these legal guarantees were clearly somewhat compromised. Nevertheless, in the end, the existence of the right to appeal against administrative decisions to higher authorities prevented the worst cases of abuse, and soon the appeals led to specific rules governing the rejection of permits which further strengthened the legal position of foreign citizens. Sweden retained the right to decide whether persons without Swedish citizenship would be allowed to reside in the country, but once permission was granted the decision could be reversed only on specific, legal grounds.

Principal aims

Immigration regulation has gradually developed a permanent character and over time its implementation has become the responsibility of a central administrative body. Parliament and the government have reviewed the regulatory system every five to ten years. In these reviews they have formulated the official aims of regulation; but, in the vague manner characteristic of political declarations, they have left considerable scope for interpretation by the government and administrative agencies. In cases where administrative decisions have been appealed, the government has created precedents for the interpretation of immigration legislation.

Citizens of the other Nordic countries enjoyed favorable treatment during the interwar years, and after 1945 the first relaxation of regulation was for them. Ever since the establishment in 1954 of a common Nordic labor market, Sweden has offered freedom of travel to its neighbors; citizens from these countries constitute the bulk of immigrants to Sweden. The desire for extended Nordic cooperation has thus taken precedence over the protection of the Swedish labor market. Nordic cooperation has remained central to policy despite the changes in immigration that occurred in 1967 and 1975. No change in the free movement now existing on the Nordic labor market is included in the 1982 agreement that replaces the original one of 1954.

The aims of Swedish immigration regulation have been expressed as sometimes vague and even partly contradictory principles in government statements and parliamentary decisions. Their content and application to particular situations have been subject to varying interpretations, which have balanced the ideas of free movement and Nordic cooperation against the necessity of protecting Swedish economic interests. The aims of immigration regulation could be considered long-term rather than short-term in the sense that the principles on which they are based have been official policy throughout most of this century. Yet, because their interpretation has varied according to Sweden's needs at different times and with respect to different national groups, they have often been altered to fit different situations. It must be emphasized, however, that protection of the Swedish labor market has consistently been the dominant aim of immigration regulation.

Before leaving this section it is important to note that discussions of immigration regulation over the years have not touched on a number of topics that might also have served as policy aims. The birthrate in Sweden is so low that since the beginning of the 1930s the population would have actually declined without immigration – yet demographic aims have never played a role in the immigration debate. Likewise, the Swedish population has a history of extreme homogeneity in language, religion, and origin, but arguments against a change in this traditional situation have not been made in the period after the Second World War.

The instruments of regulation and control

The most notable characteristic of Swedish immigration regulation is that it deals with exactly what it says – *immigration*. Foreign citizens who are granted work and residence permits for one year can count on having their permits renewed and may, if they wish, remain permanently in Sweden with their families. In this respect the Swedish regulatory system resembles the systems of traditional transoceanic immigration countries, which recruited or invited people and gave them the status of "immigrant" as soon as they received an entry visa. Yet this similarity has never been made completely explicit; in fact, no paragraph in the Aliens Act would prevent a different application of the rules. Under present law the Swedish government could decide that work and residence permits would no longer be renewed and that foreigners whose permits had expired would have to leave the country. But no government has applied the law in this way since it was first passed in 1927, and this long precedent makes such an application unlikely today.

Visa requirements are in effect (with certain exceptions) for Africa, Asia, and Eastern Europe, but not for the rest of the world. Before a visa is issued there is a check to determine if the reason for entering the country is as given (e.g. tourism or visiting friends) or whether instead there may be an intent to immigrate. In the latter case the visa application will normally be refused. Persons who intend to seek work or permanent residence in Sweden must state this when applying for a visa. This rule also applies to persons from countries not subject to the visa requirement: if they wish to reside or seek work in Sweden they must obtain the proper permits *before* entering the country. Requests for permits from persons already in the country are accepted only from political refugees, close relatives of persons living in Sweden, and other exceptional cases.

Sweden's geographical position makes the borders relatively easy to guard. Most people entering the country arrive by boat or plane; few enter across the long land border with Norway. Citizens of Denmark, Norway, Finland and Iceland do not need passports to enter Sweden – only identification documents. Since border control is the responsibility of the Nordic country first entered, the Danish–German border is most important for Swedish immigration control. It is fairly easy to enter Denmark and the number of persons crossing this border is very high. On the boats from Denmark to Sweden, non-Nordic citizens may mingle with Nordic tourists, who are not checked, and thereby slip into the country.

To stop such activities, the Swedish border control has tried since 1976 to identify non-Nordic citizens by observing the hair, shoes, clothing, etc. of tourists. Suspected persons have been stopped and asked to identify themselves, and some 2,000 persons have been refused entry each year. This procedure thus has had results, but at the cost of some embarrassing treatment of Nordic citizens with the "wrong" appearance. A further complication is that each country, despite the Nordic passport union, retains its own system of immigration regulation.

Under these circumstances a system of *internal* control has become the most important instrument of Swedish immigration regulation. In the past, employers and landlords were held responsible for reporting cases in which they hired or rented to aliens. The reporting system had many faults, however, and is no longer used for this purpose. Internal control is today based on measures that make it illegal to employ non-Nordic citizens who cannot produce a work permit and which make it generally impossible to extend social benefits to them if they are not included in the Swedish population register (this does not apply to persons awaiting asylum decisions). Aliens from outside the Nordic countries are included in the register only if they have valid residence permits and intend to remain in Sweden for at least one year.

Of fundamental importance to this system is the fact that every Swedish citizen as well as every registered foreign citizen has a personal number (*personnummer*) of ten digits. This number is requested by an employer when paying a salary or deducting taxes, by the national insurance office when paying sickness benefits, by hospitals when admitting a patient, and so forth. This system makes it difficult for illegal aliens to escape detection or for employers to hire them.

Still, there are holes in the system. A completely effective system of internal control would require extensive police action, a measure considered neither reasonable nor desirable. Strong public criticism has already been directed at police arrests of minors awaiting deportation and also at the practice of stopping people in public places for purposes of identification. Again, in the latter case, persons with "foreign" appearance are often discriminated against.

A residence permit is required of all non-Nordic citizens, aged sixteen or older, who wish to remain longer than three months in Sweden. As a rule, a work permit is required for non-Nordic citizens to seek employment. Until they reach sixteen, youths of foreign citizenship living in Sweden are considered dependants of their parents or guardians; afterwards they are entitled to receive work and residence permits individually. An immigrant who has either a work or a residence permit for at least one year can apply for a permanent residence permit, which also includes the right to work. This permit has no time limit, but it can be revoked if the holder takes up residence in another country. For this reason some persons with permanent residence permits do not register with the Swedish authorities when they move out of the country, hoping thus to retain their status for later re-immigration. Once discovered out of the country their permits may be revoked, but the rule has so far been applied in a very liberal manner.

As mentioned earlier, close family members are allowed to join persons in Sweden who hold work and residence permits. Whenever a group is granted entry permits (e.g. several hundred refugees from some part of the world), it is assumed that the additional entry of family members will increase the total number of immigrants. Family members include spouses (legally married or living under "marriage-like" arrangements) and unmarried children under 20 years of age. In a few cases a wider definition of the "family" has been adopted to reflect conditions in the emigration countries.

Almost inevitably the rules with respect to marriage or cohabitation have been used to beat the control system. The obviously "arranged" marriages are rejected, but it is often difficult to judge. Permits are issued in cases where marriage occurred prior to entering Sweden, but may be revoked if the marriage is terminated during the first two years in the country. A significant number of immigrants are affected by this rule.

Once given a permit, an immigrant's chances of being allowed to stay permanently in Sweden are quite good. As mentioned above, a permanent residence permit can be issued after just one year. After three years of legal residence, a foreign citizen is eligible to vote and run for office in local and regional elections; after five years he or she can obtain Swedish citizenship. Citizens of Nordic countries can become naturalized after only two years' residence. Thus, a non-Nordic immigrant who wants to become a Swedish citizen, with full civil and political rights, can do so in five years or perhaps six including administrative delays. For those married to a Swedish citizen the process can go even faster. Yet, in relation to the number who qualify, relatively few immigrants apply for Swedish citizenship. The reasons for this cannot be discussed here; suffice it to say that the acquisition of citizenship is not a prerequisite for planning a secure future in Sweden. Such security is already guaranteed by the permanent residence permit.

In summary, immigration to Sweden is regulated in part by visa requirements for countries in Africa, Asia, and Eastern Europe, in part by enforcing a maximum stay for tourists of three months, and in part by a system of internal control. This control system is far from airtight, however, and illegal immigration – though still small – is an increasing worry. Since 1972, when labor immigration was reduced to a minimum, immigration based on family reunion has grown and the number of persons seeking asylum has increased. Finally, Sweden continues to allow free labor immigration from the other Nordic countries, completely outside of the ordinary system of regulation.

The outcome of regulation and control

Impediments to the enforcement of immigration regulation are public opinion and the media. Political opinion in Sweden does not favor opening the borders to increased immigration. The restrictive nature of immigration regulation is supported by all political parties and by public opinion, as shown by periodic polls. Nevertheless, strong feelings arise when individuals are refused permission to remain in Sweden because of insufficient cause for refugee status, for example, and when they and perhaps their families are picked up by the police and taken into custody in preparation for deportation. Students have demonstrated in support of their fellows who were denied permits; newspapers report individual cases in big headlines. The connection between general immigration policy (which all seem to support) and decisions in individual cases (which many seem to condemn) is a difficult one for many people to make. The final word on such matters lies with the Minister of Immigration, who as a politician and a representative of a political party may hesitate to go against public opinion. For this reason some demonstrations and protests may be successful, which only encourages further attempts.

A major flaw of the present regulatory system is the long waiting periods for those who have claimed political refugee status. Because of a heavy work load decisions sometimes take more than two years. The shortening of this period has become one of the policymakers' most important aims, but it is not easy to achieve, since the legal rights of the individual alien must be protected and since all cases must be treated equally.

Applications are presently made to specialized police offices, where fact-finding interrogations are carried out. Questions regarding permits are first dealt with by the central aliens agency, the Swedish Immigration Board (SIV). Appeals may be brought to the government, where the Minister of Immigration is responsible for the final decision in individual cases. A system in which appeals are directed to a special administrative court or "council" instead of to the government has been discussed, but was not instituted. This would not shorten the waiting period, and it would make it more difficult for the government to establish immigration policy which presently develops partly through the precedents set by appeal decisions.

Immigration regulation is presently under review. A Parliamentary Commission on Immigration Policy, comprising politicians from all political parties represented in parliament, was established in 1980 by the government to propose recommendations for immigration regulation and immigrant policy. The recommendations concerning immigration regulation were published in June 1983, and in April 1984 a government bill was presented to parliament. The regulatory system is the subject of greater attention now that restrictions on immigration are severe and the existence of illegal immigration more obvious. So far there has been no discussion of numerical quotas for immigration other than the quota that was established by parliament for the acceptance and transfer to Sweden of political refugees for whom Sweden is not the first country of asylum. Policymakers are beginning to devote serious attention, however, to the long-term effects of immigration, and it is not inconceivable that plans for the size of immigration might be adopted in the future.

4. Immigrant policy

Persons who immigrated to Sweden before the middle of the 1960s occasionally express a certain envy for those who immigrated in later years. In the early period of immigration no special measures were taken to help immigrants adjust to life in Sweden. When refugees from Germany arrived near the end of the 1930s they were helped by voluntary organizations, often because they belonged to the same religious group or political party as the organization's members. The immigration of Baltic refugees at the end of the Second World War also depended heavily on voluntary efforts, although government agencies were also involved.

The establishment in 1965 of a task force on immigrant policy to propose measures to aid the integration and adjustment of foreigners was the first major change in policy. Government funds were made available to finance free instruction in Swedish; an "Immigrant Newsletter" with information on Swedish society was published in several languages; a book called *New to Sweden* was issued, giving basic information on rights and responsibilities (mainly as a handbook for officials dealing with immigrants). An investigation was begun to determine how foreign citizens could be placed on an equal footing with Swedish citizens. A definite immigrant policy began to take shape.

Of course, there had existed an immigrant policy to some extent in Sweden before 1965, based on the idea that immigrants would eventually be assimilated into Swedish society. There were no special programs for immigrants, for it was thought that access to the Swedish social welfare that developed in the postwar years was sufficient. The basis for this social welfare policy was a program worked out by the Social Democratic Party before the war was even over. This so-called "postwar program" declared that Sweden, spared the destruction of the war, would immediately begin work on the social reforms which had been postponed for so long. Family policy, housing policy, and education policy would all be formulated to overcome class differences and offer equal opportunities to the next generation. Important parts of the program envisioned improved housing standards and a uniform system of basic schooling for all children. As the following section will show, the implementation of many of these reforms had direct consequences for immigrant policy.

Principal aims

The aims of Swedish immigrant and minority policy were summarized in a decision by parliament in 1975 under three headings: equality, freedom of choice, and partnership. The goal of *equality* implies the continued efforts to give immigrants the same living standard as the rest of the population. The goal of *freedom of choice* implies that public initiatives are to be taken to assure members of ethnic and linguistic minorities domiciled in Sweden a genuine choice between retaining and developing their cultural identity and assuming a Swedish cultural identity. The goal of *partnership* implies that the different immigrant and minority groups on the one hand and the native population on the other both benefit from working together.

Parliament has expressed its unanimous support for a government declaration in which these aims are presented in some detail. The aims retain a general character, however, even in this government declaration. They serve as principles for the agencies that implement immigrant policy; they also serve to indicate the direction in which parliament wishes immigrant policy to proceed. Although in their present form they are not legally binding and could not, for example, be cited in a court of law, they have nevertheless had great influence on the course of immigrant policy reforms.

It has been noted in various connections that these three aims – which seem to paraphrase the French Revolution's *liberté, égalité, et fraternité* – are so contradictory as to be impossible to achieve at the same time. If the second aim in particular, freedom of choice, is achieved to the extent that immigrant minorities retain their cultural identity, then it could be difficult to achieve the other aims of equality and partnership. The aims are formulated, however, so that they do not specify the degree to which immigrant policy must achieve any one of them. They merely indicate the direction that policy should take.

The aim of equality was not initiated in 1975. As early as 1967, when immigration control was tightened and work permits were required prior to arrival in Sweden, the Social Democratic government maintained that this was necessary to insure that immigrants achieve equal conditions. This argument was repeated the following year when parliament approved a declaration of principle regarding future immigration regulation. In fact, when equality was officially established as an aim in 1968, this was a natural application of an ideology according to which society has a responsibility for all of its members and social inequalities should be eliminated. Thus immigrants should be accorded the same treatment as everyone else. In addition, organized labor has always demanded that foreign workers be offered the same employment conditions and wages as Swedish workers and should be organized in the same manner. Demands for equality have thus long existed in Swedish society, but were not made a general aim of immigrant policy until the end of the 1960s.

The second aim of Swedish immigrant policy, freedom of choice, was formulated in 1974 by the Parliamentary Commission on Immigration. This goal may be seen as a reflection of ethnic realities in Sweden. In many cases immigrants with the same nationality and language have sought residence in the same community and even in the same neighborhood. They have formed associations and religious congregations and have opened businesses and restaurants; their language is spoken in the neighborhood streets and taught in the schools. This development of ethnic-minority communities occurred during a period when the concept of ethnicity gained a new importance all over the world. Minority groups that seemed about to disappear were suddenly revitalized (the Lapps are an example).

The aim of partnership can be regarded as an application of the other two principles to political life. It was first pronounced by parliament in 1975, the same year that foreign citizens were given voting rights in local elections. Partnership means that immigrant and minority groups should work together with the majority population. This presupposes that immigrant and minority groups, as partners in the development of society, are not only granted full freedom of association but also the public support needed to build and maintain their own associations. At the same time immigrants must be able to participate, individually or collectively, in labor union and political activity.

In summary, one can say that Swedish immigrant policy is and will be multicultural, at least for the immediate future. The path to full political and labor union participation and to cultural exchange lies open for the first generation of immigrants, and even more so for their children. Naturally, this path can in the long run lead to assimilation; but if it does, Swedish culture will change as well.

The instruments of immigrant policy

The direct measures of immigrant policy will be discussed shortly. But first, it is important to explain how general social policy in Sweden has influenced immigrants and how it has become more responsive to immigrants' needs. This will demonstrate the great extent to which immigrant policy is furthered through the realization of the general social policy.

Housing

An excellent example of the effects of general social policy is found in the area of housing. As already mentioned, immigrants often live together in certain neighborhoods. This concentration is not the result of any conscious, direct policy. Rather, it has resulted from general housing policy, as well as from the desire of some immigrants to live in areas together with their countrymen.

On the housing market immigrants generally look for rental apartments, usually because they are neither able nor willing to spend the kind of money necessary to obtain other forms of housing. They often find accommodations in neighborhoods where, at the time of their arrival, apartments are either newly built or for some other reason ready for immediate occupancy. Housing standards in new apartments are good, but rents are high, even if they do not really reflect actual cost since a great deal of housing is subsidized by society. The result of general housing policy is, then, that immigrants often live in relatively good housing in neighborhoods with many other immigrants of different nationalities. There are, however, no neighborhoods where *only* immigrants live, just as there are no neighborhoods with only a single immigrant group, e.g. Finns. There is no special "immigrant housing" owned by corporations or by the state.

Housing concentration has been gradually noticed and discussed. Some local communities have tried to stop the further entrance of certain nationalities, but such attempts have met with strong criticism. Attempts have also been made to stimulate movement out of some neighborhoods. But these direct measures are ad hoc responses to particular problems, and there is still really no immigrant housing policy to speak of. Instead, for better or worse, the housing conditions of immigrants are similar to those of Swedes with little or no savings.

Labor market

The situation is similar with regard to labor market policy. A major concern of immigration regulation is the protection of the Swedish &labor market. To this end, non-Nordic immigrants must have work permits; these are limited during the first year to specific occupations, although thereafter they are valid for all types of work. Immigrants also receive special instruction in Swedish on paid company time. Other than these exceptions, immigrants are subject to the same rules on the labor market as everyone else.

Of course, some immigrants may be the first to go when a company decreases its personnel, reflecting the commonly accepted rule that those employed last must go first. Other immigrants, however, have already worked many years in Sweden; they tend to stay longer on the same job because they expect to encounter obstacles in finding a new one. Unemployed persons receive assistance regardless of their citizenship as long as they have paid dues to an unemployment plan for at least twelve months. Immigrants have the same rights as Swedes to the services of the state employment agency and to occupational retraining and relocation.

When unemployment increases, the greatest problem for immigrants is that employers are less inclined to hire them than to hire Swedes. Immigrants thus have an equal legal position on the labor market but a less favorable real position. In this respect, immigrants have even been handicapped by special regulations meant to help them. Through a law passed in 1972 immigrants got the right to receive up to 240 hours of free instruction in Swedish during paid working hours. The original goal of this law was to ensure that immigrants received good instruction. In addition, the law was meant to discourage employers from importing foreign labor, since they had to pay their employees wages during language instruction. The consequence of this has been, however, that in order to avoid such extra costs employers hesitate to hire immigrants who have not already undergone the legally required 240 hours of language instruction, even if they are already residing in Sweden. Besides this, there is some actual job discrimination against foreigners, which means that in many cases employers give preference to Swedish workers, even if they are less suitable or qualified in other respects.

Social welfare

General national policy, and not policies directed specifically towards immigrant groups, also determines the conditions available to immigrants in the area of social welfare. The same social welfare offices, child- and maternity-care centers, and hospitals assist both immigrants and Swedes. In general, the same rules and regulations apply for all, even though they were not originally designed with immigrants in mind (which can occasionally lead to certain difficulties). There do exist special service institutions which help immigrants find their way through the Swedish bureaucratic labyrinth and which provide translators and interpreters as needed. In all communities with a large number of immigrants there are special "immigrant-service" offices that provide general assistance to the most numerous immigrant groups in their own languages. Official agencies also must provide interpretation for immigrants, and they can for this purpose obtain the necessary personnel from the immigrant-service offices.

Direct immigrant policy

So far we have discussed mainly indirect immigrant policy in various areas: housing, labor market, and social welfare. We will now turn to the measures of direct immigrant policy, which taken together are quite substantial, and discuss the education of immigrant children.

In principle, the Swedish school system should be the same for all children, notwithstanding social class, place of birth, or mother tongue. With growing numbers of immigrant children in many local schools, this principle has been challenged, and a policy debate on multicultural education has started. In 1976, parents with native language other than Swedish received the right to request that their children be taught to speak their mother tongue and since 1979, immigrants' mother languages have been used increasingly as the language of instruction for certain school subjects. Experiments had already started with Finnish classes, Turkish classes, and so forth in schools where the number of immigrant children was large enough to form such classes. In 1981 there were about 300 mother-tongue classes in Sweden, with a total of some 4,000 pupils. This means that about 10 percent of all children whose parents have a native language other than Swedish were enrolled in such classes.

Though these classes are increasing rapidly in number year by year, the great majority of immigrant children do not receive much instruction in their mother tongue. In 1981 about 100,000 school children took part in mother-tongue courses, usually not more than two hours per week, while their classmates studied other subjects. Around the same number of children abstained from their right to do this, some because they did not have enough interest or knowledge and others because they preferred to follow the regular curriculum.

The aims of language instruction are generally summarized under the designation "active bilingualism". The schools should convey to immigrant pupils a good knowledge of Swedish so that they can compete on the Swedish labor market, yet also teach them their parents' native language so that they can maintain and develop it. The liveliest immigrant policy debate at present concerns the interpretation and application of "active bilingualism".

The success of this program often depends on the fact that mother-tongue instruction has already been given during preschool years. Mother-tongue classes often last for six of the nine obligatory years of schooling; during these six years Swedish is also taught. All instruction is from the beginning done in the parents' native language, but the students are supposed to learn enough Swedish so that it can be used as the language of instruction during the last three years. Some immigrant groups are now demanding that this development be carried further: they would like nine school years in the mother tongue, followed by an opportunity for further studies (since 1977 there have been experiments with mother-tongue classes in high schools). There are also demands that immigrant groups have their own schools instead of just their own classes in the Swedish school system.

The education of first-generation immigrants (e.g. instruction in Swedish and comprehensive occupational retraining) is even more specialized than measures taken for their children. The first generation has very specific needs and, moreover, must be able to compete on the labor market. An example of a recent measure in this area is education for illiterate immigrants.

Different attempts have been made to estimate the total cost of direct immigrant policy. For the fiscal year 1983–84 the cost will probably be between 1,500 and 2,000 million Swedish crowns (200–300 million US dollars). To get a total estimation of the cost of immigrant policy we must add to this sum the cost of indirect measures which fall within the general budgets of agencies for public welfare that aid immigrants as well. These additional costs cannot even be estimated. Of course, all costs must be seen against the significant tax revenue paid by immigrants. The question is not whether Sweden has gained or lost money on immigrant policy but rather how large the scope of that policy has been.

Direct immigrant policy consists, as we have seen, partly of the very comprehensive immigrant education system in the schools. To this one must add measures taken to teach Swedish to first generation immigrants

– on the job, in the context of occupational retraining for the unemployed, and in voluntary classes. A significant portion of direct immigrant policy provides support for immigrants' own activities. This support goes to both local and national immigrant organizations, to the newspapers they publish, and also to cultural activities, youth work, study groups, and so forth. In addition to all of this there is an extensive information and service activity aimed at helping immigrants find their way in Swedish society, giving them information about conditions in society, and so on. Radio and television assist with special programs; there are also special newsletters and informational brochures. Immigrant-service offices and interpreter services have already been mentioned. In conclusion, it should also be emphasized that special contributions are made to inform Swedes about immigration and about immigrants.

In addition to this, measures are taken to aid the groups of refugees that Sweden selects for admission to the country, at present totaling approximately 1,250 people annually. During their first few months in Sweden these refugees are placed in special camps where they receive social and medical services, job counseling and help in finding work, and basic information and instruction in Swedish. After this they are placed in various communities across the country. These activities have up to now been the responsibility of the National Labor Market Board (AMS) which has concentrated primarily upon finding jobs for refugees on the labor market. A new form of organization has been proposed that both shortens the time spent in the camps and broadens refugee orientation to include Swedish society as a whole. The Swedish Immigration Board (SIV) would supervise the new arrangement. It must be added that the same social benefits are also available to refugees other than those selected for official programs. Actually, such refugees have been more numerous than the selected ones.

The outcome of immigrant policy

Immigrant organizations sometimes complain about the gap between the high aims of immigrant policy and the results which have been achieved. They can be answered in several ways. One way is to explain that aims must always be set high: they set the standard, and the target of policy is to meet them, but there can be no complaint if they have not been reached after only a short time. Another way is to answer that the aims have in fact been achieved to a surprisingly great extent, and those who argue otherwise simply make false comparisons. One cannot compare an immigrant to the average Swede unless one also takes into account how long he has resided in Sweden, how well he can speak Swedish, what his job qualifications are, and so on. If, after making these distinctions, one compares immigrants to *comparable* groups of Swedes, one will find that differences in matters of housing, work, income, and well-being are not so great.

There are studies comparing Swedes with Finns and Yugoslavs, using a special matching procedure to create "twins" with a number of comparable qualities. These studies show that the immigrants' standard of living is relatively equal to that of Swedes in the same age and occupational groups. The Finns have a somewhat poor health record, however, indicating some stress in their living conditions, and while immigrants generally have few social contacts with Swedes, this is especially true of Yugoslavs, whose social relations and leisure activities are much more tied to relatives and friends.

The problem remains to use immigrant policy to remedy the situations revealed by these studies. Often no attempt is made to investigate whether an immigrant policy program has functioned effectively. Swedish language instruction began in 1965. The program seems to have had only mediocre results, but apart from a few minor studies there has been no serious evaluation of its effectiveness. At the same time, large sums of money have been spent on the program. Some of the problems of the language instruction program are the following: pedagogical difficulties and the need for specialized instruction for teachers have been underestimated; pupils have lacked the proper motivation; and there have been practical difficulties with instruction during working hours. Nevertheless, no one has questioned the importance of Swedish language instruction as an instrument of immigrant policy – we just know very little about its effects.

We know somewhat more about the instruction of immigrant children in schools, despite the fact that this program began at a later date. But, even here, there has been little serious evaluation. Investigations have taken place into various information efforts for newly arrived immigrants, or in connection with specific reforms, e.g. the franchise reform of 1976 in which foreign citizens, resident in Sweden for more than three years, received the right to vote and run for office in local and regional elections. The result was an increase in immigrant interest in Swedish politics and a corresponding increase in the interest of local politicians in immigrant issues.

Thus a number of individual reforms have been studied in connection with limited projects. The Swedish Commission on Immigration Research (EIFO) has attempted a more general evaluation of immigrant policy through a special project on the long-term effects of immigration (PIL). The study of comparative immigration policies presented by this book is a part of this project.

Immigrant policy and immigration regulation

The relationship between immigration regulation and immigrant policy was made explicit when control of non-Nordic immigration was tightened in 1967–68. The official argument behind this change was that if the number of resident immigrants became too large it would become impossible to guarantee them a reasonable standard of living. In other words, to achieve the aim of equality explicit in immigrant policy tougher immigration regulation was required.

However, one can raise three objections to this analysis of the 1967–68 controls. Firstly, the tighter controls did not in any way cause a halt to immigration; secondly, the Nordic labor market was not affected by the changes; and thirdly, even before 1968 immigrants could be relatively certain of their right to remain in the country.

1. In 1969 and 1970 Sweden had its largest immigration ever. Nevertheless, the most important sign of change was not the size of immigration but rather that a declaration of principle had been made with respect to immigration regulation and that certain methods of regulation had been chosen. Whether regulation would then be strictly or liberally applied depended on the prevailing economic conditions and the Swedish need for labor. But there was no change in the methods of control or in the principle that those admitted would be allowed to stay.

2. The largest immigration came from Finland and was thus completely outside of the new regulations. Immigrants from Finland already had the right to stay and live in Sweden if they wished. They did not need work or residence permits, and they had the same rights and duties as Swedes, except for the right to vote and the need to do military service. One can therefore argue that since Finns and other Nordic citizens were completely outside the ordinary regulatory system, they were not affected by the interrelations between immigration regulation and immigrant policy.

    Swedish policymakers were influenced by their knowledge of Nordic migration patterns; they knew it was large and that it occurred under favorable conditions. Therefore, the need for labor immigration from non-Nordic countries was less than it would otherwise have been and regulation was therefore necessary to keep it low. But at the same time the favorable conditions offered to Finnish immigrants raised the reasonable argument that non-Nordic citizens, once admitted as immigrants, ought to be offered the same conditions. In this way, the Nordic common labor market helped lead to the adoption of equality as an aim for all immigrants.

3. It is true that prior to 1968, in principle, no new work permits had been issued during periods of high national unemployment; on the other hand, foreign citizens who lost their jobs had not been deported either. Instead, they were offered support and relief work in the same way as Swedes. The Aliens Act has always contained provisions that allow immigration authorities to refuse to renew work permits and thus force resident aliens to leave, but these provisions were never used.

One might say, therefore, that as far as Sweden is concerned, immigrant policy limited immigration. Both because of the favourable conditions enjoyed by Nordic immigrants, particularly the Finnish, and because of the dictates of Swedish sociopolitical ideology, the aim of equality was basic. Those who were allowed to enter the country as immigrants could be forced to leave only in accordance with specific rules, e.g. if they had committed a serious crime or had threatened national security. All other immigrants had the right to remain. In order to realize this goal of equality, immigration had to be brought under control; though it remained high for several years following 1968, it was later limited.

As soon as immigration regulation was tightened, intensive work to formulate immigrant policy began. A new central aliens agency, the Swedish Immigration Board (SIV), was established in 1969 to take charge of both immigration regulation and immigrant policy. A series of different measures were taken to strengthen the position of immigrants on the labor market, to give them information and language skills, to support their organizations, and so on. In all of this activity we see that immigration regulation and immigrant policy effect each other: the aims of immigrant policy have required regulation and regulation has in turn given impetus to immigrant policy reforms.

5. Policymaking and administration

Immigration policy in Sweden is the product of a political system that can be characterized by several terms: stability, consensus, compromise, and bureaucratization.

Political upheavals have not occurred during modern times; instead, political traditions have had the chance to evolve gradually. Since 1914 the Social Democratic Party has been the largest party in Sweden, with the support of approximately half the voters. But this does not mean that the other four parties have had no influence. Political proposals are prepared thoroughly and slowly, which allows all concerned to influence the process. The goal is usually to find broad solutions acceptable to everyone. Dunkward Rustow, the American political scientist, has called

Swedish politics the "politics of compromise" because unanimity is such strong a goal. Because the attainment of this compromise is a tedious process, political debate in Sweden often seems technical, boring, and perhaps bureaucratic. State agencies with great responsibility and independence implement political decisions; government ministries are small and intended primarily for long-term planning and the preparation of parliamentary bills.

Sweden is a small political unit. The political and bureaucratic elite is small and there are close personal relations within it. This results in both strong peer control within the elite and good possibilities for unanimous solutions to problems. Finally, Sweden is a thoroughly organized society. Every interest group has an organization, and the larger organizations have much opportunity to exercise influence over policymaking and administration.

Perceptions

Immigration policy is not one of the traditionally "big" issues in Swedish politics, but it has on occasion received increased political attention. One such occasion was 1907–14, when various interest groups demanded that immigration be limited; another was 1927, when a new Aliens Act was passed. In 1938 university students demanded that an impending immigration of Jewish doctors be stopped in order to protect the academic labor market. Now, long after these events, one can easily see that the dire warnings of masses of immigrants pressing against the borders were strongly exaggerated. Much of this exaggeration was built on the understandable fear that the difficult interwar years of unemployment would return.

It is more difficult to identify perceptions in one's own time, although naturally they exist. One of them is obvious: as already mentioned, since the late 1960s Sweden has continually used the term "immigrant". The power of words over thought has often resulted in measures suitable for "immigrants", but not suitable for those who may wish to return home after a while. There is a substantial number of people within each immigrant group who return to their own countries. The proportion varies, but from experience we know that around one third of all immigrants return within four to five years while about one half remain permanently. Those who stay do not usually intend to do so from the beginning, but only after a long period of residence discover that they have become "immigrants".

One of the present perceptions of Sweden as an immigration country can be called the "multiethnic" perception, which points out that Sweden, long a homogenous society, has through immigration rapidly become a multinational society. A hundred different languages might be spoken in a single municipality, with mother-tongue instruction in perhaps fifty of them (of course, most of these languages would be spoken by only a small number of people in each place). Local associations have been formed, and they have combined to form national federations, which publish weekly or monthly newspapers in their language.

Still, the future is uncertain. Language instruction in the schools is hotly debated. A great change has occurred in Swedish society, but many of the new minorities have few representatives and lack the resources to retain and develop their language and culture. The "multiethnic" Sweden of today undoubtedly has some characteristics that will not survive and others that will endure and develop.

Policymaking
Immigration came first and immigration policy followed – this is a general description of the Swedish situation. Policymaking only started at the end of the 1960s when immigration became larger. Parliament's decision on immigration policy in 1968 and the establishment of the Swedish Immigration Board in 1969 have already been cited as important steps. Nevertheless, it is still worth asking whether Sweden today has an immigration "policy" and, if so, how old it is.

The answer is, in my view, that a "policy" *does* exist. Certainly, Sweden lacks definite plans for how large future immigration should be; as in the past, size will be adjusted to Swedish needs. But regulation of immigration is established and has functioned fairly well, even though lately there has been some increase in illegal immigration. Immigrant policy has grown into a comprehensive program. In this sense Sweden has at present an immigration policy.

This policy has been developed gradually and successively. If we go back to the period 1945–65, we find that Sweden not only lacked a definite immigrant policy but lacked planning for immigration as well. Aliens control was directed more to individual cases than to a general regulation of the size of immigration. It was fairly easy for non-Nordic citizens to obtain work and residence permits; immigration from Finland increased little by little; a few corporations recruited workers abroad, and a Swedish recruitment office was opened in Yugoslavia. But one cannot really speak of a definite, articulated immigration policy during this period. One may question, of course, whether immigration policy must be "definite and articulated" in order to exist. The laissez-faire system that Sweden had prior to 1968 certainly involved a choice of direction, a "non-policy", which is *also* a type of policy. The real issue is, how was the choice made; in other words, how did immigration policy come about?

When I argue that immigration policy received a more precise formulation through parliament's decisions of 1968 and 1975, this suggests that parliament and the political parties determine immigration policy, which is of course true in a formal and legal sense. However, the major determinants of policy are the bureaucracy and interest groups, and not the political parties. Immigration issues have never been politicized so much that the parties have fought over them. On the contrary, unity is pointed to with some pride; for instance, the 1975 decision was made by a unanimous parliament. At the same time, central agencies in charge of immigrant affairs have occasionally complained that political parties have not assumed responsibility for giving direction to immigration policy. They charge that the parties have left policy decisions to administrative bodies.

Yet, such a situation is not unusual in Swedish politics. Similar cases exist in many areas, and all reflect the tradition that decisions should be made after long preparation and unanimously if possible. Commissions have been established to deal with issues of immigration reform. The Aliens Commission (1961–68), the Commission on Immigration (1968–74), the Aliens Act Commission (1975–81), and the Commission on Immigration Policy (1980–84) are the most important examples. Members of Parliament and specialists from agencies and organizations sit on these commissions. With the help of a permanent staff they develop recommendations which later, after eliciting comments from all interested parties, form the basis for government proposals to parliament. In policy areas where the difference of opinion among political parties is minimal (e.g. immigration) the influence of specialists often becomes great.

In 1944 a central body, the National Aliens Commission, was established for immigrant questions concerning residence and work permits, deportations, and aliens control. When this Commission was replaced in 1969, the Swedish Immigration Board (SIV) received the added responsibility of organizing immigrant policy. SIV became an active force in the process that decided immigration policy; it developed expertise in the field, and its yearly budget proposal summarized the areas in need of reform. Kjell Öberg, general director from 1969 to 1980, took an active part in pushing for policy reforms. He was, for example, the first to demand publicly that foreign citizens receive the right to vote.

It is difficult to weigh the various shapers of policy, but one can say that the political parties have sanctioned decisions rather than initiated them. Employers and labor unions have been the most important factors in decisions concerning work permits. When determining where the bulk of the work has been done, one must mention in particular SIV's leadership and the Commission on Immigration. Immigrants themselves have long lacked any real influence on policy decisions, although individual immigrants have been active in the policy debate. Not until the end of the 1970s were national immigrant organizations able to put some power behind their words, thanks to increased internal organization and mutual cooperation.

Administration

As we have seen, a central agency for immigration regulation was established in 1944. This was very late – controls and regulations had already been in effect since 1917. Initially the Stockholm police were given special orders to take care of immigration regulation for the whole country. In 1932 the responsibility was transferred to the state agency in charge of social welfare policy, where it formed a large section. The regulation activity was the whole time considered temporary, i.e. it would be dropped as soon as international conditions improved and became "normal". Even the National Aliens Commission (1944–69) had the provisional character of a wartime agency. SIV is the first immigration agency with a truly permanent character.

Today SIV makes decisions about visas, work and residence permits, political asylum, and naturalization, and keeps a register for purposes of aliens control. SIV works together with a number of other agencies. The Foreign Service in some cases handles visas and applications for permits, and the National Labor Market Board (AMS) makes recommendations on applications for work permits after consultation with national and local union organizations. The police are in charge of border control and also interview aliens who request permits. Regional offices have recently been formed to improve the quality of these interviews and to reduce waiting periods for applicants. SIV has as yet no local or regional units (though such agencies have been proposed) and must therefore rely at present on the police. Finally, AMS has responsibility for the transfer of selected groups of refugees from other countries, although in time this function will also be turned over to SIV. In general, each central agency or board is responsible for policy implementation within its own sector of public life, while SIV's task is to remind these agencies about the special needs of immigrants.

Immigrant policy is administered primarily on the local level. SIV cannot give local authorities directives on how to arrange housing, social services, or other services for immigrants; it can, however, offer its experience as well as advice and small amounts of money for special projects. On the local level the main responsibility for immigrant affairs lies with the ordinary administration: the social welfare offices, the local housing authorities, the schools, and other agencies that provide services for the whole community. But sometimes additional special measures are needed for immigrants. Local schools can organize special instruction and perhaps special classes for the larger national groups, and special personnel are often employed to handle contacts with immigrants. Communities with many immigrants have special "immigrant-service" offices where immigrants can go for help and advice.

Since local municipalities have a good deal to say about the kinds of service they provide for immigrants, conditions vary from place to place. This may depend on the level of a particular municipality's overall services or on its political leadership, but may also depend on the number of immigrants living there and from which countries they come. Thus, local policy is important for immigrants, which is one reason why they are allowed to vote and run for office in local elections.

Voluntary organizations and associations do not play much of a role in immigrant policy. Organizations like the Red Cross and "Save the Children" (Rädda Barnen) provide help for refugees, and some religious groups have begun activities to help immigrants, but most work is done by immigrants themselves. They have built up their own churches and congregations and have started their own associations, which have later become national organizations that cooperate with one another. One could say that these churches and organizations rarely take responsibility for the social and economic needs of immigrants, since that is taken care of by municipal agencies. Nevertheless, they provide cultural services and a place where fellow countrymen can meet.

To be entitled to the benefits of immigrant policy a non-Nordic citizen must in principle be registered as a resident of Sweden and thus have a residence permit. With a few exceptions, only those who have passed through the immigration regulation process and have received the unofficial status of "immigrant" have a right to housing, schools, and so forth. There is also an in-between group consisting of those persons who have applied for political asylum but have not yet received a decision. Applicants are not allowed to work during that time, but they do receive economic support and free access to Swedish language instruction.

Regulation is relatively centralized in SIV, although appeals can be made to the Ministry of Labor; immigrant policy lies on the local level. Nevertheless, a certain amount of coordination exists between the two. When SIV was established in 1969, immigration regulation and immigrant policy planning were merged, and attempts have been made since then to integrate more closely these two very different aspects of immigration policy. The impediments are numerous. Civil servants in the control section have different training and get a different on-the-job perspective from their colleagues in the section for immigrant policy. Yet the merger has not been completely without meaning. The two sections are under a common leadership which reaches agreements on fundamental issues.

Joint budget priorities are made regarding the hiring of new personnel, for example, and there has been some movement of personnel between the two sections.

While SIV has approximately three hundred employees, only about fifty people work with immigration in the Ministry of Labor. The majority of these people handle the appeals against SIV's decisions on, for example, deportation or naturalization. A small group works with immigrant policy. Thus, immigration issues are integrated under one administrative unit in both the Ministry of Labor and in SIV.

6. Lessons from Sweden?

Sweden became experienced with immigrant policy relatively early, undoubtedly because of the large Finnish immigrations. It was hard not to offer to other immigrants the same economic and social conditions available to Finns, who were on equal terms with Swedes in housing and working conditions as a consequence of Nordic cooperation. In addition, the strong Swedish labor unions did not allow discrimination against foreign workers with respect to wages and working conditions. In this way Sweden gained early experience with an immigrant policy aimed at creating equality between immigrants and native Swedes. The results of this policy have been good with regard to political rights and freedom of cultural choice, but somewhat worse with regard to return migration.

A prerequisite for the exercise of political rights is the guarantee that one cannot be forced to leave the country. Otherwise an immigrant's political opponent could threaten him with deportation. The Swedish Aliens Act gave such guarantees early on. These guarantees were never absolute since there were methods of avoiding them; still, freedom of association, speech, and assembly have been a reality for the most part.

Reform of the voting laws resulted in something quite new and, as it turned out, quite positive. Immigrants in Sweden are now engaged in political and labor union activity to an even greater extent than before. This does not mean that they have been culturally assimilated; it merely means that they are no longer closed out of political life. They can and do make demands and, because they are voters, the local politicians listen, and they have paid more attention to immigrant policy, which is especially important since it is administered on the local level. Perhaps other immigration countries ought to consider a similar type of voting reform.

National immigrant organizations have become interest groups in relation to the majority society. At the same time they serve to help preserve their members' national cultural life – a prerequisite for the achievement of "freedom of choice". Even though immigrant organizations exist in other immigration countries, they often have to work under less favorable conditions. It is too seldom recognized how essential these organizations are for a successful immigrant policy. A little separation from the majority may lead to a more thorough integration in the end.

Long-term goals are an uncertain point in Swedish policy. The aim of cultural freedom of choice may be suitable for the present, but no one knows how immigrant groups will develop in the future, what position they will have relative to the rest of society, and so forth. There are different alternatives. One possibility is that a number of them will disappear as their members grow older and a new generation with perhaps less connection to the emigration country emerges. Another possibility is that the larger organizations at least establish themselves as spokesmen for national minorities with specific rights and duties. One could imagine them building completely separate communities with their own decision-making powers on certain issues, their own school systems, and so forth. Their languages might be given full minority status. One can of course think of many other alternatives between these two extremes. But no goals have been set, and no one even knows what can realistically be achieved.

This lack of future-oriented policy discussion is negative. But even more negative is the tendency to regard all foreigners in the country as "immigrants", thereby neglecting those who choose to return home. This is slightly ironic: just because Swedes have been so careful to emphasize that immigration *can* be permanent, they often forget that it is not *always* permanent. In perhaps one third of all cases immigration is only temporary, yet few measures have been taken and no programs worked out to prepare those who want to return home in the short-term. On the other hand, there do exist agreements with emigration countries allowing the payment of pensions and child benefits to those who have returned. Sweden has also begun some attempts at technical and economic cooperation with Yugoslavia to create employment opportunities in particular emigration areas. There have been studies of return migration and of remittances, but on the whole the problem of return migration has been ignored. This is a serious omission at a time when return migration, particularly to Finland, is increasing.

3

The Netherlands

HAN B. ENTZINGER

1. Immigration and immigration policy

A brief historical overview

For many years the Netherlands has had a reputation for its strong international orientation. The country's favorable geographical location enabled it to become the seafaring nation of Europe. In order to insure commercial contacts it built up a colonial empire of surprising dimensions, given the modest size of the mother country. Since the Reformation in the sixteenth century the Netherlands has also been known as a tolerant country, and it became a refuge for those who were persecuted on grounds of religious or political beliefs. Jews from all over Europe, Huguenots from France, Roman Catholics from Germany, and many other refugees have contributed substantially to the country's economic prosperity and cultural development. During certain periods there was also a substantial immigration of temporary and permanent workers from nearby countries. Many of these were employed in agriculture, while others served as mercenaries in the navy and the army.

On the other hand, commercial and other interests in many parts of the world have led to substantial emigration. Dutch people have settled in many former colonies (North America, Brazil, West Africa) and in some cases their descendants may still be traced quite easily (Burghers in Sri Lanka, Boers in South Africa). During the nineteenth century large groups of Dutch emigrants moved to the United States and to the former Netherlands East Indies. Since the Second World War, and especially during the 1950s, half a million people have left for "New World" countries like Canada, Australia, and New Zealand.

For the people and the authorities of the Netherlands this long tradition of in- and out-migration of a more or less spontaneous nature may have blurred the specific character of immigration as it has developed over

50

Table 3.1. *Annual migration of foreigners to and from the Netherlands 1967–82*

	All foreigners			Nationals of nine Mediterranean countries*		
	Immigration	Emigration	Net migration	Immigration	Emigration	Net migration
1967	23,770	27,980	− 4,210	7,340	16,290	− 8,950
1968	32,270	21,120	+ 11,150	13,870	8,560	+ 5,310
1969	42,130	18,260	+ 23,870	23,260	7,080	+ 16,180
1970	52,070	18,540	+ 33,530	31,330	8,120	+ 23,210
1971	53,430	23,290	+ 30,140	27,350	10,410	+ 16,940
1972	41,630	36,900	+ 4,730	18,710	12,020	+ 6,690
1973	44,250	37,670	+ 6,580	21,740	11,170	+ 10,570
1974	45,370	37,030	+ 8,340	21,810	10,080	+ 11,730
1975	55,250	22,090	+ 33,160	26,680	9,610	+ 17,070
1976	48,930	25,730	+ 23,200	20,120	10,870	+ 9,250
1977	49,880	24,700	+ 25,180	20,050	9,630	+ 10,420
1978	55,600	24,110	+ 31,490	22,810	8,490	+ 14,320
1979	72,170	24,380	+ 47,790	25,430	7,630	+ 17,800
1980	79,820	23,630	+ 56,190	31,850	6,890	+ 24,960
1981	50,420	24,980	+ 25,440	20,110	8,140	+ 11,970
1982	41,130	28,280	+ 12,850	14,320	11,080	+ 3,240

Source: Central Bureau of Statistics.
Note: * Algeria, Greece, Italy, Morocco, Portugal, Spain, Tunisia, Turkey, Yugoslavia.

the past decades (Table 3.1). Decolonization processes, the widening development gap between the world's poor and rich nations, the need for manpower in the industrialized countries, and the availability of cheaper and quicker transportation facilities have together brought about a new kind of immigration consisting of people who have come not only in unprecedented numbers but also with time perspectives and objectives rather different from those of earlier immigrants. Their social, economic, and cultural background, as well as the possibility they have of maintaining close ties with their home countries, have made a smooth integration into post-industrial society less natural than it was in the past.

Recent immigration

Today there are well over one million people living in the Netherlands who themselves or whose parents migrated to the country since the end of the Second World War. They constitute about 8 percent of the country's 14.3 million inhabitants, and this proportion is increasing. Just over one half of them may be considered as colonial immigrants, i.e. people that arrived around the time of their respective countries' independence from the Netherlands.

During the years 1946–58 almost 300,000 people of Netherlands nationality were 'repatriated' from the former Netherlands East Indies and, somewhat later, from Netherlands New Guinea. Some of them were European administrators and planters; others were of mixed descent but preferred not to stay in Indonesia. From a cultural point of view nearly all of these Eurasians were fairly strongly oriented towards the Netherlands, which fact, combined with their strong motivation to integrate and the prosperous economic situation of the 1950s, promoted their rapid assimilation into Dutch society.

This has not been the case with the 12,500 Moluccans, members of the dissolved Royal Netherlands East Indies Army and their families. In 1951 they were practically forced to migrate to the Netherlands and there they awaited an imminent return to their own independent Republic of the South Moluccas. The course of history has been different, however, and at present the group – which has grown to 40,000 in the meantime – still lives in the Netherlands.

Another wave of colonial immigrants arrived during the early 1970s, shortly before the independence of Surinam, which was a Dutch territory at the northern edge of South America for over 300 years. Within a few years the number of Surinamers in the Netherlands grew from a few thousands, who were mainly there to study, to 180,000 (half the current population of Surinam). Many of these immigrants came from the poorest strata of Surinamese society and tried to secure a better future as long

Table 3.2. *Annual migration of Surinamers and Antilleans to and from the Netherlands 1970–82*

	Surinamers			Antilleans		
	Immigration	Emigration	Net migration	Immigration	Emigration	Net migration
1970	7,384	1,793	+5,591	3,820	2,518	+1,302
1971	9,493	1,957	+7,536	3,461	2,731	+730
1972	8,490	2,131	+6,359	3,653	2,445	+1,208
1973	11,098	2,087	+9,011	3,500	1,897	+1,603
1974	17,902	2,166	+15,736	3,399	1,825	+1,574
1975	39,699	3,037	+36,662	4,102	1,636	+2,466
1976	5,757	5,142	+615	3,841	1,709	+2,132
1977	4,786	3,430	+1,356	4,432	1,966	+2,466
1978	7,388	2,681	+4,707	4,717	2,166	+2,551
1979	18,162	2,372	+15,790	4,478	2,294	+2,184
1980	18,994	2,290	+16,704	5,475	2,315	+3,160
1981	4,432	3,338	+1,094	4,430	2,811	+1,619
1982	3,431	3,706	−275	3,989	3,196	+793

Source: Central Bureau of Statistics.
Note: Surinamers and Antilleans in the Netherlands on 1 January 1982:

Surinamese passport holders	17,700
Netherlands passport holders of Surinamese orgin	170,000 (est.)
Netherlands passport holders of Antillean orgin	41,000 (est.)

Table 3.3. *Foreign residents in the Netherlands (1 January of selected years 1900–82)*

	All foreigners (thousands)	All foreigners as % of population	Foreigners from nine Mediterranean countries* (thousands)	Mediterraneans as % of all foreigners
1900	53.0	1.0		1.1
1910	70.0	1.2		3.5
1921	112.1	1.6	1.2	4.4
1931	175.2	2.2	6.1	5.9
1947†	103.9	1.1	4.6	18.6
1960†	117.6	1.0	6.9	35.4
1964	134.8	1.1	25.1	52.4
1968	181.3	1.4	64.1	56.0
1972	268.0	2.0	140.2	55.6
1976	350.5	2.6	196.3	56.0
1977	376.3	2.7	209.4	56.7
1978	399.8	2.9	223.7	56.1
1979	430.0	3.1	243.9	57.0
1980	473.4	3.4	265.6	58.7
1981	520.2	3.7	296.6	
1982	539.2	3.8	316.7	

Source: Central Bureau of Statistics.
Notes: * Algeria, Greece, Italy, Morocco, Portugal, Spain, Tunisia, Turkey, Yugoslavia.
† 31 May.

as their Dutch nationality still enabled them to do so without any legal restrictions. In addition, there are about 40,000 immigrants from the Netherlands Antilles, a group of small islands in the Caribbean that is still a part of the Kingdom (Table 3.2).

A second category of immigrants has been those with motives of a primarily economic nature. Shortages of labor, especially at the lowest levels of the labor market, caused Dutch industry, with the support of the authorities, to recruit foreign workers, mainly from the Mediterranean area (Table 3.3). This option was preferred to the introduction of labor-saving but costly innovations which would improve the efficiency of production. As in other European countries, the labor shortage was considered only temporary. Some people even regarded the presence of foreign workers as a form of development aid! All this turned out to be an illusion: many foreign workers stayed on as immigrants and were gradually joined by their families. At present over 300,000 Mediterranean immigrants live in the Netherlands, most of them Turks and Moroccans.

There are also several smaller groups of immigrants. Since the end of the Second World War the Netherlands has admitted about 30,000 political refugees, at first mainly from Eastern Europe and later from a wide range of Third World countries (Uganda, Chile, Vietnam, and others). Quite surprisingly, given the Dutch tradition in this field, the number of refugees accepted is rather low in comparison with the number accepted by most other Western European countries. Two additional categories of immigrants are the Chinese (some 25,000) and the Gypsies (some 2,500). Both form quite distinct communities within Dutch society.

Finally, about 200,000 other foreigners live in the Netherlands who do not belong to one of the previous categories (Table 3.4). Many of them are nationals of adjacent countries. They have recently increased in number because of the free circulation of workers within the European Community, and come especially from the United Kingdom. But since more Dutchmen have moved to other member states (especially to the Federal Republic of Germany and Belgium) the net intra-EEC migration balance for the Netherlands is negative. The presence of these foreigners in Dutch society does not give rise to any specific problems. Hence they are not subject to any form of immigration policy – except, of course, that certain regulations for their admission to the country and its labor market also apply to them.

Immigration policy in brief

In comparison with other countries in Europe a major characteristic of postwar immigration to the Netherlands has been its heterogeneity. Several waves of colonial immigrants, most of them Netherlands

Table 3.4. *Foreign population of the Netherlands by country of citizenship and by sex, 1 January 1982*

	Subtotal (thousands)	Total (thousands)	As % of all foreigners	Men per 100 women
Belgium	23.6		4.4	107
Luxemburg	0.3		0.1	*
F.R. Germany	42.4		7.8	122
Denmark	1.2		0.2	*
France	6.4		1.1	113
Greece	4.1		0.8	173
Italy	21.1		3.9	185
Ireland	2.1		0.4	110
United Kingdom	40.0		7.4	145
Total EEC		141.2	26.2	133
Algeria	0.5		0.1	*
Morocco	93.5		17.3	158
Portugal	9.4		1.7	126
Spain	22.8		4.2	147
Tunisia	2.6		0.5	225
Turkey	148.5		27.5	127
Yugoslavia	14.2		2.6	120
Total 7 Mediterranean countries		291.5	53.7	138
Surinam		17.7	3.3	106
Indonesia		11.0	2.0	120
USA		10.7	2.0	98
All other countries (incl. stateless)		67.1	12.8	142
Total all foreigners		539.2	100.0	135

Source: Central Bureau of Statistics.
Note: * No data available.

passport holders, have been admitted along with immigrants of foreign nationality who came for economic and humanitarian reasons.

For many years Dutch admissions policy was fairly liberal. It was based on the persistent but erroneous presumption that all major groups of immigrants – except for the Eurasian "repatriates" of the 1950s – would be staying only temporarily. This idea was not dropped until the end of the 1970s. Since that time admission regulation has become stricter, as the government considers this a necessary condition for developing a coordinated immigrant policy.

Certain elements of an immigrant policy had been developed, however, even before these recent changes. To a large extent these were copied from the successful Eurasian integration policy of the 1950s, in which housing was a major instrument. In addition, government-subsidized, private social-work agencies had played a crucial role in the reception of immigrants, although their resources were limited. Though some success was achieved, immigrant policy on the whole was for too long fragmented, mainly ad hoc, and not well coordinated. The current new government policy may lead to an improvement, but it is still too early to assess its effects.

Terminology

The heterogeneous nature of immigration as regards nationality together with the immigrants' reasons for coming has given rise to a rather confusing terminology. While in immigration regulation nationality has been of primary importance (Netherlands nationals from overseas being in a far better position than foreigners), the immigrants' social situation has in fact been the major justification for Dutch immigrant policy. Immigrant groups whose position in society is not considered difficult either by themselves or by Dutch society are not or are no longer subject to a specific immigrant policy. At the moment this is the case with the Eurasians, the "European" foreigners and – quite surprisingly – the Chinese. It used to be the case with Surinamers and Antilleans when theirs was still an elite and middle-class migration. The social position of all other groups (Mediterranean workers and their families, Moluccans, refugees, Gypsies and – since the early 1970s – Surinamers and Antilleans) is considered problematic. They are therefore subject to a formal immigrant policy, which in the Netherlands is referred to as ethnic minorities policy, or simply minorities policy.

There seem to be two major reasons why the Dutch prefer to use the term "ethnic minorities" rather than "immigrants". One reason is that this enables them to include the increasing number of children born in the Netherlands of immigrant parents. The other reason is that the country's population has traditionally been composed of minorities, albeit cultural (religious) rather than ethnic ones. In fact, designating immigrants as "minorities" suggests that just a few more groups have been added to the existing sociocultural patchwork. This terminology itself reflects a basic element of the political philosophy that prevails concerning immigration.

The term "foreigners", which is used in most other continental European countries, would not be adequate in the Dutch context since about half of the recent "immigrants" possessed Netherlands citizenship upon arrival. Finally, it should be noted that some people prefer to use the term "ethnic groups" rather than "ethnic minorities" because they feel that "minority" implies "inferiority" – another interesting feature of Dutch multiculturalism!

All this aside, the term "immigrant" will be used here to designate any person entering the Netherlands with the intention of staying more than three months (the formal limit for tourist and business visits), irrespective of his or her nationality. The term "immigrant policy" will be used to designate all forms of government policy that aim at improving immigrants' participation in Dutch society. It should be seen as equivalent to what the Dutch call "minorities policy".

2. General preconditions

Historical and geographical preconditions
It has been mentioned that the favorable geographical location of the Netherlands has influenced its traditional international orientation. The country is not only situated in the delta of several major European rivers and at the junction of important sea-trade routes, but it is also surrounded by several cultural "spheres" of world importance. With its limited natural resources (except for natural gas), the Netherlands has always been highly dependent on commerce and trade. In fact, half of the national income is earned through exports. Rotterdam is the world's busiest port and KLM the sixth largest international airline; some of the biggest multinationals are based in the country. It is no wonder that throughout its history the Netherlands has been a clearinghouse for foreigners, many of whom have stayed on as immigrants. It is interesting to note that in the early twentieth century the percentage of foreigners in the country's population was higher than it is now, although they came from less remote countries.

But not just the traditional seafaring activities of the Dutch have caused migration. The country has always been easily accessible through its land borders, especially from the south. Under the 1958 Benelux Treaty passport control was removed to the external Benelux borders, which means that the Dutch–Belgian border is practically unguarded. This has had an important effect on immigration regulation.

The colonial past of the Netherlands, of course, is also an important precondition for understanding its present immigration policy. When Indonesia was still a Dutch colony only a small upper class possessed full Dutch citizenship, allowing the mother country to protect itself from large-scale immigration of non-Europeans. In 1954, in an attempt to "enlighten" colonial policy, most of the remaining overseas territories became self-governing, equal partners within the Kingdom of the Netherlands under the Covenant of the Kingdom (*Statuut van het Koninkrijk*). This implied, among other things, that the inhabitants of Surinam and the Netherlands Antilles became Dutch nationals and could settle freely in "the European part of the Kingdom". This led to a gradual increase in immigration, especially from Surinam. Granting independence to that country, in 1975, was considered the best solution to stop this flow, but as independence day came nearer a real exodus to the Netherlands of Surinamers who feared the uncertain future of their ethnically divided country (40,000 new arrivals in 1975 alone) took place (Table 3.2).

Economic preconditions

Industrialization took place rather late in the Netherlands and it has never reached the level of nearby countries like Britain, Belgium, and Germany. The few coal mines in the south were closed in the 1960s and heavy industry has never really been very significant. Instead, light industry (food processing, electronics) and the service sector (banks, commerce, trade, and transportation) are of crucial importance to Dutch economic life. This may be one reason why the need for foreign workers to do the heavy and dirty work that the original population shied away from was felt later than elsewhere in Europe. Mediterranean workers have never constituted more than 3 percent of the Dutch labor force and their distribution over the major branches of industry is relatively well balanced.

Another reason for the late start in labor migration may be found in the rapid population growth resulting from high birthrates and the "repatriation" of Eurasians. Both factors guaranteed a satisfactory domestic labor supply which implied that wages could be kept lower than elsewhere in Europe until well into the 1960s. Only then did demand begin to exceed supply on the labor market, and foreign workers were needed. This rather late start of foreign labor recruitment meant that the Dutch had to rely more heavily than their neighbors on Turkey and Morocco as labor suppliers, the geographically and culturally less distant countries of Southern Europe having been more or less "depleted" by then (Table 3.4).

Social and population preconditions

The Netherlands, which is the most densely populated country in Europe (400 inhabitants per square kilometer), has never seen immigration as an element of population policy. On the contrary, during the 1950s emigration to the "New World" was encouraged, although "repatriation" from Indonesia acted as a counterbalance. High population density has long been the official argument for stressing the temporary nature of immigrants' presence in the country, a main characteristic of Dutch immigration policy until very recently.

In the Netherlands, as in most other European countries, rapid economic growth began to stagnate during the first half of the 1970s. Beginning in 1973 this caused foreign labor recruitment to drop considerably, although it was never formally stopped. Economic stagnation, however, did not reduce the number of new immigrants. On the contrary, only a few years earlier the rules for family reunification had been eased, so that about this time Mediterranean workers began to bring their spouses and children to join them. Simultaneously immigration from Surinam reached its peak.

So, paradoxically, immigration (mainly of non-workers) went up while economic activity went down. As a matter of fact, the relative increase in the number of immigrants has been higher over the past ten years in the Netherlands than anywhere else in Europe (Tables 3.3 and 3.5). This has put a heavy extra burden on the sophisticated Dutch social welfare system. Despite the presumed temporary nature of immigration a large part of the Dutch population considered it unfair to force immigrants to return home when recession started. Besides, in many cases this was either impossible for legal reasons or unwise for economic reasons. Certain sectors of the economy would collapse even further without the support of immigrant workers, at least as long as the Dutch remained unwilling to do their kinds of jobs and preferred to rely on social security. This welfare ideology, according to which the state guarantees a fairly acceptable subsistence level to all residents, has become subject to critical public discussion lately. During its heyday, however, it definitely acted as a "pull" for immigration.

It is therefore no surprise that current unemployment among immigrants, depending on their ethnic group, is up to three times as high as among non-immigrants, for whom the unemployment rate stood at 15 percent in mid-1983. Immigrants often lack an adequate educational background and they are victims of the discriminatory attitudes of employers and potential colleagues. A perception of immigrants' rather heavy reliance on the social security system, where their rights are generally equal to those of non-immigrants, has intensified anti-immigrant feelings among the Dutch. This of course makes immigrants' chances even worse in a country

Table 3.5. *Registered residence and work permit holders from seven Mediterranean countries (1961–79)**

	Residence permit holders (a)	Work permits issued (b)	(b) as % of (a)
1961	719	545	75.8
1962	2,510	1,896	75.5
1963	6,110	5,030	82.3
1964	10,803	10,275	95.1
1965	22,690	23,031	101.5
1966	39,950	33,393	83.6
1967	56,877	46,359	81.5
1968	48,511	39,245	80.9
1969	44,736	45,213	101.1
1970	70,205	53,368	76.0
1971	92,870	68,543	73.8
1972	120,150	83,724	69.7
1973	128,572	85,511	66.5
1974	139,490	89,983	64.5
1975	153,120	93,158	60.8
1976	176,056	100,997	57.4
1977	190,544	99,724	52.3
1978	207,371	105,279	50.8
1979	218,565	110,439	50.5

Source: Central Bureau of Statistics, Ministry of Social Affairs and Employment.
Notes: On 1 November 1979 a new system of work permits was introduced.
　* Greece, Morocco, Portugal, Spain, Tunisia, Turkey and Yugoslavia.

which in 1982 spent 42.2 percent of its national income on social security, more than any other European country except Denmark.

With only a few exceptions Dutch trade unions have never really taken up the immigration issue. They have been avoiding the delicate dilemma of "international workers' solidarity" versus "protection of the members' interests". They count surprisingly few immigrants as members. Only very recently has the largest workers' federation begun to take some interest in the matter; its leaders are making an effort to promote their integrationist views among the membership.

Cultural preconditions
　Pluralism may be considered a major characteristic of Dutch society. The people of the Netherlands were traditionally split into various social and cultural blocs, mainly determined by their religious affiliation (Roman Catholic, Humanist, various Protestant denominations, and a few smaller communities). These blocs – or "pillars" as they are usually called – each showed a large degree of autonomy, with their own schools,

hospitals, broadcasting corporations, political parties, workers' unions, and private associations (Lijphart 1975). This delicately balanced system of "pillarization" broke down rather suddenly during the late 1960s, partly as a result of growing secularism but also because the emancipation process of what used to be "indigenous cultural minorities" had reached its final stage.

Immigration, which started to grow during the same period, may have hastened the dismantling of traditional "pillars". To which "pillar" should immigrants have addressed themselves? This tradition of pluralism should be kept in mind in order to understand the Dutch reaction to recent claims put forward by immigrant groups for certain forms of social and cultural autonomy as a means of eventually achieving full participation in Dutch society.

Foreign political preconditions

Decolonization has been an important element of Dutch foreign policy since the Second World War. One of its immediate effects, the arrival of Eurasian "repatriates", was not really a point of discussion. Because of the 1954 Convenant of the Kingdom, "spontaneous" immigration of Dutch passport holders from Surinam and the Netherlands Antilles has never been prevented. For a long time their need for education in the Netherlands was used to legitimate free admission, even after large numbers of immigrants had started to arrive for other than educational reasons.

Immigration from Surinam and the Antilles may be seen only to a certain extent as a substitute for the recruitment of foreign workers. Except for a brief period in the mid-1960s no workers have ever been recruited from those countries. The legal position of these Dutch passport holders is much stronger and their average level of education is somewhat higher; therefore, they are less apt to act as a buffer at the lowest level of the labor market, a function that "guestworkers" were believed to assume (and in fact did assume in the beginning).

In contrast to Dutch relations with the (former) overseas territories, relations with the other group of major emigration countries, those in the Mediterranean area, have never been very strong. Historically the Dutch have never had many interests in that part of the world. Large-scale migration has of course intensified bilateral contacts at the personal level, but at the official level such contacts have been limited to the negotiation of agreements on labor recruitment, social security, and cultural and educational cooperation, in part because of the undemocratic nature of some of the regimes in that area.

Finally, one should remember that the Netherlands considers the protection of human rights as a cornerstone of its foreign policy. Consequently, certain categories of political refugees have been admitted from countries where human rights are violated. As a more general rule, however, the government prefers to help these people in other ways, mainly because of the country's high population density. The Netherlands strongly supports United Nations' activities in the regions where refugees come from. It denounces totalitarian regimes in international forums and has set up an elaborate program of development cooperation. In 1980 the Netherlands spent 0.99 percent of its Gross National Product on development aid. This was the highest percentage of all OECD countries (Sweden ranked second with 0.76 percent).

3. Immigration regulation and control

Quite paradoxically the Netherlands did not consider itself a country of immigration until the late 1970s. All categories of immigrants entering the country since the Second World War were supposed to have done so on a temporary basis, except certain refugees and the Eurasians, who were not considered immigrants but rather "repatriates". All others were expected to return home at some stage, unless they had married Dutch nationals or become naturalized citizens. The Moluccans would go back to Indonesia after it had granted autonomy to the South Moluccas. Surinamers and Antilleans would return after completing their education (the expressed purpose of stay for the majority of them), or they would integrate without much effort, since they were Dutch nationals anyway. The Mediterranean workers had been welcomed on a temporary basis and would return when no longer needed or would be replaced by other immigrants (the rotation principle).

How different the reality was! Indonesia has still not allowed the Moluccans to establish a free republic and is not likely to do so in the future. Surinam became politically independent in 1975 and economic and political conditions there have worsened. There is some commuter migration to and from the Netherlands Antilles, but as that country's independence approaches return migration is not likely to increase. Mediterranean workers did return in quite large numbers in the early years of labor recruitment; yet as their average length of stay increased, return migration decreased (except to Italy, Spain, and Greece, three labor-supplying countries of limited importance to the Netherlands).

During the 1970s this growing discrepancy between policy and reality was noted by various authors and politicians (Entzinger 1975:327; Molleman 1978:331). Only as recently as 1978, however, did the government formally recognize that most Moluccans and Surinamers should be considered permanent immigrants. Not until 1980 did it do the same for the Antilleans and the Mediterraneans. The government has even admitted now that the presence of so many immigrants may lead to some additional immigration in the years to come, mainly as a result of continued family reunification.

Principal aims

Rules for the admission of immigrants of foreign nationality are laid down in the Aliens Act (*Vreemdelingenwet*) of 1965 and in the General Administrative Orders based on the Act. These rules are primarily technical and, at least initially, were meant to regulate rather than to counter immigration, which was generally considered a temporary phenomenon, even by many immigrants themselves. The rather vague concept of "general interest" was seen as the major guideline for admissions policy. During the years that followed, however, the gradual introduction of a series of measures made it more difficult for foreign workers to enter the country, and during the 1973 oil crisis the government for the first time openly spoke of "the need to limit the number of foreigners employed in the country to a ceiling in line with economic conditions" (WRR 1979:127). From then on the recruitment of foreign workers virtually came to a halt, but the immigration of non-workers continued on a fairly large scale because the existing restrictions in this field were not easy to enforce (Table 3.5).

Later, in the 1979 Memorandum on Aliens Policy (*Notitie Vreemdelingenbeleid*), the need for an even more restrictive policy was expressed much more strongly and its scope was extended to *all* foreigners. The Memorandum stated that admissions should be "as restrictive as possible within the limits set by international obligations and humanitarian considerations, even if an upswing occurred in the economy". This tightening up of immigration policy was not without effect, as we shall see later on. As before, high population density was presented as a major argument for the restrictions. In addition, however, it was argued that "the Dutch tradition of hospitality should no longer be reflected by admitting larger *quantities* of foreigners", but rather "by setting up an immigrant policy of good *quality* for those who were in the country already" (*Notitie Vreemdelingenbeleid* 1979:8). In other words, curtailing immigration was considered a prerequisite for the development of a sound immigrant policy.

The instruments of regulation and control

Antilleans and Surinamers

Immigrants of Netherlands nationality may enter the country freely. At present the only immigrants to which this applies are the Antilleans. As usual in colonial relationships the reverse is not the case: Dutch passport holders from "the European part of the Kingdom" may only settle in the Antilles if they possess a valid work permit.

The same freedom of entry and settlement also applied to Surinamers until their country became independent on 25 November 1975. At that time all Surinamers residing outside their country were entitled to retain Dutch citizenship, which the overwhelming majority of those living in the Netherlands did. During the five years that followed, Surinamese nationals were given a form of preferential treatment comparable to that enjoyed by citizens of the EEC.

In November 1980 the bilateral Settlement Treaty (*Vestigingsverdrag*) of 1975 expired and had to be renegotiated. Three months earlier the Netherlands government, in a reaction to a renewed heavy flow of immigration, had announced that Surinamers entering would require visas. In the renewed treaty the privileged position of Surinamese entrants was revoked, and since then migration from Surinam has decreased quite sharply (Table 3.2).

Foreign immigrants

The admission and settlement of all immigrants of foreign nationality is governed by the 1965 Aliens Act. Immigrants of some nationalities, however, enjoy certain forms of preferential treatment, provided they have sufficient means of subsistence. Nationals of the Benelux partners are free to settle in the Netherlands; nationals of the other EEC member states are also free to settle, along with their families, if they engage in some economic activity. Specific rules also apply to foreigners married to Dutch nationals.

Under the most recent policy guidelines any other newly arrived foreign immigrant – except for refugees and asylum-seekers – may only qualify for a temporary residence permit if this can be justified by a fundamental Dutch interest or by humanitarian conditions. A "fundamental Dutch interest" may be the fulfillment of a vacancy that no one residing in the Netherlands is available for. In certain cases foreign artists, students, or adoptive children may also be admitted. "Humanitarian conditions" mainly refers to family reunification for foreigners that have worked and legally resided in the Netherlands for a period of up to 24 months (differences apply according to nationality) and can prove that they will continue to do so for at least one more year. In addition, certain health and housing requirements have to be met.

Under the law on Employment of Foreign Workers (*Wet Arbeid Buitenlandse Werknemers*) of 1978 a newly arrived foreign immigrant who takes up paid employment needs a work permit, which the immigrant and his or her employer must jointly apply for. The permit may be valid for a limited period and is restricted to a particular job. A permanent work permit may be granted to the foreigner and his family members after three years. This permit allows free access to the entire Dutch labor market. Under the 1965 Aliens Act, however, a minimum of five years of uninterrupted residence is required before a foreigner may apply for a permanent residence permit. Besides, certain additional requirements, like a guaranteed income, have to be met. In the case of family reunification the permits of family members are linked during the first year to the permit of the person they have joined. A permanent residence permit may be withdrawn only for serious criminal offences. Holders of a permanent residence permit no longer need a work permit and cannot be forced to leave if they are no longer engaged in an economic activity.

The years 1970 and 1971 were the peak years for the recruitment of Mediterranean workers. When recruitment dropped after 1973, jobseekers continued to come spontaneously and some were still granted the necessary permits after arrival. At the same time the number of illegal immigrant workers increased quite sharply. In November 1975 the government announced a "general amnesty" for those illegal immigrants who could prove that they had been in the country for at least one year. About 15,000 illegal immigrants made use of this amnesty, but it did not solve the problem of illegal immigration as had been hoped. On the contrary, illegal immigration increased because a repetition of the amnesty was expected. In fact, a second "regularization" measure was taken under parliamentary pressure in 1980, but on a much smaller scale. This was connected with the introduction in 1979 of the Law on Employment of Foreign Workers, which instituted much tougher sanctions than the previous law against employers of illegal workers. In 1981, for instance, 460 cases of illegal employment were taken to court, involving some 2,500 foreign workers, but thus far fines have been rather low.

In general, the authorities are not too strict about detecting and expelling illegal immigrants, provided they do not violate other laws. Certain sectors of economic activity (horticulture, restaurants, cleaning) rely quite heavily on illegal workers. The number of illegal immigrants is now estimated at 20,000–40,000.

Although regulations regarding the expulsion of unemployed regular foreign immigrants are applied more strictly now than in previous years, the Netherlands government has never really pursued an active expulsion policy. By the time the immigrants were hit by the economic recession the majority of them already possessed a permanent residence permit; moreover, public opinion generally was against forced repatriation. In 1974 the government announced plans for a 5,000 guilders departure bonus for each foreign worker who would leave the country, but this proposal was rejected by parliament. Then it was decided to study possibilities for promoting the reintegration of Mediterranean migrants who returned on a voluntary basis. This so-called REMPLOD study was followed with great attention by experts and policymakers from other countries in Western Europe (Van Dijk & Penninx 1976). Its results were rather disappointing: there was little evidence that returning migrants did or could contribute to their home country's development.

Refugees

The legal status of refugees is quite different from that of foreign workers and their families. The granting of refugee status is governed by international agreements, specifically by the 1951 Geneva Convention and the 1967 New York Protocol relating to the Status of Refugees, as well as by the Aliens Act. Two categories of asylum-seekers may be distinguished: (1) those who fulfill all conditions as defined by the international agreements, and (2) those to whom not all these conditions apply but who "for humanitarian reasons, in view of the political situation in their country of origin, cannot reasonably be required to return to that country" (*Notitie Vreemdelingenbeleid* 1979:24). People in the first category are sometimes invited by the Netherlands government. They arrive in groups or individually and in recent years most of them have come from Latin American countries and especially from Vietnam. They obtain the formal, internationally recognized refugee status (so-called "A-status" refugees). Asylum-seekers may also arrive on their own initiative. If they can sufficiently prove that they fulfill the required conditions they may be accepted as "A-status" refugees. Otherwise they may be granted a "B-status", which entitles them to residence and work permits, or they may be extradited.

Since 1977 the government has set an annual quota of 750 invited refugees, which may be exceeded in the occurrence of calamities (e.g. the Vietnamese boat people). Individual asylum-seekers, however, may be admitted even after the quota has been reached, although the number of asylum-seekers that are granted "B-status" has been decreasing in recent years. There has been a gradual increase lately in the number of asylum-seekers who seem to have fled their countries for economic rather than political reasons. The vast majority of these people, who now number in the several thousands – among them many Turkish Christians – do not qualify for refugee status. Some of them are expelled fairly quickly, while in other cases arrangements have been made for them to move on to traditional immigration countries in other parts of the world.

Moluccans

Finally, the Moluccans who arrived in 1951 and their descendants form a very special category. Some members of this group are Indonesian nationals while most have taken on Netherlands citizenship over the years. A significant minority, however, are stateless and do not want to opt for either nationality. Under the Act of 1976 concerning the position of Moluccans ("Facilities Act" – *Faciliteitenwet*) stateless Moluccans have been given the legal position of Netherlands nationals, except that they lack the right to vote and cannot be drafted into the army. This means, among other things, that a stateless Moluccan can never be forced to leave the country.

Naturalization

Any foreigner aged 21 or over who has resided permanently in the Kingdom (Netherlands plus Netherlands Antilles) for five years, who used to possess Netherlands citizenship, or who was born in the Kingdom with stateless parents or parents of unknown nationality may submit a request to the Queen for naturalization. The conditions are that there should be no objection to the applicant's unlimited stay in the Kingdom and that he or she should be "sufficiently acclimatized" to Dutch society. In the latest directives (1979) based on the 1892 Act on Netherlands Citizenship and Residence (*Wet Nederlanderschap en Ingezetenschap*), the latter condition is interpreted as meaning a "reasonable knowledge of Dutch" and a "sufficient acceptance by Dutch society". These criteria are quite obviously rather vague.

In the past decade the number of applicants for Netherlands citizenship has been surprisingly low, especially among immigrants of Mediterranean origin. Only about one thousand of them have been naturalized each year (Table 3.6). It seems that many foreigners are not willing to cut the ties with their country of origin; moreover, the possession of a permanent residence permit entitles them to the same rights as Dutch nationals – at least formally – in many fields of society. As a general rule the government does not attach a great symbolic value to naturalization. It is merely considered a step in the integration process and not its ultimate goal, as in some other European countries. It should be noted here that under the present law *ius patri* prevails for second-generation immigrants; only the third generation obtains Netherlands citizenship at birth. This latter regulation, however, will not be automatic if a controversial new bill, which was recently submitted to parliament, is passed to replace the 1892 Act.

Table 3.6. *Naturalizations by country of last citizenship, 1976–80*

	All countries	Eight EEC countries	Nine Mediterranean countries*				
			Total	Italy	Morocco	Turkey
1976	3,900	880	870	250	40	100
1977	6,990	1,450	1,270	330	50	110
1978	6,590	1,580	1,060	300	40	110
1979	9,560	1,860	1,070	330	60	90
1980	15,220†	1,870	1,180	330	110	110

Source: Central Bureau of Statistics.

Notes: * Algeria, Greece, Italy, Morocco, Portugal, Spain, Tunisia, Turkey, Yugoslavia.
† Including 9,270 Surinamers.

The outcome of regulation and control

Until a few years ago immigration regulation and control was severely hampered by the striking discrepancy between officially stated policy aims and the facts, as mentioned earlier. In the 1979 Memorandum on Aliens Policy and, more explicitly, in a first general outline of the new government policy, published in March 1980, it was finally admitted that the Netherlands had indeed become a country of immigration. This enabled the authorities not only to set up a coherent immigrant policy (see section 4 below) but also to systematize the various admission directives that had developed over the years.

Elements of the new admissions policy are: the introduction of visa requirements for nationals of certain countries with a high emigration potential (Turkey, the Maghreb countries and Surinam) and a stricter application of the rules for family reunification. People trying to enter illegally are now being refused more consistently and "pseudo-marriages" for the purpose of illegal entrance have been made more difficult, although not impossible.

The guidelines to be applied in these cases, however, are still not clear and uniform, which has led to a certain degree of legal inequality vis-à-vis people seeking entrance. In many cases it is difficult to appeal against an administrative measure if the person in question is still abroad (e.g. refusal of visa) or has entered the country illegally.

The number of regular admissions of all foreigners has gone down considerably since these new measures went into effect (80,000 in 1980, 50,000 in 1981 and 41,000 in 1982; see Table 3.1). The drop in the migration surplus (immigration minus emigration of foreign nationals only) is even more dramatic (56,000 in 1980, 26,000 in 1981 and 13,000 in 1982). Of course, the rapidly worsening state of the country's economy will also have contributed to this decrease. Yet the government is well aware of the impossibility of stopping immigration altogether. So-called "primary" family reunification will continue, especially among Moroccans (although the maximum admission age of dependent children will soon be lowered from 21 to 18). Most second-generation Mediterraneans marry someone from their country of origin, which opens up a new potential for "secondary" family reunification. Border control – especially at the Belgian border – is not strict, and the admission of refugees will continue (e.g. 2,500 boat people in 1981, most of them picked up by Dutch vessels). In addition, fears have been expressed on various occasions that if the situation in South Africa worsens it might cause the return of tens of thousands of the Dutch passport holders living there, and possibly also South Africans of Dutch origin.

But even if no new immigrants were admitted at all – except for strictly limited family reunification – it has been calculated that the number of foreign nationals will increase by almost one half over the next decade, mainly as a result of their high birthrates (Kool & Van Praag 1982).

Under the current immigration policy emphasis has been placed on limiting admissions rather than on reinforcing internal control, which for various reasons has never been terribly strict. These reasons have not been publicly stated, but one may assume that they involve the fear of accusations of racial discrimination, the wish to protect certain marginal sectors of economic activity, practical explanations (shortage of policemen), and perhaps also pressure by public opinion and the press.

4. Immigrant policy

Principal aims

The long-term official denial that the Netherlands was a country of immigration as well as the heterogeneous nature of the immigration has prevented the development of a clear immigrant policy. This is not to say that there has been no specific immigrant policy at all but rather that the measures taken in the past have been of a somewhat ad hoc nature and therefore of only limited effectiveness. Quite recently, however, the government has begun to develop an overall "ethnic minorities" policy, the basic aim of which is to increase the participation of immigrants in Dutch society. It has become clear now that this cannot be achieved simply by applying general social instruments to immigrants, even though these instruments often try to improve the conditions of life for the less-favored strata in society.

Since the early 1970s the increasing proletarization of immigration from Surinam combined with family reunification among Mediterraneans has caused a rapid growth in the social needs of immigrants. These immigrants came in contact with more sectors of Dutch society than before (schools, housing, health care, and so forth), but their weak legal and social position as well as their lack of language and other skills prevented many of them from obtaining a fair share of social benefits. The culture gap made it difficult for existing institutions to cope with the increasing numbers of newcomers. Some of these institutions were still set up along "pillarization" lines – the traditional characteristic of the Dutch social system outlined above.

The government – more precisely the Ministry of Cultural Affairs, Recreation, and Social Work – gradually developed a policy of "integration with the preservation of separate identity". In reality, however, this policy was merely a slogan; it involved little more than the extension of social assistance services and the subsidy of certain recreational facilities so that the basic idea of non-permanence would not be violated. Obviously, these measures were far from sufficient. Unemployment, feelings of isolation and apathy, criminal behavior and drug abuse spread rapidly, especially among immigrant youngsters who were caught between two cultures.

The need for a coherent policy was publicly recognized in 1979 when the Scientific Council for Government Policy, a high level advisory body to the government, recommended that the government "proceed on the assumption that [the immigrants'] residence in the Netherlands could be permanent" (WRR 1979:xvii). The Council said that in accordance with this principle a policy should be set up with two distinct aims: (1) the closing of the socioeconomic gap and (2) cultural equality in an open multi-ethnic society. Government action to achieve these aims ought to be focused mainly "on creating institutional arrangements on behalf of immigrants, on increasing their participation in society, on combating discrimination, and on improving the legal status of the foreigners among them" (WRR 1979:xxi ff).

In a preliminary statement released in March 1980 the government for the most part accepted these ideas. In April 1981 a 336 page Draft Memorandum on Minorities (*Ontwerp-Minderhedennota*) was published in which the new policy was further elaborated. The Draft Memorandum was submitted for discussion and comment to all groups concerned; the final text was sent to parliament in autumn 1983. At present, the aim of Dutch "minorities" policy is officially formulated as "the creation of a society in which all members of minority groups living in the Netherlands will have an equal place and full chances, individually as well as on a group basis" (*Ontwerp-Minderhedennota* 1981:35).

Though a clearer formulation of this aim might have been possible, the intention is obvious. The most outstanding Pfeatures of the (proposed) policy may be summarized as follows:

a.   Recognition, at long last, of immigrants as a special subject of government policy, irrespective of their nationality and reasons for coming.
b.   A mostly integrationist approach in socioeconomic matters, whenever necessary by providing extra (temporary) facilities to bridge existing gaps.
c.   A mostly *pluralist* approach in cultural matters, certainly inspired by Dutch traditions of pluralism.

Not only immigrants but the indigenous population as well have become the subject of immigrant policy. The government is well aware that changes in the social position of the former will have implications for the latter. The somewhat disputable concept of the Netherlands as a "multi-cultural society" has been introduced.

In order to carry out this policy the government will need more information on the actual living conditions of immigrants and on the effects of policy measures. It was felt that social science research might contribute substantially to this, but research on immigrant groups had long been neglected, in part because of the persistent denial that the Netherlands was a country of immigration. This is why the Advisory Commission on Minorities Research (ACOM) was created in 1978. The major task of this consultative body, whose members are independent academic experts, is to give advice on the setting up and implementation of government-sponsored research projects related to the immigrant issue, and, on the basis of research findings, to advise on policy guidelines. Though government policy is for obvious reasons not shaped by social scientists alone, it cannot be denied that the activities of ACOM have had an impact on the nature of the new immigrant policy.

The instruments of immigrant policy

Until recently direct immigrant policy had been developed in only two fields, housing and social work. In all other areas general policy instruments were meant to apply to immigrants also, at most with some minimal additional services. This may be illustrated by the following examples.

Some general policy instruments

Employment

During the years of planned recruitment of foreign labor and the early days of large-scale "spontaneous" migration from the West Indies the expanding labor market could easily accommodate immigrants. Most Mediterranean workers were employed in industry and most Surinamers and Antilleans worked in the service sector.

Partly because of their lack of vocational skills, immigrants were among the first to be hit when the economy began to stagnate. A few special training courses were set up for young Surinamers, but the results were limited, in part because of discriminatory attitudes among employers (De Graaf 1979:102). Occasionally, young immigrants of foreign nationality were denied the work permit, although they were entitled to it as a consequence of one of their parents' holding a permanent work permit. Public employment offices were not able to cope very well with the rapidly increasing supply of second-generation immigrants and foreign women, and registered unemployment among these groups rose quickly. A few special employment officers have been appointed for the Moluccan community – with some success, it appears (Veenman & Vijverberg 1982).

Education

Schools were unable to cope with the heavy influx of immigrant children from different cultural backgrounds; these children tripled in number within five years as a result of family reunification and high birthrates. At first no special provisions were thought necessary for Surinamese children since Dutch has always been the language of instruction in their country, but it soon became apparent that their potential for integration was only superficial. Certain facilities were created for children of Mediterranean origin, mostly in the form of remedial teaching, but these measures were rather haphazard (Van den Berg-Eldering *et al.* 1980:11ff).

At some schools special teaching in the children's own language and culture was introduced to facilitate their eventual return. Later, in the 1981 Policy Plan on Cultural Minorities in Education (*Beleidsplan Culturele Minderheden in het Onderwijs*), when the authorities had become aware of the permanent nature of immigration, this aim was reformulated as "developing the children's self-concept" – yet the facilities remained unchanged! (De Vries 1981:87). It should be noted here that most schools in the Netherlands are fairly autonomous in setting up their curricula – another legacy of the "pillarization" system. A few limited opportunities were offered to adult immigrants to become familiar with the Dutch language, mainly through Dutch volunteers. It should be noted as well that there is some lack of motivation on the part of many adult immigrants to learn Dutch, not only because in a European perspective it is a language of only regional importance, but also because for a long time the immigrants themselves were convinced that their stay would be only temporary.

Political participation

Political participation among immigrants is extremely limited. Of course, immigrants who are Dutch nationals possess full civil rights, but for a long time political parties and other sociopolitical institutions were hardly interested in their situation. Immigrants of foreign nationality possess fewer rights than Dutch nationals and lack the right to vote and to run for office (Groenendijk 1979:54). There have been some experiments with consultative councils of foreigners and Moluccans, but most of them failed because they lacked any real influence on political decisionmaking. In early 1983 a new Constitution came into force that removed the major obstacle to an amendment of the Electoral Law. As a result, foreign nationals with a certain residence record (probably three years) may in the future be granted the right to vote and run for office on the local level.

Direct immigrant policy

Housing

When the Netherlands emerged from the Second World War it was faced with an enormous housing shortage. Many buildings had been destroyed and rapid postwar population growth made the problem even worse. The housing shortage was declared "public enemy number one" and a large-scale building program was started, heavily sponsored by the public sector. Numerous cheap dwellings were built, generally of rather poor quality. Yet despite these measures the housing shortage has persisted up to the present day, as may be illustrated by the recent "squatter" activities all over the country. The percentage of privately owned houses is far below the European average and public authorities and "pillarized" corporations continue to have much say in the distribution of living accommodation.

This may explain why the Dutch government, when faced with the first postwar immigration wave from Indonesia, decided to make housing a central element of its integration policy. Throughout the country a certain quota of newly built houses was put at the disposal of the new arrivals. This facilitated the Eurasians' inevitable integration.

A much different policy was formulated for the Moluccans, although housing was still an important element. Since their stay was meant to be temporary the Moluccans were physically segregated from Dutch society. When they arrived in 1951 they were put into barrack camps (some of which were former Nazi concentration camps), and at first they were not even allowed to take employment. As their stay continued, however, segregation lessened somewhat. During the 1960s a policy of clustered dispersal was introduced and special neighborhoods were built in various municipalities throughout the country. The vast majority of Moluccans still live in these neighborhoods; this has enabled them to preserve some elements of their cultural identity but it has also hampered their integration.

It is no surprise that when faced with large-scale immigration from Surinam in 1974 the government again embarked on a housing policy similar to that applied to the Eurasians in the 1950s, although it was now on a more voluntary basis. Five percent of all newly built council houses were allocated to Surinamers. This time, however, success was limited because several important distinctions from the Eurasian situation had been overlooked: Surinamers were less motivated to integrate (the return option continued to exist) and work was less readily available to them, partly because they did not possess the proper qualifications. What had proved workable in the 1950s was no longer effective in the 1970s.

Surinamers, together with foreign workers for whom practically nothing has been done (after the initial provision of accommodation in hostels by their employers), have to compete with the Dutch on the normal housing market where their chances are limited. Quite often, foreign workers may only register for council houses after they have been joined by their families, but family reunification is only permitted if adequate housing is available. This vicious circle forced many immigrants to buy or rent expensive dwellings of poor quality in the private sector, mostly in declining urban districts (Nijzink 1979:16).

Social work

The long absence of an effective general policy has led to a heavy reliance on social work as an instrument of direct immigrant policy, especially as regards foreign workers. During the early years of labor recruitment foreign workers' contacts with Dutch society were kept to a minimum in view of their assumed temporary residence. Several assistance agencies were set up, mainly by private initiative and by churches, to ensure the reception and guidance of foreign workers. Later the funding of these agencies was taken over by the Ministry of Cultural Affairs, Recreation, and Social Work (now Social Welfare, Public Health and Culture) and their staff expanded rapidly. As time went by these social workers increasingly felt unable to limit themselves to assisting individual immigrants in overcoming day-to-day problems. They dropped their somewhat paternalistic attitudes and gradually assumed an important role in voicing group interests, given the lack of other means to ensure social and political participation for immigrants.

Social work agencies, however, were hardly able to improve directly the structural accommodation of immigrants in Dutch society; the instruments required were beyond the agencies' domain and in many cases did not even exist. But in an indirect way their acting as defenders of the rights and interests of immigrants has speeded up the change in policy.

Towards a general immigrant policy

As a first step certain measures were taken in the field of legislation. These were relatively easy to bring about and more important did not cost much. The 1976 Facilities Act for Moluccans has already been discussed. In 1981 the Penal Code was amended in order to strengthen antidiscrimination legislation.

The proposed overall policy was laid down in the Draft Memorandum on Minorities published in April 1981. The major instruments of the policy which, of course, also includes further restrictions in immigration as discussed in the previous section, may be summarized as follows:

1. *General policy instruments*
   a. Improve the legal status of foreign immigrants who have resided in the Netherlands for some time by reducing certain differences in the applicability of legislation.
   b. Combat discrimination through legal measures and an active information policy, and possibly by creating a special body to handle complaints.
   c. Reinforce political participation by granting local voting rights to foreigners with a certain residence record and by setting up consultative councils at the national level for each ethnic minority group.
   d. Create more facilities for scientific research into immigrants' social situations.
   e. Set up more pools of language interpreters.
2. *Labor market instruments*
   a. Various concrete measures in the field of vocational training to make immigrants, especially the young and unemployed, better qualified for the Dutch labor market.
   b. Extend subsidies to employers who hire unemployed immigrants.
   c. Create temporary jobs for immigrants in government sponsored, non-profit sectors.
3. *Housing*
   It is hoped that general policy instruments meant to stimulate construction and urban renewal will have a positive effect on the immigrants' housing. In addition, special facilities will be created:
   a. to increase the number of large houses.
   b. to improve living conditions in urban districts with large concentrations of immigrants.
   c. to offer immigrants a wider choice in cheap housing.
   Neither concentration nor dispersion will be officially stimulated by the government. In practice, however, several local authorities have taken clear positions on this matter, and they usually favor dispersion.
4. *Education*
   a. More and better reception classes to prepare newly arrived children for the Dutch school system.
   b. Certain facilities for education in the language of the country of origin of the child and/or his parents.

   c.   More remedial teachers.
   d.   Further development of curricula for "intercultural education".
   e.   Facilities for language and social-skills training for adults, usu-
        ally outside the work setting.
5. *Social welfare and health care*
   a.   Make social work agencies and health care facilities more accessi-
        ble to immigrants.
   b.   Gradually dismantle some social work agencies that are for
        immigrants only.
6. *Return migration*
   a.   Create better facilities for those who want to return without,
        however, forcing any migrant to do so.

In order to carry out this ambitious program, hundreds of millions of
guilders will be set aside annually during the years to come. This will, of
course, be in addition to the money spent on the general facilities that
immigrants may also make use of. In the 1981 government budget an
amount of fl. 720 million was set aside for the new program, and in the
1982 budget this amount was raised to fl. 830 million. The table shows
how the extra money was distributed in the 1981 budget.

General policy instruments*	fl. 20 million
Employment	80
Education	230
Housing	60
Social welfare and health care	240
Return migration	10
Funds to be spent by local authorities	80
Total	fl. 720 million†

* Including about fl. 6 million for scientific research.
† Approx. US$240 million, in mid-1983.

The outcome of immigrant policy
   It is too early, of course, to assess the effects of the new policy. It
has not even been formulated and adopted in its definitive form yet,
although certain parts of it have already become operative. Obviously
social science research, which so far has been mainly inventorial and
descriptive, will again play an important role in assessing the effects of the
new policy instruments. In fact, through earlier evaluations of the position of immigrants in housing, education, and other sectors of social life,

researchers have been able to detect some of the obstacles mentioned earlier and in so doing have contributed to formulating current immigrant policy (ACOM 1979; Entzinger 1981).

Current policy may very briefly be characterized as having two major aims: (1) to achieve greater equality in socioeconomic matters by increasing immigrants' share of goods and services; and (2) to achieve greater cultural pluralism. The second aim will be pursued in particular by the introduction of consultative councils to the national government for the various groups and by the perpetuation of certain special facilities in the field of education and social work. When the two aims appear contradictory, the "equality" aim will prevail. This is becoming more obvious now that the overall economic situation has worsened. For this reason current policy is essentially integrationist, although the term "integration" has been carefully avoided for reasons that will be discussed later (sections 5 and 6).

At the same time the concept of the Netherlands as a multicultural society has been (re)introduced. It implies the promotion of mutual respect for the cultural heritage of all ethnic groups living in the country. By applying this traditional Dutch notion to immigrant groups, however, the government may have ignored a little too easily that certain elements in the immigrants' culture may be incompatible with the requirements of life in Western industrial society (e.g. the position of women, the functions of extended-family ties, concepts of democracy). Though in many cases – but not always – a rapid integration at the individual level will be impossible, the potential for cultural change caused by immigration should not be underestimated either.

The interrelationship between immigrant policy and immigration regulation and control

Only quite recently has the government of the Netherlands become fully aware of the close links between immigration regulation and immigrant policy. Prior to this realization immigrant policy was fragmented and ad hoc – a natural consequence of an almost autonomous process of immigration based on false assumptions of non-permanence and voluntary integration. An additional, somewhat confusing factor (which is fairly typical for the Netherlands) is that immigration regulation and immigrant policy do not apply to all immigrant groups in the same way, nor has their application remained constant over a period of time. Table 3.7 illustrates this situation.

In any case, the 1981 Draft Memorandum on Minorities now states:

> The success of the "minorities" policy that the government has in mind will be increased by further restrictions in immigration

Table 3.7. *The application of immigration policy in the Netherlands*

Subject to immigrant/ "ethnic minorities" policy	Subject to immigration regulation (as defined by the Aliens Act)	
	Yes	No
Yes	Mediterranean workers plus families	Moluccans (only a specifically defined group)
	Surinamese nationals (since 1975)	Surinamers of NL nationality (since 1974)
	refugees	Antilleans (since 1974)
	gypsies	Eurasians (until 1966)
No	Belgians and Luxemburgers	Eurasians (since 1966)
	other EEC citizens	Surinamers (until 1974)
	Chinese (partly UK nationals from Hong Kong)	Antilleans (until 1974)
	foreigners not yet mentioned	

... The government is of the opinion that in the process of weighing equal opportunities of those members of minority groups who already belong to our society against the admission of foreigners living elsewhere under hard social and economic conditions, priority has to be given to the former group. (*Ontwerp-Minderhedennota* 1981:52)

For various reasons the actual implementation of this policy still may create problems, most of which have been mentioned already:

a. Earlier immigration waves have set in motion certain forms of chain migration. Since in a European perspective large-scale immigration to the Netherlands had a late start, the effect of this chain migration is still quite noticeable. An effective immigrant policy may even attract more immigrants."

b. A completely tight border control remains difficult to achieve, while it is formally impossible at the internal borders of the Benelux. It should be noted here that the Netherlands, Belgium, and Luxemburg have harmonized their regulations regarding the admission of foreigners for periods of up to three months, although certain differences persist as regards the granting of residence permits. This favors illegal immigration. On various occasions an active expulsion policy in other European countries has led to an increase in (illegal) immigration to the Netherlands. Yet, there has been little formal coordination of immigration policies within the EEC.

c. Although the government wants to counter illegal entrance and residence as much as possible it does not propose any new instruments of internal control, but only plans to increase the use of existing methods. If the current practice of a low-profile policy is continued the number of illegal residents might rise; on the other hand, if internal controls become too severe, strong opposition from several sectors of public opinion can be expected, for economic as well as humanitarian reasons.

d. Finally, the linking of admissions and immigrant policies might also be hampered for reasons of policy administration. So far there has been little cooperation between the authorities charged with immigration control and those responsible for carrying out immigrant policy. Sometimes their interests are clearly opposed, especially when it comes down to the application of guidelines and directives. Besides, there may be certain distinctions in personal motivation between officials of the two categories (Aalberts & Kamminga 1983).

5. Policymaking and administration

Perceptions

The Netherlands' long history of immigration and emigration as well as the tradition of cultural and religious pluralism has made the Dutch acquainted, at least superficially, with different life-styles. In addition, during the early years of the decolonization process there was a general feeling of responsibility toward the Dutch nationals who had become "victims" of the process: the Eurasians, the Moluccans, and (to a far lesser extent) the Surinamers and the Antilleans. This is why the immigration issue has never played a primary role in public debate or in parliamentary discussions, not even during the main years of labor recruitment. The presence of foreign workers was seen as a necessary but temporary phenomenon.

During the postwar years the Netherlands was generally perceived as a harmonious society where consensus prevailed, even in politics, and where racial discrimination did not exist and would never have a chance to develop (Bagley 1973). The brutal persecution of Jews under the Nazi occupation was abhorred both at the time and in retrospect. For a long time the specific needs of the "new" immigrants were denied by referring to the successful integration of earlier immigrants, especially the Eurasians. It was not until the mid-1970s that such misperceptions began to fade.

Around the same time several violent acts of terrorism were committed by young members of the Moluccan community whose political and social ambitions had become increasingly frustrated. These events (hijacking trains, hostage taking, an abortive attempt to kidnap Queen Juliana) drew the entire world's attention to the Moluccan problem without, however, bringing the Moluccans' political aspirations – a free and independent Republic of the South Moluccas – any closer to reality. For the government of the Netherlands these events were a very clear sign that mounting social problems had been neglected, and there can be no doubt that this realization speeded up the development of an immigrant policy (Köbben 1979:154).

The superficial observer might be surprised at the degree of understanding expressed in public reactions by the press and mass media and by many politicians for the reasons behind these terrorist acts. Again, feelings of guilt for the colonial past may have played a role here as well as a certain pride in the Netherlands' reputation for tolerance. Under the surface, however, the growing number of immigrants has led to a gradual rise in feelings of xenophobia and prejudice ("they" take "our" jobs, houses, etc.; "they" are criminals), although it is still considered improper to express such feelings in public (Bovenkerk 1978:9ff).

This may explain why all major political parties as well as other organizations have long been trying to play down the immigrant issue. Whenever they are forced to take a stand it is usually pro-immigrant, although this is more the case for issues of immigrant policy than issues of immigration regulation, where viewpoints have become noticeably tougher recently.

The making of immigration policy

There are no major differences between the larger political parties as regards immigration policy. Importantdecisions taken in the past were always supported by these parties, whether or not they were represented in the government at the time. It should be noted that in the Netherlands the regular alternation between center right and center left coalition governments has been the rule for many decades now. This system serves to prevent sudden changes in policy.

A certain tendency to emphasize the need to respect and support immigrants' rights – especially in the fields of culture and education – may now be observed among politicians more strongly than might be justified by the views of their voters. Again, one should not forget that most political

parties in the Netherlands – like many other associations – are still struc-
tured along "pillarization" lines, which means that traditional concepts of
harmonious multiculturalism, mutual respect, and help for the
underprivileged are still of primary importance. Outside the political
arena, however, these concepts are increasingly being replaced by more
individualistic views, especially in urban settings where the economic
recession as well as the effects of immigration are most direct and most
strongly felt.

In these settings there is no widespread sympathy for sophisticated
policies of multiculturalism, which is seen as an invention of academics,
politicians, clergymen, and welfare workers. This lack of sympathy
became very clear in September 1982 when for the first time in history the
extreme rightist Centrumpartij managed to obtain one seat in parliament
on a fierce anti-immigration program. It drew most of its votes from the
old districts in the large cities. As a result of this the more established
parties may be forced to elaborate upon their own immigrant policy in the
near future (Van Donselaar & Nelissen 1982).

Because of the prevailing political consensus, immigration policy was
largely determined by administrators and their advisers. The predominant
role played by the 1979 recommendations of the Scientific Council for
Government Policy (WRR) may be seen as an illustration of this. Certain
activities of the Advisory Commission on Minorities Research (ACOM)
have also had a wider impact on the shaping of government policy than one
might expect from a group of independent academic experts whose primary
task is to advise on the programming of social science research in the field.

There can be little doubt that this situation is changing rapidly at the
moment. The political parties' low-profile attitude on immigration affairs
has created a situation in which numerous interest and pressure groups
have begun to act as advocates for immigrants' needs and demands. The
press and other mass media have also played an important role here. The
Netherlands is known for its unique system of private and autonomous
broadcasting associations that dominate the radio and television networks – another legacy of "pillarization". Immigrant groups and the
groups that act on their behalf quickly find willing listeners among the
staff of some of these associations to voice their grievances and criticism
(Penninx 1981:4). Some politicians are rather sensitive to these forms of
publicity. A certain incompatibility can be noted between the need for a
restrictive admissions policy on the one hand and feelings of compassion
for individuals who have become "victims" of that policy on the other, for
instance, where the expulsion of illegal immigrants is concerned.

The government has felt the need to give immigrants a greater say in
formulating immigrant policy. A Consultative Council for Moluccan

Welfare (*Inspraakorgaan Welzijn Molukkers*) was created in 1976 for this purpose. This council, in which various Moluccan associations are represented, was given advisory powers to the Minister of Cultural Affairs, Recreation and Social Work in matters related to the Moluccan community. In its 1981 Draft Memorandum on Minorities the government announced an extension of similar facilities to other ethnic communities. A Draft Regulation on Consultative Facilities for Ethnic Minorities and Caravan Dwellers (*Wetsontwerp Inspraak Etnische Minderheden en Woonwagenbewoners*), designed to grant legal status to such bodies, has already been released for public discussion.

Though this is only meant as a temporary measure, sceptical observers have pointed out certain disadvantages. Elections for membership on these councils are impossible for legal and technical reasons. Fears have been expressed that the councils might become dominated by particular subgroup interests, as has been the case with a similar experiment at the local level in the city of Utrecht. Introducing this type of legally required consultation may also set a precedent for other groups in Dutch society (senior citizens, handicapped people, women). Although the councils' powers will only be consultative, they might undermine the tasks of parliament in the long run (*Harmonisatieraad Welzijnsbeleid* 1981:10).

Tendencies towards more "autonomy" for immigrant communities are also reflected by recent shifts in the demands voiced by certain welfare agencies and ethnic associations. Some of them not only demand more attention for immigrants' social needs and for the improvement of their legal status (their "traditional" role) but also advocate a certain degree of "autonomy" for the respective groups. In particular, they demand certain separate facilities that will enable immigrants to preserve their cultural identity. In some cases these demands go well beyond providing accommodation for religious ceremonies and leisure activities. Demands have been put forward for separate schools – which under the Dutch pluralist school system would not be impossible – for separate hospitals, and for segregated housing. Such demands are not really in line with the primarily integrationist policy that the government is now pursuing, and the authorities are increasingly worried about a possible backlash among the original population, in particular among those in the least privileged socioeconomic strata.

The administration of immigration policy

Before the Napoleonic era government in the Netherlands was highly decentralized. In fact, the Constitution of the United States of America was modelled after that of the Republic of the Seven United Netherlands (where Holland was by far the most important province). Things have changed drastically since those days and national government has become predominant in nearly all policy matters. Municipal and provincial governments are free to operate only within the fairly narrow constraints set by the state authorities, although there is increasing pressure for less centralization.

The primary role of the national government has caused most of the thirteen ministries in The Hague to develop into fairly autonomous and huge administrative bodies. Another characteristic of the system of government in the Netherlands is that outside the ministries there are only a few specialized agencies which have relatively extended powers. Since such agencies do not exist at all for immigration matters, admissions regulation and immigrant policy are basically shaped and administered by the ministries. For a long time each ministry has acted from its own particular angle, and this has contributed to the ambivalence that has characterized Dutch immigration policy.

The Minister of Justice has primary responsibility for immigration regulation and control; he decides, in individual cases, which foreigners (including asylum-seekers and refugees) may enter the country. He is also responsible for the expulsion of foreigners. Foreigners who are to be expelled or who have been refused a residence permit may appeal against the decision to a court, but in many cases the appeal will not delay the enforcement of the decision.

The diffusion of responsibility for immigrant policy is more complicated, a result of the recent history of immigration to the Netherlands and of the wide variety of motives among the immigrants for coming to the Netherlands.

The Minister of Social Affairs and Employment has always been in charge of the recruitment of foreign workers. When as a result of family reunification other ministries were also faced with the immigrants' problems, it became his task to coordinate their policies. Yet this Ministry held to its original views on the role of foreign workers as a temporary buffer in the labor market. Of course, this did not always benefit the immigrants' integration into Dutch society.

Post-colonial immigration was primarily seen as a social welfare problem. Therefore, the Minister of Social Welfare, Public Health and Culture was authorized to deal with these groups. Though he was given certain coordinating powers, he could not freely dispose of the policy instruments of his colleagues. In particular, the ministry's ideas on creating facilities to preserve the cultural identity of these immigrant groups were not welcomed with great enthusiasm.

In 1976, shortly after the first hijacking, coordination for the Moluccans was transferred to the Deputy Prime Minister, who happened to be the Minister of Justice at the time. This gave rise to the idea that policy for

Moluccans had become a "law and order" affair. Later the Moluccans' affairs were "transferred" to the Minister of the Interior.

Besides the ministries already mentioned nearly all other ministries were increasingly confronted with the immigration issue; yet any form of concerted action remained practically impossible. Some striking contradictions, for instance, appear from an analysis of the various chapters of the 1974 Memorandum on Foreign Workers, but at the time these were hardly noted by parliament (Entzinger 1975:334).

In early 1980, when the absurdity of this situation had finally been recognized, the government decided to transfer all responsibilities for the coordination of immigration policy to the Minister of the Interior, who was already in charge of the Moluccans. One of the arguments was that his ministry is also responsible for the functioning of local government, which actually has to implement some of the major elements of immigrant policy. A special Secretary of State ("deputy minister") was given charge of minorities policy for the first time in the second Van Agt cabinet, which took office in September 1981.

At the Ministry of the Interior a Directorate for the Coordination of Minorities Policy has been created, headed by a former Member of Parliament. Its main task has become to remind all other ministries of their particular responsibilities in this field and to harmonize basic policy guidelines. It also acts as a *trait-d'union* between the national government on the one side and the various ethnic groups as well as the municipal authorities on the other. At the local level things have developed along similar lines. Most of the larger cities have now placed one of their aldermen in charge of the coordination of local immigrant policy. In several cities he or she is supported by a small staff.

The administrative coordination of immigrant policy has certainly advanced over the past few years, but it still seems too early for an assessment of the effects. Although the existence of certain links between immigrant policy and immigration regulation and control has now been recognized, final responsibility for the latter has remained with the Ministry of Justice as an element of its overall aliens policy. In other words, the two faces of immigration policy have not been integrated completely, and it remains doubtful if that can ever be achieved.

6. Lessons of the past – hypotheses for the future

A brief summary

Immigration policy in the Netherlands has long been characterized by ambivalence, although the country is by no means unique in this respect. A fairly liberal policy of admissions and control and a humane social welfare policy stood in opposition to a reasonably strict employment policy and a virtual absence of specific instruments in other fields of immigrant policy (except housing).

This may be explained not only by erroneous ideas about temporariness, even among immigrants themselves, but also by the country's traditional pluralism. Some people thought that just a few more cultural minority groups had been added to the existing "pillars". In addition, no specific legal measures were considered necessary because many immigrants already possessed Netherlands citizenship. These beliefs concealed the fact that nearly all immigrants had a very weak economic position and lacked the capacity to improve it. This did not become apparent until the Dutch economy began to stagnate and the new immigrants appeared among the first victims of the decline. At that time (1979–80) some important changes were made: admissions policy became stricter and a broad policy was announced to ensure that immigrants would participate more fully in Dutch society.

Options for the future

Two basic options seem to be open for an active immigrant policy. The first option is primarily concerned with individual immigrants and aims at promoting their participation in socioeconomic life. Such a policy intends to create more room for immigrants within existing institutions – perhaps with some small adaptations – by giving them a fairer share in the distribution of goods and services. This means, for instance, that better opportunities should be created within the existing forms of education through (temporary) facilities and compensatory programs. Immigrants' chances on the labor market should be improved, possibly by "affirmative action" or "positive discrimination", which recently has become a topic of discussion in the Netherlands. Their housing conditions should also be improved; for instance, by an active policy of dispersion that includes better urban districts. Such an approach requires not only a lot of money but also a large degree of understanding on the part of the host society for the needs of immigrants.

The second option places more emphasis on the immigrants as separate ethnic groups and on their cultural heritage. Under this option immigrants should be given the opportunity, for instance, to set up their own schools, to specialize in certain professions and branches of industrial activity, and to live closely together. Inside these separate institutions the "emancipation" process of immigrants could take place; once a satisfactory level of functioning were reached, most of the partition walls would disappear automatically. This option, which may appear somewhat untenable to a non-Dutch observer, is very much in line with the traditional Dutch system of "pillarization". Increasing numbers of advocates for such a policy of "autonomy" can be found among immigrants and their leaders.

The government, however, has now decided to adopt a policy that is largely based on the first option, which could be called "integrationist". Only some concessions have been made that might enable immigrants to preserve certain elements of their ethnocultural identity (e.g. in education) and to ensure their political participation (e.g. consultative councils). Though the "mutual adaptation of majority and minorities" is another slogan of this policy, it has been admitted that "the immigrants' cultural identity can only be respected in so far as this will not hamper their functioning in Dutch society" (*Ontwerp-Minderhedennota* 1981:38). Any other solution is likely to lead to the further development of an ethnic subproletariat, which could threaten the traditional stability of Dutch society. In the long run no democracy can afford socioeconomic divisions to coincide with ethnic divisions.

4

Great Britain

ZIG LAYTON-HENRY

1. Immigration and immigration policy

Britain has traditionally been a country of emigration. Since the eighteenth century considerable numbers of Britons have moved overseas and helped establish and populate the United States and countries of the British Commonwealth and Empire. During the nineteenth century the majority of migrants went to the USA, but after 1900 most emigrated to Canada, Australia, and other Commonwealth countries. By the turn of the century migration had become a conscious part of British imperial policy, and it was felt that encouraging emigration from Britain to the Commonwealth would help the economic development of Dominion territories, strengthen the ties with Britain, and increase the power of the Empire. Land grants and assisted passages were used to encourage people to migrate. After the First World War the self-governing Dominions became more selective in their demands for migrants, requiring skilled industrial workers instead of agricultural workers. There was no halt in the outward flow, however, and between 1919 and 1930 two million people emigrated from the United Kingdom.

The depression between the wars caused a change in the balance of migration and the net flow became an inward one. After the Second World War, however, emigration resumed at a high level, encouraged particularly by the immigration policies of Australia, which was concerned to increase her population for security reasons and also to maintain its British character. Between 1946 and 1950 720,260 people left the UK, and most of them were relatively highly skilled (Cheetham 1972). The postwar shortage of labor and the resumption of traditional patterns of migration to the Commonwealth was a source of concern for the Royal

---

* I would like to thank G.C. Barclay and P.R. Jones for commenting on this chapter and for their helpful suggestions.

Table 4.1. *Net gain or loss by migration from Great Britain, 1871–1941*

1871–1880	− 257,000	1911–1920	− 857,000
1881–1890	− 817,000	1921–1930	− 565,000
1891–1900	− 122,000	1931–1940	+ 650,000
1901–1910	− 756,000		

Source: HMSO, Royal Commission on Population, Cmnd 7695, 1949.
Note: Great Britain includes England, Scotland, and Wales, but not Ireland.

Commission on Population, which the government had established towards the end of the war to assess postwar manpower requirements. Nevertheless, government policy continued to facilitate migration for economic and political reasons. Both the government and the Royal Commission failed to anticipate that the postwar economic boom would lead to spontaneous immigration from the New Commonwealth.

Considerable migration has also taken place during the past 150 years within the British Isles, especially from the peripheral countries of the United Kingdom (Ireland, Scotland, and Wales) to England. Ireland in particular was a major exporter of migrants: between 1820 and 1910 nearly five million people left the country, including the large numbers who moved to Britain. In 1861 some 3 percent of the English population was born in Ireland, as was 6.7 percent of the population of Scotland. This migration to Britain was facilitated by Ireland's geographical proximity and by historical links between England and Ireland going back to the twelfth century. In 1801 Britain and Ireland were formally united under one parliament, but the union was dissolved in 1921 with the creation of the Irish Free State. Despite the independence of most of Ireland, however, the British government has always allowed unrestricted movement between the two countries and has never treated Irish citizens as aliens. They are accorded full citizenship rights, including voting rights, and are not restricted in any way.

Between 1880 and 1914 a significant migration of Russian Jews to Britain occurred as a result of the Tsarist pogroms. Most of these refugees settled in the East End of London, where they met with considerable hostility. A vigorous campaign to control this immigration was organized and led to the first Aliens Immigration Act in 1905. This Act forbade entry to people who could not support themselves and their dependents, to people whose infirmities were likely to make them a charge on the rates, and also to some known criminals. The principle of political asylum was reaffirmed, however, and the Liberal government, elected in 1906, was able to use reports of violence against Jews to nullify the effects of the Act, although they did not repeal it (Garrard 1971).

During and after the Second World War, 120,000 Poles who had been members of the allied forces settled in Britain and for the first time a British government took positive action to assist in the integration of alien residents. A Polish Resettlement Act was passed in 1947 and a Polish Resettlement Corps established. The integration of the Polish excombatants and their families was achieved remarkably smoothly, despite initial union opposition, partly because they had established an institutional infrastructure during the war, partly due to public sympathy for wartime allies (which facilitated government support), but mainly because the acute labor shortage enabled their rapid absorption into the economy. The acute shortage of labor was endangering postwar reconstruction and the expansion of the economy. A number of schemes were devised to encourage European Volunteer Workers to come to Britain, but these were not very successful (Tannahill 1958).

The background to New Commonwealth immigration

Britain has traditionally favored the free movement of capital and labor within the Empire, although by the turn of the century all the self-governing Dominions had acted to control immigration to their territories, largely because of concern over the potential of Indian immigration. Britain alone had no restrictions, a principle reaffirmed by the Nationality Act of 1948. A year later a Conservative Party policy document stated that "There must be freedom of movement among its members within the British Empire and Commonwealth. New opportunities will present themselves not only in the countries overseas but in the Mother country and must be open to all citizens" (*The Right Road for Britain* 1949). The assumption was, however, that the major population movement would continue to be an outflow from the United Kingdom to the Empire and Commonwealth.

Before the Second World War there already existed small settlements of colored people in such ports as Liverpool, Cardiff, Manchester, and London's East End. These had been established by colonial seamen during the First World War. The heavy unemployment during the interwar years provided no incentive for migration to Britain, and those who came were largely return migrants unable to establish themselves in the Dominions due to the world recession. The outbreak of war in 1939 dramatically changed this situation and set in train the events that were to lead to the major postwar migration of West Indians and Asians to Britain. During the war, colonial labor was recruited to work in forestry and munitions factories and the services. Most notable were the 10,000 West Indians recruited to work as ground crews in the Royal Air Force. Considerable numbers of West Indians, Asians, and Africans served in the allied forces during the war and in the Merchant Navy as well.

After the war every effort was made to repatriate the colonial labor that had been recruited to work in Britain, but a minority decided to remain; moreover, many who returned to the West Indies quickly came back to Britain to seek work and a higher standard of living. The war had given many West Indians experience of life in Britain, and the continued shortage of labor after the war meant that there were plenty of jobs for those wishing to escape poverty and unemployment. In 1948 the British government had set up a working party on the Employment in the United Kingdom of Surplus Colonial Labour "to enquire into the possibilities of employing in the United Kingdom surplus manpower of certain colonial territories in order to assist the manpower situation in this country and to relieve unemployment in these colonial territories" (Ministry of Labour Report 1949). The government was reluctant to accept colored immigrants out of concern over the problems of racial prejudice and discrimination that the newcomers might face. However, by the end of 1948 the first immigrant ships began to arrive from the West Indies and a largely spontaneous movement of people had begun.

In discussing immigration policy in this chapter I will be mainly concerned with the immigration of British subjects from Britain's former colonial territories, in particular the West Indies, India, Pakistan, and Bangladesh. I have chosen this approach because "New Commonwealth" immigration has both constituted the major part of immigration and has caused the greatest public concern and dominated the thinking and actions of policymakers.

A note on terminology

The development of New Commonwealth immigration has radically changed British nomenclature as regards key terms in everyday use and &has also caused new ones to be invented. Before the war immigrants were overwhelmingly either "aliens" (foreign born with foreign nationality), "Irish" (who were treated as British), or "British" (white Commonwealth or returning migrants, soldiers, or administrators) and therefore not considered immigrants. Since all these groups were European it was assumed that they would be easily assimilable; while some aliens might have difficulties adjusting to the English language and way of life, it was assumed that their British-born children would be completely British. There were very few non-white immigrants before New Commonwealth immigration created the first substantial settlement of non-Europeans in Britain. In everyday language the term "immigrant" has now come to mean a black or brown person who is either a New Commonwealth immigrant or a person of New Commonwealth descent. The use of the term "immigrant" to describe non-white people of British birth and

Table 4.2. *Estimated net immigration from the New Commonwealth 1953–62*

	West Indies	India	Pakistan	Others	Total
1953	2,000	–	–	–	2,000
1954	11,000	–	–	–	11,000
1955	27,500	5,800	1,850	7,500	42,650
1956	29,800	5,600	2,050	9,350	46,800
1957	23,000	6,600	5,200	7,600	42,400
1958	15,000	6,200	4,700	3,950	29,850
1959	16,400	2,950	850	1,400	21,600
1960	49,650	5,900	2,500	– 350	57,700
1961	66,300	23,750	25,100	21,250	136,400
1962*	31,800	19,050	25,080	18,970	94,900

Source: House of Commons Library Research Paper No. 56, *Commonwealth Immigration to the UK from the 1950s to 1975 – A Survey of Statistical Sources.*
Note: * First 6 months.

nationality suggests that they are not "fully" British and because of their color cannot be completely assimilated. It is clear that young black British citizens face as much discrimination and prejudice as their immigrant parents or grandparents did (HMSO, *Racial Disadvantage* 1981).

In the gradual formulation of immigration policy a new term, "patrial", has been invented to distinguish those Commonwealth citizens that have a close link with Britain through descent from a British parent or grandparent. They are overwhelmingly white and have privileged access to the United Kingdom; they do not need work permits to take up employment or to settle permanently. They do not require resident permits for periods of stay in excess of six months, nor do they have to register with the police. The concept of patriality was first introduced into legislation by the Commonwealth Immigrant Act of 1968, although the term was not defined in legislation until 1971 in the Immigration Act of that year.

2. General preconditions

Geography and population

Before the Second World War the British population could be considered relatively homogenous despite the fact that four "nations" inhabited the British Isles. Virtually all were white, English-speaking, and Protestant – except the Irish, who were Roman Catholic. The independence of the Irish Free State in 1921 partially accommodated the national aspirations of the Irish. There has been considerable intermarriage between the different national groups. For the most part they live harmoniously together, except in Northern Ireland where a majority composed of the descendants of English and Scottish Protestant settlers is in favor of remaining within the United Kingdom while a minority composed of Catholic Irish would prefer a united Ireland. The campaign being waged by the Irish Republican Army for a united Ireland is almost wholly confined to Northern Ireland.

The United Kingdom is a highly urbanized industrial country with a population of nearly 56 million. It has a high population density – 229 persons per square kilometer. The population is concentrated in England, with 46.5 million inhabitants and 356 persons per square kilometer. The major centers of population are in southeastern England in the Greater London area, the Midlands, South Lancashire, and West Yorkshire. Central Scotland and South Wales are also substantial population centers.

As in other countries British society has been changing rapidly since the war, with a falling birthrate, longer expectations of life, a higher divorce rate, widening educational opportunities, and a rising standard of living. In 1980 there were 754,000 live births, which outnumbered deaths by 93,000. The birthrate declined from 18.0 live births per thousand in 1966 to a historic low point of 11.8 in 1977, but thereafter rose to 13.5 in 1980. Life expectation is now about 70 years for men and 76 for women. Thus, although the total population has remained stable during the past decade, there have been significant changes in its age and sex structure, including a decline in the proportion of young people under 16 and an increase in elderly people. At present some 18 percent of the population is over the normal retirement ages of 65 for men and 60 for women.

Migration has also contributed to changes in the British population. Between 1971 and 1980 some 2.25 million people emigrated from Britain and 1.9 million immigrated. Most British emigrants left for North America, Australia, and the European Community, while about one third of all immigrants came from New Commonwealth countries. In 1980 the number of inhabitants of New Commonwealth and Pakistan ethnic origin was estimated at approximately 2.1 million, of whom over 40 percent were British born.

The establishment of a significant ethnic minority population in Britain was neither planned nor anticipated by policymakers. The Royal Commission that published a report on population needs in 1949 had been concerned with the disadvantages of a falling population, especially as it did not wish to recommend discouraging British emigration to other parts of the Commonwealth. It concluded that "a systematic immigration policy could only be welcomed without reserve if the migrants were of good human stock [presumably European] and not prevented by religion or race from inter-marrying with the host population and becoming merged with it" (HMSO, *Royal Commission on Population* 1949:226–7). The Commission doubted the capacity of an established society like Britain to absorb immigrants of an alien race and religion. The ability of colonial workers to integrate with and be accepted by the native population was a matter that had concerned the Colonial Office in recruiting such labor during the war, but as it turned out wartime conditions had facilitated their acceptance and integration. Once New Commonwealth immigration developed after the war the government proved very reluctant to intervene with a policy of either management or control. On the one hand the government did not wish to seem to be encouraging such immigration; on the other hand, policies of control would have disrupted relations with Colonial and Commonwealth governments.

History and foreign policy
The most important factors facilitating the migration of New Commonwealth immigrants to Britain and constraining the freedom of action of British policymakers have been the historical and imperial links between Britain and its colonies in the West Indies and former colonies in South Asia. This imperial relationship meant that Colonial and Commonwealth citizens were British subjects and as such were not subject to any immigration controls. Once their identity and citizenship were established at the port of entry they were free to enter, settle, and seek employment. As British subjects they had full civic rights and could vote, run for parliament, and serve in the armed forces and public service. The imperial connection seems to have given West Indians in particular a high expectation of the wealth and benevolence of the Mother Country and feelings that they would be well received, treated as full and equal citizens, and achieve a high standard of living. Many had good memories or reports of the welcome and treatment that West Indians had received in Britain during the war.

Many postwar migrants, however, were ill-prepared for the harsh conditions experienced by unskilled workers in an urban industrial society. Indians and Pakistanis appear to have migrated with more realistic expectations limited to gaining jobs, a better standard of living, and better prospects for their children. Asian settlers in Britain have thus been less disappointed with poor housing and work conditions than West Indians and express higher levels of satisfaction with life in Britain (Rex & Tomlinson 1979).

The historical links between Britain and the sending countries meant that many immigrants had some knowledge of English language, education, cultural traditions, and history. This was most obviously the case in the West Indies where language, religion, the educational system, culture, and sports owed so much to centuries of British influence. The impact of British culture was much less pervasive in India and Pakistan, although many of the early Asian migrants had experience in the British armed forces and some knowledge of English.

The importance to British policymakers of a peaceful process of decolonization, as far as this was possible, and of maintaining Britain's position in the world through leadership of a Commonwealth of independent nations increasingly composed of "Third World" countries was a crucial factor constraining British politicians from introducing immigration controls before 1962. British efforts, for example, to establish a Federation of the West Indies in the 1950s involved long and complicated negotiations between Britain and the various colonial administrations. British attempts to control immigration would have made these negotiations even less likely to succeed. The West Indian economies were weak, the islands suffered from heavy unemployment, and traditional West Indian migration to the United States had been substantially reduced by the Walter–McCarron Immigration Act of 1952. Leading West Indian politicians lobbied strongly against control whenever the issue was raised in Britain. They argued that controls would be economically disastrous for the islands and would undermine not only Britain's leadership of the Commonwealth but the foundations of the Commonwealth itself.

Colonial and Commonwealth governments were to some extent directly represented in the British cabinet; the ministers for Colonial and Commonwealth Affairs represented their views. There was also sympathy among policymakers for the Colonial and Commonwealth territories since many of Britain's political elite had served in these countries as administrators, politicians, or soldiers or had relatives who had done so. A final factor influencing British policy was a sense of obligation or guilt towards Commonwealth countries for the legacy of colonial exploitation perpetrated by past British governments. This was most strongly felt on the left of British politics and can be illustrated by the Trade Union Congress's explanation for New Commonwealth migration: "Congress . is of the opinion that these coloured workers are driven from their homeland by poverty and social insecurity which are due mainly to unbalanced economies created by long years of colonial exploitation" (Trade Union Congress 1955).

Economy
Britain is a trading nation, exporting a higher proportion of its production of goods and services than any other industrial country of comparable size. It exports some 31 percent of its Gross National Prod-

uct. The traditional economic strength of the country has been based on the manufacturing industry, but it has been declining relative to the service sector. In 1981 some 39.1 percent of the working population was engaged in engineering, manufacturing, construction, mining, and related industries. Service industries employed 59.3 percent. Agriculture engaged only 1.6 percent of the workforce, a lower proportion than in any other major industrial country; nevertheless, agriculture is highly efficient and produces more than half of the nation's food. Even so, Britain is one of the world's largest importers of agricultural products and also of raw materials and semi-manufactured goods. The major exports are aerospace products, electrical equipment, finished textiles and services such as banking and insurance. Britain has recently become self-sufficient in oil due to production from wells in the North Sea.

New Commonwealth immigrants came to Britain in search of work and a better standard of living. The expansion of the British economy in the 1950s and 1960s created a substantial shortage of labor, particularly in the relatively stagnant sectors of the economy; for example, textiles, metal manufacture, and transport where low pay, long hours, and shift work made the jobs unattractive to native workers. These industries were unable to compete for the short supply of native labor with expanding sectors. In periods of economic expansion the more prosperous regions with expanding industries quickly developed labor shortages, which were partly filled by immigrant workers that concentrated in the major conurbations of Greater London, the West Midlands, Manchester, Merseyside, and Yorkshire.

They found work mainly as unskilled or semi-skilled workers. In the most extreme case it was found that 58 percent of Pakistan men were doing unskilled or semi-skilled work compared with 18 percent of white men, while 8 percent of Pakistanis compared with 40 percent of whites were doing non-manual jobs. For Indians and West Indians the contrast is less extreme with 36 percent of Indians and 32 percent of West Indians doing unskilled or semi-skilled manual work. All groups, particularly West Indians (59 percent), are well represented in skilled manual trades, but only Indians (20 percent) and East African Asians (30 percent) are well represented among non-manual occupations (Smith 1977).

New Commonwealth immigrants are strongly over-represented in shipbuilding, vehicle manufacture, textiles, the manufacturing industry generally, and also in transport. West Indian women are heavily over-represented in the Health Service where they have been traditionally recruited as both nurses and domestic staff. The Health Service has also recruited significant numbers of New Commonwealth doctors.

Immigrant workers thus formed a replacement labor force and found work mainly as semi-skilled and unskilled workers. They came in a period of labor shortage made more acute by the continued emigration of Britons to Commonwealth and other countries, which was not discouraged. Once the Poles and European Volunteer Workers had been absorbed there were no easily available sources of European labor for the British economy (except Ireland) because the faster growing West European economies were absorbing surplus labor from Southern Europe. It was under these conditions that immigration from the West Indies began in 1948, quickly followed by immigration from India and Pakistan.

One interesting contrast between Britain and other major European countries like France and Germany was the lack of government planning and involvement in immigration policy once the migration developed. Freeman argues that British leaders, unlike the French political elite, failed to recognize the contribution of immigration to the national economy and to economic growth (Freeman 1979). From the very beginning the British government was concerned with "the problems arising from the immigration into this country of coloured people from British Colonial territories" (Secretary of State for the Colonies 1950). These problems related to housing, employment, and law and order; the remedy was seen as restriction and control.

Colored immigration was not to be welcomed as contributing to national wealth and economic growth but to be discouraged as far as possible. British policymakers were very aware, from the beginning, of the problems of racial prejudice and discrimination that colored migrants would face in Britain as well as of the dangers of racial disturbances. They were much more aware of the social and political costs of immigration than of its economic benefits, which explains why Britain moved to a position of instituting legislative controls rather earlier than other West European countries. The perception was that of an already overcrowded island with limited resources facing a potentially limitless stream of immigrants from the Indian subcontinent, rather than that of a dynamic and growing economy being held back by a lack of young, fit workers.

The growth of the British economy in the 1950s and 1960s was slow and punctuated by crises over the balance of payments and the role of sterling and by worries about inflation. It was also a period of rapid withdrawal from imperial commitments and a realization by British leaders and people of their declining world status. In such a situation immigration was seen as an added burden – not as a valuable asset.

Trade unions
British unions have traditionally been suspicious of and hostile towards high levels of immigration. In the 1890s the TUC passed several resolutions demanding the control of Jewish immigration. After the Sec-

ond World War strict conditions were imposed on the employment of European Volunteer Workers before the unions would allow their recruitment. They had to join the appropriate union, be the first to lose their jobs in case of redundancy, and their opportunities for promotion were limited. In practice these conditions were never enforced because of continued economic expansion and full employment. Even so, in some industries like mining the employment of foreign labor proved impossible because of union opposition (Garrard 1971).

The reaction of the trade unions to New Commonwealth immigration was surprisingly positive, at least at the national level. The TUC Congress in 1955 welcomed the new immigrants to Britain and deplored attempts to erect a color bar against Commonwealth citizens (Trade Union Congress 1955). Clearly union leaders felt an obligation towards immigrants; they felt that immigrants had been forced to come to Britain due to colonial exploitation and lack of investment in their territories. In addition opposition to colored immigration might be interpreted as racist. Nevertheless, trade union leaders were not confident about the reaction of their members towards colored workers. The Working Party on the Employment of Colonial Labour reported that

> The Leaders of the Trade Union movement generally take the line that while they themselves have no objection in principle to the introduction of coloured workers from British territories, the decision whether or not to go on with a recruiting scheme must in every case be left to the local branch in the area of prospective employment. The local Trade Union Officials usually say that they would help if they could, but that the workers in their particular area are not prepared to accept coloured workers in their place of employment. (Ministry of Labour Report, 1949)

Beetham has described the efforts by local branches in the transport industry to exclude black workers (Beetham 1970). Such resistance was gradually overcome as the problem of labor shortages continued. New Commonwealth workers in Britain have a surprisingly high level of trade union membership, much higher than native workers, but in several cases the unions have proved reluctant to defend immigrants' interests, especially when these appear to conflict with the interests of native workers. The major problem the migrants faced was a combination of indifference at the national level and hostility in local union branches where ideological inhibition to racial exclusion was weaker (Miles & Phizacklea 1977).

Social welfare

The British social welfare system in 1980 was about 18 percent of GNP, and the largest program was the social security system, designed to secure a basic standard of living for people in financial need. Medical services are available to all residents irrespective of means through the National Health Service. The local authority social services and voluntary organizations provide advice and help to elderly people, disabled people, and children in need of care. New Commonwealth immigrants as British subjects have been entitled upon arrival to the whole range of social welfare services. However, the British Nationality Act of 1981 means that Commonwealth citizens are no longer automatically British citizens as well. Those who are accepted for settlement can receive all the services.

In the housing market, like employment, immigrants tended to fulfill a replacement role. They were forced to buy or rent cheap older housing in inner city areas that were being vacated by native white families moving to new suburban housing estates away from the city centers. They did not qualify, unless homeless, for local authority housing because it required local residential qualifications, often 5 years' residence, and this excluded new migrants. The outward flow from urban areas to suburbs, dormitory towns, and semi-rural areas has continued leaving inner city areas populated by immigrant families and poor, often elderly, whites (Ratcliffe 1981).

New Commonwealth immigrants have now achieved the residential qualifications necessary for local authority housing, resulting in a large movement of West Indian families into such housing. Nearly 50 percent are now housed in this way. Asians have preferred to remain in owner occupation and continue to suffer from overcrowding, although this is declining. The educational system in Britain is comprehensive, although a tiny but significant private sector also exists. Asian and West Indian children therefore go to the same state schools as native white children. Because of the residential concentration of immigrant families, however, their children tend to go to schools where a majority of the children are also Asian or West Indian (Rex & Tomlinson 1979).

The presence of substantial ethnic minority populations with their own cultural traditions presents a considerable challenge to the social services. The assumptions underlying the service hitherto provided for a homogeneous population with shared cultural and linguistic codes are being undermined. Moreover, distinctive cultural patterns are not being rapidly eroded, as happened with previous immigrants; they are being maintained by such factors as childhood socialization, residential segregation, and as a result of reaction to the hostility of the majority population. While in many respects immigrant families, because of their relative youthfulness, make less demands on the social services than the host population does, one must remember that they live in areas of urban decay. Their children may have special educational needs, and they suffer high levels of unemployment, especially in periods of recession. Their cultural distinctiveness may require ethnically sensitive provisions that are resented by parts of the native population that feel the minorities should assimilate. Special provisions may also be seen as reducing scarce public resources and may result in political conflict (Ballard 1979).

3. Immigration regulation and control

British immigration policy has been ad hoc and reactive rather than centrally planned and managed. In fact, one could argue that before the Second World War Britain had a laissez-faire attitude towards immigration, although the Home Secretary has had, since 1905, powers to control the entry and settlement of aliens. Immigration in this period was small and often composed of refugees and returning British migrants. Before 1939 migration policy was perceived as being concerned with facilitating emigration from the United Kingdom to the Dominions. Between 1945 and 1948 immigration was centrally planned to the extent that European Volunteer Workers were specially recruited, under stringent conditions, to meet the needs of labor-starved industries. The more substantial immigration of Irish workers was, of course, uncontrolled.

Between 1948 and 1962 the substantial immigration of West Indians and Asians was uncontrolled because the migrants were British colonial and Commonwealth citizens. In the late 1950s the British government put pressure on the Indian and Pakistani governments to control prospective migrants by restricting the issuing of passports; this was done for a short time but was relatively ineffective. In 1962 the first Commonwealth Immigrants Act was passed; it made Commonwealth immigrants subject to control through the need to obtain employment vouchers.

Since 1962 the policy of successive governments has been to institute tighter and tighter controls in an attempt to end the primary immigration of non-white immigrants from the New Commonwealth but at the same time allow the secondary immigration of close dependants. Patrials continue to have privileged access to the United Kingdom. The 1971 Immigration Act and subsequent changes in immigration rules have strictly controlled New Commonwealth immigration and it is now largely dependants who are being admitted and the remaining UK passport holders (Asians) from India and East Africa. In fact, the major flow of these passport holders now comes from India, although they originate from East Africa. This flow as well as the flow of dependants is beginning to fall rapidly, however, as families are reunited and the queue in the Indian subcontinent is reduced. In addition some groups have been admitted on humanitarian grounds, such as Vietnamese refugees.

Once New Commonwealth immigration began the government was confronted with conflicting policy aims. From the beginning it was concerned that prejudice and racial discrimination should prevent the integration of colored workers. As early as 1947 an interdepartmental working party based in the Home Office was set up. It concluded that West Indian immigration would increase and expressed concern at the possibility of an "inassimilable minority" being created by migration. The working party concluded that control was the only practical solution and was reconvened in 1948 to consider how controls should be introduced (Deakin 1972). Thus it is clear that even before political agitation against colored immigration gained public support the government was prepared to consider racially discriminatory controls.

At the same time, however, the government also wished to preserve its leading position in the Commonwealth, maintain good relations with the sending countries, and benefit from the manifest economic advantages that immigration gave to the British economy. Plans for control, although occasionally raised in the cabinet, were shelved until the racial disturbances in 1958 focused public attention on the issue and fueled the political campaign against colored immigration. Since the Commonwealth Immigrants Act of 1962 both Conservative and Labour governments have tightened controls on New Commonwealth immigration while continuing to allow certain white groups privileged access to the United Kingdom. This policy has been justified on the grounds that equality and integration can only proceed smoothly for the ethnic minorities within the United Kingdom if the public is assured that New Commonwealth immigration is strictly controlled. Successive governments, especially Labour governments (but generally with Conservative party support), have passed legislation against racial discrimination and have established institutions to combat racial prejudice. These institutions have not been very successful and the emphasis of government policy has been focused on tough controls (Layton-Henry 1984). In 1981 the Conservative government introduced a new British Nationality Act that defined British citizenship more restrictively than before and linked the right of abode in the United Kingdom more closely with citizenship.

Principal aims

Immigration legislation before the Second World War was wholly concerned with regulating the immigration of foreigners. The 1905 Aliens Act gave the Home Secretary powers to control the entry of undesirable and destitute aliens. While in practice the Act was liberally administered it nonetheless ended the previous policy of free immigration. In 1914 much tougher legislation was introduced for security reasons and the Home Secretary was given powers to refuse aliens permission to enter the country and to deport them. For the first time all aliens had to register with the police. The right to political asylum was reaffirmed, however.

The aims of postwar immigration policy have been much more variable depending on the size and type of immigration and the internal political reaction. The principal aim with regard to the Polish excombatants was to integrate them as quickly as possible. From the beginning it was recognized that their chances of returning to Poland were remote; in fact, many had already married British wives. Help was provided for the teaching of English and retraining and integration proceeded slowly but smoothly. The process of adjustment was helped by geographic dispersal, inter-marriage, and the labor shortage. The aim of recruiting European Volunteer Workers was purely economic; the conditions were strict, and many migrated further to North America. In the 1950s other European workers, mainly Germans, Italians, and Spaniards, came to Britain under the same work-permit scheme as the Volunteer Workers, but they were quickly allowed to bring in their families and have settled down more successfully (Rees in Kubat 1979). It has always been assumed that European immigrants can assimilate if they wish. The Macdonald Report stated that "It is in our view of the greatest importance that the immigrant should from the earliest possible moment after his arrival in his new country, regard himself as a citizen of that country with all the rights and obligations of such citizens" (HMSO, Macdonald Report 1934). Though this was stated in the context of emigration from Britain it was clearly also applicable to immigration and underlay the thinking of the Royal Commission on Population.

Instruments of regulation and control

In the seven years up to 1962 nearly 500,000 New Commonwealth citizens settled in Britain, most of whom were later joined by their wives and other dependants. The 1962 Commonwealth Immigrants Act was introduced to regulate this flow by using a system of employment vouchers to control the number of arrivals for settlement. There were three categories of vouchers: category A for Commonwealth citizens with a specific job to come to; category B issued by British High Commissions overseas to those with such recognized skills or qualifications as were in short supply; and category C for anybody at all on a first-come, first-served basis with priority to those with war service.

Between 1962 and 1965 vouchers were issued liberally in accordance with previous rates of immigration. The importance of the immigration issue in the 1964 general election, however, caused the new Labour government to determine to stem the flow of New Commonwealth immigrants. In August 1965 the government arbitrarily restricted the number of employment vouchers to 8,500 (of which 1,000 were reserved for Malta). Category C vouchers, for which there was a waiting list of over 400,000, were abolished.

In 1968 additional controls were introduced to reduce the flow of British passport holders of Asian descent from East Africa. The "Kenyanization" policies of the Kenya government had resulted in increasing redundancies among Asian holders of United Kingdom passports, and the numbers of Kenyan Asians coming to Britain rose from 6,150 in 1965 to 13,600 in 1967. Some 12,823 arrived in the first two months of 1968, by which time a campaign against the movement had been mounted by Duncan Sandys and Enoch Powell.

The government capitulated to this campaign and controls were introduced in the form of the Commonwealth Immigrants Act of 1968. This required all citizens of the United Kingdom and colonies with no substantial connection to the United Kingdom (for example by birth or descent) to obtain an entry voucher before arriving. This was the first time a distinction was made between patrial and non-patrial citizens of the United Kingdom, and the clear intention of the distinction was to control colored immigration from the Commonwealth while allowing most white Commonwealth citizens of British descent unrestricted access. At first 1,500 vouchers were made available per annum for heads of households from East Africa. In 1971 this was raised to 3,000 with an additional 1,500 vouchers for people in special difficulty issued on a once and for all basis. In 1975 the quota was raised to 5,000.

Before the Immigration Act of 1971 came into force the system of control over the entry of foreign nationals (as opposed to Commonwealth citizens) derived from the Alien Restriction Acts of 1914 and 1919 and rules drawn up under the Acts to cover admissions, supervision, and deportations. Foreign nationals were admitted to Britain to take employment provided they held a work permit issued by the Department of Employment. A permit was issued for a particular job with a particular employer. Employment was limited to a maximum of one year in the first instance but could be extended on application by the employer. Unlike Commonwealth citizens, foreign nationals were required to register with the police. After a foreign national had been in approved employment for four years he or she could apply to the Home Office for cancellation of the conditions imposed on that employment and length of stay in the United Kingdom, which was normally granted. The foreign national could then stay indefinitely and engage in any kind of employment. Between 1960 and 1968 some 15,000–20,000 people had their conditions cancelled annually (HMSO, *Immigration into Britain* 1981).

The Immigration Act of 1971, still in force today, replaced all previous legislation with one statute that made provision for control of the admission and stay of Commonwealth citizens and foreign nationals. The Immigration Act recognized a "right of abode" that citizens of the United Kingdom and colonies, and certain Commonwealth citizens, are entitled to because of a close connection with the United Kingdom by birth, descent, or marriage. People who have this right are known as "patrials" and are entirely free from immigration control and may live and work in the United Kingdom without any restriction. The Act defines patrials as:

1. Citizens of the United Kingdom and Colonies that have citizenship by birth, adoption, registration, or naturalization in the United Kingdom or that have a parent or grandparent who was born in the United Kingdom or has acquired citizenship by adoption, registration, or naturalization.
2. Citizens of the United Kingdom and Colonies that have come from overseas, have been accepted for permanent residence, and have resided in the United Kingdom for five years.
3. Commonwealth citizens that have a parent born in the United Kingdom.
4. Women that are Commonwealth citizens (including citizens of the United Kingdom and Colonies) and are or have been married to a man in any of these categories.

Everybody entering Britain, including patrials, needs a valid passport or other recognized identity document. In addition, visas are required in the case of foreign nationals or an entry certificate in the case of Commonwealth citizens that wish to settle in the United Kingdom; visas are also required from nationals of Eastern Europe, Cuba, and some African and Asian countries. Visitors are admitted for six months (with six months' extension) if they satisfy the immigration officer that they intend to stay for the period stated, can maintain and accommodate themselves and their dependants without working or recourse to public funds, and can meet the costs of their return journey. Overseas students are admitted for the period of their courses of study.

Work permits are required for all foreign nationals seeking employment except patrials, nationals of the EEC, immigrants of independent means seeking to establish themselves as self-employed businessmen, and young Commonwealth citizens on working holidays. Work permits are only available for overseas workers holding recognized professional qualifications or a high degree of skill or experience. For most occupations they are only issued to workers aged 23 to 54 with a good command of the English language. They are issued for a particular job with a specified employer when there is no suitable worker in the United Kingdom or other EEC country. Work permits are initially issued for twelve months and extensions of stay are granted by the Home Office. After four years permit holders can apply for the removal of the time limit and if granted they are regarded as settled and are free to take any employment with approval. Certain categories of employment are exempt from these restrictions such as doctors, ministers of religion and representatives of overseas firms with no branches or subsidiaries in the UK.

Wives and children of men settled in the United Kingdom may be admitted subject to the possession of an entry certificate; other elderly dependant relatives may also be admitted, provided their kin have the means to maintain and accommodate them. Husbands of women settled in the United Kingdom will be admitted unless there is reason to believe it is a marriage of convenience.

Refugees are a special category and may be admitted if the only country that they could be sent to is one where they are unwilling to go for fear of prosecution. The main examples of refugees being admitted since the war are the Hungarians in 1956, Ugandan Asians in 1972, and most recently Vietnamese. The British government, of course, had special obligations towards the Ugandan Asians, most of whom were British passport holders.

Citizenship of the United Kingdom may be acquired by a Commonwealth citizen through registration and by foreign national naturalization. The conditions are five years' residence, good character, a sufficient knowledge of English, and an intention to reside in the United Kingdom. Foreign nationals and citizens of Commonwealth countries of which the Queen is not Head of State must take an oath of allegiance. The grant of naturalization or registration is at the discretion of the Home Secretary.

Commonwealth and Irish citizens that were settled in Britain on 1 January 1973, when the Immigration Act of 1971 came into force, have the right to be registered as citizens at any time after completing five years' continuous residence in Britain without satisfying any other requirements. A Commonwealth citizen who is patrial has an absolute right to be registered after five years' residence. A woman who is not a citizen has the right to acquire citizenship by registration if she marries a citizen.

Once a person gains admittance to the United Kingdom he or she is relatively free from internal controls. There are no identity cards or other system of internal controls and such controls as there are apply only to aliens (excluding the Irish). The Irish Republic forms a Common Travel

Area together with Britain, and the two governments cooperate in a joint system of frontier controls. The substantial coastline of the United Kingdom is a possible source of illegal immigration but does not seem to have been a significant factor thus far, even though in the late 1960s considerable publicity was given to the arrest of small parties of Asians that were landed on quiet beaches from small boats, but the numbers involved were insignificant. Evasion of controls has occurred particularly in the period 1962–65. The most common form of evasion is probably overstaying. The long distance and therefore cost of travel from the West Indies and Indian subcontinent does not appear to have been a deterrent to migration; communications between Britain and the Colonies or former colonies were naturally very good. In fact, communications between Britain and many West Indian islands were better than communications between the islands themselves.

The outcome of regulation and control

Recent British governments have found it difficult to limit the inflow of New Commonwealth immigrants as much as they would wish, mainly because there are still significant numbers of dependants, especially in the Indian subcontinent, who have the right to join husbands and fathers settled in Britain. There are also smaller numbers of East African Asians now resident in India that hold United Kingdom passports and thus have the right to come to Britain. In recent years immigration from the New Commonwealth has been about 40,000 per year.

Colored immigration remains a political issue despite the strictness of controls, and successive governments have made every effort to keep the figures as low as possible. Various methods have been used to achieve this. One method has been the strict enforcement of immigration rules at the ports and the deportation of people that break the conditions of entry. Another method has been the issuance of entry vouchers by the British High Commissions or Embassies in the countries of origin. Through demands for documentary proof and careful scrutiny of applications, prospective immigrants have been made to wait long periods before gaining permission to enter. Some prospective immigrants may give up the attempt and others may be disqualified by the waiting period (Moore & Wallace 1975).

The strain and anguish suffered by separated families must be very great. There have been a number of highly publicized cases where after a public campaign Home Office decisions in such cases were reversed, for example in 1981 Anwar Ditta, a British born woman of Pakistani origin, won her case to bring her three children to Britain after a six year campaign. Evidence of parentage, including blood tests, was provided by the

Table 4.3. *Immigration to the UK from the New Commonwealth and Pakistan, 1962–82*

1962*	16,453	1969	44,503	1976	55,013
1963	56,071	1970	37,893	1977	44,155
1964	52,840	1971	44,261	1978	34,364
1965	53,887	1972	68,519	1979	36,597
1966	48,104	1973	32,247	1980	33,700
1967	60,633	1974	42,531	1981	31,000
1968	60,620	1975	53,265	1982	30,300

Source: HMSO, *Control of Immigration Statistics 1981*, Cmnd 8533, 1982.
Note: * Second half of the year.

television program "World in Action". In general, however, public opinion appears to be less concerned with the suffering caused by controls than with the enforcement of them. External controls in the countries of origin have the advantage of removing harsh decisions far from the view of politicians, the media, and public opinion. It means that High Commission staff and Embassy officials have the difficult job of administering the harsh government policy.

Growing restrictions on New Commonwealth immigrants have progressively undermined the rights that non-patrial citizens have enjoyed in the past, such as freedom from immigration control, freedom to settle, the right to family life, and the right to pass in and out of Britain without let or hindrance. British citizens of Asian and West Indian descent may have difficulty bringing in dependants due to the need to prove their relationship in order to gain an entry certificate, and they may be anxious about going abroad for fear of problems when they try to re-enter the country. Attempts to reduce colored immigration have thus resulted in the refusal of people entitled to come, harsh treatment at the ports of entry, and the long separation of families where dependants are waiting for entry certificates. Some immigrants, e.g. East African Asians, have been admitted on temporary visitors' permits so that their entrance does not show up on the numbers accepted for settlement, until they apply for the removal of conditions that reduce their right to work (Moore & Wallace 1975).

Internal control has not been a method much used in Britain in the past, but it may be in the future. Contact with the police may result in colored people being asked to prove their immigrant status. There have also been cases of passports being demanded before free hospital treatment was given. In 1980 there were a number of well publicized cases of police raids on hotels and stores to search for illegal immigrants, but these appear to have been isolated cases. Certainly tough immigration policies were an important part of the Conservative administration's electoral promises in 1979, and publicity showing that they were being tough would not be unwelcome to many on the right of the party.

There have been a number of amnesties for illegal immigrants, but they have not been entirely successful. In 1974 the Labour Home Secretary announced an amnesty to overcome the retrospective nature of the 1971 Immigration Act. Yet many immigrants came forward who were overstayers rather than illegal entrants and found that they were not covered. A number were deported. Perhaps partly because of this, relatively few people have come forward as a result of amnesties; moreover, the figures do suggest there are relatively few illegal immigrants compared with overstayers.

At present the Conservative government has shifted the emphasis of its control strategy from immigration to nationality. The British Nationality Act (1981) defines citizenship so that it relates to close connection with the United Kingdom. The Act removes the imperial obligations of *Civis Britannicus sum* under which all colonial and Commonwealth citizens were British subjects with full rights of citizenship. There are now three types of citizenship: (1) British citizenship, (2) citizenship of the British Dependent Territories, and (3) British Overseas citizenship.

British citizens are people that have a close personal connection with the United Kingdom either because their parents or grandparents were born, adopted, naturalized, or registered as citizens of the United Kingdom or because of their own permanent settlement in the country. As a general rule British citizenship from now on will only be transmitted to the first generation born abroad. Citizenship of the British Dependent Territories is acquired by citizens of the United Kingdom and Colonies that have their citizenship by reason of their own or their parents' or grandparents' birth, naturalization, or registration in an existing dependency or associated state. They do not have the right to enter and settle in the United Kingdom. British Overseas citizenship is a residual category intended for citizens of the United Kingdom and Colonies that do not qualify under either of the first two categories. It relates mainly to persons of dual citizenship who live in Malaysia. British Overseas citizens will not be able to pass on this citizenship nor will they have the right of abode in any British territory. In reality it is an invitation to those British subjects permanently settled abroad and with no close connection to the United Kingdom to acquire their full local citizenship as quickly as possible; since this citizenship cannot be passed on to descendants, some children might be born stateless if their countries of birth refused them citizenship. This residual category – a citizenship without rights – is a clear indication that the Conservative government wishes to divest itself of the remaining obligations related to the imperial status of British subjects.

Table 4.4. *Ethnic minority population of Britain, in thousands and as percentage of total population*

	1961*		1966*		1971*		1976†	
	no.	%	no.	%	no.	%	no.	%
West Indians	223	0.5	390	0.8	549	1.1	604	1.1
Asians‡	223	0.5	389	0.8	461	0.9	636	1.2
Other New Commonwealth§	227	0.5	320	0.7	331	0.7	531	1.0
Total population	46,104		47,135		48,749		54,389	

Source: *Ethnic Minorities in Britain*, Home Office Research Study, no. 68, HMSO, 1981.
Notes:
* England and Wales.
† Great Britain.
‡ Asians here include Indians and Pakistanis and, after 1973, Bangladeshis.
§ "Other New Commonwealth" includes those from Africa (including African Asians) and Mediterranean Commonwealth countries, and those from Sri Lanka, Hong Kong, Malaysia, Singapore and other New Commonwealth territories in Asia and Oceania.

4. Immigrant policy

Britain has been slow to develop an immigrant policy. In the early post-war period special help was given to integrate the Poles, and later special arrangements were made for the Hungarian refugees in 1956, the Ugandan Asians in 1972, and the Vietnamese refugees in 1979–82. The mass of New Commonwealth immigrants, however, were largely left to fend for themselves. They had come, predominantly, of their own accord, and as British subjects had full civic and legal rights; therefore, special measures were not considered appropriate. In addition, there was concern that positive action might lead to popular resentment.

Yet by the early 1960s, when controls were first introduced, it was becoming evident that colored immigrants suffered from substantial levels of discrimination, especially in housing and employment. To compensate for its decision to tighten controls the Labour government passed in 1965 the first Race Relations Act making discrimination in public places unlawful. This linking of tough controls with positive measures towards ethnic minorities has been a constant theme of successive governments. For example, the election manifesto of Mrs Thatcher's government stated that "firm immigration control for the future is essential if we are to achieve good community relations ... and will remove from those settled, and in many cases, born here, the label of immigrant" (*Conservative Party Manifesto* 1979). Since controls are now widely accepted as being as tough as practicable the emphasis of government policy is changing towards policies for a multiracial society that contains substantial ethnic minorities suffering particular difficulties.

Principal aims

The major declared aim of government policy is the integration of ethnic minorities through ensuring that they receive equal opportunities and equal treatment. It is now widely recognized that the integration of New Commonwealth immigrants and their descendants will not result in complete assimilation as has been the case with past influxes of European migrants.

The new ethnic minorities are keen to preserve their own cultural and religious traditions. The size and geographical concentration of the West Indian and Asian settlements will also help to preserve their distinct identity, which may be reinforced by their experience of racial prejudice and discrimination. All major political parties, with the partial exception of the far right of the Conservative Party, are now committed to a multiracial society in which the various communities live and work harmoniously. The major parties are also committed to the removal of racial disadvantages suffered by ethnic minorities, although there is considerable disagreement as to how this can best be achieved. Many on the left would favor positive discrimination, but this is highly unpopular with public opinion.

The basis of immigrant policy has been a series of race relations acts aimed at combating racial discrimination. Institutions to enforce the acts and promote good race relations have been established. The Commission for Racial Equality is a statutory body established under the 1976 Race Relations Act to enforce its provisions, to promote the elimination of racial discrimination, and to foster equality of opportunity and good race relations. It succeeded two earlier bodies, the Race Relations Board and the Community Relations Commission.

Good community relations and racial harmony can be considered major aims of government policy. Racial tension may easily break out into sporadic acts of violence that could escalate into racial disturbances, which the government would naturally wish to avoid since such outbreaks further increase racial tension, involve the police in confrontations with members of the public, and damage the country internationally. As a result of the racial disturbances of 1981 and the subsequent report of Lord Scarman (HMSO, Scarman Report 1981), the government is giving a high priority to police–minority relations. The relations between the police and the ethnic minorities in some areas are very poor. This is partly because some communities feel they suffer from public harassment and partly because some feel inadequately protected against racial provocation and attacks (Home Office, *Racial Attacks* 1981).

Instruments of immigrant policy

Housing
The allocation of housing in Britain is predominantly a function of private market forces and local authorities, who own about 30 percent of the housing stock. Migrants were initially forced to seek whatever accommodation was available – usually privately rented accommodation in run-down inner city areas. Accommodations in better residential areas were expensive to buy and difficult to rent due to discrimination and a lack of availability. In the short term, local authority accommodations were unavailable to immigrants, except the homeless, since most local authorities would not accept on their waiting lists people who had not been resident for a period. Once on the list, people who had been waiting the longest had priority depending on needs and circumstances.

Since private rents were often high, many immigrants were forced to buy cheap leasehold or freehold property in inner city areas vacated by white families anxious to move to the more desirable suburban estates being built at a rapid rate in the 1950s and 1960s. These inner city houses were then often rented to or shared with later arrivals. Homeless people and families are routinely housed by local authorities in their poorest accommodations, in part because low quality housing is more likely to be available and in part because the homeless have little choice but to accept what is offered. Homelessness is, in other words, not a good way of gaining accommodation.

There is some evidence that the housing situation is changing rapidly, especially for West Indians. In 1978 the National Dwelling and Housing Survey found that the proportion of West Indian households in council housing had risen from 25 percent in 1971 to 45 percent in 1978 and for Asians there was a rise from 4 percent to 10 percent. Redevelopment of inner city areas may be a contributing factor as well as the fulfillment of council requirements by minority families.

One further factor in the housing market is the high concentration of immigrant communities. In a Department of the Environment report it was found that 10 percent of the census enumeration districts housed 70 percent of the black population. In these districts they formed 20 percent of the population. These districts also contained three times as many people living at a density of 1.5 persons per room, which is the statutory definition of overcrowding (DOE, *Census Indicators of Urban Deprivation* 1976).

There has been considerable controversy over the concentration of black immigrants and over whether a policy for dispersal in the allocation of housing, as was operated for a time by Birmingham council, or the busing of immigrant children to schools in other areas to achieve a more racially balanced mix of children, as happened in Ealing, would help integration. It has now been decided that the costs of "forced" dispersal are too high to the minority communities; the policy has now been declared discriminatory and has been ended.

Rex and Tomlinson in their survey of Handsworth found to their surprise that immigrants did not even mount a campaign for equality of access to suburban housing on the new estates. The social development department in Birmingham found that 90 percent of immigrants interviewed preferred inner city areas and that there was a marked unwillingness to move to estates located on the fringe of the city. What immigrants did oppose as discriminatory was the dispersal policy itself, in part because it effectively reduced the number of offers they were likely to receive but also because it involved the forced break-up of black communities (Rex & Tomlinson 1979).

Employment

In 1971, people born outside the United Kingdom accounted for just under 6 percent of all economically active persons; of these, 2.2 percent (5,520) were from the New Commonwealth and 1.7 percent (421,130) from Ireland. The proportion of immigrants in the workforce varies from 1.3 percent in the north of England to 15 percent in Greater London. New Commonwealth immigrants work in a wide variety of mainly manual occupations and industries and tend to be concentrated in unskilled and semi-skilled jobs. They have traditionally taken jobs rejected by native workers due to low pay, long and unsocial hours, or unpleasant work conditions. New Commonwealth workers are over-represented in ship-building, vehicle manufacture, and textiles. In London, West Indians are concentrated in transport and laboring jobs and Pakistanis and Bangladeshis in the clothing trade; over half the workers in the catering industry are also immigrants. In the West Midlands, Asians are concentrated in furnace, forge, foundry, and rolling mills. In the north of England, Asians work mainly in the textile industry. In Yorkshire and Humberside, where 6 percent of the general population work in textiles, 62 percent of Pakistanis do so. This is often permanent nightshift work (Smith 1977).

The National Health Service is a major employer of New Commonwealth immigrant workers, and this appears to contribute significantly to the proportions of Indian and East African Asians in professional positions. One third of hospital medical staff and one sixth of doctors in general practice were born overseas. This is also true of 20 percent of student nurses. Smith found that New Commonwealth men had generally little success in penetrating white collar and professional jobs: 40 percent of native whites held such jobs as compared with only 8 percent of West Indians, Pakistanis, and Bangladeshis; the proportion of Indians was 20 percent and East African Asians 30 percent. Many of the immigrants were in lower paid professional jobs and many of the Indians and African Asians are shopkeepers. However, despite the attention given to Asian entrepreneurs, the vast majority of Asians are not businessmen and many that are have markets restricted largely to the supply of their own communities.

Due to their relative youthfulness a higher proportion of New Commonwealth men are working (91 percent) compared with the general male population (77 percent), although this distinction disappears in the 15–54 age group where 93 percent of immigrant males are economically active compared with 91 percent of indigenous males. Among women 50 percent of New Commonwealth migrants were working compared with 43 percent of adult women. There were considerable discrepancies between different groups of immigrant women, with 74 percent of West Indian women working, 45 percent of Indians, and only 17 percent of Muslim women (Pakistani and Bangladeshi). In the later case cultural, religious, and language barriers inhibit employment (Smith 1977).

All the major studies show a high level of trade union membership among immigrant workers. Amongst immigrant men 61 percent are members of a trade union compared with 47 percent of native men. Despite high levels of immigrant worker membership, however, and despite union rhetoric in favor of equality of opportunity for black and white workers as well as union resolutions against racism at union conferences, few positive initiatives have been taken on behalf of immigrants. If anything, there has been a reluctance to support industrial action promoted by immigrant members. British unions are also somewhat uncertain about positive action policies, as this might be interpreted as discrimination against white members. Only a handful of black workers have achieved union office and some unions increasingly appear to represent a privileged white aristrocracy of labor (Rex & Tomlinson 1979).

It is illegal for employers to discriminate against job applicants on grounds of race or color; nevertheless, there is considerable evidence that such discrimination takes place. Members of ethnic minorities are particularly vulnerable to unemployment in periods of recession, and this is particularly true for West Indian men. Once unemployed, members of ethnic minorities respond by taking less desirable jobs, which reinforces their position in the lowest sections of the labor market.

Education

The government and local authorities were slow to respond to the growing number of immigrant children entering the schools in areas of New Commonwealth settlement. The education system was changing from a selective grammar school system to a comprehensive one, but the system was well established and assumed cultural and religious homogeneity. At first the influx of immigrant children was seen as causing problems only when the children were Asian non-English speakers. In the past it had been assumed that foreign children would quickly pick up English in the schools, but the geographical concentration of New Commonwealth immigrants caused white parents in areas of immigrant settlement to protest at the holding back of native children. This caused the Department of Education to recommend, in 1965, that immigrant children should not form more than 30 percent of the pupils in any school (*Britain's Black Population* 1980).

In the 1960s provision began to be made for additional resources to help with language teaching for immigrant children and modest funds were allocated in the Local Government Act of 1966. In 1976 local educational authorities spent 20 million for additional teachers, liaison officers, interpreters, clerical staff, ancillary school staff, social workers, and educational welfare officers. Some 15 million was contributed by central government. Financial help with school buildings has also been available under the urban aid program that began in 1969 and also from the EEC social fund, but such aid has been very small.

The geographical concentration of the immigrant community has resulted in a considerable amount of segregation of immigrant children. Some authorities for a time resorted to busing to get a better mix of children but this brought resentment from both immigrant parents whose children suffered long school hours (to include travel) and from white parents. Segregation is often increased in inner city areas because many of the white families living there are Irish and their children go to parochial Catholic schools.

The presence of immigrant children in the schools has challenged the assumptions underlying school curriculum and has exposed the ethnocentric and even racist bias of courses and textbooks, especially in subjects like history, English literature, and religious education. Serious research is now being done into multicultural education.

There is increasing evidence that West Indian children are performing badly and despite a number of inquiries and studies the reasons for this are unclear. Attention is being given to language problems caused by the use of Jamaican patois or Creole; cultural and consequently behavioral problems that cause West Indian children to be classified as educationally subnormal and dumped in "problem" schools; and problems of family background (HMSO, *West Indian Children in our Schools* 1981). In marked contrast to West Indian children the Asians appear to perform well in school, despite language problems and deprived family backgrounds. There appears to be no problem of underachievement here, which is surprising given the Asians' relative disadvantage in housing and cultural distance.

Thus, instead of a national policy on ethnic minority education, there has been only a number of ad hoc expedients. Some of these, such as the establishment of Education Priority Areas and the Center for Information and Advice on Educational Disadvantages, cover ethnic minority children as part of general programs. The Department of Education has established a Multi-Ethnic Inspectorate and a number of local authorities have appointed staff responsible for multiethnic education provision.

Inner city policy

A further instrument of policy with particular reference to ethnic minorities is the various programs known as inner city policies. These programs apply to all residents, both black and white, who live in inner city communities; but since these are areas of high minority concentrations, the programs are considered to apply particularly to immigrants. Thus, while the Labour government's White Paper on Inner City Policy in 1977 did not mention race relations, the Minister of the Environment argued that inner city policy was an important contribution to the fight against racism. This political ambiguity is deliberate: the policy can be defended as universally applicable in the designated areas while, in practice, resources can be steered to areas of racial stress.

A variety of such programs have been initiated but have all been limited to relatively small resources. The 1974–79 Labour government made more initiatives in this area than previous governments; between 1976 and 1979 approximately 20 million per year was made available to inner city areas under the Urban Aid Programme. This has now been substantially increased to improve inner city investment. The Conservative government has since 1979 also considered various initiatives to aid the inner cities, but the schemes developed, like Enterprise Zones and Urban Development Corporations, are extremely limited and not specifically aimed at helping ethnic minorities. The urban riots that occurred in Bristol in 1980 and London and Liverpool in 1981 are likely to result in similar small-scale initiatives, although a government so committed to public expenditure cuts is unlikely to provide the massive investment that inner city areas require.

Discrimination legislation

The Labour government elected in 1964 was concerned, for ideological reasons, to balance its "about turn" on immigration controls by positive measures against discrimination. In 1965 the first Race Relations Act was passed outlawing discrimination in public places and substituting conciliation procedures for criminal sanctions. The crucial areas of employment and housing were excluded. The Act set up the Race Relations Board and the National Committee for Commonwealth Immigrants.

After considerable evidence of continuing discrimination, especially in employment, the second Race Relations Act was passed in 1968. This Act made it unlawful to discriminate on grounds of color, race, or ethnic or national origins in recruitment, training, promotion, dismissals, and terms and conditions of employment. Complaints were to be referred first to the relevant industrial machinery; if the complainant was dissatisfied with the decision of the approved industrial machinery, appeal could be made to the Race Relations Board. The Board would then seek to form an opinion as to whether discrimination had occurred and, if it had, seek to conciliate. It was hoped that by these means discrimination would be reduced not only in the conciliated cases but in numerous others where knowledge of the Board's work would have a preventive and educative effect.

A Parliamentary Select Committee on Race Relations and Immigration was also established in 1968. Since then the Committee has collected considerable evidence on a wide variety of topics concerned with ethnic minorities and has published a large number of reports. One of these reports reviewed the administration of race relations legislation and was influential in determining the content of the 1976 Race Relations Bill which greatly strengthened anti-discrimination legislation.

By 1975 both the Race Relations Board and the Community Relations Commission were arguing that existing legislation was insufficient to deal with widespread discrimination, especially in housing and employment. Extensive surveys by Political and Economic Planning confirmed that discrimination in the areas of rented accommodation and employment remained high and that the problems of disadvantage suffered by ethnic minorities also added greatly to their social deprivation. The additional recommendations by the Select Committee caused the Labour Home Secretary, Roy Jenkins, to introduce a very strong race relations bill.

The new bill represented a considerable advance on previous legislation. It extended the definition of discrimination to include not only direct discrimination but also indirect discrimination where unjustifiable practices and procedures that apply to everyone have the effect of putting people of a particular racial group at a disadvantage. It allowed individuals who felt they had been discriminated against on racial grounds to take their complaint to the County Court in all cases except employment, which could be submitted to industrial tribunals. It abolished the Race Relations Board and the Community Relations Commission and established a Commission for Racial Equality with greatly increased powers of investigation and enforcement to enable it to make wider strategic use of the law in the public interest. In 1980–81 the CRE had a staff of 224 and a budget of £7 million with which it was expected both to promote good race relations practices in the community, especially with employers, local authorities, and other major institutions, and to enforce the Race Relations Act. Not surprisingly the CRE has failed to live up to the expectations of its liberal supporters. The environment within which it works – a deeply prejudiced society – is hostile to its aims, and its resources are insufficient to challenge powerful organizations like building societies, banks, multinational corporations, and local authorities without powerful government backing. Such backing was lost in 1979 when a Conservative government, unsympathetic to the aims of the CRE, was elected. Attempts to introduce racial monitoring into the Civil Service, to investigate the immigration service after the "virginity testing" scandal at Heathrow airport, and to introduce a code of practice for employers have all been resisted by the government, although an experiment in racial monitoring has now been introduced, and, after an appeal to the courts, an investigation of discrimination in the procedures of the immigration service has commenced.

The outcome of immigrant policy

The aims of immigrant policy have been poorly defined and government policy lacks coordination, so that a wide range of government departments, local authorities, and organizations like the police play important but autonomous roles in dealing with immigrants and especially with ethnic minorities. The Parliamentary Home Affairs Committee was highly critical, in its report on racial disadvantage (HMSO 1981), of the passive role of the Home Office, which it felt should play a more positive role in coordinating and assessing the government's policies for combating racial disadvantage. But the Minister of State in charge of race and immigration matters rejected the notion that anybody in government should be in charge of monitoring race relations performance in different departments. He told the Committee that he saw the Home Office as exercising only a liaison role – not a leadership role.

Even after fifteen years of aid to local authorities with large ethnic minority populations, no national policy on minority education has emerged. The government often prefers to do good by stealth; thus, for example, the various initiatives on the inner city are general schemes because the government is wary of pursuing policies that may be seen as positively discriminating and therefore electorally unpopular. A number of studies have indicated that there is considerable resentment against the Race Relations Act, which is seen as positive discrimination rather than as protection from unfair discrimination for the minorities (Moore & Wallace 1975).

Much of the initiative regarding race relations policy is in practice left to the major government agency, the Commission for Racial Equality, but so far it has had little success in promoting fair practices in housing and employment. In spite of its legal powers and powers of enforcement it has met considerable resistance from employers and even some local authorities. It has also been subject to considerable political criticism regarding its own management and general competence. However, the all-party Select Committee has recognized the continuing disadvantages and discrimination experienced by the new ethnic minorities, and there is some evidence that the government is beginning to give these matters higher priority.

The interrelationship between immigrant policy and immigration regulation and control

As government policy changed in the 1960s and 1970s towards tighter immigration controls, many politicians felt that greater efforts should be made to promote integration within Britain. In many cases the policy of control was directly linked with integration because it was frequently argued that control would reassure people in Britain that their culture and identity was not being "swamped" by large numbers of non-European immigrants; indigenous citizens would be less hostile to immigrants if it was widely appreciated that immigration was strictly controlled. It was also believed that smaller numbers would reduce competition for housing, jobs, and social services so that their visibility would decline and resentment against them would be reduced. Integration could then proceed slowly and smoothly.

5. Policymaking and administration

Immigration policy in Britain is the product of a highly centralized and elitist political system. Policy is determined by the executive, legislated and legitimized by parliament, and administered by the bureaucracy or local authorities. The Civil Service plays an important role in the formulation of policy, especially in advising the key ministers what policy options are practicable. Through consultation with a variety of interested and campaigning pressure groups, the Civil Service also advises the ministers of the likely reaction of such groups and of public opinion to policy initiation. Politicians naturally are also open to lobbying and feel themselves experts on public opinion and pressure groups. The administration of immigration control is a complicated and difficult job and ministers are bound to take serious account of the expert advice of their officials. It is clear that such advice was crucial in the Conservative government's decision to drop the proposed register of the overseas dependants of immigrants settled in Britain.

One important aspect of the British political system is that the single member simple majority electoral system favours the dominance of two major parties who tend to be elected with overall parliamentary majorities despite securing only minority electoral support. As the Conservative and Labour Parties support rather different policy positions on most issues and as they rarely remain in office for more than two elections the result is substantial changes in policy as governments change. This has had some influence on race relations and immigration policy, although not as much in practice as might be expected. In the 1960s, when Labour was in office for most of the period, tough immigration controls and moderately positive policies on race relations were favored. In the period 1970–79, the Conservative Party tightened controls, but despite internal opposition within the Party allowed the Ugandan Asians to come to Britain. After 1974 the Labour government slightly relaxed certain aspects of the immigration rules and introduced the strongest race relations legislation that Britain had ever had, but it failed to repeal the Immigration Act 1971 as the Labour Party had promised. Since the Conservative electoral victory in 1979 the major government initiative has been the British Nationality Act of 1981. The re-election of the Conservatives in 1983 is likely to result in the continuation of existing policies unless particular events force special initiatives. But the new government is content with existing controls and is opposed to special policies for the ethnic minorities which, they argue, increase separation rather than aid integration. This is a high risk strategy given the continuing evidence of discrimination, the high levels of unemployment, particularly among the young, and as a consequence the feelings of rejection experienced by so many of the second generation.

Perceptions
Immigration has become one of the most important issues in Britain. Both immigration regulation and immigrant policy receive extensive coverage in the media and in parliament. The reason for this is the view that colored immigration is an issue which the electorate feels very strongly about and which there is substantial consensus on. Although there is considerable evidence to suggest that the British people are deeply racially prejudiced, some liberal academics have attempted to portray them as generally tolerant and fairminded (Rose 1969) – in part, one suspects, from a desire to influence policymakers in a liberal direction.

Lawrence, for example, re-analyzed Rose's *Colour and Citizenship* data for Nottingham and found that, out of 500 respondents, 65 percent believed that West Indians took more out of the country than they put in, 61 percent believed the same of Asians and 38 percent the same of Greeks. Sixty-six percent considered the British superior to Africans, 58 percent considered them superior to Asians, and 25 percent considered them superior to Americans. Asked whether they thought color distinction would ever become unimportant in the way people felt about each other, 8 percent agreed but 62 percent felt color distinctions would always be important. Fifty-five percent felt that there should be special immigration regulations against colored people (Lawrence 1978/79).

It is clear that politicians and civil servants were concerned about the acceptability and assimilability of colored immigrants from the beginning of the migration but perceived Britain's world role and economic prosperity to be more important issues. The racial violence of 1958, the increasing evidence in opinion polls of public hostility to colored immigration, and an internal campaign inside the Conservative Party led to the 1962 Commonwealth Immigrant Act. Nevertheless it was the electoral victory of Peter Griffiths in the General Election of 1964 that had the most decisive impact on policymaking. After a strong anti-immigrant campaign Griffiths captured the Labour constituency of Smethwick, unseating Patrick Gordon-Walker, the prospective foreign secretary. His achievement was dramatic because he gained a swing to the Conservative Party of 7.5 percent in an election where the national swing to the Labour Party was 3.2 percent. Dependent on a majority of only five seats, reduced to three when Gordon-Walker lost another "safe" Labour seat at Leyton in 1965 after the sitting member had been asked to step down, the Labour government reversed its opposition to the 1962 Act and in 1965 introduced stricter controls (Layton-Henry 1984).

Public concern over immigration was assuaged by the Labour government's change of policy, but only temporarily. Enoch Powell and Duncan Sandys successfully campaigned against the influx of Asians from Kenya in 1967–68. Enoch Powell's "rivers of blood" speech in April 1968 had a dramatic impact and raised the salience of race and immigration to such a level that it is believed to have contributed substantially to the Conservative victory in the general election of 1970. It was no surprise that the Conservative government introduced further legislation tightening control in 1971. It is clear that public opinion has had a major impact on policymaking in this area (Studlar 1974).

Politicians frequently claim that immigration controls have been introduced and strengthened to ensure that native British do not feel threatened by New Commonwealth immigrants. The reality is that most people feel that such controls have come too late to be of very much value. In each of the three national samples studied by Butler and Stokes in 1963, 1964, and 1966, it was found that over 80 percent of respondents felt that too many immigrants had already been let into the country (Butler & Stokes 1969). So despite politicians' arguments that they are responding to public disquiet, each tightening of controls can be seen as confirmation of the inadequacy of past policies and the failure of politicians of all the major parties to respond to popular wishes. What is remarkable is the stability of the findings of opinion polls. As recently as February 1978, the National Opinion Poll found that 86 percent thought that too many immigrants had come to Britain. Majorities exceeding 80 percent were against the admission of parents, brothers, and sisters of those who had settled here (Lawrence 1978–79). The result of New Commonwealth immigration has been to create a substantial minority of British citizens that are seen by many as intruders and illegitimate competitors for scarce resources. Recent studies of mixed samples in inner city areas tend to confirm these views (Phizacklea & Miles 1980). In contrast – and despite high levels of prejudice and discrimination – large majorities of Asians and West Indians claim to be satisfied with their jobs, housing, and circumstances in Britain (Rex & Tomlinson 1979).

These perceptions of popular prejudice have also been a factor constraining the actions of employers, trade union leaders and the police, but since the prejudices are so widely disseminated among the population it is clear that they are shared by many of the elite as well.

One argument used by politicians, especially Conservative politicians, has been that to ignore right-wing populist demands for an end to colored immigration would result in growth and support for the National Front and other far right groups. This was a clear implication of Margaret Thatcher's "swamping" speech in January 1978, and it was noticeable that in the general election of 1979 the electoral support for the National Front collapsed and appeared to go to the Conservatives (Layton-Henry & Taylor 1979). Mrs Thatcher's attempt to win back these voters to the Conservatives appeared to have been successful. One major problem has been that every concession to the far right has been received as confirmation of the justice of their case and has thus led to increased demands.

As has already been emphasized, Commonwealth citizens (including those from the New Commonwealth) have full civic rights by virtue of their status as British subjects. They are able to vote in local and national elections, stand for political office, and serve in the armed forces and the public and diplomatic service. In the early period of immigration their numbers were small, many failed to register on the electoral rolls, and participation in British politics was low. Many remained more interested in the politics of their countries of origin, and branches of the major Indian, Pakistani, and Caribbean parties were established in Britain. After 1958 when immigration became a political issue of some significance it was the impact on the white electorate that was crucially important. This remains true today. When members of the ethnic minorities stand for office they tend to do badly.

In the 1970s it gradually became clear that because of their geographical concentration and increasing numbers, immigrant electors were able to play a significant role in a small but growing number of constituencies. In 1975 the Community Relations Commission published an influential pamphlet on the growing electoral importance of the ethnic minorities, which contributed to the first positive efforts by the Conservatives to recruit members of the ethnic minorities (Layton-Henry 1978). By this time large numbers of Asians and West Indians were on the electoral rolls and election studies were showing very high rates of electoral participations in both local and national elections. By the late 1970s significant numbers of Asians and West Indians were being elected to local councils predominantly but not exclusively as Labour councillors. In some areas large numbers of Asians appeared to be joining constituency Labour parties and exerting some influence in the election of local council candidates. All election studies of the voting behavior of New Commonwealth voters show incredibly high levels of support for the Labour Party and little support for any other party. Independent minority candidates have not done well. Asian voters have the highest rates of participation, followed by native whites; West Indians have relatively low rates of turnout (Layton-Henry 1984).

In attempting to examine minority organizations and their political role and impact, one is struck by the incredible number and range of such organizations, many with little support and often the creation of personally ambitious individuals. The Asian community in particular has strong communal organizations, especially religious, that are very influential within their communities. Many organizations, such as the Indian Workers Association, are riven by internal political disputes. Attempts to form all-embracing Afro-Asian organizations have not been successful. There has been some support for Marxist organizations that have campaigned on anti-racist, anti-fascist platforms and for far-left sponsored groups like the Anti-Nazi League. Support for such groups may grow among the second generation, if the racial harassment and attacks of right-wing groups continues. At present many West Indians, particularly the young, are disillusioned and seek refuge in various forms of apathy and withdrawal. British Asians on the contrary appear to be becoming more involved in the politics of the Labour movement.

The making of immigration policy

The determinants of immigration policy are political. British politicians have adopted highly exclusionist policies towards colored immigrants in response to public opinion. Wide powers have been delegated by parliament to immigration officers at the ports of entry and to officials in British High Commissions and Embassies abroad, and these officials carry out the policy of the government. Their decisions are subject to a system of adjudication, with tribunals that hear appeals. Applicants can also appeal to the courts and to sympathetic politicians for assistance. The Home Office is the department of state with responsibility for immigration and one of the ministers at the Home Office is given special responsibility for race relations and immigration matters. He will normally review the decisions that come to the Home Office for final appeal. Final responsibility rests with the Home Secretary and the government.

Because immigration and race relations are so politically sensitive the Home Secretary devotes considerable time to this part of his work. There is also a Junior Minister at the Home Office whose major responsibility is immigration control and race relations matters.

Since the first control bill was passed in 1962, considerable parliamentary time has been devoted to race and immigration matters. The first bill was highly controversial and the government was forced to make a number of concessions, one of which was that legislation would lapse if not reviewed by parliament. Between 1963 and 1970 there were thus annual debates on immigration policy as the legislation came up for renewal. This ceased with the enactment of the 1971 Immigration Act. In the 1970s the activities of the far right, especially the National Front, kept immigration to the fore as a political issue even though controls were very tight. In the general election campaign of 1979 the Conservatives promised to strengthen controls even further and were subject to a backbench revolt because of the harshness of the new rules (Layton-Henry & Taylor 1980). Because of this the government was forced to make some concessions. The Parliamentary Select Committee on Race and Immigration, now succeeded by a sub-committee of the Home Affairs Committee, has been very important as a means of collecting evidence on immigration matters and has been an influential and progressive force on immigration and race relations issues.

The administration of immigration control

Immigration control is organized in the sending countries by the need to gain entry certification and at the ports of entry by the need to satisfy immigration control officers of the right to enter. The Foreign Service controls immigration by the issuing of entry certificates, visas, and passports to British citizens and applicants overseas. The Home Office controls immigration at the ports of entry and decides on applications to change conditions of entry, applications for naturalization, and the deportation of criminals and illegal immigrants, and those who have violated immigration control. There is a government funded agency, the United Kingdom Immigration Advisory Service, which helps prospective immigrants with appeals against administrative decisions, but many applicants prefer the Joint Council for the Welfare of Immigrants, an independent body that helps prospective immigrants with immigration problems and also campaigns for more liberal immigration policies. The only special arrangements made for particular national groups have concerned political refugees such as the Poles, Hungarians, Ugandan Asians, and most recently the Vietnamese boat people.

Critics of government policy feel that it is becoming increasingly harsh.

More people are being refused entry into Britain and more people are being detained at detention centers while their appeals against refusal of entry are considered. The policy is clearly discriminating: Asians are 50 to 60 times more likely to be refused entry compared with travelers from Canada and Australia. Moreover, internal controls are increasing, with a growth in police raids on places where illegal immigrants are thought to be employed and an increase in deportations.

6. Lessons of the past – hypotheses for the future

In the postwar period the debate has focused on colored immigration, while immigration as such has not been an issue. In the future it may become one, if there is an expansion of migration within the EEC from Southern Europe. This could become significant, if Spain and Portugal are admitted to EEC membership. White immigration, whether of kith and kin (former British settlers overseas) or aliens, is not an issue at all, while the immigration of even relatively small numbers of colored immigrants is an important political issue. British governments have been hampered in their efforts to control colored immigration by the colonial legacy, the lack of a precise definition of citizenship, and the lack of internal controls whose imposition would be highly controversial. Even legislation defining British citizenship tightly and restrictively, which has now been introduced, is politically controversial due to the large numbers of Britons settled abroad that wish to keep dual nationality and maintain their right of entry and abode in the United Kingdom. Millions of Britons have such relatives abroad, especially in the United States and in "Old Commonwealth" countries.

The major failures of British immigration policy concern the lack of government action. Successive British governments failed to give priority and resources to ensuring the successful settlement and integration of New Commonwealth immigrants or even to develop a policy on immigration before 1962, when the policy adopted was control. Once settlement had occurred on a substantial scale, positive policies were again needed to ensure equal rights and opportunities. Little has been done, and it has been halfhearted and sporadic. The major problem facing future British governments will be to ensure that the second and third generations of Black Britons are not alienated from their country of birth but feel full and equal citizens.

5

France

GILLES VERBUNT

1. Immigration and immigration policy

Historical backround

France has a long tradition of immigration. Since the second half of the nineteenth century thousands of foreigners have been recruited or granted admission in an effort to compensate for the country's insufficient labor supply and low birthrate. The low birthrate has created a permanent demographic need and has together with periodic labor shortages served to motivate immigration. Immigration policy has tried to regulate the arrival, residence, and departure of foreign workers and their families, according to the interests of the moment.

The effects of immigration policy, however, have never been exactly those expected or planned for. When French governments wanted immigrants to come, as in 1919 and 1945, only a few responded; when they tried to send them home, as in 1932 and 1978–79, only a small number cooperated, and many chose to be naturalized instead. The two periods of heavy immigration, 1921–31 and 1956–72, escaped the control of political authorities almost totally. Today, illegal workers are still entering France despite firm border controls and generally increasing unemployment. "In spite of the efforts undertaken by the international organizations and by concerned governments, on a worldwide scale spontaneous migrations are rather the rule and organized migrations the exception" (Costa-Lascoux & de Wenden-Didier 1981:352).

In Table 5.1 immigration policy appears as only one of the regulating elements. Immigration reaches its peaks when employers want to augment the insufficient supply or avoid the excessive cost of domestic labor by replacing it with available and cheap foreign labor. Their needs are conveyed by "natural" information networks formed either by immigrants or by sources in the emigration countries. Through the channels created by

Table 5.1. *The development of immigration and immigration policy in France*

Year	Societal context	Policy	Results
1850–1913	Industrial development; rural exodus	Naturalization facilitated; after 1890 employers recruit collectively from distant countries; beginnings of state control	Immigrants take places left by French peasants. Immigrant population increases from 380,000 in 1850 to 1,160,000 in 1911
1914–18	First World War		2 to 3 million casualties
1919–21	Repair of war damages: need for population (young males) and construction (housing and industry)	Immigration encouraged; rotational immigration from China and Vietnam	Small increase in the number of resident immigrants
1922–31	Economic growth; need of manpower; reduction in rural exodus	Authorities create framework to facilitate and up to a certain extent control recruitment organized by employers	Increase in immigrant population from 1,532,000 in 1921 to 2,715,000 on 1931; more and more immigrants arriving from distant countries
1931–39	Economic crisis; widespread unemployment and a slow recovery	Protection of national labor market; efforts to encourage departures	Few returns and many naturalizations (30,000 per year)
1939–45	Second World War		
1945–55	Need of young males to repair war damages; emphasis on population and construction	Plans for an active immigration policy controlled by the state; preference for assimilable Italians; new Nationality Act to increase naturalizations	More than one million casualties 1,670,000 foreigners in 1945 and 1,553,000 in 1954; naturalizations and deaths exceed arrivals, which were 54,000 annually from 1946 to 1949 and 18,000 annually from 1950 to 1955
1956–61	Economic development, especially in building; war with Algeria leads to many repatriations	State permits no longer so effective; half of all immigrants come spontaneously	Arrival of 432,000 permanent workers (majority are repatriates and uncontrolled Algerians)

1962	Algerian independence; French need of manpower	Efforts to reintegrate the repatriates from Algeria	270,000 foreign immigrants plus 270,000 repatriates and Algerians (now considered foreigners)
1963–73	Rapid economic growth in labor-intensive sectors; need for unskilled manpower; more and more social problems	Laissez-faire policy: only 10 to 30 percent of immigration is controlled, first steps to control admissions come in 1972	An average of 130,000 arrivals annually; first efforts in social services; end of the large *bidonvilles* (self-built slums)
1974–80	Economic recession, with unemployment in the labor-intensive industries; restructuring of French industries; development of dual labor market (one protected and one vulnerable)	Immigration stop in 1974; 25 new social measures; vice-minister for immigrant affairs; from 1977 immigrants encouraged to leave; protection of national labor market; restrictions on family immigration	Foreign population does not decrease (4,200,000); small increase in returns; many naturalizations (30,000 per year); 70,000 children born each year to foreign families; increase in number of illegal immigrants
May–June 1981–1983	Political change: Socialist president and majority; no industrial reorientations other than nationalizations; steps to establish new relations with the Third World and especially with emigration countries	Efforts to stop illegal immigration and "black" labor; offer to legalize illegal workers; firm border control; liberalization of family immigration; measures to give better security and more rights to resident immigrants	c. 120,000 illegal workers are made legal (out of a total of c. 200,000 to 400,000); increase in family immigration and perhaps also illegal immigration; stabilization of the foreign population

this tradition immigrants keep coming to France, thinking it better to be an illegal worker (even unemployed) in France than to be a legal (sometimes employed) worker in a Third World country.

The table insufficiently indicates the different composition of the immigration trends. Until the First World War immigration to France was from her neighboring countries. In the agricultural provinces near the Italian border, North Italian peasants took the place of French peasants who had migrated to the growing French industrial centers. A similar movement of Belgians in the north and Spaniards in the south of France also took place.

Between the two world wars employers went as far as Southern Italy and Eastern Europe, and sometimes to North Africa, to recruit the manpower they needed. These immigrants were employed in groups throughout the whole country (except the western part) in agricultural, mining, and industrial (especially building) centers.

After the Second World War immigration from the former colonies increased in volume. The familiar Italian and Iberian immigration also increased, especially from Spain in the 1950s and Portugal in the 1960s, although North Africans and later West Africans became more and more numerous. Algerians had been coming to France for many years, but since they were French citizens until 1963 they were not considered or counted as immigrants (Tapinos 1975:55–62).

In more recent years the variety of nationalities and cultures has increased. Immigrants come from countries that are often totally unfamiliar to the French people; some of them, e.g. Turks, Indians, or Pakistanis, come to France after residing in a neighboring country. Cultural differences are growing and integration is becoming a major issue in France, a country where unemployment breeds attitudes of rejection.

Terminology

In France only foreigners can be called "immigrants". For example, Antillians from the islands (*départements*) of Martinique and Guadelope, although they have many problems in common with immigrants that do not have French nationality, are called "migrants". On the other hand, not *all* foreigners are "immigrants" – tourists, seasonal workers, students, and refugees all have special status (which may sometimes serve as a screen for an illegal worker).

The English word "immigrant" can be translated into two different French words: *immigrant* (present participle) and *immigré* (past participle). The first word is not used as a noun; instead, it is replaced by "migrant", which has, as we saw, a wider meaning. By using the past participle *immigré* as a noun, one emphasizes the result of the action more than its movement; in other words, one refers to "someone, a foreigner, who has come to live here" rather than "someone who moves around, i.e. whose nature it is to go from one country to another". The latter meaning is better rendered by the word "migrant".

When this chapter presents statistics, all foreigners are included, even EEC citizens. But when it discusses laws, EEC citizens are excluded because they enjoy special treatment, as do Algerians and in some respects various African nationalities. The term "Africans" includes both North Africans (also called Maghrebians; not to be confused with "Arabs": Maghrebians come from Tunisia, Algeria, Morocco, and Mauretania) and West Africans (black Africans from Mali, Senegal, Ivory Coast, Cameroons, etc.).

2. General preconditions

Geography and population

For a long time France was the most industrialized Mediterranean country. It is situated simultaneously in the cultural area of peoples that speak Latin languages, in the economic area of commercial exchanges with countries in North Africa and the Near East, and in the industrial area of Western Europe with its similar political and social organization. Unlike most other industrialized European countries, however, until recently France received many immigrants from neighboring or culturally similar countries, e.g. Italy.

The borders are hard to control because of intense traffic (tourism is very important for the French economy) and because of their shape and size. The border with Spain, formed by the Pyrenees mountains, is full of gaps, as smugglers demonstrated when they brought across tens of thousands of Portuguese workers during the 1960s. The borders with Belgium and Germany are easy to cross, as shown by the number of Pakistanis, Turks, Indians, and others that have come since France changed its immigration policy. The control of African immigration, especially from West Africa, is difficult because the border police have a hard time detecting exchanges of identity documents. It is generally admitted that networks of smugglers dealing in human merchandise are still active.

France has several small territories overseas: the islands of Martinique and Guadelope in the Caribbean and the Ile de la Réunion in the Indian Ocean. Together they have a population of 1,200,000. France has a total population of approximately 53 million; its population density is 96 inhabitants per square kilometer, less than half that of its neighbors. Demographic problems have been persistent, not only with regard to population growth but also because of an unfavorable balance between rural and urban areas. Population increased from 30 million in 1810 to 40.1 million in 1890, and to 40.5 million in 1946, but only because the mortality rate declined and immigration took place (the generations born between 1820 and the First World War did not even ensure their own reproduction). During each world war more than one million people, mostly young males, were killed in France.

After the Second World War measures were taken to re-establish demographic equilibrium through immigration and special social measures, the so-called *allocations familiales* ("family allowances"). The French age pyramid is very irregular and also top-heavy: the third age group (60 years and above) is over-represented. The birthrate in 1936 was only 14.6 per thousand; it climbed up to 21 per thousand in 1947 and remains at present between 18 and 19 per thousand, even in rural areas. Assessing the importance of immigration for the French population since the Second World War, Lebon writes that immigrant families have directly contributed 2.6 million inhabitants and, with the birth of 65,000 children per year, have indirectly contributed 1.3 million inhabitants. One must also include 1.3 million repatriates, mostly from North Africa, in the population growth that has occurred since the 1950s (Lebon 1981:34).

Immigration was also intended to balance the very unequal distribution of population within the country. Nine million people live in the region of Paris, several million more are concentrated in other industrial areas, e.g. the regions of Lyons, Marseille, and the north and northeast; however, population is much lower in the south and southwest, where industries are less numerous, and still lower in the central regions and in the west. Consistently low birthrates have caused a rural exodus that has in some areas resulted in the desertion of entire villages and the decline of small towns. Between 1968 and 1978, one million farmers left their land; the total number of farmers declined from five million in 1954 to two million in 1978. Immigrants often take the place of those who leave for the cities. Of 350,000 wage-earning farmworkers today, 20 percent are immigrants, and an even larger number are "black" workers (i.e. workers without residence and work permits).

The admission of young foreign families has made possible a better equilibrium in the age pyramid, avoiding the danger that an old, unproductive population would someday become too heavy a burden resting on too small a base.

Economy

Compared with its industrialized neighbors France is still an agricultural country. However, French agriculture does not provide young people with a good future. This situation is traditional and has led, in some regions, to several waves of immigration during the past century.

As mentioned previously, the industrial sector is concentrated in a few regions. It employs 40 percent of the active population and accounts for half the national income. The steel, automobile, aeronautical, ship-building, and chemical industries also produce for export; their raw materials are often imported. A great deal of French trade, more than that of any other European industrialized nation, goes to Third World countries.

The service sector employs 40 percent of the active population and accounts for 35 percent of the national income. The service sector is developing because of the modernization of French industry.

The most recent wave of immigrants, in the 1960s, was necessary for France's industrial expansion. This expansion occurred particularly in the labor-intensive industries: building and agriculture since 1956 and steel, automobiles, textiles, and chemicals in later years. The unskilled labor force was also necessary to balance the upward mobility of French youth, whose higher education allowed them to take more qualified jobs. Whole units of production were left to immigrants, whose presence soon became a *structural* necessity (Briot & Verbunt 1981:21).

Since 1974 efforts have been made to decrease the country's dependence on immigrant labor. Old industries have disappeared or been modernized; working conditions have been improved for unskilled jobs and pressure has been placed on French youth and on unemployed workers to take them. The need for peasant immigration has decreased because of the abandonment of labor-intensive industries in favor of modern, capital-intensive ones. The unskilled jobs created by the latter are acceptable, at least so far, to French workers and to the children of immigrants. The evolution of French industry from labor-intensive to capital-intensive has been encouraged by the state, which is incidentally the most important industrial employer through its ownership of nationalized enterprises.

Despite these developments, however, France still retains a number of small, archaic enterprises, many of which can survive only because they offer low wages and poor working conditions. Small enterprises often work for large, modern ones and supply their day-to-day needs. "Black" labor is frequent among these small enterprises.

Trade unions try to intervene, especially regarding working conditions, but they do not have the kind of influence that similar organizations in Northern Europe have. CGT and CFDT (which are the most important unions for immigrants) proclaim, of course, the necessity of international solidarity and the "ontological" unity of the working class across national borders. But putting these theories into practice is not always easy. After all, the unions are organized on a national level, and even there the interests of the workers are not always identical.

Society and culture

France was originally a mosaic of cultures, and rulers since Louis XIV (1643–1715) have tried to unify it into a single nation. This policy of unification has led to centralization, an example of which can be seen on any highway or railroad map: all roads and railways begin or end in Paris. Regional cultures have been suppressed as much as possible in the cause of national unity, and it is only recently that regions outside Paris (*la Province*) have been able to develop certain aspects of their own cultural identity. One of the consequences of centralization has been the concentration of state power and the development of intermediaries that bridge the great distance between national rulers and local administrators. Since local authorities must respond to the desires of lobbies, pressure groups, and traditional power groupings, differences often exist between national decisions and local implementation.

Since the second half of the nineteenth century the French school system has stressed uniformity as a means of promoting absolute equality among all citizens. Yet this system, in its promotion of social equality, has not always respected religious or cultural (regional) differences. Immigration policy has often reinforced this tendency because of the country's demographic need of foreigners. Becoming French is not only a practical decision but also includes an emotional adherence to French values and ways of life.

Belief in the universal values of French institutions has caused a certain inadaptability to the constantly changing problems of immigration. Belief in the universality of French values led older institutions to deny the existence of any specifically new problems. The principle of equality of treatment, i.e. the tendency to treat unequal things equally, led to the worst exclusions. This changed gradually, however, in the 1970s.

The importance of human rights and of the principles of the French Revolution has impregnated French society; the French people know, or believe, that they are judged by other countries on the basis of how well they practice these principles. Therefore, the pressure for more justice for immigrants does not come only from the political left. In the struggle for more justice, religious convictions, the *grandeur de la France*, and, especially for jurists, the transcendental principles of legal justice have sometimes been as important as the actions of activists. In other words, there are some things that one "just cannot do", or admit, if one is a lawyer, a Christian, or a defender of the principles of the French Revolution.

International relations

Vietnam, Algeria, and some West African countries south of the Sahara were French colonies until recently. Other countries were protectorates: Tunisia, Morocco, Laos, and Kampuchea. French colonization was more than just political or economic. The French language and the French model were introduced in the colonies, and French institutions replaced local ones. Colonial citizens served as French soldiers in both world wars and a certain number remained in France afterwards. When the country needed manpower these former soldiers brought in their neighbors or members of their families. Other colonial citizens came to France when their countries became independent. Colonial or postcolonial immigrants have had the advantage of knowing the French language, but the French people have at the same time had a tendency to continue the manners of colonization, i.e. to treat these immigrants in France in the same spirit as the inhabitants of the former colonies were once treated.

Algeria became independent only after a long war (1954–62) and a great number of European colonizers (now repatriated) were present in the country until 1960, which continues to make the relationship between French and Algerians a pretty complicated mixture of feelings and economic interests. Juridical complications and emotional implications, especially for Algerian descendants born in France, serve to focus public attention on Algerians more than on any other nationality; for many people, "immigrants" means "Algerians", even though the 850,000 Portuguese immigrants are more numerous than the 800,000 Algerians.

France is a member of the European Community, which has not significantly affected immigration (Italians are less and less numerous among entrants and they return home or naturalize more often). On the other hand, EEC membership has improved the situation of immigrants from the other member states, giving them more security and rights. Restrictive measures are or will be taken towards countries that enter (or plan to enter) the Community in order to avoid a massive immigration of Greeks, Spaniards, and – especially for France – Portuguese.

3. Immigration regulation and control

International migration occurs without the prior intervention of any national policies. The differences in economic development between the rich industrialized nations and the rest of the world creates a macro-economic framework in which thousands of individual decisions by peasants in one country and employers in another determine the course of migration. Because of its geographical position and economic structure, France cannot remain apart from this movement; the best it can do is try to realize the benefits and avoid the prejudices. Immigration policy attempts to determine the degree of state intervention and to decide which interests should be saved and which should be sacrificed.

Principal aims

In France, there was little state control as long as interests of different parties coincided. Since 1956, and especially in the 1960s, economic expansion created a need for massive amounts of unskilled manpower. This manpower was available in the Third World – peasants from Portugal and Africa were willing to come. Because employers needed these workers rapidly and in large numbers the official channels of immigration were neglected. At the end of the 1960s, 70 to 80 percent of all immigrants entered the country illegally (at that time they used the word "spontaneously"). This was the policy of laissez-faire.

Conflicts of interests began in the 1970s. State intervention increased and led to the official immigration stop of 1974, and interventions have multiplied since then as the interests of the different factions become more and more divergent. The state is one, but because it is governed by different political parties it supports different interests based on political ideology and temporary needs. The aims of immigration policy in France have thus changed very often. We can summarize these aims under three headings: demographic, economic, and social.

After the Second World War France greatly needed young males. Projects were begun and institutions created to attract immigrants, especially Catholic Italians. The principal immigration act and the new Nationality Act both date from this period. They not only tried to encourage new immigration and naturalization but also wanted it to take place under good conditions (particularly with regard to employment and housing). At the same time, immigrants were needed to help reconstruct the devastated country.

After 1956 the need for unskilled labor began to be important, especially in the building sector. Other industries developed in the following years (automobiles, textiles, ship-building, chemicals) and rapidly increased this need. The official channels worked too slowly and were not well appreciated by employers and prospective immigrants; therefore, more and more immigrants came as tourists and later had their situation "legalized" after finding an employer. In these circumstances the authorities could no longer control work and housing conditions. Since the national economy needed the contribution of foreign labor, however, the government took a laissez-faire attitude and even gave its legal recognition to the situation. There was no time left for social or demographic considerations (Fontanet 1970:4–7).

This lack of state intervention was increasingly questioned at the end of the 1960s. Scandals concerning work and housing conditions combined with the obvious expansion of an indigent proletariat brought demands for a new immigration policy. At the same time, unemployment began to increase among French workers. Some measures were taken earlier, but only since 1974 has a new policy been formulated in detail.

Giscard d'Estaing (neo-liberal) became president in 1974 and initiated the new policy by establishing a new institution, the Secrétariat d'Etat aux Travailleurs immigrés.* The head of the institution, Paul Dijoud, announced two aims: stopping all new immigration, even family immigration, and improving the social situation of the established immigrant population. Dijoud emphasized that the second aim could not be achieved without the first. As long as new arrivals kept creating new housing, education, and sanitary problems there would be no resources available to improve the situation of their predecessors. The first aim also reflected a general policy of encouraging the modernization of French industry.

After 1977 Lionel Stoleru, the successor to Dijoud, took a series of measures that revealed a third aim: high mobility of immigrants, especially international mobility, in order to be able to adjust as closely as possible, at any moment, the number of immigrants to the changing labor needs of French industry. This goal envisioned a sort of international rotation system – a global extension of temporary jobs in which the sending countries assume responsibility for their workers as much as possible while they are unproductive. Stoleru wanted to restore to the receiving country the benefits of international migration resulting from permanent mobility and the permanent renewal of the immigrant labor force. It appears that after three to five years of residence in France immigrant labor is almost as expensive as native labor. The attempt to achieve this kind of flexibility is one reason why illegal immigration was tolerated as long as it served economic needs.

The election of François Mitterand and the victory of the Socialist Party in May–June 1981 did not, of course, change the international system or the industrial orientation of the country, i.e. its reliance on capital-intensive industries. Nevertheless, more attention is being paid to the social impact of industrial restructuring and especially to the existence of "black" labor (and "black" employers) in small, old, and badly equipped enterprises, particularly in the building and service sectors. The government's economic aim is to pressure these enterprises to modernize their production and employ their workers legally or else go out of business. Its social aim is to eliminate underpaid, illegal jobs and to offer security to immigrant labor.

To achieve these aims the immigration stop has been maintained, although family immigration has become easier, expulsions have been reduced, and measures have been taken to establish greater equality of rights for all workers in France.

* A Secrétaire d'Etat is a sort of vice-minister. In this case he functioned in the framework of the Ministry of Labor.

Instruments of regulation and control

Apart from the mechanisms of the labor market, immigration regulation and control has been carried out by laws, institutions, procedures, and pressure groups. Because the aims of regulation change constantly the executive branch makes the decisions that determine immigration policy without consulting the National Assembly, a procedure made easier by the fact that immigrants cannot vote. Since 1975 more than a dozen of the measures taken by ministers or vice-ministers in the area of immigration policy have been nullified because of their conflict with existing laws (Mangin 1982:49).

The fundamental law regulating the residence and employment of foreigners in France was passed in November 1945. According to this law a foreign citizen who wishes to engage in a steady occupation in France must obtain a residence permit and a work permit. The procedures for obtaining these permits do not apply in the same way to the citizens of EEC member states, to Algerians, or to the citizens of certain West African countries.

Before the Second World War immigration to France was organized by the Société Générale d'Immigration, which included those employers most affected by immigration. After the war, however, the government prohibited private recruitment and made it a public monopoly in order to avoid bad working and housing conditions. The law of 1945 created the ONI, Office National de l'Immigration, to act as a state-controlled intermediary between employers and future immigrants. A foreign citizen who wanted to immigrate to France had to apply to the ONI office in his or her home country. The ONI organized the journey and also ensured that legal procedures were followed if the immigrant was offered a job by a French employer. Employers also had to apply to the ONI, which required them to provide suitable housing and working conditions before being allowed to hire immigrants who were planning to enter the country.

However, the system did not work, at least not after 1956. From then on, "regular" immigration was increasingly ignored in favor of "irregular" immigration, i.e. immigrants and employers made contact without an intermediary and the ONI exercised only ex post facto control. At present the ONI only becomes involved with the admission of the families of established workers.

Immigration regulation is based on residence and work permits, each valid for either one, three, or ten years. Based on their respective durations, residence permits are called temporary, ordinary, or privileged; work permits are designated "A", "B", or "C". Permits "A" and "B" allow an immigrant to work only in specified occupations and specified areas. Until a "C" permit is obtained an immigrant must seek authorization to change occupations or to work in another area. This authorization is not always granted. Ideally, an immigrant's work and residence permits should be of the same duration, but in practice this is not always the case since two different ministries, the Home Office and the Ministry of Employment, issue the respective permits.

There are a number of exceptions to this system. Citizens of EEC member states may come to France freely and look for work; if they find a job they are automatically granted both permits for five or ten years. Algerians were French citizens until 1962 and thus subject to no restrictions. After 1962 they could still enter France freely, but in 1968 a bilateral agreement established an annual entry quota. In 1973, Algeria decided to stop all labor emigration to France because of the growing racism against the Algerians already living there. Algerians have a special permit, the certificate of residence, that may also serve as a work permit if so indicated. The certificates were originally valid for five or ten years, but since 1978 they have been renewed for only one-year intervals because of the negotiations taking place between France and Algeria concerning re-migration. These negotiations led in September 1980 to renewals of three years and three months, i.e. for the period lasting until the end of 1983, when new negotiations are scheduled to begin.

Finally, some of the former colonies in West Africa have retained special ties with France. Bilateral agreements specify the rights of citizens from these countries and there is a great deal of variation from country to country. The tendency is, however, to make these immigrants increasingly subject to the ordinary immigration regulations.

Expulsion

During the 1970s, the use of expulsion caused many scandals, which is why the government in October 1981 modified the law of 1945. In general, a foreign citizen in possession of all the required permits can be expelled if he or she threatens the *ordre public* (public order), which is an imprecise juridical notion subject to many possible interpretations. For a time, many foreigners who had been in jail for six months or more were threatened with expulsion. The Conseil d'Etat then stated that there should be no systematic relation between prison sentences and expulsion. Therefore, the new government decided that persons who have been sentenced to less than one year in prison cannot be expelled.

Some categories of persons can no longer be expelled at all: foreigners who were born in France or arrived before the age of eleven; foreigners who have spent twenty years in France or have close relatives (parents, children, spouse) who are French citizens. This change, also introduced by the new government, aims at avoiding the inhumane expulsion of young foreigners who, at the age of nineteen or twenty, were forced to leave alone for countries that they generally were not familiar with and where they could not speak the language.

The new government also decided that the bureaucracy is no longer responsible for expulsions; instead, decisions are to be made by a commission, presided over by a judge, with no members from the bureaucracy. It is also now possible for an expelled person to return to France after ten years, unless the commission objects.

Family reunification

The law of 1945 is practically silent about the admission of families. For this reason the general immigration stop of 1974 could also be applied to the spouses and children of immigrants that were already resident in France. Under the pressure of many organizations, however, special rules were established in 1976 to allow for the admission of families. But because of its stringent conditions the official entry procedure was used in less than half of all cases; most families tried instead to enter illegally as tourists and then to "regularize" their situation afterwards, although by the end of 1980 even this had become almost impossible. The new government immediately began a more liberal policy, but family reunification still remains difficult because of the problem of finding acceptable housing.

To discourage families from joining immigrants in France the government after 1978 refused to grant work permits to newly arrived spouses or children. They received only residence permits. The new government ended this practice, but in some cases the *opposabilité de la situation de l'emploi* can still be used as a reason for refusing a work permit. This notion, introduced in 1972, allows the authorities to refuse to issue a work permit to an immigrant in an occupation where there are unemployed French workers. At present, all occupations fall under this description.

Naturalization

The Naturalization Act of October 1945 aimed at increasing the population of France through the automatic naturalization of two categories of immigrant children: children born in France of foreign parents and children born in France of parents who were themselves born in France. The former become French citizens at the age of eighteen if they have resided in the country permanently since the age of thirteen; the latter are French citizens from birth. This second provision has applied to some Italians and has been especially important for young Algerians born in France after 1963 whose parents were born in Algeria while it was still a French colony.

Strictly speaking, the term "naturalization" applies to only those foreigners that obtain French citizenship by decree. Other foreigners "re-integrate", i.e. they were French citizens at one time but lost their nationality (e.g. through marriage). Other foreigners (almost half of all naturalizations) simply "declare" themselves French; they have this possibility because they are married to a French citizen or because they come from a former French territory. This procedure sometimes leads to marriages of convenience, arranged in order to obtain citizenship (or residence and work permits). Such marriages usually end in divorce after a year or so.

Naturalization is possible after five years of residence in France. Eighty percent of all applications are approved; the others are rejected because of lack of assimilation or lack of loyalty. The charge of "lack of loyalty" seems to have been used – most frequently at the end of the 1970s – to deny citizenship to those who did not agree with the politics of the prevailing majority, although no official cause was actually necessary in order to reject an application. The new government will perhaps follow a more liberal policy, even toward its political opponents. On the other hand, a French government always seems to see itself as the embodiment of "the nation" and easily confuses loyalty to the government with loyalty to France.

Illegal immigration

Illegal immigration was accepted until the beginning of the 1970s when social problems and menacing unemployment raised demands for greater state control, i.e. that the ONI once again act as the sole intermediary between employers and prospective immigrants or, in the case of family reunification, between resident immigrants and their families abroad. But it is not easy to reverse a tradition established for almost twenty years. Peasants in the Third World do not believe that it is nearly impossible to obtain work and residence permits once in France; besides, they consider it better to be illegal and unemployed in France (with a chance to find work someday) than to be stuck in their own countries with little hope for the future. Therefore, it was not enough just to declare an immigration stop. Several additional measures have been necessary to detect illegal immigrants and prevent their entry.

The most important measures involve border control. The former government passed a law in 1980 that gave the border police extensive powers to send home all tourists suspected of being "phony". A new law passed in October 1981 by the Socialist majority confirmed the severity of the previous law on one point: in order to enter France, tourists may be requested to produce piles of documents and guarantees. However, the border police do not make such requests from citizens of EEC member states or from American or Japanese tourists. At the borders or at airports the police are meant to be selective and should not interfere with genuine tourists or businessmen.

Until the change of government in May 1981 there were many police controls in France, especially aimed at young African immigrants in the big cities. One of the odious aspects of these controls – other than the discriminatory ones – was the way in which controls were carried out. Racism was so clearly evident that it shocked many French citizens. Several times the police surrounded a home or neighborhood or block of houses to carry out systematic controls, but this always provoked violent reactions from French organizations and labor unions. Controls were carried out again at the end of 1981, although in a less harsh manner.

Previously, illegal workers who were apprehended could be expelled following a trial and a one-year prison sentence. To improve the situation inherited from the previous government, the new government decided in June 1981 to allow all illegal workers to "regularize" their status. But the conditions that illegal workers were required to fulfill effectively excluded most of them. Employers who agreed to declare their illegal workers before the end of 1982 would not be punished. In October 1981 the National Assembly passed a law that confirmed the penalties for illegal employers. This law also gave illegal workers the same social rights as legal workers. If apprehended, they could claim their rights as if they had been legally employed.

Both the present and past governments have considered improving the visa system, which already applies to Turkish visitors. Efforts are being made to convince other countries to control the departures of their citizens (Algeria may possibly do so again). Bilateral agreements should lead to more control in the emigration countries.

Return

From 1977 to May 1981, the French government tried to reduce the size of the immigrant population with several measures. An allowance of 10,000 francs was promised to certain categories of immigrants if they and their families would return to their countries of origin and never come back to France. France and Algeria signed an agreement in September 1980 to encourage the resettlement of Algerian workers with aid both from France (loans, vocational training) and from Algeria (housing, employment, etc.). The aim was to induce the return of 35,000 Algerians per year.

In an indirect attempt to reduce the number of foreigners the government in 1980 reinstituted a 1932 law giving it the power to fix a ceiling on the number of foreigners employed in certain professions or industrial sectors. Under this law, which had not been applied since 1945 (its existence was generally unknown!), the administration was able to refuse the renewal of numerous work permits, which subsequently led to the refusal of residence permits.

It was especially common during this period for administrative agencies and the police to receive many informal instructions "from above". Decisions were often arbitrary and the decisionmakers were protected from being overseen. This situation led to a great deal of insecurity among immigrants (Mangin 1982:31–49) and induced a certain number to leave or to choose naturalization.

The outcome of regulation and control

As mentioned previously, migration to a country like France has its own dynamic. The movements are not created by the authorities and policy measures can only limit, encourage, or modify them. The demographic goal defined in 1946 to encourage immigration of culturally similar groups like Italians was accomplished only to a small extent. French politicians lacked the requisite motivation while the newly created institutions did not have the necessary powers. In Italy there was little interest among the population (Tapinos 1975:28). Short-term economic interests prevailed most of the time over long-term demographic or social interests (especially between 1956 and 1970). The laissez-faire policy was successful because it responded well to the immediate needs of most of the parties and of the nation as a whole.

Efforts to stop immigration were less successful. Family reunification continued on a regular basis despite the many attempts to hinder it. It proved impossible to stop the entrance of new workers. Although control of the borders is efficient at established checkpoints, such as harbors, airports, and border stations, it is less effective along the length of the borders themselves, especially in the mountains. Networks of experienced *passeurs* have long existed (smugglers or ferrymen who specialize in bringing foreign workers illegally to France), and it is hard to thwart them; they go on recruiting in the underdeveloped countries, making false promises and then abandoning their human cargo in France. Their task is all the easier because in underdeveloped countries, especially in Africa, emigration is regarded as a normal way to resolve the financial problems of the family or village.

These newcomers – most of whom are young people – are already in France, and if the authorities refuse to give them permits it is not certain that they will agree to leave voluntarily. With the help of activists they will undoubtedly cause great problems for the French authorities. The recent change in the rules governing expulsion has alleviated one of the most dramatic problems faced by second-generation immigrants. Now, most of the children of immigrants cannot be expelled, which allows them to live in greater security than before. Another positive development for the second generation is that they now are able, in almost all cases, to obtain a work permit. Nevertheless, these improvements do not solve all the problems, particularly not the problem of unemployment. A work permit is fine, but it does not supply a job (Gisti 1981).

The outcome of the battle against the "black" labor market is still unclear. In the second half of 1981 the government offered illegal immigrants a "one-time" opportunity to be "regularized". Yet many will nonetheless remain illegal, since the conditions attached to the offer allow probably only 30 percent of all illegals to take advantage of it (probably about 100,000–120,000 out of a total of 300,000–400,000, as no precise figures exist here). Many others will lose their jobs because of the heavy sanctions imposed on those who employ illegal workers.

Efforts to induce return migration have met with very little success. The allowance of 10,000 francs convinced 100,000 persons (60,000 of them workers) to leave the country. More than two thirds were Spaniards and Portuguese, however, which was contrary to the government's hope that mainly Africans would leave. The return-migration agreement with Algeria did not produce any results, partly because of difficulties in organizing vocational training and finding housing in Algeria, but also because many Algerians in France were simply unwilling to leave. The annoyance and frustration brought about by police controls, arbitrary bureaucratic decisions, and racism induced some immigrants to return home, but not as many as the authorities had hoped. Most have chosen to remain in France as illegal workers rather than leave. This has led to social tensions, however, particularly if delinquency becomes the only way for the illegals (especially the young ones) to survive.

The number of naturalizations is steadily increasing, in part because of economic insecurity and in part as a result of the assimilation of older immigrant groups, i.e. those that arrived more than ten years ago. Spaniards, Italians, and Portuguese constitute the majority of the 30,000 annual naturalizations as well as close to half the annual declarations of French nationality (usually through marriage); the latter means of naturalization is the one most used by Africans and Asians. Under the Nationality Act of October 1945, most of the 70,000 children born in France will receive French citizenship. Around 1.5 million of the French citizens now living in France were previously foreign citizens, and more than 10 million of the country's 53 million inhabitants are able to recall having at least one foreign ancestor.

4. Immigrant policy

"We called workers and human beings came." This sentence by Max Frisch, which describes the Swiss situation, can also characterize French policy, at least until 1974. Some special measures had been taken and institutions created, but only to cope with partial problems; there was no overall immigrant policy. At the end of the 1960s the Minister of Labor was still able to pretend that as long as the economy needed the presence of foreign labor, French society would spontaneously create the structures needed to make it possible for immigrants to live in France. The result of this laissez-faire social policy was that immigrants *survived* more than they lived.

This belief in the creativity of French social and educational institutions and their adaptability to all human beings and all social situations led to shortcomings in almost all sectors of social life. New specific and specialized institutions remained scarce and those that were did not adjust themselves to the new problems. Most social work was done on a voluntary and private basis. The institutions created in this informal fashion found it difficult to be recognized as valuable and useful by the official and professionally staffed institutions.

One of the fears constantly expressed by officials of social and cultural institutions was that the creation of special immigrant-welfare organizations would lead to segregation. By forcing immigrants to address French traditional institutions, it was hoped that assimilation would be favored.

Ideas like "positive discrimination" are still in their infancy in France. Most people working in the official institutions believe that a formal guarantee of access to legal rights and social participation is sufficient to create equality. Equality is assumed to exist and is therefore not considered a goal.

Thus there is in France, theoretically, a preference for general institutions. Yet because these institutions in practice did not or could not cope with immigrant problems, specific institutions had to be created that in the end actually encouraged segregation because their existence was not recognized as valuable by the official institutions. Finally, the French authorities accepted this situation and almost all immigrant affairs were placed under the control of the Secretary of State for Immigrants, who deals with housing, vocational and other training, cultural expression, social care – and immigration regulation as well.

The laissez-faire policy towards immigration was finally abandoned in 1974. A series of twenty-five measures accompanied the immigration stop, aiming at a better integration of immigrants into French institutions and society. New institutions were created to improve the reception of immigrants, to promote immigrant cultures, and to improve relations between immigrants and French natives. Only some of these measures have been effective; because of a lack of financial resources a great deal of the many policy proposals that were made never produced any results.

Principal aims

Besides the very vague official goal of "improving the social situation of the immigrant population and their relations with the French population", two principal aims – one positive and one negative – have guided French immigrant policy. The positive aim concerns the integration or assimilation of "suitable" immigrants; the negative aim concerns maintaining social peace: troubles like those caused by blacks in the United States (as seen through French eyes) must be avoided.

After 1974 officials often made a distinction between "good" and "bad" immigrants. European immigrants who lived in France with their families were usually considered "good", and because of France's demographic problems they were encouraged to stay permanently. Portuguese families in particular had been willing to accept assimilation, and they were better accepted than the Africans by the French population. Though there was no official discrimination against African workers who wanted to bring their families to France, in practice the administration, police, and social services treated requests of Europeans with more openness than those of Africans. Identity controls by the police affected Africans more than Europeans. Employers preferred Portuguese workers because they demanded less than Algerians and Tunisians. These "good" immigrants were encouraged to stay, raise children, and add to the population of the country.

The "bad" immigrants were those that caused trouble and insecurity (Mangin 1982:29). The majority of them were young Africans, labor union activists, and/or unemployed. Three methods were used to maintain the social peace and keep them quiet: the threat of expulsion (or "encouragement" to leave the country), segregation, and repression. Each method reinforced the others. The goal of immigrant policy for the "bad" was *return*, not integration and assimilation. In fact, by the end of the 1970s the public authorities had almost convinced the French population (and many immigrants as well) that departure (to Africa, of course) was the natural and expected outcome of the migratory chain.

Thus we can conclude that immigrant policy has had either a positive or a negative aim for each immigrant group and that the distinguishing criterion has been the possibility of the group's integration or assimilation. Demographic interests demanded the assimilation of some immigrants while social peace demanded the exclusion of others.

At the end of the 1970s a third aim became apparent: the maintenance of a feeling of insecurity among resident immigrants in order to increase their mobility. Immigrant policy would aid the labor market by giving it the flexibility needed during the period when national industry was to be restructured. To achieve this aim a policy of non-integration, i.e. segregation, was applied to certain groups of immigrants, especially single men and new arrivals.

In early 1977 the Vice-Minister for Immigration, Paul Dijoud, introduced another goal: immigrant policy should help immigrants return to their countries of origin if they wanted to do so. He insisted on freedom of choice and on the opportunities that should be offered to returning immigrants, especially young ones, to help prepare them for life in their home countries. This policy led to the encouragement and development of immigrant cultures by the schools, by television, and by cultural organizations. In time the original aim of preparing immigrants for return was forgotten; cultural activity continued for its own sake, maintaining and reinforcing immigrants' cultural identities.

The socialist majority promised to abandon the policy of social and economic segregation. Cultural pluralism and political participation by ethnic minorities figured in the socialist program announced before May 1981. This program acknowledged that immigrants were going to remain permanently in France; it emphasized their right to live and work without having to give up their cultural identity and without having to face discrimination in employment or housing. Special efforts were urged to speed the social and vocational incorporation of young immigrants. The program recognized, however, that general measures concerning housing, the right to association, and the growing role of the labor unions might be more important in the long run than specific, limited measures.

Since May 1981 the new majority has been too busy with the struggle against "black" labor and with improvements in agencies that treated immigrants poorly in the past to be able to define more precise aims for immigrant policy. All attention has been focused on the short-term aim of restoring to immigrants their elementary rights and abolishing the arbitrariness that characterized the policy of the previous administration.

The instruments of immigrant policy

Housing
Housing policy reflects the above-mentioned complexity of aims and reveals the discriminatory approach used against certain immigrant groups. Since the end of the Second World War France has suffered a great shortage of residential housing. Immigrant families arrive on an

already overcrowded housing market, and their position is made even worse by two additional factors:

- French houses are designed for families with two or three children, yet immigrant families often have more than four children.
- Most immigrant families congregate in certain areas because of lower rents (often only *apparently* lower) or because the poor quality of the buildings induced the previous French residents to move out, making them available to immigrants.

During the 1950s one of the first "solutions" to the problem was the construction of the so-called *bidonvilles*, i.e. improvised slum housing similar to the kind that surrounds urban centers in the Third World. Another early "solution" was for immigrants to live in the overcrowded, furnished rooms owned by the so-called *marchands de sommeil*, or "merchants of sleep" (Hervo & Charras 1971). At the end of the 1960s three institutional "solutions" replaced these improvised ones: resettlement in normal dwellings, in temporary housing, or in special homes for single workers.

Normal dwellings were secured by the immigrants themselves in old houses and old neighborhoods already abandoned by the French population. The richest immigrants (particularly the Portuguese) bought or constructed private homes. Many immigrants, however, were admitted to the HLM, the "cheap housing projects" (*Habitat à Loyer Modéré*). Economic and social mechanisms led to the concentration of immigrants (as well as of Antillean and Moslem French citizens) in certain suburbs, towns, and neighborhoods, which created tensions between the different populations.

Both the mechanisms that caused the tensions and the tensions themselves were later politically exploited (by the Communist Party as well as by the liberals and conservatives) and led to debates about the so-called *seuil de tolérance* or "threshold of tolerance": when does the percentage of foreigners in a population become so high that hostile reactions automatically develop? This unscientific, racist notion is still cited by municipalities as an excuse for avoiding the admission of immigrant families to the HLM.

Cultural differences characteristic of peasant and African (or Asian or Antillean) immigrants do create real problems in this kind of standardized housing, which is designed for a homogeneous population. The buildings are not intended for residents with different life-styles and daily rhythms (e.g. smells and sounds, work, sleep, and leisure schedules, family size, and so on). European families naturally cause fewer problems in this kind of housing, and the housing offices admit them more readily than Africans or Antilleans.

When the *bidonvilles* were gradually destroyed at the end of the 1960s and the beginning of the 1970s, there was not enough cheap housing available for everyone, and many African families were judged to be "unadaptable" to life in modern French dwellings. To accommodate these families (mostly North Africans) the government built the *cités de transit*, housing complexes where the immigrants were to live for two or three years and receive an intensive education that would facilitate their integration into French society. In practice, however, these poorly built *cités* were not at all provisional; families have lived there for ten and twelve years as a segregated group and are perhaps less "adjusted" now than in the beginning. Most of the *cités* turned into ghettos, and the children who grew up there posed difficult questions for French society.

When the *bidonvilles* were destroyed a third group of immigrants was sent to the *foyers*, the homes for single workers then being built all over the country by different organizations with public funds (there are approximately 700,000 single workers in France). The *foyers* were originally intended to house Algerians during the war of independence (1954–62). After the war they were used for other immigrants as well, but their original character remained unchanged: the residents lived like soldiers in barracks or students in a boarding school, with former soldiers as supervisors and many restrictions in personal liberties.

Conditions changed after 1975, however, when the residents led powerful strikes and protest actions against the most important organization, the SONACOTRA. This has been the most important social conflict led by immigrants themselves, and their action caused a rent-strike by several thousand residents which lasted for several years. As a result, the country's 600 *foyers*, with an average of 300 beds each, now all provide single rooms, although a great many residential services are still provided on a group basis (Benot 1979:*passim*). Because they represent a concentration of (foreign) men, the *foyers* are not appreciated by the neighbors, and this leads to segregation. Immigrants who live in the *foyers* do not integrate and usually remain on their own.

These three institutional "solutions" to the housing problem – the HLM, *cités de transit*, and *foyers* – correspond neatly to the different aims that immigrant policy has for different immigrant groups: the HLM dwellings for those who are to remain, the *cités* for those who may or may not remain but are kept segregated until the choice is clear, and the *foyers* for those who are not desirable as permanent residents.

The housing problem has not been the same in small cities or in rural areas, where in most cases old but decent housing has been available. This has not really alleviated the overall problem, however, since the number of immigrants is proportionally much higher in most of the industrial and urban centers. Foreigners constitute eight percent of France's total population, but they are unevenly distributed: some departments have 17 percent foreigners while others have only 1 or 2 percent. In some suburbs the proportion of foreigners is 25 percent and in some neighborhoods even higher. The same unevenness exists in the project housing: immigrants reside in 10.3 percent of the total number of HLM dwellings, but in particular neighborhoods this may mean that the proportion of immigrants is 50 percent or higher, without even counting the number of Antilleans.

Education and vocational training

For a very long time nothing special was done to integrate immigrant children into the very French school system. Assimilation was not only an aim but considered the natural outcome of a long-term process in a non-discriminatory situation, and nothing was done to maintain the individual cultures of the different immigrant groups. In addition, the heavy emphasis on equality as a basic principle has led the French school system to condemn privileges and segregation. Until recently teachers generally agreed that the greatest service the schools could render immigrant children was to "Francisize" them as quickly as possible and that to do so it was necessary to cut them off from their parents' language and culture.

This mentality has gradually changed over the past ten years. One reason for the change has been the observation that compared with French pupils only a small proportion of the almost one million immigrant pupils ever finishes school. Foreign children constitute 10 percent of pupils that complete the first degree (4 to 11 years of age) and 6.3 percent of those that complete the second degree (12 to 18 years of age). Only 3.3 percent of the latter group follows the "long cycle", i.e. the most theoretical line of education. It is now admitted that special classes to which foreign children can be sent upon arrival to receive special instruction, especially in the French language, are valuable aids to education. Thus far 1,100 such classes have been formed, and they are integrated into French schools in order to avoid segregation.

Another reason for the change in attitude is the growing acceptance of the idea that teaching the mother tongue and the parent's culture can help immigrant children in their development. Many now have an opportunity to receive such instruction, either in official courses organized by French schools in collaboration with the consulates or embassies of the emigration countries, or in private courses organized by humanitarian organizations or (in the Algerian case) by the Amicale des Algériens en Europe, a government association for the immigrants.

Despite these changes in attitude, the level of education in immigrant areas is still poor. To reduce the potential for unemployment among immigrant children when they leave school and to avoid the social consequences of such unemployment, a new kind of pre-vocational training has been developed in the past several years, the so-called *préformation*, which is designed to allow immigrant children to continue directly with vocational training for adults after they leave school. *Préformation* is also open to adults. It is interesting to note that instruction in the mother tongue and *préformation* were both originally aimed at preparing immigrant children to return to their parents' home country, although this aim was later abandoned.

The introduction of French language courses for adults has long been the principal effort made for the social promotion of the immigrant population. Knowledge of French is necessary to participate in vocational training. Language courses are often taught by more or less qualified teachers after working hours two or three evenings a week. It takes a long time before immigrants can express themselves in French and are able to follow vocational training for adults. Because of the language barrier one finds that most of the immigrants at the vocational training centers come from former French colonies.

During the past few years the French government has organized "return training". Several hundred immigrants, mostly Algerians, have undergone six months of training designed to give them the qualifications needed to find employment after returning to their countries of origin. "Return training" is very expensive; it will not be applied generally.

Labor market

Once in possession of a work permit a foreign worker, whether employed or not, theoretically has the same social rights as a native worker. After three months of employment a "documented" or legal foreign worker is entitled to unemployment compensation and to social security insurance for illness for himself and his family. Numerous conventions with the different emigration countries govern the payment of benefits for illness, accident, disability, pension, and so on if the worker returns to his country of origin. If the worker remains in France he has the same rights as a French worker.

Special mention should be made of the family allowances. If a foreign worker brings his family to France he receives the same allowance as a French worker; but, if his family stays behind, his wife and children receive an allowance that is close to the amount offered by the country of emigration and is also limited in most cases to no more than four children. Because allowances paid in the home countries are normally much lower than those paid in France the state saves almost two billion francs per year, a third of which is made available to the Social Action Fund (FAS; see below) and used for social work.

Foreigners can attend vocational training (the law on adult *formation* is the same for all), and if unemployed they can benefit from the services of the state employment agency. But in practice these rights are often illusory. In enterprises like Renault, unskilled workers (mostly immigrants) have gone on strike because after ten or fifteen years they were never promoted and had never had the same opportunity to attend *formation* as their French colleagues, who did not have to stay many years at the bottom of the ladder. In employment agencies the few available jobs are offered first to French workers (even though this is illegal) because most employers feel that hiring foreign workers will lead to tensions in the workplace.

Until recently a "black" labor market was tolerated where work conditions and social rights were, of course, not respected at all. Thousands of immigrants work(ed) in small building firms, the textile industry, the confection industry, and agriculture. Most people who work as domestic personnel are employed without any social security. As mentioned above, measures have been taken recently to suppress the use of "black" labor. But implementation of the new immigration policy has been difficult.

Political rights

Foreign workers in France have the same *social* rights as the French, but they have *no political rights*. Prior to May 1981 activists belonging to the labor unions or the associations were deported on the grounds that they had not "respected the political neutrality that is expected of any foreigner residing on French territory". When one speaks in France of granting foreigners the right to vote in local elections the reaction of the French population is very hostile. In the Socialist Party's electoral program immigrants were promised that their right to vote in local elections would be a first step towards their participation in French political life. After the socialist victory in June 1981 the government declared that granting the municipal franchise to immigrants in 1983 was out of the question. The Immigrant Councils that exist in some municipalities are the only direct political channel now open to immigrants. These councils are supposed to give an opinion on matters concerning immigrant interests, but in most cases they are little more than a formality.

It should be noted that on the subject of political rights for foreigners there has been little progress in the two centuries since the French Revolution. An article from the Constitution of 24 June 1793 states that:

Every foreigner over 21 years of age, settled in France for more than one year, who earns his livelihood by working, or acquires property, or marries a French wife, or adopts a child, or nourishes an elderly person; every foreigner who has demonstrated the merits of humanity, is permitted to exercise the rights of a French citizen.

The outcome of immigrant policy

The results of French immigrant policy have lagged far behind expectations for two main reasons. First, Giscard d'Estaing tried after 1974 to control by financial means the initiatives made in the different fields of immigrant policy. Less and less support was given to organizations that did not "fit into" the overall political orientation. The French executive branch easily regards itself as an embodiment of "the nation". This meant that voluntary organizations with involvement and motivation suffered from a lack of funds while the official, bureaucratic organizations – which had the funds – lacked the motivation and were also subject to frequent interference "from above".

Second, the resources made available to immigrant policy were very insufficient. Thus, the housing problem remains; the *cités de transit* and the *foyers* are still in use. Some progress has been made in the field of vocational training, but improvements in the education of immigrants has been confined more to immaterial than material matters.

Whatever positive changes have taken place in the social situation of immigrants is more a result of work done by motivated individuals, immigrant organizations, labor unions, and other organizations than of the efforts of official policy. The government was forced to finance activities that deviated from its political orientation as long as the activities enjoyed sufficient political support; when the support declined, the subsidies were reduced. At the same time the government subsidized activities that were in line with its political orientation but were otherwise ineffective.

In judging the mediocre results of immigrant policy we should remember, however, that it attempts to improve conditions that are not unique to the immigrant population. The native French also have a housing problem; French workers are also unemployed; the school system has also failed in the past few years to respond to the problems of French working-class children. Yet, these problems are in general a bit worse for immigrants.

The interrelationship between immigrant policy and immigration regulation

One fundamental relationship between immigrant policy and immigration regulation was noted at the time of the immigration stop. It was then argued that it is impossible to improve the situation of resident immigrants, particularly in the areas of housing, work, and education, as long as new immigrants continue to arrive and create the same problems all over again. The 1974 immigration stop was said to be necessary because of the calamitous social conditions that uncontrolled immigration had brought about, and this argument was strengthened by fears of growing unemployment.

At the end of the 1970s pressure was exerted on immigrants to encourage them to leave France. Politicians made sure that people understood that there was a connection between the presence of two million immigrant workers and the unemployment of one million French workers. It was insinuated that there was a connection between the presence of immigrants (i.e. young African males) and the insecurity in the cities.

This type of psychological pressure was difficult for immigrants to bear. Insecurity about the possibility of staying permanently in France together with the state's emphasis on the "natural return" had consequences for their social integration. Some returned; others refused to be integrated; but most, unable to return for material or psychological reasons, just became more and more aggressive towards French society.

5. Policymaking and administration

Since immigrants have no political rights their destiny is determined by civil servants more than by elected politicians. With few exceptions politicians are interested in immigrant issues only if popular pressure exists on the part of French voters or if social conflicts are threatening.

Perceptions

The structural character of immigration escapes the understanding of most French workers and a large part of the middle class, and for this reason immigrants are blamed for taking jobs away from Frenchmen. This in turn leads to the perception described at the end of the previous section; namely, that a connection exists between unemployment and the presence of immigrants. Another common perception, also mentioned in the previous section, is that a connection exists between insecurity in the cities, delinquency, and the presence of African and young immigrants. Everyone "knows" that foreigners are more delinquent than French people; all the studies showing the inaccuracy of this belief are ignored (Mangin 1982:11–14).

Since France's culture is considered "universal" and popularly seen as superior to all other cultures, different ways of behaving are regarded as deviant and as proof of lack of adjustment. "Different" takes on the meaning "inferior" or "abnormal". This perception makes it easy to use immigrants as scapegoats for unemployment and housing problems. The French people have always felt very insecure when faced with different cultures, as can be illustrated by comparing their method of colonization to the British or Dutch. They have always exerted great moral pressure on foreigners to "assimilate", to become "good Frenchmen". In French eyes it is a great honor to be considered "well assimilated"; other cultures are respected as folklore and the subject of museum displays but are not taken seriously as a way of life.

These perceptions vary among the French. People whose employment is threatened, who are poorly housed, and whose children have bad results in school perceive immigrants as rivals; other people do not perceive them as rivals but rather as persons who need to be educated, who disturb normal social life, and who may be dangerous. The main concern of this latter group is social control.

The notion of a *seuil de tolerance*, a "threshold of tolerance", is popular. For instance, it is generally believed by politicians, journalists, and those working for housing departments (and most other people as well) that if the proportion of immigrants living in a housing project exceeds 12 to 15 percent then there will sooner or later be trouble. It is assumed that the French are able to tolerate the presence of only a limited number of foreigners. In a similar fashion people believe that if the proportion of foreign children in a school class exceeds 25 percent the level of instruction and classroom discipline will decline. This notion has been refuted many times by social scientists, who have proved that it is impossible to establish such a *seuil*. Nevertheless, the myth seems to correspond so closely to French perceptions that it is impervious to rational arguments.

Immigrants are also seen as rivals in the area of social welfare, i.e. the rebuffs that Frenchmen experience at the welfare offices are caused by the presence of foreigners. Immigrants are often blamed for the deficit in the social security system. The people who believe they would get better treatment if they were Arabs do in fact see a large number of immigrants in the welfare offices, although they refuse to see the perfectly normal explanation for this: only very few French families run the high risks faced by many immigrants, who have more children, less income (lower wages), poor housing, dangerous or unhealthly jobs, language problems, and a host of other difficulties. If foreigners are compared with the French population as a whole they are more frequent recipients of social welfare, but this is certainly not true if they are compared with a comparable subgroup of the French population (Cordeiro & Verhaeren 1977:*passim*). The same argument can be made concerning the perception that most immigrants are delinquents.

Among middle-class French the concern is not about individual rivalry with immigrants but instead involves general security. They do not regard immigrants as dangerous elements in society but as "poor people" who need help and education. To this group of Frenchmen the presence of immigrants generally seems a moral or national (economic, social, and cultural) issue rather than the menacing physical threat that it seems to most of the working class. They treat immigrants with charity and soon reduce them to the status of "helped people". They do not respect the demands of immigrants to be treated as adults having their own culture, rights, and opinions. Even if this may contribute to the improvement of their social conditions, it does not help them acquire political rights. The charity approach assumes that immigrants do not demand – they ask nicely; they remember their position as guests in France and, like good guests, are thankful for the privilege of being allowed to live and work in such a fine country.

The different perceptions discussed thus far exert a dual pressure on institutions and politicians. On the one hand, politicians (or other elected representatives) may risk defeat in the next election if they appear too generous in giving immigrants housing or social welfare, or if they defend foreigners against their landlords or employers too publicly or too often. On the other hand, however, it is not advantageous to try to make immigrants into scapegoats, in part because of the common bonds shared by French and foreign workers and their families and in part because of the moral or religious scruples of the middle class. The socially most accepted opinion on the immigrant issue seems to be the following: do not expel the "good" immigrants, but do not let the "bad" ones enter our neighborhood, our children's school, or our country.

Thus, popular perceptions limit politicians' freedom of action in different ways. The government of Giscard d'Estaing could not expel immigrants too vigorously because of the humanitarian or religious opposition of its own voters. Yet the freedom of action of the socialist majority is also limited by the opinions of its own voters, i.e. the working class. The government of Mitterand cannot go too far in helping immigrants, a constraint that has slowed the fulfillment of promises of municipal voting rights, regularization of all illegals, and so on.

The making of immigration policy

As mentioned previously, immigration policy in France has been the product of the economic needs of the moment, tempered by political, demographic, social, and cultural interests. For a policy (or several policies) of this nature the heavy decisionmaking apparatus of the National Assembly cannot provide the necessary flexibility. When the national situation changes rapidly, policy must keep pace. For this reason the

National Assembly has been able to exercise only limited control over immigration policy.

Only the executive branch seems to have the ability to reach quick decisions, and as long as it works within the general guidelines laid down by the National Assembly there are not many problems. After 1972, however, the government introduced many measures which did not correspond to the laws then in effect; though eventually annulled by the Council of State, these measures were nevertheless applied, perhaps with slight modifications. In practice the administrative agencies obeyed these illegal or questionable measures more often than the law. Whatever limits were placed on executive power came from the judiciary (e.g. the Council of State), which received its impetus from the trade unions and the activist organizations. Politicians exerted little control over the formation or implementation of executive decisions.

Thus for a great many years the executive acted alone in the area of immigration policy. The issue did not become politicized until around 1972. From 1974 on, however, the government of Giscard d'Estaing launched a new policy designed to modify or eliminate France's traditional labor-intensive industries. This policy favored huge international and modern industries at the expense of small enterprises. The restructuring of the national labor market in order to reduce the country's dependence on immigrant labor was a measure aimed at serving the interests of the huge enterprises (Briot & Verbunt 1981:22). The restructuring policy had to be moderated in the face of humanitarian and ideological resistance, but the government eventually resolved this problem by increasing the gap between its generous statements in public and its cynical actions in private. Since only a few people could know what really happened in the administrative offices and agencies, public opinion and even members of the National Assembly were not aware of the actual treatment being meted out to immigrants. Only a few influential newspapers, such as *Le Monde, Le Matin* (socialist), and *Libération* (leftist), discussed these problems; television programs as a rule repeated the government's official position.

Concentration of policymaking in the hands of a few members of the government was also reflected by the absence of advisory committees or other forms of consultation. For example, the official commission on the employment of immigrants, in which the labor unions participated, conducted their discussions solely within the very narrow limits defined by the government and thus ceased to interest anyone by the end of the 1970s. In a similar fashion the labor unions had participated in the ONI between 1945 and 1947 and had then disappeared from the organization (Gani 1972:42). Advice was only accepted from those who agreed with the government's policy.

Since May–June 1981 the National Assembly has debated various legislative projects, although once again these debates have been marked by a concern for employment needs rather than by an overall view of what today's immigration really is. The preparation of these projects has, once again, occurred without seeking the advice of competent organizations or specialists, not even those within the Socialist Party. Politicians from the executive branch, particularly those from the Home Office (Ministère de l'Intérieur), have succeeded in imposing their will on the National Assembly and on government ministers who are concerned by social issues.

Until May 1982 the labor unions were opposed to the government's immigration policy, which served the interests of the employers and caused divisions among the working class. The presence of immigrants was used to weaken the power of the unions and to force French workers to accept wages and working conditions that they would have rejected if competition from foreign labor had not been present. Nevertheless, the unions' freedom of action was limited by the negative view that most of their members had about immigration. To the leaders at union head-quarters, immigration was a manifestation of the new international division of labor, a new type of exploitation that could be avoided only through international solidarity. To the members at the grassroots level, however, immigrants appeared as rivals whose exclusion was dictated by national or professional solidarity.

Despite this division of opinion the strongest opposition to the immigration policy practiced during the 1970s came from the labor unions CGT and CFDT and from some activist organizations. Religious authorities and organizations of lawyers also influenced policymaking.

It is important to remember that there exist in France a certain number of activist groups that are more or less politicized. Most of these local or national organizations were created to offer material aid to immigrants; they began by solving housing problems, giving French lessons, and helping resolve administrative problems. As time passed many of them grew frustrated at dealing only with the effects of the problem and began to search for the causes. They demanded more justice for immigrants and changes in immigration policy.

The activists have been a tremendous help to the organizations that immigrants created for themselves in the 1970s. These immigrant organizations are called "autonomous" because they strive to be independent of any political party and of the authorities in their home countries. Their action has a real political base, but they move particularly on the cultural and social level (Verbunt 1980:369–88). They would like to be recognized as the representatives of their respective national groups in France, but even the new government fears the diplomatic difficulties that such recognition could entail.

Almost all the important nationalities have their own organizations, and some nationalities have several. Because of the repression that the organizations suffered under the previous government only very motivated activists were members, which meant that each organization was either very politicized or very passive. Since October 1981 a large number of new organizations have been created. They pay a great deal of attention to cultural events, which both reinforces their internal unity and at the same time makes them known to the French population.

National associations have also been created by foreign governments, and they are called *amicales* in France. The translation of the French word is "friendly" or "amicable", but in reality the associations are far from friendly. The *amicales* of the Moroccans and Tunisians are in fact more feared than respected. The Amicale of the Algerians in Europe has a better reputation, although as a representative of Algeria's single political party it has its defenders and attackers. The *amicales* are regarded by the governments of these countries as a means of maintaining control over the emigrated population.

Immigration is a troublesome issue for the political parties in France. The right-wing parties have no special institutions that define immigration policy. The moderate right wing talks about immigration in terms of economic necessity or humanitarian exigency. The socialist, communist, and leftist parties have special working groups on immigration. The leftist parties demand total equality between foreign and French workers, political rights included.

The immigration issue has been embarrassing for the Communist Party, which has regarded immigrants as temporary workers actually belonging to the working class of the sending countries. This doctrine contradicts the facts. As a grassroots organization the Communist Party has also experienced tension between the proclamations of international solidarity from its leaders and the practical attitudes of its members, which led at the end of 1980 to party approval of racist ideas in several municipalities. The communists also insist on the national organization of the working class; international solidarity is expressed on the level of the national representatives of different countries rather than on the level of the workers themselves. In the communist framework foreign workers have to adapt to the national structures of France, i.e. as long as they are in France they should subscribe to French aims and respect French methods. This framework leaves immigrants no place for individuality or autonomy as regards their problems in France; such notions exist only as regards the countries of emigration. The Communist Party is dominated by the fear that the presence of immigrants weakens the strength and unity of the working class – a not unjustified fear, in fact. Immigration has been used by employers and by the right wing to divide the working class, and immigrants have been used by the extreme leftists to disparage the Communist Party.

The Socialist Party created a special commission on immigration policy that published its proposals and conclusions at the end of the 1970s. It said that immigrants are probably in France to stay and that French society must respect their identities. Individuality and autonomy were not rejected. Nevertheless, the party's performance as the most important member of the government since May–June 1981 has demonstrated that it is not guided by a coherent doctrine agreed upon by the entire party. The proposals of the special commission went too far for the bulk of the party, and internal struggles between the different ministers and advisers have delayed the program that the special commission presented.

It also appears that the policy followed by the socialist administrators responsible for immigration has been built on a series of responses to urgent problems rather than on a long-term, coherent program. The socialists theoretically consider immigration an aspect of the international economic order, yet the concrete measures adopted thus far hardly take into account the overwhelming importance of the international context. There is also a lack of coherence between the struggle against "black" labor on the one hand and, on the other hand, the ineffective approach to the existence of the dual labor market required by France's combination of modern and old-fashioned industries and techniques. The separation of the immigration issue from other international economic and social issues has led to a weakness in policy. On the other hand, though, immigration is not automatically taken into consideration by the individuals and groups that determine the outcome of international issues.

The administration of immigration policy

Political decisionmaking is very centralized in France, and superiors leave to inferiors only the decisions that they for some reasons (time, local situation etc.) are not able to make themselves. There are many intermediaries before a decision is implemented at the grassroots level and each one of them understands and transmits the decision in his own way. For this reason immigration policy may be applied very differently from one province to another and even from one official to another.

France is a presidential republic. The president not only appoints the government but intervenes as much as he likes in any particular policy area. The practical decisionmaking as regards immigration regulation is the responsibility of the Minister of the Interior. Until May 1981 immigrant policy was formed by the Ministry of Labor; now it is formed by the Ministry of National Solidarity (formerly the Ministry of Health and Social Affairs) in conjunction with the Vice-Minister for Immigration (Secrétaire d'Etat à l'Immigration). The only ministries that maintain some responsibilities are the Ministry of Education (responsible for immigrant education in the school system) and the Ministry of the Interior (responsible for the admission, control, and expulsion of immigrants). All other aspects of immigrant life are controlled by the Ministry of National Solidarity.

The decisions of the ministers are communicated to the *Prefets*, i.e. the chief administrators in each of the 90 *departements* or "provinces" of France. The *Prefets* are appointed by the Ministry of the Interior, and it is their job to implement government policy. They are assisted by some councils (that do not always work) and especially by the Service de la Réglementation, which is in charge of issuing residence permits. Work permits are issued in each department by the Direction de la Main-d'Oeuvre, which follows the instructions laid down by the Ministry of Labor. This system is now being reformed so that the power of the *Prefets* will decline in favor of the power of the elected officials of the departments. This is intended to give politicians better control over what happens in their departments.

The Vice-Minister of Immigration has created his own policy instruments while trying to coordinate those of the other ministries. One of the most powerful instruments created was the FAS, the Fund for Social Action, whose mission is to promote all activities that might improve the social conditions of immigrants in France. Until 1974 its support was given primarily to the improvement of housing conditions, and even at present more than half the available annual funds (890 million francs in 1983) are used for the maintenance of the *foyers*, thus affecting only about 150,000 immigrants and refugees (IGAS Report 1982). The placement of immigrant families in housing projects is financed by a general fund that receives 0.1 percent of the salaries paid by the employers.

Social and cultural activities have been developed since 1974. The International Social Service has had a branch in France for a long time, which is called the Social Service for Aid to Emigrants (SSAE). Two institutions were also created in 1974 for cultural activities, and some years later they were merged into one, the ICEI (Information and Culture: Immigration). The purpose of this institution is to aid immigrant groups in developing their culture, but until 1981 only expressions for ethnic traditions and folklore were allowed. The ICEI also handled the Sunday morning television programs for immigrants, which explained the official immigration policy and presented information by the authorities of the sending countries on the situation there. Recently this institution has changed its name to become the Agency for the Development of Intercultural Relations (ADRI).

For a long time instruction for newcomers in reading, writing, and the French language was organized both by voluntary organizations and by a more or less official one, the Amicale de l'Enseignement des Etrangers or Club for the Teaching of Foreigners (AEE). This institution was dissolved in 1977. The voluntary organizations have grouped themselves into several federations that try to exert an influence on the politics of *formation* (vocational training).

6. Will France adjust to immigration?

In contrast with neighboring immigration countries, France has developed a policy of admitting foreigners not only as temporary labor but also as an addition to the permanent population. This is why family immigration has been encouraged, or at least tolerated, for such a long time. Only in the past several years has immigration been presented as a "temporary" phenomenon. Yet nothing can change the fact that permanent settlement and family immigration has been and remains the rule and return migration the exception.

The official inducements to leave France have not been very successful. Not only were many of those who decided to return Europeans and skilled workers, but a large number later decided to come back to France because they found insufficient means with which to resume life back at home. They felt like strangers in their country of birth and suffered from the lack of housing and job opportunities. A poorly housed, unemployed immigrant still considers his situation better in France than it would be in his country of origin, as we have seen. As long as this perception continues, foreign workers will do anything to remain in France.

In spite of the measures to reduce the number of illegal workers, these remain numerous. More will arrive. The government now admits that it is a mistake to regard illegals as a homogeneous group; many different problems exist and they call for different kinds of solutions. On the whole, in fact, the problem cannot be solved by a single nation, but only by cooperation between groups of nations and by a change in the international division of labor. The only long-term solution lies in the economic development of the emigration countries, although an increase in the coordination of the immigration policies of Western Europe might also be useful.

France has traditionally "assimilated" its immigrants in the long run. But the process has not been so easy this time; housing and unemploy-

ment problems have led to segregation and younger immigrants in particular feel left out of the French society. This situation, placed in an overall
context of growing recognition of regional and especially cultural identities, has caused immigrants to demand the right to maintain their culture
and preserve their identity. Younger immigrants demand the opportunity
to develop a "new" identity.

These demands conflict with the French tradition of assimilation and
the very centralized structure of French society. Even the regional movements that promote the cultures of Bretons, Corsicans, Occitans, etc.
rarely identify with the demands of immigrants, who are seen as people
with no territory and as members of a "lower" social stratum. For
instance, young Algerians claim the right to live as young Algerians in
France (i.e. not as Frenchmen and not as Algerians in Algeria), but
France is anything but prepared to become a "multicultural" society.

It is significant that the demand during the past few years for cultural
rights has become as strong as that for social rights, although the distinction between the two is hard to define exactly. Part of the reason for the
emphasis on cultural rights can be found, of course, in the concentration
of ethnic groups in certain housing areas. Yet other phenomena are also
becoming apparent: the French industrial society leaves people isolated
with their problems, it provides no model for the education of the younger
generation, and there is in general a lack of human relations and personal
security. Because of these tendencies there is an increase in the number of
groups that defend educational values, "original" cultures (i.e. mother-
tongue instruction), cultural expression (theater, dance, music), and so
forth. The demands of these and other similar groups are becoming
increasingly political (Culture Immigrée, *Autrement* 1977).

Immigrant organizations demand recognition as the formal representatives of their respective national groups. In the past, such recognition was
extended only by labor unions and humanitarian and religious organizations. But in May–June 1981 the socialist Vice-Minister for Immigration
met with delegations from the most representative immigrant organizations. This recognition, and the possibility that they will be able to extend
their activities, is perhaps more important for the future of immigrants in
France than would be the right to vote in local elections. French immigration policy is today faced with two problems of growing intensity: "black"
labor and second-generation immigrants. The future will depend heavily
on the strength that immigrant organizations can develop.

But the outcome will also depend on whether the new government has
the flexibility and intelligence to cope with a changing situation. If this is
to be the case, the authorities will have to change some traditional attitudes:

- Immigration is not a field for specialists but a part of political life; it is the intrusion of international economics into the social and cultural situation of the locality and the nation.
- Immigration *cannot* be stopped by decree; the international migration of populations escapes the control of individual governments. The real causes that initiate and guide these movements are still insufficiently studied and understood.
- Immigration today is *not* the same as immigration in the past. It is not certain that the newcomers of today and their children will eventually (and "automatically") be assimilated. Immigrants may have to adapt to French society, but France must adapt just as much to immigration.

6

Federal Republic of Germany

HARTMUT ESSER and HERMANN KORTE

1. Immigration and immigration policy

In many respects the present situation in Germany in regard to immigration and immigrants is unprecedented. A great number of immigrant families are preparing for a permanent stay and some form of "integration"; moreover, easing the tension between integration and cultural autonomy is being considered on a political level. The situation now differs fundamentally from that of the past, when foreign workers were either clearly defined as seasonal workers and subjected to rigid Germanization during their stay (and in the Second World War forced into war production) or else used as an easily transferable labor pool to compensate for manpower shortages in certain branches of the economy. Yet policymakers have found it difficult to grasp this difference and to act accordingly, which is why the current reorientation of immigration policy has been so difficult.

To understand the novelty of the present situation and to appreciate the obstacles faced in changing from a "guestworker" policy to an "immigration" policy, one must begin by examining the varied history of population movements and foreign labor migration into the German Reich and the Federal Republic of Germany (FRG).

Until 1885 Germany was mainly an emigration country (Armengand 1971:163ff). Germans emigrated primarily to the United States and, to a lesser extent, to Canada, Australia, and South America. A number of Germans settled down to work as administrators and merchants or founded new settlements in the Baltic, Poland, and Russia. By 1776 about 200,000 Germans lived in the area that later became the United States, and after the American Revolution many former mercenaries decided to stay permanently. From that time on the stream of emigrants from Germany grew considerably and was only briefly interrupted by the Napoleonic

165

Wars. The main reasons for emigration were political unrest and oppression and economic problems, especially in the agricultural sector.

The peak of emigration was reached between 1881 and 1885 when 857,000 migrants left Germany. Afterwards, as economic expansion began, the number of emigrants dropped rapidly and after 1896 emigration was less than 150,000 per every five-year period. The actual history of immigration begins only after the decline of emigration movements around 1890. This history can be divided roughly into five phases: the period before the First World War; the First World War; the era of the Weimar Republic (1919–33); the era of National Socialism (1933–45); and the postwar era from 1945 to the present (which will be the major subject of this chapter).

In the German Empire after 1871, manpower shortages that could not be met by the indigenous population first occurred in the eastern provinces of Prussia, especially in the agricultural sector (Dohse 1981:29–53). At first the labor shortage could be compensated for by employing Poles from Russia and Austria, but this policy – which was economically unavoidable – soon caused a severe political problem. Since 1872 the government of Prussia had been forcing a rigid policy of Germanization on the Poles living in the previously Polish areas annexed by Prussia in order to unite them with the Prussian State. The government feared that the employment of "foreign" Poles would jeopardize this policy, and reacted by ordering mass expulsions and the closing of the borders, against which the big landowners and the owners of the Upper Silesian mines protested vehemently. This conflict between economic necessity and political interest is characteristic of the first phase of immigration.

The conflict was settled by a "compromise". On 26 November 1890 the Prussian government suspended the immigration ban on foreign Poles for three years. By that time the shortage of agricultural workers was becoming acute; the migration of Germans from the countryside to the cities had increased and there was a change in progress to the highly profitable but labor-intensive cultivation of potatoes and turnips. To prevent the Poles from taking up permanent residence they were ordered to leave the country every year during the so-called *Karenzzeit* (waiting period) from 15 November to 1 April. Furthermore, they were not permitted to move from the agricultural and industrial areas in the east to the industrial areas in the west.

Since Polish workers were obviously indispensible, in 1894 their further entry was authorized and their status as seasonal workers, which was the means of controlling the political consequences of their employment, was reconfirmed. Continued economic development gradually pushed back political opposition and immigration restrictions were relaxed: the

Karenzzeit was shortened and the employment of Poles in areas other than agriculture was made easier. An attempt was also made to avoid nationalist opposition by replacing Poles with other foreigners, especially Ruthenians. But the great supply and "adaptability" of Polish workers combined with the needs of the economy overcame any political demands that other foreigners be employed. In the end the restrictive program of nationalist politicians gave way to additional liberalizations in the employment of Poles. In 1908 309,000 foreign agricultural workers were employed in Prussia and 80 percent of them were Poles. Despite a loosening in restrictions for recruitment, however, the general controls over the residence of Polish workers were retained.

The immigration of Polish workers to the Ruhr district, often regarded as a model of successful integration, is a special case (Wehler 1976:437–55). The growing mining and industrialization in the Ruhr district caused manpower shortages that, as in the agricultural sector of East Prussia, could only be filled by the immigration of additional workers. These immigrants were ethnic Poles, but they were also legal citizens of the German Reich and therefore not subject to the restrictions mentioned above. The cutback in the number of "foreign" Poles caused by these restrictions, which was motivated by domestic interests, could thus be fully compensated for, especially since most of the new immigrants had already worked as miners in Upper Silesia. By 1907 over 100,000 Poles worked in the Ruhr district, where they constituted one third of the total labor force.

Because they were German citizens nationality conflicts did not affect the Ruhr Poles before the turn of the century. Until then they were treated, like all other Germans, as *Reichsdeutsche*. The turning point began with the *Bergpolizeiverordnung des Königlichen Oberbergamtes Dortmund*, a decree issued in 1899 by the Royal Mining Office of Dortmund, which made command of the German language a prerequisite for employment in a senior job. In 1908 the *Reichsvereinsgesetz* was passed. Paragraph 12 of this act, the "language paragraph", made German the official language in all organizations. This regulation was mainly intended to check the rapidly developing cultural, religious, and even political life of Poles in the Ruhr district.

The "language paragraph" was the final stage in the Prussian language policy directed towards Germanization. Yet the result of this strategy was instead to strengthen ethnic solidarity and national consciousness among the Poles and thus to retard the process of assimilation that had gradually taken place. This was not to be the last time that a policy aimed at forced assimilation would result in an increase in ethnic identity.

The First World War brought about a drastic change in the policy towards Polish workers (Dohse 1981:77ff). In a virtual reversal of the *Karenzzeit* regulation Poles were forbidden even to return home. On the day the war broke out passports were made compulsory to prevent their leaving the country. During the war, when manpower was in increasingly short supply, foreign Poles were no longer prohibited from working in the industries of the western provinces, and new Poles were recruited after the occupation of the Russian part of Poland. The Deutsche Arbeitszentrale (German Labor Center) obtained a monopoly on the recruitment of workers from the occupied areas in the east. As soon as the Poles crossed the German border they lost their right to return or to change jobs. About 700,000 Poles were "recruited" in this fashion, and in the course of the war they were increasingly subjected to violence and oppression. Besides the Poles a large number of Hungarians and about 150,000 Belgians were forced to work in the German war economy. The legal and political situation of foreign workers in the Empire during the First World War was exclusively determined by the state of the war.

With the breakdown of the German Empire and subsequent economic problems there was no significant employment of foreign labor in the Weimar Republic. Between 1918 and 1933 the number of foreign workers in the German Reich never exceeded 250,000. Nevertheless, the events of this period have great significance for the Federal Republic's present attempt to restructure immigration policy; the consequences of what happened then can still be felt today (Dohse 1981:85–112).

The most important regulations of this period were based on demands of the Social Democratic Party: equal pay and security from arbitrary expulsions on the one hand, and the principle of preference for German workers over foreign workers (*Inländer-primat*) on the other hand, a preference which is still valid today. Very important also was that the Deutsche-Arbeitszentrale was given a monopoly to recruit foreign workers.

The phase of National Socialism must be divided into two sub-phases, the first running from 1933 to 1938 and the second from 1938 to the end of the Second World War. The gradual economic revival from 1934 onwards brought about a rise in the number of foreign workers from 100,000 to almost 400,000 in 1938. Agriculture and the armaments industry, in particular, suffered increasingly from a lack of workers.

It became obvious by 1938, at the latest, that the German National Socialist Reich could not make up for its lack of workers by voluntary recruitment: the Reich had long ceased to be attractive for immigrants. The problem was finally "solved" by the Aliens Decree of 1938, which prohibited foreigners, especially citizens of "enemy" countries, from leaving the Reich and also gave the police total control over their liberties. The threat of internment or confinement in a concentration camp was in the following years the most effective means of disciplining the foreigners forced to work in the Reich.

Compulsory labor assumed its most dramatic form during the Second World War. By the year 1945 approximately 8,000,000 foreigners worked in the German Reich, about half of them in industry and one third in agriculture. Of these, 6,000,000 were civilian forced labor recruited in the occupied areas; about 2,000,000 were prisoners of war. Without this system of compulsory work, supported by terror and a complete lack of rights and liberties, the German war economy would not have been able to keep providing food and armaments until 1945. The breakdown of production and supply occurred only after the war when compulsory workers and prisoners were liberated.

The development after 1945 can be divided into five phases. The first, from 1945 to about 1955, is marked by two problems: the treatment of former forced labor who did not return home, and the expulsion of almost 9,000,000 persons from the former German eastern districts, in addition to the immigration of about 3,000,000 refugees from the GDR, which lasted until 1961.

The 1951 Act on the Legal Status of Homeless Foreigners basically guaranteed the legal equality of those who had done forced labor and had remained in Germany (Dohse 1981:137ff). The regulation of the right of asylum, a topic of recent interest, should also be noted in this context. Article 16, section 2 of the German constitution of 1949 guarantees the right of asylum to all victims of political persecution.

The integration of the expelled persons and refugees, once initial mass unemployment was eliminated at the beginning of the 1950s, had the effect of severely reducing the need for foreign workers. As a result of this there was an interruption in the employment of foreign workers during the years between the Second World War and the beginning of the recruitment of "guestworkers" later on.

This interruption had an important political consequence: the regulations concerning foreign workers could be "reconstructed" at a temporal distance from the experience of National Socialism and without any pressing need, since the employment of foreign workers was not yet significant.

The new immigration regulations were reconstructed with explicit reference to the Aliens Control Decree of 1938, which was declared "reusable" in 1951. In this way continuity was achieved concerning the right to residence (Heldmann 1974:26ff). The second pillar of immigration regulation and control, the access to the labor market, was based on the 1933 *Verordnung über ausländische Arbeitnehmer*. The new regulation now stated that decisions were to be made by the *Bundesanstalt für Arbeit*

(Federal Institute of Labor, BfA), in which the Federal Government, the employers, and the unions would each hold one third of the votes. This regulation made the BfA in the following years one of the most effective control instruments of the Federal Government.

The year 1955 marked a certain change because it was then that the reservoir of easily recruitable German workers began to dry up (Korte 1981:538ff). From 1961 on, when the labor shortage caused by the so-called "economic miracle" began, requests for the recruitment of foreign labor came first from agriculture and then from industry. Though foreigners were not recruited on a large scale during the period 1955–61, important decisions were made that determined the nature of future immigration policy. The first bilateral recruitment agreements were reached; for example, the one with Italy was made in 1955 (Mehrländer 1978:115). Furthermore, the unions changed their mind and consented to the employment of foreign labor – on certain conditions.

By the end of July 1960 the number of foreign workers in the FRG totaled 280,000, of which 45 percent were Italians. Around the same time, recruitment agreements were signed with Spain (1960), Greece (1960), and Turkey (1961). When the GDR closed its borders and built the Berlin Wall in August 1961, the stream of refugees ceased.

This marked the beginning of the "uncontrolled expansion" of immigrant labor (*Bodenbender*), the third phase in the employment of foreign labor after 1945. Though this phase actually lasted until the recruitment stop in November 1973, it is usually dated from the construction of the Wall in 1961 to the first major postwar recession in 1966–67. During this period the number of foreign workers rose continuously to a peak of 1.3 million. Additional recruitment agreements were entered into with other sending countries: Portugal (1964), Tunisia (1965), and Morocco (1963 and 1966).

In April 1965 the most influential immigration regulation was passed, the Aliens Act, which is still in force today (along with its implementation act of June 1972; for details see section 3). This act lays down the terms under which foreigners may be "permitted" to take up residence in the FRG. It gives the authorities broad discretionary powers and does not grant foreigners any legal right to residence. This act, backed up by the regulations on work permits (see section 3), was intended to make immigrant labor in the FRG a maneuverable resource, easily controlled and regulated, for the solving of economic problems (primarily that of manpower shortages).

This situation did not change fundamentally during and after the 1966–67 recession. We can see that until then even immigrant workers themselves regarded their stay as temporary from the fact that during a

Table 6.1. *Foreigners of selected nationalities residing and working in the Federal Republic of Germany, 1955–82 (thousands)*

| | Total foreigners | | Selected nationalities | | | | | | | | | | |
| | | | Greek | | Italian | | Yugoslav | | Spanish | | Turkish | |
Year	Resident population	Number employed	Resident population	Number employed	Resident population	Number employed	Resident population	Number employed	Resident population	Number employed	Resident population	Number employed
1955	485	80	4	1	26	8	21	2	2	1	2	
1961	686	549	52	42	225	197	16		62	44	7	
1966	1,807	1,314		195		391		97		178		161
1967		991		140		267		96		118		131
1970	2,977	1,949	343	242	574	382	515	423	246	172	469	354
1973	3,966	2,595	399	250	622	450	673	535	286	190	894	605
1975	4,090	2,039	391	196	601	292	678	416	247	125	1,077	543
1980	4,450	2,070	298	133	618	309	632	357	180	87	1,462	592
1981	4,630	1,917	299	122	625	285	637	336	177	81	1,546	584
1982	4,667	2,038	301	129	602	296	632	350	174	82	1,580	652

Blanks indicate no data available.

single year, 1966–67, when jobs were scarce, the number of foreigners employed in the country dropped by 320,000 (see Table 6.1). After the economic recovery in 1967 the number of foreign workers again rose rapidly, reaching a peak of 2.6 million at the end of the fourth phase in 1973. At that time the total number of foreigners in the country, both workers and family members, was almost 4 million. It is worth noting that the employment rate among this group stayed at about 66 percent, which significantly exceeded the rate among the German population.

The period between 1966–67 and 1973 was distinguished by a very low rate of unemployment among both Germans and foreigners. Because of the continual shortage of labor Germany drew up an agreement in 1968 with Yugoslavia to provide for the employment of Yugoslav workers in the FRG. At the same time the national composition of the immigrant population began to change: the proportion of Italians gradually decreased while the number of Yugoslavs and, after 1969, the number of Turks rose drastically. This change proved to be greatly significant later on. At the beginning of the 1970s Turks constituted about 13 percent of all foreigners in the FRG; by 1980 this figure had risen to 33 percent. It is important to note that during the period of "overemployment" and even up to 1976 the unemployment rate was lower among foreigners than among Germans, a statistic that underscores the economic indispensability of immigrant labor. In 1973 foreigners constituted 11.9 percent of all employees; this figure has dropped only slightly since then and was in 1983 just under 10 percent.

The main branches where foreigners are employed are industrial production (especially metal processing, mechanical engineering, and textiles), construction, and services (Rist 1978:66f). In contrast to the past situation in the Empire and the following periods only a few foreigners are employed in agriculture. Not many immigrants work in mining either, although their proportion is still significant (especially in the Ruhr area).

The heavy increase in the employment of immigrant workers did not produce an expansion of total employment but instead a *substitution* of immigrants for German workers. In this process of substitution, immigrant workers gradually took over the least skilled and most strenuous jobs. Besides facilitating reductions in working hours this substitution enabled an increasing number of German youths to receive a better and longer education without causing shortages on the labor market. Moreover, the reconstruction of the German army after 1955 could never have taken place so smoothly without the addition of foreigners to the labor force. On the whole the process of substitution resulted in a "collective mobility" of the German population, a phenomenon that, in the beginning, was not recognized by immigrants as being disadvantageous to them.

The oil embargo and the world economic crisis put an end to the expansion of foreign employment. The 1973 recruitment stop was designed to combat rising unemployment problems, and it was hoped that the number of foreign workers would, as in 1966–67, decrease considerably. And indeed, the number of workers did drop after 1973 from 2.6 million to a low of 1.87 million in 1978, which meant a drop in foreign *employees* of about 700,000. This reduction was overshadowed, however, by another process that moved in the opposite direction. Because of family reunifications and a higher birthrate, the total number of foreigners resident in the FRG dropped only from 4.1 million to 3.9 million in 1976–77 and has actually been *rising* since then (up to 4.6 million in 1981). This means that, at the moment, foreign citizens constitute 7.7 percent of the total population in the FRG. During the same period the employment rate dropped continually among foreigners, from 67 percent to about 42 percent, and is now even *lower* than among Germans. The employment rate is lowest among the Turks (just over 40 percent) and highest among the Italians (50 percent) and the Yugoslavs (56 percent). The decrease in the number of foreign employees is thus not solely a result of remigration but also a result of increased unemployment among the foreign population.

Instead of reducing the foreign population the recruitment stop brought about an increase and – what is most significant – changed its composition through an increase in family immigration. This development had not been anticipated, and the official immigration policy reacted only late and reluctantly. Though the employment of foreign workers had been seen merely from the economic point of view up to the beginning of the 1970s, social questions were now gradually considered. When the Federal Government in 1973 presented a "Program for the Employment of Immigrant Labor" it was the first official attempt to deal with the social implications of long-term immigration.

The first generation can no longer be considered "guestworkers"; the average length of stay has steadily increased and is at present (1981) almost ten years. This trend has been reinforced by the recruitment stop: more and more immigrants do not consider returning home because they fear that they will not be permitted to remigrate to the FRG once they have left. With the deterioration in the global economic situation and, in particular, the elimination of many unskilled jobs, immigrant workers were more severely affected by unemployment than German . workers. Since 1976, the unemployment rate among foreign citizens has been higher than among German citizens; in the past, the opposite was true. The use of the social services by foreign children and youths has become more and more significant. Their uncertain legal position, cultural marginality, and lack of skills has become, albeit reluctantly, a subject of interest.

In the face of these problems a committee was set up in 1975 at the Federal Chancellery to formulate some guidelines for immigration policy. The resulting *Thesen zur Ausländerpolitik* demanded – not without contradiction – that a clear priority be given to the social over the economic aspects of immigration (see section 3). At the same time, however, these guidelines demonstrated once again the inconsistent and amorphous nature of German immigration policy by also demanding the integration of immigrant families and a stronger promotion of remigration.

In all its decisions and statements until now the Federal Government has officially emphasized that the FRG is *not* an "immigration country". In 1982 it is still implicitly assumed that the residence of 4.6 million foreigners is basically a temporary phenomenon. Recent measures have been primarily directed towards stopping the further immigration of youths and elderly family members, although in reality the policy aims at stopping the further immigration of Turks and asylum-seekers. Further uncontrolled immigration must not be allowed to jeopardize the integration of the foreigners who already live in the FRG. Since the residence of immigrants is not yet perceived as a permanent phenomenon, it is not surprising that official policies generally lack long-term planning and are clearly oriented towards the labor-market interests of the German economy. In this respect not much has changed since the beginnings of immigration policy in the German Empire.

2. General preconditions

The FRG attracts immigrants for two main reasons: its economic opportunities and its comparatively liberal political situation, free of direct political oppression. Social institutions (e.g. national insurance, health insurance, child allowance, welfare aids) and the education system have also attracted immigrants in recent years.

The economic opportunities were the main reason for the classic "guest-worker" immigration during the expansive phase of the economy from 1961 to 1973. The political situation – in addition to economic opportunities – is the primary motive for the immigration of refugees. After 1973, with the consolidation of labor immigration and the advancing age of the second and third generations, social and educational institutions will be more and more important as reasons for immigrants' remaining in the FRG, even if the economic situation seems less promising than before.

The political regulations governing the employment of immigrant workers must be understood within the framework of the FRG's special geographic, political, demographic, legal, and socioeconomic conditions (Schäfers 1979:97ff). The FRG is *geographically* distinguished by its location in Europe's center and by its common border with the Eastern bloc. This is one of the reasons for the considerable regional differences within the FRG. There are huge industrial conglomerations in the west (Ruhr) and southwest (Rhein–Main), and less developed rural areas in the east and southeast (lower Saxony, parts of Bavaria). Because of its geographical isolation and special political status, the situation in West Berlin is different. The highly disproportionate number of old people caused a large demand for workers, which together with its geographical isolation resulted in an extremely high concentration of immigrants (especially in some quarters close to the Wall). In the rest of the country immigrants are concentrated mainly in the great industrial areas of the west and southwest as well as in some smaller industrial cities.

The general political situation in the FRG is defined by its being divided, and by its membership in NATO and the EEC. All of these factors have had a great influence on the employment of foreign workers. At the time of its division Germany lost large agricultural areas in the east that had previously been important for the employment of Poles. Furthermore, after the division it was no longer possible to fall back on the traditional Polish labor reservoir. Membership in NATO had linked certain developmental aspects of immigration with military aims; the most obvious example is Turkey. Membership in the EEC resulted in freedom of movement for Italian workers. The right of free movement has been an important issue in negotiations on expanding the EEC because the admission of Greece, Spain, and Turkey (among others) would undermine the recruitment stop. For this reason the Federal Government has advocated a restriction on the right to free movement, particularly if Turkey is allowed to enter the Community.

The political system of the FRG is characterized by four main features: it has a federal structure; it is based on parliamentary democracy; it is organized as a social welfare state; and it is supported by "socially concerned groups". The country's historically rooted federal structure rests on a division of political decisionmaking between the Federal Government, the eleven *Länder* (States), and the local governments, with legislative priority existing at the Federal level. The most important effect of this structure as regards immigrant policy is that education lies within the sovereignty of the *Länder*. This structure also affects housing policy and the general implementation of immigrant policy: though Federal institutions are in many respects responsible for legislation, the interpretation of laws and acts is primarily in the hands of the administration. This means that local authorities have broad discretionary powers in applying the regulations passed on the Federal level (see also section 5). The coordination of decisions on immigration policy is especially complicated by the bicameral system, which divides legislative power on the Federal level between the Bundestag (Federal Parliament) and the Bundesrat (*Länder* representation). This system accounts for a number of the inconsistencies in recent immigration policy.

Foreigners are not represented in parliament. They do not have the right to vote or to run for office on either the Federal, *Länder*, or local levels. The greatest influence on immigration policy is exerted by "socially concerned groups", which mainly include the Deutsche Gewerkschaftsbund (DGB, German Federation of Trade and Labor Unions), the Bund Deutscher Arbeitgeber (BDA, Employers' Federation), the Protestant and Catholic Churches, welfare organizations, and the political parties. The formulation and institutionalization of immigration regulation is an outcome of the different interests and relative political weights of these groups, which explains some of the inconsistency and weakness of many decisions in the past.

Productivity and national income are comparatively high; this is the main reason why the FRG attracts immigrants. The country's economic structure is mainly determined by its lack of mineral resources (except coal) and of productive farmland. As a result, the "secondary sector" predominates, especially steel production, mechanical and electrical engineering, and the chemical industry. A major part of production is destined for export.

The development of immigration after 1961 cannot be explained without reference to the FRG's demographic structure. The population is 61 million and the population density is 247 persons per square kilometer. This total includes about 12 million expelled persons and refugees from the GDR, about 100,000 international refugees, 750,000 German emigrants from Poland, Rumania, and the GDR, and 4.6 million immigrant workers and their families.

The unevenness in the age structure is primarily caused by the lack of births during the two world wars and by the global economic crisis. After the Second World War the birthrate rose until 1964, leading to a surplus of approximately 370,000 births after 1965. But then the birthrate among the German population began gradually to drop, and from 1972 on it has been negative. During the same period there has been a large surplus of births among the foreign population, which has almost compensated for the low birthrate among Germans. The consequence of this trend has been a drop in the relative proportion of German children in the total population.

The losses during the wars (and other developments, such as the improvement of the education system and the reconstruction of the army) resulted in overemployment during the 1960s, which in turn caused the recruitment of immigrant labor. In later years, however, the surplus of births that existed until 1964 began to swell the labor force and is at present aggravating the problem of underemployment. In addition, more and more foreign youths, having come to Germany as a result of family reunifications, are demanding training placement and jobs. On the other hand, because of the low birthrate since 1972 it is probable that a shortage of labor will occur once again after 1988. The political decisions concerning integration, especially for the second generation, must be viewed against this background.

The FRG has developed an elaborate system of social security that includes national insurance, pension plans, health insurance, child allowances, rent subsidies, and welfare aid. The social-spendings rate (i.e. the proportion of the GNP spent on "social security") has risen continually from 1950 (17 percent) to 1980 (about 34 percent). Immigrant workers have the same social and industrial rights as Germans (Mehrländer 1978:127f). They are legally entitled to rent subsidies and to unemployment benefits and child allowances; the latter two are especially relevant to the current immigration policy debate. It must be added that immigrant workers, because of their age structure, have not used the social security system to the same extent as the rest of the population; during the phase of expansion, in particular, they contributed more to the system than they received.

The regulations governing child allowances had a great influence on restructuring the foreign population after 1973. As with the other social benefits, child allowances are paid according to the territorial principle. Under a regulation issued in January 1975 the allowances for children living in the FRG were raised considerably while the ones for children living in the sending countries remained low. This regulation made the most fundamental contribution to the dramatic restructuring of the immigrant population after the recruitment stop; families were reunited more and more often, especially after 1975.

Generally, immigrant workers are eligible for unemployment benefits on the same basis as German workers. Yet immigrants are subject to additional regulations that do not apply to Germans, so that the general requirement that a worker be "available" for employment means that an immigrant must have valid work and residence permits. This condition gives the authorities a means of restricting unemployment benefits for immigrants (see also sections 3 and 4).

Numerous multinational agreements guarantee immigrant workers equal social security benefits. In other words, despite the territorial principle the benefits of the rent scheme and health insurance are continued after return migration. But these agreements have not had much significance until recently since foreigners have used the German social security system to such a small extent.

We will conclude this section on general preconditions with an outline of the general legal situation of foreigners, mainly as a background to the discussion in the following two sections of the specific regulations of immigration policy (Franz 1974:39–55; Rittstieg 1974:56–79; Becker & Braasch 1980). The basis of all immigration regulation is the Aliens Act of April 1965 (and the Implementation Act of June 1972), which together determine the legal status of foreigners in the FRG. Though they are in general subject to the provisions of the constitution, some of the rights guaranteed – especially freedom of movement – may be restricted.

According to the Aliens Act the right to reside in the FRG depends on the possession of a residence permit. Whether or not a residence permit is issued and whether or not it is restricted as to duration or location are matters completely within the discretion of the immigration authorities. Certain offenses – also a matter of official discretion – may lead to expulsion. The residence permit is linked with the work permit, which is granted by the labor authorities according to the principles of economic priority and preference for Germans. These restrictions are not applied to the citizens of EEC member states. Naturalization is only possible after permanent residence of at least ten years and is granted at the discretion of the Naturalization Office. Refugees have the basic right of asylum guaranteed in article 16 of the constitution ("Victims of political persecution have the right of asylum"), but in reality asylum status is granted only after lengthy legal proceedings and a two-year employment ban.

The brief discussion in this section already reveals the restrictive nature of immigration policy in the FRG and how it is related almost exclusively to the country's national and economic interests. The development of immigration policy can only be understood against the background presented here, the roots of which reach back into the German Empire and the period of National Socialism.

3. Immigration regulation and control

The FRG has never had a long-term, coordinated immigration policy. In this respect it continues the tradition of the German Reich, whose immigration policy was restricted to controlling the entry and residence of foreigners in accordance with the economic interests and/or national political aims of the time. Foreign citizens today are still not regarded as either "immigrants" or "minorities", but rather as "foreigners" or, at best, as "guestworkers".

This general orientation in immigration policy derives from two historical peculiarities. First, unlike France, Belgium, Great Britain, and the Netherlands, the German Reich virtually lacked a colonial tradition. Second, the burden of having employed *Fremdarbeiter* under National Socialism has complicated all attempts to develop more than a merely economic and utilitarian relationship with immigrants and ethnic minorities. Thus, it is not surprising that national and especially national economic interests are as predominant in the immigration policy of the FRG as they were in the policy of the German Reich.

Furthermore, the fundamental regulations governing immigration were passed at a time when all parties were concerned only with economic interests. Workers were recruited as *Gastarbeiter* – note the absence of the taboo word *Fremdarbeiter* – with the explicit intention of *not* instituting permanent immigration. This aim was known to all persons involved and was generally accepted. The original intention was clearly to provide temporary compensation for labor shortages followed by eventual return migration. Plans were also made – even by the sending countries – to establish a rotation system. The "integration" of immigrant workers into the political and social system of the FRG was never intended, and one of many reasons given for this policy was that the temporary employment and eventual return migration of immigrants would promote economic development in the sending countries.

That some of these aims have changed is not the result of a conscious shift in priorities but rather of certain unforeseen changes in the international situation and in the domestic development of guestworker employment. It might also be added that policymakers never expected immigrant workers to become an indispensable part of the German economy or that they would increasingly use the social services. In short, circumstances dictated that something more than just a guestworker policy was needed after 1973.

Principal aims

Against the background of the general goals mentioned above, the basic elements of the FRG's immigration policy can be summarized in the following three points:

- the employment of immigrant workers depends on the general labor situation, on shortages in the labor supply in certain sectors, and on the difficulties that demographic development is expected to cause;
- the policy of permanent immigration is still rejected; and,
- the FRG is committed to its membership in the European Economic Community.

The dominant aim of all policymakers, especially during the period of reconstruction, has been to supply a steady stream of labor to the economy. According to the *Arbeitsförderungsgesetz* (Labor Promotion Act), the Federal Institute of Labor has the main responsibility for regulating the supply of labor. The employment of immigrant labor served the aim of economic growth from the very beginning; since all interested groups (government, employers, and unions) accepted this, it was relatively easy to agree on the conditions for the recruitment and residence of immigrant workers. In February 1970 the Federal Government established principles for the integration of immigrant workers and thereby indicated the first subtle shift toward an integration policy; yet, it still declared that the extent of immigrant employment must comply with "the development of the labor market and of the economy". Other issues, such as housing, family reunification, the education and training of youths (see section 4), were only to be considered within this framework. All agreements concerning the recruitment of foreign labor confirmed the priority of German workers.

The 1973 recruitment stop was the clearest manifestation of the central role that economic interests have in the employment of immigrant labor. The apparent broadening of policy from merely economic aims towards more "social" aims, beginning in the 1970s, was basically just an adaptation of the original aims to different conditions. Immigrants had become indispensable in many segments of the economy and employers were increasingly interested in stabilizing their foreign labor force; the integration of immigrants into the social system of the FRG had become inevitable, the "social costs" of a second generation caught between two cultures threatened to exceed the benefits of immigrant employment; and finally, another labor shortage was expected for the 1990s due to the lower birthrate of the German population after 1964. Because of these changes in conditions economic objectives could no longer stand alone and had to be complemented with "social" aims, although the latter were nonetheless still closely oriented towards the goals of national interest and growth.

The "practical" view explains why official policy still refuses to acknowledge that the FRG has become a country of immigration. The arguments used to justify this refusal are several; the country's relatively high population density; the fear that permanent residence for ethnic minorities may cause conflict (especially in industrial centers); the country's lack of preconditions for integration; and – last but not least – the belief that permanent immigration is not in the interest of the sending countries either. All arguments aside, however, the fact remains that the FRG actually *is* an immigration country. As a result of family reunification and longer periods of residence, more and more immigrants are preparing to stay permanently.

The third principle of the FRG's immigration regulation was expressed by the standing conference of the *Länder* Ministers of the Interior in a 1965 decision that prohibits (with certain exceptions) citizens of non-European and Eastern bloc countries from staying in the FRG. The justification for this so-called "European principle" was that non-Europeans would have difficulties adapting to German conditions. But there is little doubt that the decision was also politically motivated; the exclusion of the Eastern bloc countries proves this, as does the inclusion of Turkey among the recruitment countries, which can certainly be explained by its significance for NATO.

The "European principle" is part of the regulations that were adopted later on governing freedom of movement within the European Economic Community (they are only relevant in the FRG for the Italians). These regulations guarantee citizens of EEC member states a relatively free choice of employment within the Community. Residence is authorized on the condition that work is found; a residence permit is not needed. These regulations obviously limit to a certain extent the FRG's ability to control the immigration of EEC citizens. They were accepted in fulfillment of the higher political aim of creating an EEC citizenship according to article 48 of the Rome Treaties. Nevertheless, it should not be assumed that the existence of these regulations reflects any desire to give preferential treatment to EEC citizens as regards immigration policy.

The only part of the FRG's immigration regulations that expresses clearly non-economic and non-practical aims is the special regulation concerning political refugees: under article 16, section 2 of the *Grundgesetz* (German Constitution), the victims of political persecution have a right to asylum in the FRG. After the experiences of National Socialism and the fate of emigrants and refugees from Germany during the Second World War, the legislature decided that the FRG be unconditionally open to all victims of political and racial persecution. This regulation politically complicates the enforcement of the ban on further immigration. On the other hand, it makes possible a distinction between "real" applicants for political asylum versus economically motivated immigration. The latter is more frequent and is to be treated differently.

The "utilitarian" aims of immigration policy are especially characteristic of the expansive phase that lasted until the recruitment stop in 1973 (Meier-Braun 1980:23ff). Though the general goals have not changed fundamentally since then, specific goals have been increasingly adapted to the new situation described above. There is in fact an inconsistency about the general aims that has, until now, been the main cause of the problems and contradictions in German immigration policy. On the one hand, the economic crisis and unemployment after 1973 reinforced the idea of solving the problems of the labor market by a reduction in the employment of immigrants and by their increased repatriation. The recruitment stop was mainly intended to reduce the problems on the labor market. On the other hand, it soon became obvious that most of the immigrants did *not* compete with Germans on the labor market but had become instead an indispensable economic factor in a "segmented" labor market, some parts of which (mainly heavy industry, mining, and services) were interested in stabilizing the employment of foreign workers. An "integration" of these groups had already been contemplated at the beginning of the 1970s.

Increased family reunification after 1973, especially among immigrants who had lived in Germany for a long time, as well as the expected social problems of the second generation, led to another policy, which proposed that these groups be integrated into German society while still keeping open the possibility of return to their home countries for those who desired it. The inconsistency of official policy was most recently reflected in the cabinet decision of December 1981 (mentioned above), which refers to the economic and social integration of immigrants in the FRG and, at the same time, to the reinforcement of the "desire to return".

This was the last stage in a drawn-out discussion, and the result shows on the whole the difficulties that complicated the shift from the original guestworker policy towards an integration-oriented policy. After the above-mentioned "Principles for the Integration of Immigrant Workers" in 1970, the Federal Government in 1975 presented a program for immigrant employment that for the first time systematically outlined "social" aims and the idea of integration. The program not only confirmed the priority of economic concerns but also attempted to bring the continuing interest in employing immigrant workers "into accord with their adequate integration". The FRG was still not regarded as an immigration country; on the other hand, compulsory rotation was not accepted either. The aim expressed was "consolidation of immigrant employment", i.e. its reduction to a minimum, and the idea of "temporary integration" (*Integration auf Zeit*) was made explicit for the first time.

This program was controversial. Even more controversial were the "Guidelines for an Immigration Policy" drawn up in the same year by an interministerial committee in the Federal Chancellery. They reaffirmed the aim of "consolidation" and called for a balance between the "social and humanitarian demands" of the immigrants and the "social and economic benefits" for the FRG. This meant turning away slightly from the overwhelming predominance that economic aims held over the policy of the 1960s, while at the same time supporting the recruitment stop and justifying it with reference to the situation on the labor market. On the whole, however, these guidelines reflected a further tendency towards controlling the stay of immigrants. They even supported the idea of compulsory rotation and suggested revoking the improvements in the right of residence announced in the program of 1973 (see below).

Another document of great importance was the memorandum on the "situation and further development of the integration of immigrant workers and their families in the Federal Republic of Germany", which was issued in September 1979 by the commissioner on immigrant issues, Heinz Kühn (SPD). This post had been set up by the Federal Government only shortly before and has since been taken over by Lieselotte Funcke (FDP). Heinz Kühn demanded – for the first and last time – the development of a consistent integration policy governed neither by the idea of "temporary integration" nor by encouragement of return migration nor by predominantly economic-utilitarian goals. He called for retaining the recruitment stop as a means of supporting integration. Furthermore, he demanded more legal security for foreigners and an end to all "segregating" policies.

In November 1979 a list of guidelines for the "integration of second-generation immigrants" was presented by the Coordination Committee on Foreign Workers, which had been set up by the Federal Ministry of Labor and Social Affairs. In general, these guidelines were very much in line with the Kühn memorandum, stating that there is no alternative to the integration of the second generation. Nevertheless, the practical demands (e.g. concerning naturalization) referred primarily to the second generation and ignored such essential fields as housing and aliens rights. The "radical" change in immigration policy proposed in the Kühn memorandum was not supported by this committee. On the basis of its recommendations the cabinet decided in March 1980 on the "development of immigration policy". As stated in this decision, the "future priority" of immigration policy should be the "social integration of the second and third generations" in *all* areas of life.

At the same time the recruitment stop of 1973 was reaffirmed as a means of supporting efforts at integration. The government decision stressed more strongly than the Kühn memorandum that ties should be kept with the countries of origin. The idea was not only to reduce the cultural "alienation" of foreign youths; the government also wanted to strengthen their willingness to return home as well as to support reintegration and investments in the sending countries. With these two contradictory aims, immigration policy became a definitely ambiguous compromise between a labor-market oriented policy and a policy directed towards integration and improvements in immigrants' social situation.

The dilemma of recent developments is that any measure supporting one of these aims excludes the other. Only one measure seems to have a clearly positive effect; namely, the ban on further immigration. It is hoped that this measure will improve both the state of the German labor market *and* the conditions for integration, especially for the second generation. Thus, it is not surprising that there is wide agreement on retaining the recruitment stop and, increasingly, on reducing family reunification (especially as regards the Turks). Yet it is still disputed whether or not and on what conditions the recent official – but impractical – policy of promoting *both* integration *and* "desire to return" at the same time should be replaced with a consistent integration policy.

The instruments of regulation and control

The instruments regulating and controlling the immigration and residence of foreigners in the FRG can be divided into two groups: the general regulations, which apply to all foreigners (including immigrant workers), whether recruited or not, and the specific measures concerning the recruitment of immigrant workers and the control of family reunification. There is of course a close relationship between the two groups since the general regulations largely serve to control labor immigration. The recruitment measures were in force only until 1973, but the general regulations are – with slight modifications – still valid today.

The general regulations are in the first place based on the requirement to hold a residence permit, contained in the Aliens Act of 1965, and the requirement to hold a work permit, contained in the Labor Promotion Act of 1969 and the Work Permit Decree of 1971. These regulations are closely interdependent (Dohse 1981:chaps. 6,7; Heldmann 1974; Mehrländer 1978:116ff; Rist 1978).

On the whole the Aliens Act does not grant foreign citizens any legal right of immigration or residence. This means that all foreigners who want to reside and/or work in the FRG for more than three months must possess a residence permit. A residence permit is issued *at the discretion* of the immigration authorities, whose decision is based on the "interests" of the FRG. The permit may be restricted as to duration or location; this was the rule in the case of immigrant workers, who mostly received work permits valid for one year only. After a stay of more than three years a work permit *may* be issued for durations of two or more years. After a minimum residence of five years a permanent residence permit *may* be granted; it is not restricted as to duration or location but may be linked to certain other conditions. Foreigners are subject to expulsion if they violate the "considerable interests" of the FRG (e.g. through criminal actions, impoverishment, or immorality).

Citizens of EEC member countries are entitled to residence without any restrictions in location and only minimal restrictions in duration. In general, children and youths under 16 years of age do not need a residence permit.

These regulations were altered in 1978 with a change in the Implementation Decree of the Aliens Act. An indefinite residence permit may now be issued after five years and a permanent residence permit after only eight years if three conditions are met: adequate housing according to the local standards, obligatory school attendance, and sufficient knowledge of German. Minor children and spouses may be granted the indefinite residence permit before the five-year period is over if their linguistic competence is satisfactory.

Foreigners who want to work while in the FRG must also possess a work permit, which may be granted "according to the situation and development of the labor market with regard to the individual case" and as long as there is no German applicant for the same job (priority for German workers). A foreigner must have or obtain a residence permit in order to receive a work permit. Work permits may be specific or nonspecific. A specific work permit is issued, based on the labor market situation, for a particular job at a particular place of employment. A nonspecific work permit, which does not depend on the labor market situation and is not restricted in location or duration, is granted only to those who have resided in Germany for eight years and have been employed for five uninterrupted years in the FRG. A permanent work permit is only granted to foreigners with at least ten years' residence.

The connection between the residence and work permits and the practice of restricting them to only short durations makes it possible to check regularly whether a permit holder's residence is still in the interest of Germany. In this way immigration authorities and labor officials (who issue the work permit) have strong control over the length and scope of labor immigration. For example, attempts have been made to stop the increasing concentration of immigrants in some urban areas by restricting residence permits to certain regions. Five cities have used this regulation (Berlin, Frankfurt, Hannover, Cologne, and Munich), but none has succeeded in solving the problem (Rist 1978). The regulation was introduced in April 1975 and applied as follows: when the residence permits were renewed that year, a ban on these areas was proclaimed. But since the "criteria of congestion" were not clear enough and the number of exceptions too high (e.g. for EEC citizens, family members, workers holding indefinite or permanent residence and work permits), the regulation was abolished after two years.

Citizens of EEC member states do not need a work permit; they merely need to prove that they are employed.

Regulations were tightened after the recruitment stop in 1973. The priority of German workers was stressed, and spouses who immigrated after November 1974 and children who immigrated after 1976 were no longer allowed to take employment. This so-called *Stichtagsregelung* (i.e. regulation based on the date of arrival in the FRG) was replaced in April 1979 by something called an "individual residence requirement": subject to the priority of German workers and regardless of the date of entry, spouses were granted a work permit after four years and children after two years for employment in branches that suffered from a severe manpower shortage (e.g. restaurants and hotels). Children who have taken part in vocational courses for at least six months may be exempted from this residence requirement.

In addition, the following groups of persons are legally entitled to a non-specific work permit: foreigners married to German citizens, political refugees, and the spouses of Greek, Spanish, and – if employed before October 1978 – Turkish immigrant workers who have resided in the FRG for at least five years.

In sum, both of these measures reflect how the "interests" of the FRG, especially as regards the labor market, dominate immigration regulation. They permit the authorities to dispose of the foreign labor force relatively freely; nearly all decisions are a matter of administrative discretion and legal appeal against them is hardly provided for. Regulation after 1973 (e.g. the *Stichtagsregelung*) was mainly characterized by efforts to intensify the control exercised by the authorities. Only out of concern for the further development of the labor market (see above) was residence made easier for young people, children, and long-term residents.

Recent developments are also marked by attempts to restrict the relatively liberal immigration of family members. The Federal Government made the following decisions in December 1981: immigrant youths will only be admitted if they are under 16; the immigration of children will be prohibited if only one parent lives in the FRG; spouses will not be granted entry if they are married to persons who immigrated as children or were born in the FRG. An attempt has been made to reduce the flow of applicants for political asylum by waiting two years before issuing them work permits (there was a one-year waiting period after 1980 and none previously). On the whole, the most recent regulations have been directed towards preventing further immigration and encouraging return migration; but, at the same time the conditions for integration have been improved for those willing to stay as well as for the second and third generations (see also section 4).

The majority of immigrants living in the FRG did not make a totally "individual" decision to come but were instead recruited by specific measures (this is not true, of course, for EEC citizens). The recruitment measures were the main instruments for controlling labor immigration. They allowed – and in certain respects guaranteed – an exact coordination between the German economy's need for particular kinds of workers and the "supply" available in the sending countries. Recruitment agreements were signed with Italy, Spain, Greece, Turkey, Morocco, Tunisia, and finally Yugoslavia.

There were two different procedures: state recruitment (also called the "first way" or "anonymous recruitment") and visa recruitment (also called the "second way" or "individual recruitment"). Both of these procedures combined in different ways two types of registration: registration on the labor market and registration by the aliens police. They also utilized three elements of immigration control: visas, residence permits, and work permits. Under both procedures the labor authorities made certain that the priority of German workers had not been violated before allowing any recruitment to take place (Dohse 1981:181ff; Rist 1978:91f).

With state recruitment the labor authorities collected applications from German firms which wanted to employ immigrants and checked that the priority of German workers was not threatened, that the applications were in accordance with certain model contracts of employment, and that the wages promised were equal to those for Germans. Finally, the prospective German employer had to prove that "adequate housing" (e.g. dormitories) would be provided for the immigrants. Recruitment contracts approved by the labor authorities were passed on to the recruitment offices in the sending countries, in Athens, Belgrade, Lisbon, Madrid, and Istanbul. The recruitment offices used three criteria in making their selection: qualifications, health, and employment record (i.e. "registered labor offenses"). They also arranged the necessary formalities (residence and work permits, valid for one year only) and organized group transport to the FRG.

The German recruitment offices also assisted with visa recruitment. Under this procedure, the older of the two, the employer stated that a specific immigrant was willing to work for him and ordered his visa from the appropriate German consulate abroad. The consulate then had to obtain the approval of the German immigration authorities. The local immigration authorities checked that the legal conditions allowed the issuance of a residence and a work permit; when the national immigration authorities had approved their decision, the consulate granted the visa. After that the immigrant entered the FRG and obtained the necessary residence and work permits, usually valid for one year only.

The employers were charged 300 DM, and later 1,000 DM, for each person successfully recruited. Obviously, the great influence that the German authorities exercised over the selection of workers assured that the interests of German employers prevailed over those of the sending countries. In fact, the procedure led to the selection of the healthiest and best-qualified, in sharp opposition to the interests of the sending countries, which had hoped for a reduction of their labor market problems, not an exodus of their best workers.

Recruitment ended after November 1973. Since then the recruitment stop has been the cornerstone of immigration regulation in the FRG and will not be abolished in the near future. As a result, the emphasis of regulation has been shifted from the selection of workers in the sending countries to the control of the foreign labor force already residing in the FRG.

After the recruitment stop, family reunification became more significant (Mehrländer 1978:131ff). An immigrant can only obtain a residence permit for his family (spouse and dependent children under 21) if he has worked in the FRG for at least three years and is able to provide housing "suitable for a family". Children under 16 do not need a residence permit. Citizens of EEC member states are not subject to these regulations and can even bring their relatives along with them. In the mid-1970s family reunification was made more difficult in order to prevent the strain on social services from becoming too great. After 1977, however, some of the restrictions were liberalized again. Nevertheless, decisions made by the Federal Government in December 1981 point once again in the direction of a more restrictive admissions policy for family members. The aim of these measures is to avoid the creation of a situation that might jeopardize the integration of long-term residents, particularly the second generation (see also section 4).

The outcome of regulation and control

All instruments of regulation and control in the FRG's immigration policy have been aimed at assuring and maintaining an immigrant labor force completely subject to the demands of economic development. This goal was fully accomplished during the phase of expansion before 1973. When conditions later changed, state control of immigrant labor became more and more limited, in part because of new regulations granting a certain security of status to immigrants who had resided in the FRG for a long time. For example, between October 1978 and September 1979 the authorities granted 156,000 indefinite residence permits and 4,200 permanent residence permits; 550,000 immigrants had obtained this secure status by 1979, i.e. almost 23 percent of all foreigners subject to the residence permit requirement. Nevertheless, general insecurity still prevails among immigrants because of the discretion available to the authorities in issuing residence permits.

Other unplanned and unintended developments have further reduced the state's power to dispose freely of the immigrant labor force. Because of the increased segmentation of the labor market, some industries could not survive without immigrant workers. Another factor is the increase in family reunification after 1973. Since family members, particularly the young ones, are much less subject to controls, there is no alternative but to encourage their integration (for details see section 4).

It has furthermore been realized that a tightening of the regulations for foreign youths, as exercised through the *Stichtagsregelung*, does not reduce immigration; instead, it allows the authorities to control the situation within the FRG. Another reason for the inefficiency of immigration controls is the freedom of movement enjoyed by EEC citizens, which has recently led to an influx of unskilled immigrants from Italy.

On the whole, the legal regulations on immigration have created a lasting insecurity concerning future life in the FRG, and this in turn affects the everyday life of immigrant families. The continued uncertain situation of the immigrants has jeopardized the recent integration measures. The dilemma of the present situation is that, on the one hand, integration is sought for some immigrants while, on the other hand, control over the legal status of immigrants is still used as a means of regulating the foreign labor force.

Immigration regulation, especially regarding recruitment, has also produced external effects. The gap in economic development between certain sending countries (especially Turkey) and the FRG has widened drastically, in part because of the systematic recruitment of the best-trained workers. The recruitment stop put an end to the (intended) voluntary rotation that had occurred to some extent before 1973, thus making more permanent the loss of qualified workers of the sending countries. Since this process prevented or delayed the development of social services in the sending countries, projects that promote return migration face considerable obstacles (Korte 1983). At present, return migration is encouraged; yet, since conditions in the sending countries hardly encourage return, the success of the campaign remains doubtful. Return migration is further hindered because it seems that the best-qualified workers in particular have decided to stay permanently in the FRG, despite all the legal and political uncertainties.

4. Immigrant policy

All aims and instruments of the German "immigrant policy" are based on the official position that the FRG is *not* an "immigration country". Nevertheless, there are some slight steps towards an immigrant policy because immigrants in the FRG – *contrary* to the official position – have in fact become an integral and permanent part of the German population. Such a short-sighted policy has hardly led to the coordinated, coherent program which is needed. The dilemma of immigrant policy stems from its nature: unlike immigration regulation it is formed by numerous authorities with different interests, aims, and responsibilities. Immigrant policy is part of the "home affairs" of the FRG and therefore much more affected by the different interests of employers and unions, the Conservative, Liberal, and Social Democratic Parties, the local authorities, the *Länder* governments, churches, and welfare organizations. Its implementation is connected with other much-disputed policy problems, such as equal opportunity in education and housing.

Principal aims

Until 1969 there was little that deserved the name "immigrant policy". During the expansive phase of immigrant employment the employers were only required to provide "adequate" housing. By the end of the 1960s, however, the longer periods of residence for some immigrants began to produce the first consequences. Because of increased family reunifications, the problems of the "second generation" began to receive attention. When the socialist–liberal coalition came to power in 1969 it began to consider the sociopolitical aspects of labor immigration instead of only the economic ones. The first clear result of this orientation was a tightening of the regulations concerning housing conditions.

Social aspects were stressed in the 1973 action program of the Federal Government (mentioned previously), which realized that the growth of social services has not been commensurate with the growth in the number of immigrant workers – who have been admitted only on the basis of economic considerations. The program pointed primarily to deficiencies in the fields of housing, pre-school education, and education generally. The position that the FRG was *not* an immigration country was reaffirmed, but the aim of "temporary integration" was also expressed. Full integration was expressly rejected, but "everything should be done to provide the immigrants with humane conditions during their stay".

Because of the increase in family reunification after 1973 the discussion about a new immigration policy has turned to the problems of the second and third generations. The idea that there is no alternative to the integration of foreign children and youths is becoming more and more accepted. Two reasons are given why political efforts ought to concentrate on integration. On the one hand, it is feared that the social, cultural, and structural partial integration of the second generation will result in crime and great social and political conflict; on the other hand, the demographic development of the German population is expected to lead to a shortage of workers – especially qualified workers – that cannot be compensated for by an unskilled foreign sub-proletariat. Still another reason may be that the German Army's main problem after 1985 will be a shortage of recruits. Naturalization of the second generation is, in part, intended to remedy this imminent manpower shortage of the army.

Full political and legal equality beyond the existing equal pay and equal social rights is still rejected. The official assumption is that full integration is only possible – if at all – through naturalization, which should therefore be made easier to obtain. This attitude shows the assimilationist character of what official immigrant policy calls "integration". Programs and aims directed towards preserving ethnic identity and autonomy are in most cases closely linked to the aim of strengthening the ability to return. The concept of an evolving "multicultural" German society is not discussed officially but is discussed in less influential church and academic circles. The FRG's immigrant policy is primarily aimed at dealing with, and, preferably, avoiding short-term problems; there is no distinct policy for handling the permanent residence of ethnic minorities.

The instruments of immigrant policy

The following section outlines German immigrant policy in four areas: working conditions and social rights; political rights and political participation; housing; and education and vocational training (especially for the second generation).

Foreigners are granted equal pay and trade union rights. Equal treatment is also guaranteed in the area of social security: all insurance and pension claims acquired in the FRG are fully paid, even after return. Immigrant workers in the FRG are equally eligible for unemployment benefits as long as they hold valid work and residence permits (Mehrländer 1978:127f; Rist 1978; Lohrmann 1974:129ff).

The relatively good position of immigrants in regard to working conditions and social rights is mainly to the credit of the unions. As soon as they overcame their initial resistance to the use of immigrant labor they established and promoted several integration and vocational training measures within the firms. Under article 9, section 3 of the Constitution, foreigners have the right of association; yet they did not have the same union rights as their German counterparts until 1972, when they became eligible for election to shop committees. Nevertheless, union membership is higher among immigrants than among Germans. A sample conducted in Berlin in 1976 estimated that about 27 percent of the Turkish workers as opposed to only 18 percent of the German workers were union members.

Foreigners in the FRG are virtually excluded from political participation. It is true that the Constitution prohibits discrimination based on sex, race, language, nationality, or religion and also guarantees the rights of assembly, organization, and franchise. But some of these rights are limited in regard to foreigners. The most important limitation concerns the right to vote, which is granted only to German citizens and naturalized foreigners. The problem of political participation has only partly been solved by giving foreigners the opportunity to work in local committees, the so-called *Ausländerbeiräte*. Though the regulations vary from *Land* to *Land*, in general these committees are only advisory and do not have any decisionmaking powers (Lohrmann 1974:131f; Bartels, Delbrück & Wiegel 1976:214ff; Kevenhörster 1974).

Another restriction concerns the right to organize and the right to form political parties. Under paragraph 6, point 2 of the Aliens Act, organizations of foreigners may be prohibited if they "jeopardize" the interests of the FRG. Similarly, German law prohibits the formation of foreign political parties. Foreigners may join German parties, however, and gain the right to vote and run for office within a party if it so allows. As of 1982, all parties except the CSU in Bavaria accepted foreign citizens as party members.

The housing policy has changed gradually over time. In the 1960s, immigrant workers were mostly housed in dormitories provided by the employer; bad or even inhumane living conditions often prevailed. This situation improved when minimal requirements for housing migrants were promulgated in 1971 and 1973, although the main problem remains the lack of sanctions to enforce these requirements.

Guidelines were passed in 1967 for the granting of loans to promote the construction of housing for foreigners, but such programs have never really been implemented. Recent housing policy is instead based on the assumption that special housing projects for foreigners are an obstacle to integration and should therefore be avoided.

With the increase in family reunification the housing situation of foreigners has worsened. The promotion of public housing programs, urban renewal, and home modernization lies within the administrative and financial jurisdiction of the *Länder* and the local communities. The federal authorities grant financial assistance, but the Federal Government has stressed that special housing programs for foreigners only inhibit integration and should therefore be abandoned. Only a few communities, mainly cities, have worked out special programs to improve the housing situation of foreign families.

This general inertia concerning housing also stems from the period when the employment of immigrant labor was understood merely as the short-term recruitment of "workers". The housing problems of immigrants were aggravated by the regulation that made proof of "adequate" housing a prerequisite for obtaining an indefinite or permanent residence permit. The fact that housing for foreigners was limited anyway increased the tendency toward ghettoization. It is difficult to attack this problem of ghettoization. One solution for immigrants is to move to the satellite towns and high-rise apartment buildings on the outskirts of the cities, which are not popular with the German population.

Even 35 years after the war, there is a housing shortage in the cities. But this shortage has also produced some positive effects: since German tenants do not have much of a selection either, the "flight" of one group from an area when another moves in, which happens in Anglo-Saxon countries, is less prevalent. Nevertheless, the increasing ethnic concentration, especially in the centers of German cities, is becoming a problem. To prevent such concentration from placing too great a strain on social services and to encourage integration, the Federal Government decided in the mid-1970s to prohibit immigrant workers from moving into "congested" areas, which were defined as districts and cities where the proportion of foreigners exceeded 12 percent of the total population. However, this strategy failed to succeed and it was abandoned after two years.

The only real "immigrant" policy exists in the area of education (Rist 1978). It was developed relatively late on and has in the early 1980s evolved into a consistent integrationist policy. The first steps toward improving the education of immigrant workers were a number of measures to promote the knowledge of German. Adult education centers, welfare organizations, and unions were the first to offer immigrants courses in German. Since these courses were not compulsory, attendance was poor. These efforts were coordinated after 1972, first by a central federal office for German classes for immigrant workers and then, after 1974, by a language association called "German for Immigrant Workers". The language courses are financed by the Federal Government. The number of participants has remained low, however, and on the whole these courses have not proved very successful.

Immigration policy in the schools can be divided into three phases. The first phase came at the beginning of recruitment when the number of foreign children rose from less than 2,000 in 1954 to about 35,000 in 1964. School attendance was made compulsory for the children of immigrants living in the FRG, although it was emphasized that retaining linguistic and cultural links with the countries of origin should have equal priority. These aims led to the establishment of the so-called preparatory classes, which were held in the mother tongue and were to be attended prior to entering all-German classes. This program was introduced in May 1964 by the ministers of education of the *Länder*. The fear that immigrant children would become educationally isolated was already being expressed at this early date. Another problem was that the education of immigrant children remained rather unsystematic; a form of bilingual education was intended, but the necessary guidelines, curricula, and teaching materials were lacking. This problem was not considered too serious, however, because the permanent residence of immigrants was not yet foreseen.

As the number of foreign children increased, the deficiencies of this policy became more and more obvious. In December 1971, two alternatives were discussed: the establishment of separate schools for foreigners versus full integration into the German school system. It was finally agreed that immigrant children should be fully integrated into German schools, even if they did not intend to stay in the FRG for long. Those with sufficient knowledge of German would be placed in normal German classes according to their age and proficiency; those without sufficient knowledge of German would attend preparatory classes before entering the normal school system. Though it was recommended that the proportion of foreigners per class not exceed 20 percent, this guideline could not easily be implemented. German teachers were offered financial assistance to give extra courses for immigrant children. In a reversal of policy, foreign teachers were now used to teach immigrant children in their mother tongue, especially in preparatory classes.

All these regulations – instituted successively – brought education policy in line with the new immigration policy (which had changed from a mere "guestworker" policy to a policy based on "temporary integration"). The main problem was and still is, however, that the regional concentration of immigrants is so high, and thus the concentration of immigrant children as well, that nearly all educational measures aimed at integration are doomed to failure. Moreover, the sending countries were permitted to establish supplementary national courses (more or less supervised by the school authorities of the *Länder*), and this further reduced the chances for full integration into the regular school system.

The ambiguity of educational policy – full integration on the one hand and specific education according to nationality on the other – was actually reaffirmed by the *Länder* ministers of education in a decision of April 1976. This decision developed the idea of enabling foreign children to live in "two worlds" – certainly an attempt to keep return migration a viable alternative. This ambiguous policy has not yet been changed, even though the Kühn memorandum of 1979 stressed that current policy is largely to blame for the disastrous state of immigrant education and urged the adoption of a consistent policy of full integration.

It must be added that since the *Länder* are responsible for education and culture, the priorities of education differ considerably from place to place. For instance, the policies of city-states (Hamburg, Bremen, Berlin) and the *Länder* with social-democratic governments (Northrhine–Westfalia and Hessen) tend towards integration while those of Bavaria and Baden-Württemberg emphasize separation and national instruction in order to strengthen the ability and willingness to return.

The area of vocational training has steadily become more important. In 1977 the Bund-Länder-Kommission (a committee established by the Federal Government to coordinate the education policies of the Federal and *Länder* governments) decided to intensify efforts at integration. The language association "German for Immigrant Workers" has since offered vocational training courses for unemployed foreign youths. Since 1980 these courses have been linked with the vocational courses of the Bundesanstalt für Arbeit; BfA pays 75 percent of the costs while the other 25 percent is raised equally by the Federal and *Länder* governments. The Federal share of the cost was four million marks in 1980 and ten million in 1981. Young immigrants who have completed the full-time training course do not have to wait two years to obtain a work permit. This type of legal entitlement to a work permit was further extended in October 1980 to immigrant youths who had completed secondary school.

All these measures pursue integration as far as equal opportunities in education and on the job are concerned. But beyond this, the question arises of what status to grant foreign youths who tend to identify with the FRG and plan to stay there permanently.

Since there are scarcely any ideas about a "minorities policy" in the FRG (and it would be almost impossible to carry one out at the moment anyway), policy considerations are restricted to the aim of making naturalization easier. Naturalization has been handled restrictively until now, with individual decisions completely at the discretion of the naturalization office. The requirements for naturalization are vague; for example, that the citizen "participates in and supports the national community". Applicants must have "as a citizen developed close ties with and a commitment to his community", and on the basis of this a residence requirement of ten years has been established. Other conditions for naturalization are renunciation of previous nationality, a clean police record, and broad integration into German society – for example, as proved by good knowledge of German.

In sum, neither the instruments nor the aims of immigrant policy in the FRG are based on permanent immigration or on a special minority status for foreigners. They are merely intended to tackle such specific problems as better job training and to prevent conflicts resulting from, among other things, the cultural marginality of the second generation. They aim at integration, including full political participation gained through naturalization, or at the encouragement of return migration. The problems resulting from this ambiguity in, for example, the areas of leisure-time activities and family life, are mainly dealt with by the welfare organizations (Arbeiterwohlfahrt, Caritas, Innere Mission with about 500 counseling centers and a staff of 700 in 1983).

It is generally agreed that these measures are not sufficient, let alone capable of fighting the causes of the problems. In the near future there is no hope for programs or even measures that would in practice provide guaranteed residence, improve educational and vocational qualifications, and – at the same time – accept cultural autonomy without espousing return migration. In short, there is at present no hope for a minorities policy in the FRG.

The outcome of immigrant policy

The present situation is characterized by the evolution of a system of ethnic stratification between Germans and foreigners. There is an internal hierarchy among the foreigners themselves, with the Yugoslavs at the top and the Turks at the bottom. This stratification affects nearly all areas of social life: jobs, education, qualifications, unemployment, housing, social prestige, and so on (Kremer & Spangenberg 1980). The second and third generations suffer a great deal of discrimination as regards education, vocational training, and position on the labor market. Their problems are further aggravated by the stiff competition that results from the entrance of the "baby-boom" generation into the labor market. Potential conflicts in the future can easily be foreseen: an increase in juvenile delinquency and political and religious radicalization as well as increasing hostility to foreigners from the German population, especially in the large industrial centers.

The extent to which these problems reflect a failure in immigrant policy can be disputed; but, it is clear that the measures introduced thus far have not been sufficient. At first glance, it seems that this does not hold true for the housing situation. According to surveys carried out in 1980, far more than 100,000 foreigners had by then been supplied with homes financed under public programs. But since many of these homes lie in satellite towns on the outskirts of large cities with high ethnic concentrations, and since they are mostly in the neighborhood of German families on the lower end of the social stratum, a sound "solution" to the housing problem has not in fact been found yet.

The number and quality of language courses for foreigners varies widely from region to region. They are generally not very successful, in part because of the work habits of immigrants (shift work, overtime) and in part because of deficiencies in teaching method. The German language is most often learned through personal contacts with colleagues and neighbors rather than through formal courses. Knowledge of German depends mainly on such factors as the number of contacts with Germans, job situation, residential area, education, length of stay, and age of the immigrant. In fact, according to various surveys the language courses contribute very little to linguistic ability.

The school situation is extremely bad. It is estimated that more than 25 percent of foreign children do not regularly attend school, and as a whole they are considerably under-represented at the secondary level. Measures to encourage school attendance are more or less restricted to primary and secondary modern school (which contain about 400,000 foreign youths at the moment). In areas where immigrant children form the majority, German children are also considerably disadvantaged. German parents often react by sending their children to private schools and by showing open hostility towards immigrants as regards education. The situation is extremely problematic in the case of children and youths, especially from Turkey, who immigrate at a relatively late age. Even if they previously attended secondary school in their home countries, an education in a German school can hardly be successful. German primary schools lead up to a final examination of great importance for continued studies, but only a small group of immigrant children can pass it.

There is no doubt that all these problems reduce the opportunities for gaining a qualified job, and for this reason special training courses were introduced. It should be added that at least half of the 120,000 foreign youths who leave school each year have complied with compulsory vocational school attendance, but only every fourth one can obtain an apprentice position at a regular place of employment. As a result, the unemployment rate among foreign youths is much higher than among German youths. Moreover, the foreign youths that *are* employed mostly work in traditional immigrant branches or in unskilled or semi-skilled jobs. Though the effectiveness of vocational training cannot be assessed at the moment, the failure of previous vocational measures does not leave much room for optimism.

Finally, it is even doubtful that the previously mentioned proposal to simplify the naturalization process will be accepted. Up to 1980 only a few of the over one million immigrants who had lived in Germany for more than ten years chose to apply for naturalization. There were 130,000 eligible Turks in 1978, but only 318 applicants for citizenship (i.e. 0.3 percent).

Because the aims of immigrant policy in the FRG are contradictory and uncoordinated, one cannot expect success from the measures taken. When all is said and done, however, the main fault still lies in the refusal to accept, legally or politically, the fact that immigrants will be staying *permanently* in the country. As long as this uncertainty persists, even better-financed and more intensive measures will have no more than slight success.

The interrelationship between immigration regulation and immigrant policy

That immigration regulation and immigrant policy are connected is an observation rarely made explicit in the FRG, primarily because the aims of the two are in direct contradiction: immigration regulation aims at maintaining the state's ability to dispose freely of immigrant labor in response to economic needs, while immigrant policy aims at integrating immigrants and supporting their non-economic demands. Most of the measures that encourage immigrants to use the social services run counter to economic interests and diminish the state's ability to dispose of immigrant labor. Therefore, any "coordination" of these two sides of immigration policy has been merely accidental. Tendencies towards regulating immigration on the basis of the aims of immigrant policy have emerged only recently.

An immigrant policy hardly existed during the expansive phase of immigrant employment. Whatever measures were taken – for example, to ensure an adequate supply of housing – were aimed only at providing the minimal conditions necessary to keep immigrants on the job. With the stabilization of the foreign workforce, more and more employers became interested in prolonging the residence of the immigrant workers they already had instead of recruiting new ones. Furthermore, the increased length of most immigrants' stays and the immigration of family members after 1970 brought about a growth in social demands.

This is the background against which the first deliberations about a more consistent immigrant policy took place – still motivated, of course, by mainly economic interests. The initial measures certainly conflicted with immigration regulation, which was still aimed at keeping tight control over the immigrant workforce. This contradiction was not considered serious, however, because of the new policy's general orientation toward return migration. The major policy contradiction of this period was expressed in the ideas of "consolidation" and "temporary integration".

After 1973, when the recruitment stop put an abrupt end to many immigrants' illusions of eventual return migration, family members were brought to Germany and the second and third generations began to grow up there.

Policymakers soon realized that many immigrants had become indispensable to the economy, and the problems of the second generation – especially in the areas of education and training – began to demand public attention. Moreover, it was foreseen that the demographic development of the German population would lead to severe manpower shortages in the 1990s, and therefore economic and even military interests would be served by the permanent residence of foreign youths. The contradiction between maintaining the ability to dispose freely of immigrant labor on the one hand and integration on the other was reflected in the attempts to limit family members' access to the labor market (see section 3). Yet it soon became obvious that this would jeopardize the integration of the second generation. The result of these conflicts was a policy that promoted integration for those who wanted to stay and, at the same time, tried to limit any further immigration. Even the restrictions on family reunification, though in opposition to humanitarian aims, were considered necessary in order to reach the aim of integration.

This relationship between immigrant policy and immigration regulation has a certain logic: immigration is stopped so as to facilitate integration. Yet it is incomprehensible that, *at the same time*, overall immigration policy still explicitly aims at ensuring the free manipulation of labor, which is reflected by the refusal to admit that the FRG has in fact become an "immigration country" as well as by the various recommendations for maintaining and strengthening the immigrants' willingness to return to their countries of origin. The problem is, of course, that the political regulations and controls refer to *all* immigrants while the measures of integration are intended only for some of them – in particular, the second and third generations. Integration is not pursued wholeheartedly, but always with the reservation that its results must not be allowed to harm the aims of immigration regulation.

5. Policymaking and administration

Perceptions

It was thought that the economic growth and standard of living in the FRG could only be maintained and improved through the employment of immigrant labor. Other alternatives, such as improvements in the efficiency of production or lowered economic growth, were regarded as untenable. To abstain completely from economic growth was completely out of the question.

Until the late 1960s there was broad agreement on this point between the government, the employers, and the unions, and it was supported by the theory that the employment of immigrant workers would be only a temporary phenomenon, as it had been in the German Reich and the Weimar Republic. Yet the instruments applied to immigration did not produce the expected result; limited residence and work permits did not prevent immigrants from staying longer and longer.

In the 1970s the Federal Government introduced the idea of "temporary integration", which held that immigrants could be temporarily integrated into German society but at the same time could retain their desire to return to their home countries. The provisional way that immigrants lived and their hesitation to accept integration measures was misinterpreted as a fundamental orientation in favor of return migration. Policymakers did not consider that immigrants' actions were based on the uncertainty of their status, which made it impossible to form long-term plans.

"Social integration" – i.e. assimilation to German habits, standards, and values without a reduction in ethnic and cultural identity – is a process often related, especially in the media, to the historical model of the Poles in the Ruhr district (see section 1). Unfortunately, the fundamental differences between the situation of the Polish population and the situation of the foreign population living in the FRG today, especially the Turks, are usually neglected.

The Poles who immigrated into the Ruhr district at the end of the nineteenth century came from a part of Poland that had been subjected to a massive policy of Germanization for over 100 years. They were already Prussian citizens when they arrived, with the same political rights as other Germans; in particular, the right to vote and run for office at all levels of political representation. It is important to remember that the integration of the Poles was a long process that lasted for several generations and was not actually completed until the Second World War, when all autonomous Polish organizations (banks, cooperatives, press) were crushed. In contrast to today's Turkish population, the Poles were Catholic and had a western-oriented culture. These factors assisted their integration. Moreover, much of the momentum towards the Poles' integration was gained through their joint struggle with the German working class at the end of the nineteenth and beginning of the twentieth centuries. Considerable pressure for assimilation was exerted through government measures of forced Germanization; for example, there was a language act which prohibited the use of the Polish language at Polish meetings. The peculiar features of the Polish situation demonstrate that, contrary to public opinion, the often-cited example of the integration of the Poles in the Ruhr district cannot serve as a model for the integration of today's immigrant population.

It is widely thought that the Turks in the FRG are neither willing nor able to integrate into German society. This perception is based on three arguments. First, it is argued that the cultural and religious differences between Turks and Germans are so great that the Turks must necessarily remain an alien element in German society; integration will remain an illusion, and the idea of altering German society to accommodate to Turkish society is out of the question because the two are so different. Second, the fact that most of the Turks come from underdeveloped rural areas with a traditional social structure makes their adaptation to life in a modern industrial society almost impossible. This argument is often supported by the claim that Turkish families are satisfied with very low-quality housing and that "normal" German tenants and landlords cannot be expected to accept their way of life. Third, it is argued that the Turks, because of their distinct national and religious identity and close family ties, have developed such a strong group feeling that they do not want to integrate into German society and in fact try to avoid it.

These arguments ignore many facts. The Turks are not at all the least qualified immigrant group; since they were the last to arrive, however, they had to accept the jobs and housing that was left. This led to a process through which they became stratified *below* the immigrants already living in the FRG. Family reunification brought about a rapid rise in the non-working Turkish population, and for this reason the social services have been utilized more by Turkish than by other foreign children. Their increased number made them a more visible minority, and also gave them a good opportunity to organize themselves as an ethnic group, which led to the misperception that they were against integration on principle. The Turks' efforts to demarcate an ethnic boundary can at least in part be interpreted as a *reaction* to open discrimination and to the widespread belief that the Turkish and German cultures are too different to allow successful integration.

Despite these views, however, only a small number of Germans expect an end to the employment of immigrant labor in the FRG. Social scientists and politicians have conclusively stated that there is no viable alternative. Germany's need for immigrant labor will not be eliminated in the near future by technological or economic innovations. Nevertheless, this economic need has not yet been translated into the proper political and administrative policies.

The making of immigration policy

There is such a lack of planning in the FRG's immigration policy that it could be described by the expression "non-policy". If immigration policy is "made" at all, it is only to solve problems as they arise through ad hoc measures. It is important to remember that immigration policy is not equal to policies in other areas but is still used as a means of reaching other (especially economic) aims or of preventing further mistakes.

Those who make immigration policy have been described in detail above (see sections 2 and 3). The following paragraphs will merely sum up the various institutions and committees involved.

Immigration policy is primarily shaped by the Federal Government (Ministry of Labor and Ministry of the Interior), the unions (DGB), and the employers (BDA) (Lohrmann 1974:113–17; Unger 1980). The guidelines for immigration policy are drawn up in committees where the DGB (federation of trade unions), BDA (employers' federations), and the Federal Government exert the greatest influence; the legislative branch is largely excluded. The other members of these committees – representatives of organizations dealing with immigrant issues – have input but cannot get their ideas accepted. Most policy conflicts are resolved between, on the one hand, the Federal Government, DGB, BDA, and the Federal Institute of Labor (BfA) and, on the other hand, the welfare organizations and federations of local communities. On the *Länder* level there are fundamental differences between those governed by the SPD and those governed by the CDU/CSU. Conflicts about legal issues arise between the Ministry of Labor and the Ministry of the Interior.

One should not forget that the Aliens Act gives individual agencies broad discretionary powers as regards decisions about work and residence permits, and they therefore exert considerable influence on the interpretation and actual implementation of policy. On the whole this tends to have the restrictive effect of supporting the dominant aim of maintaining the state's ability to freely manipulate the immigrant labor force.

Besides the Federal Government, the bodies that have the most influence in shaping immigration policy are the coordination committee at the Bund-Länder Commission and the BDA and DGB's joint committee on immigrant issues.

The Ministry of Labor's coordination committee on immigrant workers has existed since the beginning of the 1970s. It is designed to "coordinate measures and programs between the various organizations on the Federal and *Länder* levels". It is composed of representatives from the Federal Chancellery, Federal Ministries, Foreign Office, Press and Information Office of the Federal Government, Ministries of Labor in the *Länder* Baden-Württemberg and Northrhine-Westfalia, BfA, BDA, DGB, churches, welfare organizations, federation of local communities, and parliamentary parties. It meets two or three times a year. Its guidelines were not passed until 1978, and immigrants were in general not asked for their views of the guidelines. At the end of 1978 the committee presented a paper endorsing "the integration of immigrant workers and their families".

The administration of immigrant policy

Besides the recruitment and immigration control authorities (see section 3) and the coordination committees, the Federal Government has not established any special institutions to carry out immigration policy. Political measures for immigrants are introduced by the appropriate bodies (e.g. school issues by the *Länder* Ministries of Education, labor issues by the BA and the *Länder* Ministries of Labor, and so on). Social care is performed by churches and welfare organizations: the Catholic Caritas takes care of the Spaniards and Italians, the Protestant Innere Mission takes care of the Greeks, and the social-democratic Worker's Welfare Association takes care of the Turks and Yugoslavs.

The immigration authorities that control the residence of foreigners are part of the FRG's internal administration, and were established according to the legal regulations of each *Land*; for example, in Berlin the police are responsible for the immigration office while in Northrhine-Westfalia it is the responsibility of the municipal and communal authorities. Because the administrative agencies have broad discretionary powers, the Aliens Act receives a different interpretation in the internal regulations of each *Land*. *Länder* governed by the SPD tend to administer the Act rather liberally, while those governed by the CDU/CSU tend to administer it rather restrictively.

In general, foreigners have no legal entitlement to residence in the FRG unless they are citizens of EEC member states. They may bring legal action in the Administrative Courts against decisions by the authorities that have not gone in their favor; but such proceedings do not delay expulsion in cases where renewal of the residence permit has already been refused.

After demands by the *Länder* Ministries of Labor, the Bund-Länder Commission on Immigrant Labor was established by the Federal Ministry of Labor in 1976. Its task was to develop a comprehensive political plan for the employment of immigrant labor. The Commission is composed of representatives from the *Länder* Ministries of Labor, *Länder* Ministries of the Interior, Federal Government, BA, and federation of local communities. Members of the DBG and BDA also take part in the discussions. A program was drawn up in the spring of 1977 that both called for "social integration" and proposed measures for return migration.

The BDA and DGB's joint committee on immigrant issues has existed since 1973 and meets every two months. Representatives from the Ministry of Labor and from other concerned ministries take part in the discussions. According to the DGB this committee is supposed to be restricted to exchanging information. Nevertheless, positions are taken and actions coordinated, which means that the meetings of this committee actually have significance.

The main problem in administering immigration policy is twofold: responsibilities are not centralized, and the different interests of the Federal Government, labor authorities, *Länder*, communities, and organizations makes it almost impossible to achieve any coordination in aims and methods. Much of the weakness and inconsistency of German immigration policy stems from this administrative division.

6. Conflict potential

Political discussion in the FRG has always revealed two contrasting viewpoints on immigration: one side demands stronger measures to promote return migration while the other side demands integration leading ultimately to naturalization. These contrasting views have until now been combined in a single policy – a policy considered sufficient for dealing with labor immigration.

Those in favor of return migration are oriented towards the traditional model of the seasonal worker. In the past this was a normal arrangement enforced, if necessary, by legal measures. Modern guestworker policy was based on the idea of the seasonal worker but seldom used legal measures to bring about return migration.

Those in favor of integration and an easier naturalization process are oriented towards the other traditional view of immigration, whereby immigration is seen as an addition to the permanent population. They have advocated in recent decades the introduction of preference categories for naturalization (e.g. according to profession or age group).

But the situation of the immigrants living in the FRG as well as in other Western European countries can no longer be adequately explained by the two traditional perspectives: seasonal workers versus permanent immigration. It can be assumed that a small number of the immigrants who have definitely decided to stay permanently will want to acquire a new citizenship while another small number will in fact change their minds and return home. Most of the "guestworkers", however, have settled down quite permanently, yet they do not want to change their citizenship.

In the two traditional patterns, no serious conflicts could occur. Seasonal workers have hardly any chance to acquire social positions already occupied by citizens. They are powerless, both as individuals and as a group. Because of rotation, solidarity or political power does not develop among seasonal workers. Regulated and controlled immigration also rarely leads to conflicts that can threaten the position of native citizens. Immigration quotas, residential limits, and other forms of government control prevented immigrants from becoming serious competitors with the indigenous population. As politicians like to put it in reference to the Poles in the Ruhr district, immigrants were "tolerated".

It is obvious that political decisions and administrative measures based on either of these two traditional perspectives cannot get to the heart of current immigration problems and are not capable of reducing the increasing public animosity. Quite the contrary, most suggestions and measures only increase social conflicts by forcing each group – but particularly the immigrants – to become internally more cohesive. Politicians who are oriented towards these perspectives inevitably argue from a position of power. They can neither recognize evolving social conflicts nor intervene in any way that benefits the welfare of the people involved. Political measures based on the traditional perspectives will fail in two respects: they will not accomplish their aims and, at the same time, they will aggravate the conflicts between immigrants and the indigenous population.

The German public and particularly the German politicians must once and for all realize that the presence of immigrant workers and their families is not a temporary problem that will eventually disappear with "integration" or "return migration". An important step in this direction would be an official recognition that independent ethnic minorities will form a *permanent* part of the future German society.

Prospects have long been rather bleak for smooth co-existence between Germans and foreigners, and the political measures that have been adopted reflect the ineffectiveness of official policy. Still, it is not yet clear what direction policy will take in the second half of the 1980s. This will only be decided when the second generation, the children of the former guestworkers, comes to the fore.

Germans and immigrants are together involved in a long-range process of change that can turn in any number of future directions; they can move "with each other" or "against each other". Between these extremes lie many alternative paths. If the alternatives are not explored and the necessary solutions found, considerable conflicts will arise in the future. The conflict potential could grow and turn existing mutual aversions into open aggression and mutual agitation and violence. One must remember that this future scenario is not like the past: it will not be only a one-sided affair where the Germans use violence against the immigrants. The time may come when immigrants' hatred and aggression against the Germans may also explode into violence.

7

Switzerland

HANS-JOACHIM HOFFMANN-NOWOTNY

1. Immigration and immigration policy

Historical background

Considering its economic capacity Switzerland was long over-populated. The problems arising from this situation were dealt with by the systematic promotion of emigration. Military emigration, i.e. enlistment as mercenaries, was the preferred form of emigration, and it had become institutionalized by the sixteenth century. Between 300,000 and 350,000 mercenaries emigrated from Switzerland in the eighteenth century (Bickel 1947:91).

Compared with the huge emigration of this period, immigration was of little importance. The only significant immigration resulted from religious persecution in neighboring countries. Between 100,000 and 150,000 Huguenots rushed to Switzerland after the revocation of the Edict of Nantes (1685), but only about one tenth remained there permanently (Bickel 1947:88,106f; Ludwig n.d.:14). Civil immigration never came close to military emigration in importance; only 40,000–50,000 persons immigrated in the eighteenth century, a time when Switzerland's total population was 1.7 million (Bickel 1947:50,99). The main reason for this low immigration rate was probably that Switzerland had little economic attraction at the time. In addition, the extremely restrictive immigration policy of the cantons and communities, which tried to keep out even other Swiss, may also have played a role (Bickel 1947:102; Langhard 1913:3f).

In the first decades of the nineteenth century Switzerland had no centralized immigration policy. A short phase of leniency during the Helvetic Republic (1799–1802) and the Mediation Period (1803–14) was followed in 1815 by a return to the extremely restrictive policy of the eighteenth century (Moser 1967:331). The granting of a Permit of Permanent Residence to foreigners or even to citizens of other cantons was left to the judgement of the canton in question. Several cantons tried through inter-canton treaties to regulate the bilateral immigration of their citizens, but no general intra-Swiss policy was established.

The liberalization of migration

Increased leniency towards immigrants began after the establishment of the Swiss Federation. Through the Constitution of 1848 all Swiss obtained the right to settle anywhere in the country. The Federation was empowered to act for the whole country in setting the conditions, by means of international treaties, for the immigration of foreigners. By 1914 such treaties had been concluded with 21 states, and practically all of those resulted in immigration (von Waldkirch 1923:63af). About 98 percent of all resident foreigners could refer to an immigration treaty (Fehrlin 1952:70; Petitmermet 1923:109a). These treaties stated that natives and foreigners would be economically and legally equal in every respect. The right of free immigration and emigration was taken for granted and many European states even abolished passports (Fehrlin 1952:29f). The only evident difference remaining between foreigners and Swiss was the exclusion of the former from political rights (as was the case in other countries as well). But otherwise, control of immigration or refusal of permanent residence was legally impossible under the liberal immigration treaties.

The first wave of immigration

Paradoxically enough, these treaties, initially designed to assure a legal *emigration* from Switzerland, provided at the same time a framework for the immigration that began in the second half of the nineteenth century (Table 7.1). An immigration surplus was registered for the first time in the census of 18, although heavy emigration still continued. Thereafter, the foreign population increased steadily and reached a peak in 1914 when foreigners constituted 15.5 percent of the total population (Bickel 1947:166).

The rapidly increasing number of foreigners gave rise to fears on several levels. The expression *Überfremdung* (over-foreignization) first came into use at this time (Schlaepfer 1969:61f). What is now interesting is that proposals for controlling foreign penetration, in contrast to the situation today, provided almost exclusively for the promotion of naturalization. A concern that annual naturalizations would lag far behind annual increases in the foreign population can be found throughout the relevant publications of this period (Burckhardt 1913:24). Another issue of concern in the literature was that foreigners had a higher birthrate than the Swiss (Burckhardt 1913:31).

The relative failure of the naturalization policy was at the time interpreted as reluctance on the part of the Swiss to accept new citizens. This reluctance was due to economic rather than nationalistic motives (preservation of *Bürgernutzen* – communal income – for the citizens of the community and avoidance of economic support for the poor), especially since it also applied to the naturalization of Swiss from other communities. Other reasons for the failure of the naturalization policy were the bureaucratic and economic costs that candidates were subject to (Schlaepfer 1969:102,179f) and, finally, the lack of interest on the part of foreigners themselves (Ilg 1922:5f).

After 1900 the introduction of *ius soli* was demanded in order to increase naturalization and reduce the number of foreigners. Under this law all children born in Switzerland of foreign parents would no longer have the option but would receive Swiss citizenship automatically (so-called compulsory naturalization). This demand gained impetus when the census of 1910 showed that 38 percent of the foreigners living in Switzerland had in fact been born there (Burckhardt 1913:48). Several organizations endorsed in one form or another the introduction of *ius soli*. All these advances prompted the government to begin a revision of the Federal Constitution in order to make the introduction of *ius soli* possible. The preliminary work was practically concluded by 1914; a bill could have been submitted to the Federal Parliament if work had not been interrupted by the outbreak of the war. The revision work was begun again after the war, but in a completely different climate.

This short survey of efforts made before 1914 to facilitate naturalization shows that the solution sought for the "aliens question" was exclusively a more intense integration of resident foreigners. Tendencies towards isolationism, which arose near the end of the First World War, had not been noticeable previously, at least not on a political level (Schlaepfer 1969:129,155f). Thus, a report by the Federal Department of Justice and Police, dated the summer of 1914, which considered measures against foreign penetration, dared not even mention the possibility of a restrictive settlement policy (Ruth 1934:5).

The first wave of immigration was composed largely of people recruited from the neighboring countries of Germany, France, Italy, and Austria. In 1860 these countries provided 97.3 percent of the total number of immigrants (Germany 41.6 percent, France 40.5 percent, Italy 12.0 percent, Austria 3.2 percent). In 1910 the share of these four countries still amounted to 95.2 percent, although important shifts had occurred in the proportional distribution of the nationalities (Germany 39.7 percent, Italy 36.7 percent, France 11.5 percent, Austria 7.3 percent). The interwar years were marked by a sharp decline in the number of incoming

Table 7.1. *Foreign residents in Switzerland, by nationality, 1860–1982 (thousands)*

Year	Germany	France	Italy	Austria	Other Euro-peans	Other non-Euro-peans	Total	Percent of total popula-tion
1860	48	47	14	4	3	1	115	4.6
1880	95	54	42	13	6	2	211	7.4
1900	168	59	117	24	11	4	383	11.6
1920	150	57	135	22	35	4	402	10.4
1941	78	24	96	–	17	7	224	5.2
1960	93	31	346	38	43	33	585	10.8
1970	116	51	527	43	134*	112	983	15.9
1980	86	46	421	32	140*	168	893	14.2
1982	85	47	417	31	351*		926	14.6

Source: Statistical Yearbook of Switzerland.
Note: * Whereof Spaniards: 1970: 102; 1980: 97; 1982: 103.

foreigners, caused in part by the Great Depression. In 1941 the percentage of foreigners in the population was only slightly higher than in 1860 (Table 7.1).

The second wave of immigration

Immediately after the Second World War a new wave of immigration began. In 1950 there were 285,000 foreigners living in Switzerland (6.1 percent of the total population). This figure rose to 585,000 (10.8 percent) in 1960, and reached a peak of 1,065,000 in 1974 (16.8 percent). When the second wave started the overall nationality composition was similar to the first wave, i.e. the majority came from the four countries that have a common border with Switzerland. In 1910, 95 percent of all immigrants came from Germany, France, Austria, or Italy; in 1950 these countries still supplied 86 percent, although the proportion of Germans and Frenchmen had decreased while that of Italians had strongly increased (49.1 percent of all immigrants in 1950). As immigration continued the proportion of Italians increased steadily and reached a peak in 1960, when they accounted for 59.2 percent of all resident foreigners.

By 1980 the proportion of immigrants from neighboring countries had decreased to 65.6 percent. Roughly three quarters of these came from Italy, whose share in the total foreign population has decreased to 47.1 percent; after the Italians were the Spaniards (10.9 percent), followed by the Germans (9.7 percent), the French (5.2 percent), the Yugoslavs (4.9 percent), and the Turks (4.3 percent). It is worth mentioning that only the Yugoslavs and Turks increased both in absolute numbers and as a share of the foreign population from 1970 to 1980, despite the fairly strong reduction in the number of foreigners that took place as a consequence of the dramatic shift in policy after 1970. This shift, which will be described in more detail later in this chapter, has led to strict immigration control, a drastic reduction in the number of persons accepted as immigrants, and a certain liberalization in the situation of the resident immigrant population.

Strict immigration control is also applied to persons seeking asylum. Though Hungarians in 1956 and Czechs in 1968 were allowed to enter the country freely, this is no longer the case today. In recent years, several thousand Vietnamese were permitted to come to Switzerland, but otherwise it has become difficult to obtain permission to enter the country as a refugee.

Terminology: immigrants or foreign workers?

Of all European countries, with the exception of Luxemburg and Liechtenstein, Switzerland has by far the highest percentage of foreigners in its population. But this does not mean that Switzerland considers itself an immigration country. The official terminology does not use the term "immigrant" but instead uses the terms *Ausländer* (foreigners), *ausländische Arbeitskräfte* (foreign labor), *Fremdarbeiter* (foreign workers), or *Fremde* (alien), the latter appearing in the term *Fremdenpolizei*, for example. The same is also true as regards everyday language, where mainly *Ausländer* or *Fremdarbeiter* are used.

2. General preconditions

Switzerland is a country with many unique features, some of which will be described and discussed in the following pages. As general preconditions of immigration, some of these features may be important and some may not. Since such relationships are not easy to delineate, however, it seems advisable to discuss as many of Switzerland's features as possible to determine which of them might be considered relevant as preconditions of immigration and immigration policy.

Land and population

Switzerland is a small country in both surface area (41,300 square kilometers) and population (around 6.4 million). The average population density is relatively high (154 inhabitants per square kilometer). A considerable part of the country lies in the Alpine region and population density is therefore extremely high in those cantons situated in the so-called midlands. For example, the canton of Basel-Stadt has 5,562 persons per square kilometer, the canton of Geneva has 1,207 persons per square kilometer, and the canton of Zurich, with about 18 percent of the country's total population, has 648 persons per square kilometer.

If one considers immigration as an instrument of population policy used to fill empty spaces, as is or was the case in traditional immigration countries such as the United States, Canada, and Australia, one can easily understand why Switzerland does not consider itself an "immigration" country. The population argument – the attraction of population as such – has in fact never been brought up in discussions on immigration. It has been raised only in a reversed sense by those groups opposed to immigration, which argue that the country is already overpopulated.

Cultural heterogeneity

As Stein Rokkan has correctly observed, Switzerland can be considered a "microcosm of Europe" (1970:v). Its native population consists of four ethnic groups that coincide more or less with the country's four language groups. Of all Swiss citizens, 74 percent are German-speaking, 20 percent are French-speaking, 4 percent are Italian-speaking, and 1 percent are Romansh-speaking (if one includes immigrants the figures are as follows: 65 percent German, 18 percent French, 12 percent Italian, 0.8 percent Romansh, and 4.3 percent other languages). Despite this considerable number of minorities, political scientists believe Switzerland to have one of the most stable political systems of modern times. Almond and Powell's hypothesis (1966:259ff) that segmented democracies tend to be more unstable than homogeneous democracies has been refuted with regard to Switzerland by Lijphart (1967), Lehmbruch (1967), and Steiner (1970).

One reason that Switzerland has succeeded in mitigating the problem of native ethnic minorities, finding acceptable compromises and thus maintaining a dynamic equilibrium, is probably that ethnic division is only one of several others cutting across society in the vertical and horizontal directions. Some of the other divisions concern religious affiliation, the development level of a region, political affiliation, membership in one of the 26 highly autonomous cantons, social position, and so forth. These divisions do not all coincide with ethnicity; rather, they tend to overlap in various ways and create a large number of subcultures combining different characteristics.

It would, however, be misleading to argue that Switzerland's cultural heterogeneity has made immigration an easy process. One could argue on the contrary that a small, multicultural society has a fragile identity that can be easily endangered by immigration; the term *Überfremdung* (overforeignization) was probably coined in Switzerland and is constantly used today. It thus seems reasonable not to give too much weight to the multicultural nature of Swiss society as a source of *stimulation* for immigration.

It is important to note that common frontiers *and* common languages seem to have made immigrants regard their stay as mainly for working purposes, returning home if and when the circumstances made it desirable or necessary. This might explain why reductions in the number of foreigners in Switzerland caused by the two world wars, the Great Depression, and the recession of 1975 produced no adverse reactions from these foreigners. It might also help explain why a policy of rotation was adopted after the Second World War as well as why Switzerland has never defined itself as an "immigration" country.

Economic development

To understand Switzerland's economic development, which has made it one of the richest countries in the world, one has to realize that the process was due not to the possession of natural resources but mainly to a "cultural, social, and political environment highly favorable to economic growth" (Siegenthaler 1978:91). Switzerland is extremely poor in coal, iron, nonferrous or precious metals, oil, and natural gas. Conditions for agriculture are also rather unfavorable.

Even towards the end of the nineteenth century agriculture could only provide about half the nation's demand for calories (Siegenthaler 1978:91). Economic development thus had to depend on services and industrialization, on the one hand, and foreign trade on the other. As a landlocked nation Switzerland has no direct access to the important nautical trade routes, but it is nonetheless a kind of European crossroads and the continent's most important country of transit. A service economy developed very early (transport, trade, hotel industry, repairs); as a result, knowledge about foreign countries, goods, and techniques was widespread, which contributed to the development of handicrafts and later of industry. In addition, geographical and political conditions helped Switzerland become a financial center of international importance. Since the country's economic development relied mainly on the factors of labor and, especially, capital, industrial production of high quality goods and services (especially banking, insurance, and tourism) predominated.

Thus, immigration to Switzerland is best explained by:

- rapid economic development and a shortage of manpower, and
- the difference in economic development between Switzerland and the adjacent countries of Germany, Italy, France, and Austria, as regards the first wave of immigration, and mainly Italy and other Mediterranean countries as regards the second wave.

The liberal admissions policy outlined previously is thus an explanation for heavy immigration to Switzerland only in the sense that it simply erected no obstacles to immigration until the grassroots movement against immigration appeared (see section 5). Before the first popular initiative was launched Swiss immigration policy was a function of the needs of the economy. Immigration has always been seen as an instrument to supply the economy with sufficient labor; this is still the case today, although the grassroots movement has brought about a great number of restrictions.

Polity and society

"Like all federal systems, the Swiss version, too, is rich in intricate complexities" (Frenkel 1978:323). Today Switzerland consists of 26 highly autonomous cantons (among them six so-called half-cantons, which only differ from the full-cantons in that they send one *Ständerat* (Senator) to the second chamber of the Federal Parliament instead of two). The Swiss Confederation dates back to 1291, when three agrarian mountain communities (Uri, Schwyz, and Unterwalden) concluded a treaty of alliance lasting more than 500 years. There were many internal and external struggles before modern Switzerland came into being in 1848. Geneva was the last canton to join the Confederation in 1815.

The autonomy of the cantons and the reluctance of the Federation to intervene in their affairs are two factors that help explain why the federal executive, the *Bundesrat* (Federal Council), has only seven members. The Council acts in unison, and the "subordination of the individual member to the collective will of the government may go so far that he is forced to advocate publicly solutions to controversial problems which he rejects personally" (Gruner 1978:339).

This arrangement is all the more remarkable because the Council is formed by a coalition of the four largest parties: two members from the Social Democratic Party (SP), two from the Liberal Party (FDP), two from the Christian Democratic Party (CVP), and one from the Swiss Peoples Party (SVP). The regional (language) background of the members is as important as their party affiliation, since the cultural heterogeneity of Switzerland is also expressed in the composition of the government.

Because of the organization of the government on the one hand and elements of direct democracy on the other, it may well happen that one of the parties represented in the Council is in opposition to the government as regards a particular problem; or, one of the small parties may successfully launch a referendum against a law already passed by a large majority of the Federal Parliament. This is exactly what happened in the early 1980s with a proposed new Aliens Law: the National Action group launched a referendum against it after a compromise had been reached by all the major parties. Because of this referendum the Swiss voters had to decide in June 1982 whether or not the new law would take effect; it was rejected by the extremely small margin of 50.4 percent against versus 49.6 percent in favor.*

The referendum and the constitutional initiative are the two most notable characteristics of the plebiscitary element in Swiss democracy. The referendum gives the Swiss people the opportunity to react immediately to the outcome of parliamentary decisionmaking. If 50,000 voters can be mobilized to sign a petition regarding a law already passed by parliament, then the Federal Government is obliged to submit that law to a popular vote. Because of the possibility that parliamentary decisionmaking may afterwards be submitted to a popular vote, it is attempted to obtain the consensus of all interested groups concerned with a particular bill as early as possible (Gruner 1978:348).

The referendum can force the rejection of laws already accepted by parliament, but it cannot be used to directly force parliament to pass a certain law. This can be accomplished indirectly, however, through the constitutional initiative, which can be used to change or amend the constitution. If 100,000 voters endorse a proposed constitutional amendment, the government must submit the initiative to a popular vote. If the initiative receives a majority, the government and parliament must thereafter act in accordance with the new constitutional article(s).

Initiatives that are rejected by only small majorities, such as the overforeignization initiative of 1970, usually force the Federal Council to change its policy; in fact, this is how the change in immigration policy came about. It is thus correct to state that the plebiscitary element of the Swiss political system has proved a very important precondition for past and present immigration policy.

In the social and economic sectors there is a "typically Swiss aversion to governmental regulation of problems" (Burckhardt 1978:195). To give only two recent examples: in March 1976 more than two thirds of the voters rejected a constitutional initiative that would have made possible

* Had the proposed law been accepted it would have brought an improvement in the terms of residence and employment offered to immigrants. Three major changes were envisioned. First, a reduction in the residence requirement for a Permit of Abode from 36 months to 32 months. Second, a guarantee that immigrants residing in Switzerland with a Permit of Abode for five or more consecutive years would thereafter have a *right* to the annual renewal of the permit; at present no such guarantee exists. Third, a reduction from 15 months to 6 months in the residence requirement that an immigrant living in Switzerland must fulfill before being allowed to bring his or her family into the country.

federal legislation allowing participation by workers and their shop organizations in the decisionmaking process both of business enterprises and of the public administration. In December 1976 a majority of four to one rejected another initiative that demanded the immediate introduction of the forty-hour work week in all enterprises throughout the country. The defeat of the two initiatives illustrates the widespread attitude that solutions to these kinds of problems should either come from negotiations among the groups directly involved or else be left to private initiative.

This pattern of conflict solution, however, does not and did not function in the case of the "over-foreignization" problem. None of the initiatives launched since 1965 related to this problem (see section 5) demanded, for example, that solutions be sought through negotiations between the interested parties (i.e. unions and employers), with the government only acting to control the correct implementation of the resulting agreement – as it already does with, for instance, collective labor agreements. On the contrary, it can be shown that the Federal Government has gradually acquired more and more power in the field of aliens affairs – although the legal basis for this is fairly weak – and that the cantons only execute federal regulations.

The Swiss attitude towards government intervention also has an impact on the social security system. The ideology of the welfare state has never been developed to the degree found in other European countries and probably never will be. In principle, health insurance is voluntary. Until 1977 unemployment insurance was also voluntary; it was then made compulsory, but the number of insured days per year is limited to 180. The public old-age and survivors' insurance (AHV) only came into effect in 1948. It is based on the so-called three pillars theory: the basic pension (which should provide the means of subsistence) comes from the AHV, the second part should come from funds provided by voluntary pension plans in the business enterprises, and the third part should come from private savings.

Although the Swiss social security system may appear rather underdeveloped from the viewpoint of an orthodox welfare-state ideology, in Switzerland the view is often expressed that the Swiss must ask themselves whether they have not reached the bearable and reasonable limit to which social security can go. Even if one does not share this opinion, one must still in all fairness say that the system seems to work sufficiently. Moreover, any judgement of the system has to take into account the fact that Switzerland is a wealthy country with relatively high wages and salaries and low taxes, which gives an individual the means to insure himself adequately and the freedom to decide, to a certain degree, which risks he wants to cover and to what extent.

3. Immigration regulation and control

The Federal Law of Abode and Settlement of Foreigners (ANAG), enacted in 1931, is still valid today (with minor alterations). The most important points of this law are:

- the creation of three main categories of foreigners: those with a Permit of Abode (*Jahresaufenthalter*), those with a Permit of Permanent Residence (*Niedergelassene*), and those with a Seasonal Permit (*Saisonarbeiter*);
- the dual nature of the Permit of Abode, which serves as both a work and a residence permit. The juridical literature refers to this linkage as the main characteristic of the Swiss system (Moser 1967:371);
- the great discretionary powers of the *Fremdenpolizei* (the law contains practically only rules of procedure);
- the unfavorable legal position of the foreigner, who basically has no *right* to a Permit of Abode, although Article 19 does state that cantonal law has to provide foreigners with the right to appeal decisions against them.

Principal aims

As regards the aims of immigration regulation there is a *general* consensus in Switzerland that "only the interests of the country are relevant for the admission of foreigners" (BIGA 1964). Article 16 of ANAG stipulates that when deciding about immigration and immigrants the authorities should take into consideration the nation's cultural and economic interests, the situation on the labor market, and the degree of over-foreignization.

There is no doubt that immigration since the Second World War has primarily been seen as an *economic* phenomenon; in other words, immigrants have been desirable only as manpower. Because the postwar economic boom was expected to last only temporarily, immigration policy aimed at "rotation" as a means to prevent immigrants from staying permanently. In addition, it was believed that a rotation policy would protect Switzerland from becoming "over-foreignized". Thus, one instrument could be used to accomplish two aims. "Over-foreignization" is officially defined as the situation that results when the influence of non-assimilated, or not satisfactorily assimilated, members of other cultures is so strong that the essential and basic values that form the foundation of the native culture are influenced by foreign values and the population's way of living is subsequently no longer based on its own traditions (BIGA 1964:136).

The longer immigration to Switzerland lasted and the larger the proportion of foreigners grew, the more the dominant aim of immigration regulation and control became protection against over-foreignization. This was already officially stated in the BIGA report of 1964. It is quite correct to say that the introduction of the global ceiling (*Globalplafonierung*) in 1970, which was the same as a far-reaching immigration "stop", was not dictated by economic interests at all. It was instead the result of grassroots pressure based mainly on the issue of over-foreignization and expressed in a series of constitutional initiatives. These initiatives, which were barely rejected by plebiscite, proposed a drastic reduction in the number of foreigners in the country. Although "over-foreignization" is a vague concept, political and economic actors have nonetheless had to take into account that it can be used at any time to mobilize a broad segment of the Swiss population.

"The country's interests", however, is another vague concept. There is in fact a widespread consensus that immigration should be strictly controlled and the number of foreigners living in Switzerland should not be allowed to increase, but behind this consensus there are a number of different motivations. The over-foreignization parties (see section 5) give their consent only because the stabilization of the number of foreigners is for them just a first step towards the ultimate reduction that remains their final demand. The Federal Government and the labor authorities have proposed stabilization as a compromise, acceptable to the majority, between the employers' demand for more labor and the grassroots' demand for a drastic reduction in the number of foreigners in the country. This compromise comes close to the opinion of the trade unions, although they would also favor a reduction (albeit a slow one) if it could be accomplished without endangering Swiss jobs; for example, in cases where an entire company might have to close if it lost its foreign workers.

Employers and their associations know that their demands will provoke grassroots reaction if strongly stated. Therefore, most employers' associations have declared themselves in agreement with the Federal Government's compromise, particularly the associations of large industrial enterprises. It is relatively painless for them to agree to the compromise; since they offer better working conditions and higher wages, they can still recruit foreign workers from smaller enterprises and small businesses. On the other hand, the government's compromise places the associations of restaurant owners, the tourism industry, and the building industry under heavy cross-pressure: they both lose workers to the large enterprises and at the same time cannot recruit new immigrants.

To summarize, one can say that "national interest" means above all "economic interest", but that this interpretation is confronted by a grassroots movement that considers the main aim of immigration regulation to be the prevention of over-foreignization through a reduction in the number of foreigners.

The instruments of regulation and control

Since the outcome of the referendum on a new Aliens Law was negative, the current law (ANAG) remained in force. It provides for Permits of Abode (*Aufenthaltsbewilligung*), Permits of Permanent Residence (*Niederlassungsbewilligung*), and Permits of Tolerance (*Toleranzbewilligung*). A foreigner is allowed to remain on Swiss territory only if he or she possesses one of these permits; if the permit is lost or withdrawn, the holder must leave the country. Foreigners that stay only a short period of time, on holidays or visits, do not need permits.

A foreigner who enters Switzerland and plans to work must obtain a Permit of Abode. This permit is never valid for longer than a limited period of time, normally not more than one year when granted for the first time. The duration of the permit depends on the purpose of residence, the situation on the labor market, and, for renewal, on the foreigner's conduct as well. Certain conditions may be attached to the Permit of Abode. The permit can be withdrawn if any of the conditions are not fulfilled.

A foreigner with a Permit of Abode still needs special permission from the Police of Foreigners in order to:

- take another post within the same occupation (change of post);
- engage in a different occupation than the one specified, whether with the same employer or a new one (change of occupation);
- Take on an additional occupation (part-time job) on a regular basis, whether with the same or another employer; or,
- engage in an independent activity.

The Permit of Abode is the main instrument of Swiss immigration regulation. Under the global ceiling, introduced in 1970, there is a quota of only about 10,000 Permits of Abode for foreign workers per year for the whole country. These workers may then be joined after fifteen months by their families, who can then also receive Permits of Abode allowing them to work. As a result, one could say that the quota actually allows an annual influx of approximately 30,000 holders of a Permit of Abode who take up or – in the case of family members – may take up work. The quota is revised each year so that the total number of new entrants is kept roughly equal to the total number of those who return. The determination of the quota and its distribution among the cantons is one means of immigration regulation. A second means of regulation is the requirement that an immigrant renew the Permit of Abode regularly (each year during the first five years of residence and afterwards every two years). Since foreigners have no right to renewal, the authorities can refuse an application and thus force the holder to leave the country, which happens especially if he or she is unemployed and not likely to find a new job very soon.

Table 7.2. *Foreign residents in Switzerland by permit of stay, 1960–82*

Year	Permit of Abode %	Permit of Permanent Residence %	Total no.	%
1960	76.5	23.5	584,739	100.0
1965	75.1	24.9	810,243	100.0
1970	62.8	37.2	982,887	100.0
1975	35.4	64.6	1,012,710	100.0
1980	23.4	76.6	892,807	100.0
1982	23.5	76.5	925,826	100.0

Source: Statistical Yearbook of Switzerland.

Regular renewal of the Permit of Abode also provides a means for the internal control of immigrants. The cantonal *Fremdenpolizei* renews each permit in conjunction with the authorities in the commune of residence of the permit holder, which allows them to control whether the holder is still in Switzerland and whether the conditions of acceptance are still being observed.

The mainly economic aims of immigration were evident in former restrictions on the occupational and geographical mobility of immigrants during the first five years of residence. Foreigners were not allowed to change employer or occupation. They had to remain domiciled within the canton issuing the Permit of Abode and could not bring family members to Switzerland until after at least three years of residence. In addition, the Permit of Abode might be withdrawn if a foreigner changed employers too often. The *Fremdenpolizei* could alter these conditions but seldom did so. In recent years these conditions have been reduced to one year for change of employer or canton and fifteen months for the resettlement of the family. At the same time, however, the administration and control of the Permit of Abode has become rather more restrictive.

The Permit of Abode can be limited to a season. This Seasonal Permit is granted to foreigners with seasonal jobs in an occupation that has an expressly seasonal character. It is granted for the seasonal term and is normally valid for a maximum of nine months.

As the name indicates, the Permit of Permanent Residence entitles the holder to stay in Switzerland for good. It puts foreigners, as employees, on a par with Swiss citizens and also allows them to take up independent activities (with the exception of certain occupations that are reserved for Swiss citizens only or that demand a special Swiss examination). In all other respects, foreigners that hold Permits of Permanent Residence are treated like Swiss citizens. The only exception concerns the right to vote, which only citizens have. The Permit of Permanent Residence is unlimited and must not be restricted by any conditions.

The Permit of Permanent Residence is granted at the discretion of the pertinent authorities, usually after a stay of ten years. The permit has to be renewed regularly (every three years), but this is merely a formal administrative procedure to control the holder's physical presence in the country. The permit can only be revoked under special circumstances; for example, if the holder commits a serious crime.

The Permit of Permanent Residence is also issued to immigrants that request asylum and are subsequently accepted as refugees. At the end of April 1983 there were 33,166 acknowledged refugees in Switzerland. In 1978 there were 1,389 applications for asylum, in 1980 this figure amounted to 3,020, and in 1982 to 7,135. By the end of April 1983 7,130 applicants were waiting for a decision on their application for asylum.

The rights of asylum applicants were improved considerably by the passage of a new law on asylum on 5 October 1979. Under this law, however, the legal procedure leading to a final decision takes much more time than in the past. Because of this and because of the increasing number of applicants for asylum, the Federal Government will again revise the law, making it more restrictive.

The Permit of Tolerance is granted, when a foreigner cannot be refused residence and when none of the other permits is applicable, either because of the foreigner's conduct or for other reasons having to do with the individual foreigner.

Permits for employment as a border-commuter are granted in accordance with existing conventions with neighboring states. The rules and considerations observed when granting a Permit of Abode are also valid for border-commuters, who only need a work permit (BIGA 1964:40f).

When considering applications for a Permit of Abode the authorities first try to determine whether a Swiss worker or a worker with a Permit of Permanent Residence can be found who is suitable for the job in question. This search is not limited only to persons registered with the Employment Bureau; an employer must prove that he tried actively and over a period of time to find a suitable person to fill the job.

The policy described thus far has been in effect since the end of the Second World War and was intensified when the global ceiling and the quota system for Permits of Abode were introduced in 1970. A second quota system has been established for seasonal workers; it is meant to ensure that no more than 110,000 of them work in Switzerland at the same time. Not all seasonal workers stay in the country for the maximum allowable time of nine months, however, which means that the quota actually allows more than 110,000 entrants to work annually. Seasonal

Table 7.3. *Seasonal workers and border-commuters in Switzerland, 1960–82*

Year	Seasonal workers	Border-commuters	Total
1960	139,538	39,419	178,957
1965	184,235	45,600	229,835
1970	154,732	74,779	229,529
1975	86,008	99,373	185,391
1980	109,873	100,404	210,277
1982	116,012	111,509	227,521

Source: Volkswirtschaft.

workers are not entitled to bring spouses or other family members with them although sometimes husbands and wives both come as individual workers. Seasonal workers are not counted statistically as part of the foreign (resident) population (Table 7.3).

The recession of 1975–76 showed that instruments that allow the authorities to manipulate the number of foreigners in the country are being used for that purpose. Yet manipulative instruments lose their effectiveness as the percentage of foreigners with a Permit of Permanent Residence rises – at present more than 75 percent of the foreign population has such a permit. Because this percentage has grown continuously, the quota system has increasingly become the only instrument available to regulate the number of foreigners in the country. However, since the quota for Permits of Abode is very small in relation to the total number of resident foreigners, even this instrument does not provide immigration regulation much scope.

The same is true as regards the quota for Seasonal Permits, even though it is much higher than the quota for Permits of Abode. It seems, however, that the quota for seasonal workers could not be reduced even in case of a recession since the demand for these workers already exceeds the given quota. Moreover, they take jobs that Swiss citizens would not be likely to take. In any event, seasonal workers are not considered contributors to over-foreignization since their residence is only temporary.

The *Fremdenpolizei* is in charge of the internal control of immigrants in cooperation with the regular local control of inhabitants. As one means of internal control the Federal Government has decreed that employers and landlords must report to the communal authorities if a foreigner (with any kind of permit) leaves a job or moves out of an apartment. The latter requirement applies, however, to Swiss citizens as well, i.e. a landlord generally has to give notice that tenants have moved.

There are controls on employers, either on a random basis or with the use of an informer, to find out whether all employees have a valid work permit. If a foreigner is employed without a permit the employer may have to pay a fine up to 10,000 Swiss francs and/or be sentenced to up to six months in prison. To give an example: recently a restaurant owner in Zurich who had illegally employed a Yugoslav woman in the kitchen was sentenced to a fine of 4,000 francs and fifteen days in prison (with two years' probation). In addition, the employer was put on the so-called "black-list" of the *Fremdenpolizei*, which means that for three to twelve months he was not allowed to apply for a permit to employ a foreigner.

Naturalization is a further means of regulation – not of the number of immigrants but of the number appearing in the statistics as "foreigners". During the movement for equal rights for men and women about 30,000 children born to foreigners received citizenship on the grounds that they lived in Switzerland and their mother was Swiss. The regular process of naturalization, however, is difficult, and citizenship is hard to obtain. Naturalization is explicitly not considered a means of solving the so-called foreigner problem.

A foreigner has to have lived in Switzerland for at least twelve years before applying for naturalization. Since cantons and communes also have their own regulations concerning minimum length of residence and since time spent in one commune cannot be transferred to another, naturalization may take even longer if, for example, a foreigner has moved from one commune to another during his first twelve years in Switzerland. Many communes charge very high fees for naturalization; these may amount to several tens of thousands of francs and thus present an impossible obstacle for an applicant to overcome. The naturalization procedure as such takes about two years and ends with an examination where the applicant has to prove that he or she is "sufficiently assimilated". The final decision on whether or not citizenship in the commune should be granted (which would then be extended to cantonal and Swiss citizenship) is taken by the communal parliament or, in the small communes, by an assembly of the citizens. It is quite obvious that this procedure does not encourage foreigners to apply for Swiss citizenship, and so far there are no indications that any major change will occur in this situation.

The outcome of regulation and control

The instruments of immigration regulation and control discussed thus far are certainly designed to be efficient, and it seems that they have been utilized effectively since the shock of the Second Initiative Against Over-Foreignization and the subsequent introduction of the global ceiling (Table 7.2). At least, this is the impression one gets from the statistics. Between 1960 and 1970 the foreign population increased from 585,000 to 983,000 (from 10.8 percent to 15.9 percent of the total population). By 1974 it had increased to only 1,065,000 and in 1982 was only slightly above 900,000. This means that a restrictive immigration policy is still being consistently applied. Nevertheless, as mentioned previously, while the new policy measures taken since 1970 can prevent another increase in the number of foreigners, it is unlikely that they will result in a large reduction. If a reduction were considered opportune it could only be achieved if voluntary return migration were to exceed the quota for Permits of Abode.

The figures given above also do not reveal to what extent foreigners (with a Permit of Abode) were forced to leave Switzerland in the course of the recession, or to what extent they themselves decided to return to their home countries. Since one can show that among return migrants there is always a considerable number that have a Permit of Permanent Residence, it is evident that the decrease in the number of foreigners in Switzerland is not solely the result of the application of instruments of regulation. There are always some who leave the immigration country for reasons that are not, or are not exclusively, related to the situation there. The impression is gained, however, that during the recession foreigners also returned (though they were not and could not be forced to do so) because of the low amount of unemployment compensation and the short payment period. It thus seems that this characteristic of Switzerland's economy operates as an indirect and additional means of immigration regulation.

A look at the statistics gives no answer to the question of whether and to what extent immigration regulation measures and internal immigrant controls can and eventually are being circumvented. Interviews with officials of the *Fremdenpolizei* reveal that illegal immigration does in fact occur and that every now and then firms are discovered that employ illegal immigrants. It is impossible, however, to estimate the number of illegal immigrants in the whole country.

In 1980, the director of the *Fremdenpolizei* in the canton of Ticino estimated that between 2,000 and 3,000 illegal immigrants work there and that the police detect about three out of ten immigrants who enter illegally. But it was also pointed out that Ticino is not typical of the whole country. It has a common border with Italy which is difficult to control and enables illegals to return quickly as soon as there is danger of being detected; moreover, there is a common language on both sides (Italian), which makes it easier to remain undetected. As far as Switzerland's other cantons are concerned, crime statistics may give some hints regarding the employment of illegal immigrants. In 1979, 569 employers in the canton of Zurich, 192 in the canton of Basel-Stadt, 187 in the canton of Bern, and 131 in the canton of Geneva were prosecuted for the illegal employment of immigrants.

Still, it is impossible to judge whether these figures are only the tip of the iceberg or whether most illegal immigrants are in fact found by the police. Recent estimates by the construction workers union put the number of immigrants working illegally in Switzerland at between 30,000 and 50,000. Yet the general opinion still is that the number of illegal immigrants is not very significant. Since the country is small and the controls effective, the danger of being discovered is great, and illegal immigration is thus discouraged.

4. Immigrant policy

Max Frisch has best expressed the dilemma of Swiss immigrant policy: "We called workers, and human beings came" (Frisch 1967:100).

Principal aims

It can be said that Switzerland has no "immigrant policy" in the strict sense of the term, i.e. a well-defined and legally guaranteed set of special measures designed to meet the specific needs of immigrants and to help them solve their problems. The Swiss attitude could be expressed as follows: foreigners are meant to work, behave in an unobtrusive manner, and adapt themselves to Swiss standards and conditions. It must be added, however, that this attitude does not apply only to foreigners; most Swiss demand (mutatis mutandis) similar behavior from themselves as well. It should also be mentioned that – with the exception of school problems – there seems to be no urgent need for an immigrant policy, since the integration and assimilation of foreigners in Switzerland is already relatively satisfactory.

ANAG contains only regulations for immigration control, rules for administrative procedures, and references to restrictions on foreigners. One main reason for this lack of an organized immigrant policy is obviously the Swiss tradition of laissez-faire, under which as many problems as possible are left to self-regulation and market forces. Not even among liberal groups that oppose discrimination against foreigners is there much support for special measures in their favor; according to the liberals, special measures would result in positive discrimination, which would conflict with the principles of laissez-faire and might also strengthen the grassroots movement against "foreignization". Another reason for the absence of an immigrant policy is that its presence would contradict the official position that Switzerland is *not* an "immigration" country. There is no indication whatsoever of a change in this attitude. Finally, one must remember that the lack of an immigrant policy has to be seen in connection with the initial Swiss opinion that immigration would be only a temporary phenomenon and that an immigrant policy would therefore not be needed.

The defeated legislation on foreigners would not have brought much change in the direction of a more explicit immigrant policy: under the heading "Care and social integration" (Section 6) the law contained three paragraphs which stated only that "foreigners .2.2. will be informed adequately about the conditions of living in Switzerland and about their legal position". One recently formulated aim in the area of immigrant policy is to give all foreigners equal social rights and equal rights on the labor market. This aim relates especially to seasonal workers, who would be allowed to choose a certain employer (from one season to another) or to change employers during a seasonal stay. With the recent fulfillment of another aim in this area, seasonal workers gained the right to unemployment compensation.

The instruments of immigrant policy

The progress made in recent years in the treatment of foreigners has not involved taking special measures on their behalf; instead, it has involved the gradual abolition of a series of restrictive regulations affecting foreigners who did not hold Permits of Permanent Residence. But the fact that foreigners in Switzerland – no matter what permit they hold – have no legal right to any kind of special assistance does not mean that they are left completely on their own. This is especially true for refugees. There are special centers where they can live for three to four months, participate in language courses, and receive instruction about life in Switzerland. They are then moved to communes where groups of volunteer helpers take care of them.

In fact, there are many organizations for counseling and practical help at the disposal of foreigners. These organizations vary much in sponsorship, in structure, and in the kind of help they offer. There are also great variations from community to community and from canton to canton. In some communities and cantons a foreigner may find relatively good services while in other places services may be completely non-existent. Only the schools are at all prepared systematically to meet the special difficulties of foreign children via supplementary language training or homework assistance. In this case the recommendations of the Conference of the Cantonal Ministers of Education are available for guidance. Since they are only recommendations, however, the extent to which they have been followed differs greatly from community to community.

The outcome of immigrant policy

Since there is no "immigrant policy" in the strict sense of the term, it is difficult to evaluate the results. Nevertheless, the situation of resident foreigners can be described on the basis of a comparative study

Table 7.4. *Foreign labor by occupation, 1941–70*

Year	Self-employed	Directors and leading employers	Lower employers	Skilled and unskilled workers	Other	Total
1941	21.4	2.4	12.3	60.3	3.5	100.0
1950	10.8	2.4	11.0	73.1	2.8	100.0
1960	3.3	2.5	9.3	83.7	1.2	100.0
1970	2.3	1.9	16.8	77.8	1.2	100.0

Source: Federal census.

recently carried out in Switzerland and in the Federal Republic of Germany (Hoffman-Nowotny & Hondrich 1982). Foreigners in Switzerland seem better integrated and assimilated than foreigners in Germany. This is shown by virtually all of the indices developed in the study. Foreign workers in Switzerland stay in the country longer; they enjoy better education and training; they immigrated at an earlier age; they intermarry more frequently with the local population. There is a greater number of complete family units than in Germany as well as a greater number of families with fewer children; moreover, these families enjoy much better housing conditions.

Professionally, foreign workers in Switzerland are closer to their Swiss peers than guestworkers in the Federal Republic are to the Germans: foreign workers in Switzerland have higher qualifications and the proportion of unskilled workers is smaller (Table 7.4). Foreigners also enjoy greater upward mobility and can earn higher incomes in Switzerland; they are less prone to feel disadvantaged professionally and are a great deal more optimistic about finding better jobs and higher incomes. Finally, a greater number of foreigners in Switzerland have established relationships with native citizens; they are more likely to have Swiss neighbors, and they have more social contact both with the Swiss and with foreigners from other countries. They are also more inclined to join organizations and associations, either mixed or ethnically homogeneous.

More foreign workers in Germany (55.6 percent) join labor unions than in Switzerland (29.6 percent). This, incidentally, points to a significant and characteristic difference between Switzerland and the Federal Republic: in Germany, foreign workers find their way into society via formal membership in mass organizations, while in Switzerland they assimilate in informal ways through the relationships they develop.

How can one explain the relatively satisfactory degree of integration and assimilation of immigrants in Switzerland? It is definitely not the result of a special "immigrant policy", since there is none. It is also not the result of the ethnic and social backgrounds of immigrants in Switzerland. The situation of immigrants seems to be rather the outcome of a specifically Swiss interplay of general politics, politics of immigration regulation, and market forces. General politics tends to leave societal problems as much as possible to mechanisms of self-regulation. The gradual abolishment of the once numerous internal restrictions and discriminations that foreigners were subject to reflects this tendency, although it must be seen against a background of restrictive immigration regulation and control. Finally, efficient market forces have reacted to immigration in what seems to be a very effective fashion.

The only measures of positive discrimination to benefit foreigners are found in the school system, where it seems that some of the specific problems faced by foreign children have been successfully tackled. But otherwise, it cannot be assessed how well the various social services that work with the individual problems of foreigners are coping with the task. One can assume that in many individual cases this service was and still is helpful. Nevertheless, it would be an overstatement to say that the individual help given to foreigners by service institutions has contributed very much to the relatively positive situation described above. For this reason it seems quite obvious why no need is felt for a change towards any kind of special immigrant policy.

The interrelationship between immigration regulation and immigrant policy

Until the first half of the 1960s Swiss immigration policy was characterized by two orientations: a liberal one towards the exterior and a restrictive one towards the interior. In other words, the borders were open to immigrants, but they met hard restrictions once inside the country. Permits of Abode were administered so as to cause frequent rotation. After the middle of the 1960s these orientations shifted: immigration regulation became more restrictive and internal control gradually became more liberal. The rotation model – which did not work anyway – was officially abandoned.

It has been shown that the policy of stabilizing the foreign population, begun in 1970, and the lifting of internal restrictions, have brought about a better assimilation and integration of immigrants (Hoffmann-Nowotny & Hondrich 1982). The individual success of many foreigners, which is related to their length of residence, has also helped prevent a build-up of tensions. Such tensions could have developed if foreigners had remained stuck in the lowest positions of society.

Nevertheless, before receiving a Permit of Permanent Residence (after ten years) an immigrant is still in a state of constant insecurity regarding continued residence in Switzerland. During this time an immigrant has to consider himself a person on probation; he cannot freely decide whether to regard his residence as temporary or permanent, which has been shown to hinder his integration and assimilation (Hoffmann-Nowotny 1973:171f). Today, however, only a minority of less than 25 percent of the foreigners living in Switzerland do not have Permits of Permanent Residence (Table 7.2).

Though it cannot be said that the immigration regulations in existence since 1970 have stimulated thinking and action regarding immigrant policy, the fact remains that a legal improvement in the position of immigrants has occurred through changes in discriminatory internal restrictions. This seems to be a good example of a political paradox: the over-foreignization movement, which at least partially reached its aim of reducing the number of foreigners in Switzerland, contributed at the same time to an increase in the number of permanent immigrants as well as to a considerable improvement in their legal situation.

5. Policymaking and administration

The intensely federal structure of Switzerland makes the formation of any kind of policy a complex phenomenon (a population of only 6.4 million is divided among 26 cantons and more than 3,000 communities, each enjoying a high degree of autonomy). The formation of immigration policy is even more complex because it is guided by both economic interests and national identity interests, the latter highly emotional. Therefore, the following analysis can only present some general characteristics of the policymaking process.

Perceptions

There is no doubt that the majority of the Swiss consider their country "penetrated by foreigners" and "over-foreignized" – yet it is extremely difficult to explain just what this means. The picture does not become much clearer when one examines representative definitions of over-foreignization, some of which have Switzerland losing its identity (*Eigenart*); that customs, mores, moral values, and so on would be endangered; that the political system would be undermined if too many foreigners lived in the country; that it would be yet even more undermined if the foreigners became naturalized citizens. These definitions could – under different circumstances – have some rational basis, especially if one were to accept the idea that Switzerland has many unique features and can only function as a highly heterogeneous society as long as these features remain unaltered.

The fear of being "over-foreignized" loses its rational basis, however, when one points to the sociological fact that a fairly well-assimilated foreign lower class has neither the potential nor the desire to fundamentally change the cultural, social, or political system of the host country. Yet despite the existence of this fact and its validity for Switzerland, the fear of "over-foreignization" can still be mobilized for political purposes.

In the past, the fear that Switzerland would be penetrated by foreigners could be kept within certain limits as long as it was assumed and declared as official policy that foreigners would only stay for a short period of time (the policy of rotation). In addition, immigration could be explained as a short-term phenomenon caused by the economic boom. But as soon as the number of immigrants began to reach almost one million and their residence began to assume a more permanent character, the phase of initiatives against foreign penetration started and the politicization of the immigration question at the grassroots level resulted in the founding of two parties against foreign penetration. These parties rapidly gained considerable influence on the community, canton, and federal levels and are still represented in several parliaments.

This development was probably the result of an erroneous assessment of immigration and its possible consequences by political and economic figures. In this light the global ceiling of 1970 is comparable to an emergency brake. If the ceiling had not been introduced one can be sure that the next initiative against foreign penetration, which demanded a halving of the number of foreigners, would have been passed by the Swiss voters.

How is immigration policy made?

As already mentioned, Swiss legislation does not determine policy definitely and has therefore allowed very liberal (prior to 1970) as well as very restrictive (since 1970) immigration regulation. Swiss immigration policy is not logically deduced from a "theory" or from abstract general principles; as an upper-level administrator told us in an interview, policy was "not *made*, but *grew* out of a permanent trial and error process". Swiss policy is extremely pragmatic in that it tries to find compromises between dominant economic interests (employers and cantons), the grassroots movement, and the interventions from sending countries.

As the government stated in its 1958 report, the admission of foreigners should be governed by the necessities of the economy as long as they are parallel to the overall interests of the country. Today a corresponding statement would not be phrased in the same words (in order to avoid grassroots reaction), but it is quite clear that any restrictions on immigration are designed to do as little harm as possible to economic interests. This has never been a well-defined political concept; immigration policy became a problem for politicians only after market forces began to create significant side effects. Before then, policy was determined by administrative rather than political decisionmaking and resulted in the free admission of immigrants coupled with systematic rigid discrimination against them once they were in the country.

The political apparatus was challenged at the beginning of the 1960s when public opinion rose against further uncontrolled immigration. The government and the Federal Parliament eventually came under strong pressure. In 1965 the Democratic Party of the Canton of Zurich launched the first constitutional popular initiative against "over-foreignization"; it demanded an amendment to the Federal Constitution stating that the total number of foreigners with a Permit of Abode and a Permit of Permanent Residence should not be allowed to exceed 10 percent of the *total* population of Switzerland. This initiative was withdrawn in 1968; that is, it never came to a vote because the initiators declared themselves satisfied with the measures already taken by the authorities.

When it later became obvious that the number of foreigners continued to increase despite these measures, a second initiative was launched by the "National Action against the Over-Foreignization of the People and the Fatherland" (*Nationale Aktion gegen die berfremdung von Volk und Heimat*). James Schwarzenbach was the campaign leader. This initiative went much further than the first one: it demanded that foreigners not be allowed to exceed 10 percent of the *Swiss* population in any canton, with the exception of Geneva. The plebiscite took place in June 1970 and the initiative was defeated by a narrow majority (54 percent opposed versus 46 percent in favor). If this initiative had been accepted by the voters it would have been necessary, at that time, to reduce the number of foreigners by 44 percent.

This threat made such an impression that vigorous and effective political action became imperative, and the global ceiling was introduced. Without stating any numbers the global ceiling proposed that a balanced relationship be sought between the size of the Swiss and the foreign populations. It was added as a specification that a stabilization of the foreign population was to be reached first, and afterwards would come a gradual reduction in its size. The introduction of the global ceiling, together with the reduction in the foreign population brought about by the recession, proved sufficient to take the edge off the grassroots movement.

But National Action did not give in. It successfully launched another initiative in 1972 even more drastic than its previous one: this initiative demanded that the number of foreigners in Switzerland not be allowed to exceed 550,000 and that the necessary reductions to achieve this figure be completed before 1 January 1978. It led to a split in National Action, whose most prominent figure, James Schwarzenbach, left and founded another "over-foreignization" party, the Swiss Republican Movement (*Schweizerische Republikanische Bewegung*). The radical 1972 initiative was supported by 34 percent of the voters in the plebiscite of October 1974.

In the same year, but before this plebiscite took place, two more over-foreignization initiatives were launched, one by the Republican Movement (no. 4) and one by National Action (no. 5). The Republican Movement's more moderate initiative demanded that the number of foreigners in Switzerland not be allowed to exceed 12.5 percent of the Swiss population. National Action's initiative demanded that not more than 4,000 foreigners be allowed to be naturalized each year as long as the total population of Switzerland exceeded 5.5 million (the actual population at that time was well above 6 million). The plebiscite on these two initiatives took place in March 1977 and both suffered considerable defeats. The Republican Movement's initiative was turned down by 70.9 percent of the voters and National Action's initiative by 64.9 percent.

On the same date another initiative, also launched by National Action, was presented to the voters. It did not directly refer to the so-called over-foreignization problem; instead, it demanded first that international treaties be made subject to the referendum and, second, that this provision apply even to already existing international treaties if at least 30,000 Swiss citizens so demanded. The initiative was clearly aimed at the 1964 treaty between Switzerland and Italy, which established regulations concerning immigration between the two countries. It was rejected by 76.3 percent of the voters.

Though none of this series of initiatives was ever passed, the narrow margin of defeat for the 1970 initiative made it quite clear that the Swiss government had to hold strictly to the policy of the global ceiling. And caution is still required – a constitutional initiative that demanded an improvement in the status of foreigners (especially seasonal workers) was rejected in April 1981 by 84 to 16 percent.

It is quite clear from this discussion that immigration policy in Switzerland has for the past fifteen years been primarily a reaction to the grassroots movement; the Federal Government formulated and proposed the policy and the administrative agencies executed the measures taken to prevent passage of the over-foreignization initiatives. The Federal Parliament and the political parties played only a minor role in this process. The parties obviously did not want too much exposure in order to avoid internal conflicts among their members as well as conflicts with those of their constituents who supported the over-foreignization initiatives. This problem was especially salient for the Social Democrats because a considerable part of their traditional constituency voted for the over-foreignization initiatives and – to a lesser extent – even for the over-foreignization parties. Since immigration policy is now and will probably remain a precarious matter, it will no doubt be left as much as possible to the Federal Government and the bureaucracy, both of which have gained power as immigration policy has become more restrictive.

When the restrictive immigration regulations were introduced in 1970, the Federal Government created a commission whose task was to advise the administration and to formulate recommendations regarding an improvement in the relations between Swiss and foreigners. This commission, the Federal Consultative Commission for the Foreigner Problem (Eidgenössische Konsultativkommission für das Ausländerproblem – EKA) is composed of representatives from all relevant social groups – political parties, churches, unions, and so forth – and has a permanent secretariat. Since its creation the commission has published a number of valuable studies on the foreigner issue as well as many documents containing recommendations, e.g. regarding the school problems of second-generation immigrants. It seems that the EKA has not so much directly influenced Swiss immigration and immigrant policy, but has served more as an extra-parliamentary body of discussion and has contributed – at least to a certain extent – to a rational public debate on the so-called foreigner problem.

Commissions similar to EKA also now exist in many communes and cantons, and many of them include foreigners among their members, which EKA does not. Commissions on the local level have proved especially useful as instruments for the solution of many problems.

Finally, the role that immigrants themselves play in the policymaking process must be examined, even though it has been relatively marginal thus far. Foreigners have formed many cultural and political organizations in Switzerland, the most important of which is the Colonie Libere Italiane (CLI), which has more than 10,000 members. The CLI attempts in particular to articulate the social and political interests of foreigners and to mobilize them to participate actively not only in foreigners' associations but also wherever possible in Swiss *Gremiums* and organizations; for example, in workers' commissions in the firms, in the commissions on foreigners' problems that exist in many communes and cantons, in Swiss associations, clubs, unions, and so forth.

According to the declared intentions of the CLI (and also of other foreigners' associations), the aim behind the attempt to mobilize foreigners is twofold: (1) to further the integration of foreigners into Swiss society and (2) to encourage foreigners to use all possible channels of influence to make their voices heard and thereby influence the decision-making process on all levels of society.

The general impression is that the foreigners' associations, which at first organized themselves in a fashion analogous to political organizations in their home countries, have now come to understand the special features of Switzerland's political system and have adapted accordingly. One can thus expect that foreigners will have improved chances of having their interests taken into consideration in the future, even if they are not granted formal political rights.

How is immigration policy administered?

During the First World War the Federal Government began to regulate immigration with emergency decrees; that is, with laws that had no constitutional basis. Before that time immigration had been practically free and whatever internal controls there were had been administered by the cantonal *Fremdenpolizei*. The constitutional basis for immigration regulation was established in 1925, followed by the already mentioned federal aliens law (ANAG) in 1931. Since then immigration policy has been a federal matter, although it is executed to a considerable extent by cantonal and communal administrative bodies.

If a foreigner comes from a country whose citizens need a visa to enter Switzerland, the visa is issued by the appropriate embassy or consulate. The Federal Department (Ministry) of Justice and Police (Eidgenössisches Justiz- und Polizeidepartement) is ultimately responsible for visa matters.

Foreigners who want to enter the country in order to take up an occupation must first have been granted a Permit of Abode or a Seasonal Permit. Every year the Federal Government determines the total quota of permits and how it should be distributed among the cantons and the Federal Office of Industry, Small Business, and Labor (Bundesamt für Industrie, Gewerbe und Arbeit – BIGA). For the period 1 November 1983 to 31 October 1984 the quota for Permits of Abode is 10,000 and for Seasonal Permits 110,000. In order to have continuous data on the number of foreigners present in Switzerland, the Federal Government recently established a Central Register of Foreigners (Zentrales Ausländerregister).

The federal and cantonal *Fremdenpolizei* grant Permits of Abode, Settlement, and Tolerance within the scope of their respective legal authority. The federal labor market authority (BIGA), the cantonal labor authorities, and some municipal labor authorities empowered by the cantons together examine permit applications from an economic and labor market point of view.

The system established by the *Fremdenpolizei* Law is characterized by two features. First, there is the combination of residence and work permits in one document, the Permit of Abode. This dual purpose requires that there be close cooperation between the *Fremdenpolizei*, who decide about residence, and the labor market authorities, who examine permit applications before any decision is made. Second, the individual cantons have extensive authority in this area due to the federal structure of the country, which presupposes cooperation between the federation and the cantons. The Federal Department of Justice and Police and the federal *Fremdenpolizei* give necessary instructions to the cantonal *Fremdenpolizei* and to the border officials regarding the application of aliens legislation.

When granting permits the *Fremdenpolizei* must follow the opinion of the cantonal labor authorities, whose advice is usually binding. The cantonal authorities decide how and to whom the cantonal quota is distributed; in other words, they make the final decision as to whether or not a foreigner may be allowed to immigrate, either with a Seasonal Permit or a Permit of Abode. As regards the distribution of the cantonal quota among employers, the cantonal labor authorities usually consult commissions composed of representatives of employers and unions as well as of leading officials of the labor authority itself.

The Federal Department of Economics and BIGA establish the rules and principles followed by the cantonal labor authorities in order to guarantee a homogeneous labor market policy for the whole country (BIGA 1964:42). About 30 percent of the total quota for Permits of Abode, and about 6 percent of the quota for Seasonal Permits, is administered by BIGA. This is done mainly to meet the labor demand of federal institutions (e.g. federal universities) and enterprises (railroad, post, etc.), but it may also be used to meet an urgent need that cannot be filled under the cantonal quota.

As we have mentioned, Switzerland has no institutionalized immigrant policy, and therefore there are no institutions based on any specific laws or regulations with the task of meeting the problems of foreigners. Foreigners have access, however, to all of the social institutions that serve inhabitants of Switzerland; moreover, in many communes there exist private as well as public institutions – mainly of an advisory nature – that try to help foreigners deal with any problems they may encounter.

6. Lessons of the past – hypotheses for the future

Switzerland's immigration experience has taught one main lesson: although immigration was primarily seen from an economic perspective, it proved to have social, cultural, and political consequences of an unforeseen nature. Switzerland has had to learn that immigration and the economy are parts of a complex societal system with multiple interrelations and that changes in one subsystem induced changes in other subsystems

Table 7.5. *Foreign residents in Switzerland by language regions, 1980*

	Foreign population		Foreigners as percent of total population
Language region	no.	%	
German-speaking	563,074	63.1	12.3
French-speaking	263,292	29.5	18.0
Italian-speaking	66,441	7.4	25.5
Total	892,807	100.0	14.2

Source: Die Volkswirtschaft, March 1981, p. 126.

and in the societal system as a whole. It has had to learn that immigration can be left to market forces only up to a certain point and, after this point is passed, there is a reaction calling for severe restrictions on immigration, which means, in other words, braking the change in one sector in order to reduce its impact on other sectors. In short, Switzerland has had to learn that immigration is not only an economic phenomenon but also – and even more so – a social and political phenomenon.

It seems that this lesson is now understood as far as immigration regulation is concerned. During the past ten years state intervention has becomethe dominant instrument in this field, while market forces have played only a marginal role. An opposite development has occurred, however, regarding internal controls over the occupational and regional mobility of foreigners. Discriminatory restrictions have been abolished or reduced and market forces have gained in importance. Formal immigrant policy has never been important in Switzerland for ideological as well as pragmatic reasons; there was and is no urgent need for it, since market forces have been able to solve most problems (e.g. housing and social mobility). This does not mean, however, that special measures to help immigrants would not have been useful.

After what has been said about the grassroots movement, it is clear that a legally institutionalized immigrant policy would immediately create internal tensions, which would not be in immigrants' best interests. For the same reason it seems quite improbable that the barriers against naturalization will be lowered or that any political rights will be granted to foreigners. The slightest concession would immediately prompt a referendum or constitutional initiative that would surely find a majority to support it. Because of the restrictive naturalization procedure it cannot be expected that a large number of foreigners will soon become Swiss citizens. In any case this is more a problem of the second generation; it seems that the expectations of the largest part of the first generation are satisfied as soon as a Permit of Permanent Residence is obtained.

An end to the restrictive immigration policy and the quota system, i.e. an opening of the borders to immigrants in the future, should hardly be expected. It seems that the number of foreigners now living in Switzerland has already reached an upper limit that cannot be exceeded. Finally, the available studies indicate that the integration and assimilation of foreigners will progress even without a special policy, unless there is a catastrophic economic setback. Such a setback would undoubtedly lead to a flow of return migration, as happened during the recession of 1974–75.

PART II

Comparative analysis

TOMAS HAMMAR

8

Economy and ideology

During the twentieth century, immigration policy has progressed along similar lines in all of the project countries. Though their modern political histories differ in many respects, they have all been affected by the two world wars, and by the same long- and short-run economic trends. This shared experience is fundamental for any comparison of our six immigration countries.

As countries with at least de facto immigration, they may affect each other through their policy decisions. If, for instance, one state closes its borders, potential immigrants may try to be admitted to a neighboring state instead, which then experiences more immigration and may react with stricter controls or perhaps even close its borders completely. Immigration countries may make use of techniques already applied in other countries, such as the manipulation of residence and work permits or the alteration or enforcement of legislation concerning deportation or citizenship. The six countries studied are thus not independent cases, for the simple reason that they establish and implement their immigration policy under the same economic and political conditions and under the influence of the same prevailing ideologies.

Liberalism and nationalism

From the middle of the nineteenth century until the First World War two ideologies of great importance for international migration existed uneasily side by side: economic liberalism and political nationalism. Great Britain was the standardbearer of liberalism and led the way in 1846 with a systematic free-trade policy. France followed this lead in the years after 1860. Several other countries also reduced their tariffs and removed restrictions on international trade. In the 1880s, however, protectionism once again predominated, although Britain, the Netherlands, and Denmark retained free-trade policies. Yet previous mercantilist regulation of the economy was not reimposed, nor was foreign travel controlled as it had been before. On the contrary, travelers could move without restriction during the latter part of the nineteenth century and until the beginning of the First World War.

During this period Switzerland gained a growing number of foreign citizens (15.4 percent of the total population by 1914). The German Empire, Denmark, and (to some extent) Sweden used Polish farmworkers during the summer and autumn months as field laborers on large agricultural estates. France actively recruited foreign labor, and its foreign population reached 1,160,000 in 1911. Yet, despite its growing importance, immigration was almost insignificant at the time in comparison with *emigration*, particularly with the great movement of Europeans to North America. Emigration to other continents came from all of the European project countries, although it was far more significant in Great Britain, Germany, and Sweden than in France, Switzerland, and the Netherlands (see Table 8.1).

Approximately 34 million people migrated to the United States during this period; an almost equal number migrated from Europe to South America, Australia, New Zealand, Canada and to the Asiatic parts of Russia. In contrast to the labor migration to Europe in the 1960s and 1970s, transoceanic migration went to regions that needed increased population in order to cultivate and develop new land. It was simultaneous with the successful industrial development and rapid population growth then under way in Europe, and it was made possible by new methods of travel and communication. But equally important to its success was the freedom of movement encouraged by liberal ideology, which swept away the restrictions of the past.

New restrictions were imposed at the end of the century, however, as national conflicts increased and the ideas of protectionism once again found support. Demands were made in both the United States and in Europe for protection against "undesirable" aliens. In 1885 the United States stopped the immigration of workers whose trans-Atlantic transportation had been paid by their employers (contract labor). In 1905, Great Britain passed an immigration law that prevented foreigners from entering the country unless they could support themselves. Similar legislation was demanded in Sweden and in other countries. Yet not until during the First World War did systematic immigration regulation and aliens control appear in almost every country. Legislation was later passed in the 1920s to make permanent the provisional measures taken during the war.

The second half of the nineteenth century was a time of nationalism as well as liberalism. The unification of Italy was completed in 1861, and in

Table 8.1. *Emigration to other continents from selected European countries, 1846–1932*

	Total emigration
Great Britain and Ireland	18,000,000
Italy	10,100,000
Austria-Hungary	5,200,000
Germany	4,900,000
Spain	4,700,000
Portugal	1,800,000
Sweden	1,200,000
France	520,000
Switzerland	330,000
Netherlands	220,000

1870 the German Empire was proclaimed. In 1890, when Poles were employed as foreign farm and mine workers in Prussia, the result was an open conflict between economic liberalism and German nationalism (see Chapter 6). The Poles were not allowed to take up permanent residence but had to leave Prussia for a period each year (*Karenzzeit*), lest they jeopardize the policy of Germanization under way in Prussia at that time. But the employers would not accept the loss of indispensable manpower, and they finally won the day for economic liberalism.

But nationalism grew stronger during the following decades, as highly self-conscious nation-states came to dominate Europe. When standing armies were established and voting rights were expanded, national citizenship took on new significance. Patriotic, nationalistic feelings were strengthened by growing international tensions, by increased defense expenditures, and finally by the First World War. The international ideas of peace and brotherhood advocated in the prewar years by socialist parties did not prevent citizens from answering the national call to arms in August 1914.

With the increase in nationalistic feeling came a corresponding increase in demands that "foreigners" be clearly identified and controlled. This attitude continued to affect immigration policies throughout the interwar period, although in somewhat different ways in each country. The United States drastically reduced immigration when it imposed quota systems in 1920 and 1924, although immigrants from Northern Europe retained relatively liberal entry conditions. Germany and Switzerland successively tightened their immigration control; France did the same, but still remained the most liberal immigration country during the interwar period. All countries reacted to the Great Depression with additional controls designed to protect the domestic labor market against foreign competition.

Nationalism was not the only ideological force at work during this period. Vague conceptions of race were also present. Well into the darkness of the 1930s, it was not an extreme position but a common belief that science had "proved" that certain races had qualities that placed them over and above others. Racism was one of the moral justifications cited in favor of colonialism, but it had domestic importance as well; one of its "scientific" theories was that different races should not be mixed. A people possessing a clean, pure racial heritage ought to protect themselves against the immigration of peoples with different origins.

The postwar period

Following the Second World War a radical change occurred in the immigration policies of the European countries, a change that is not easy to explain. Massive movements of people, both forced labor and refugees from war zones and occupied territories, had taken place during the war. Millions of people were uprooted, and there were fears that Western Europe would be unable to absorb the approximately ten million refugees and other displaced persons after the war. Emigration programs were even introduced to alleviate pressures caused by this surplus population. But the countries involved in the war had also lost millions of working-age men, and immigration could fill these gaps in the labor force. This became especially necessary because the pressing need to rebuild destroyed areas required a good supply of labor.

West Germany admitted refugees and persons who were forced to leave former German-speaking regions, e.g. territory that today belongs to Poland. Later on a much larger number of people came from East Germany. France placed heavy emphasis on the need for population increase and made plans for large-scale immigration. However, the official recruitment agency (ONI) never functioned as intended, and immigrants arrived spontaneously and only afterwards obtained the necessary permits. Great Britain introduced a modest program to recruit workers from Europe, but it was soon abandoned and labor needs were met by unrestricted immigration from the colonies. Sweden had found that during the war when large groups of refugees were thrown on to the labor market, this did not take away jobs from native Swedish workers. Economic policy there after the war centered around "full employment". An expansive economic policy was used, which tended to create a shortage of labor that made the recruitment of foreign workers a tempting alternative for Sweden.

Below we will continue this short history and examine the circumstances surrounding the turning point of 1970 to 1974. But first, it is important to note that immigration and immigration policy prior to this turning point had followed a similar path in all the project countries, and this pattern continued for several years after the Second World War until a whole new phase began in international migration.

During the first years after the Second World War, rapid economic growth and shortages of labor in Germany, France, and Great Britain led to various programs for recruiting foreign labor. Sweden, Switzerland, and the Netherlands met their manpower needs mostly through spontaneous immigration. No country really planned to have large-scale immigration (except possibly France), but all were ready to accept and make use of people that arrived on their own initiative. A liberal, laissez-faire ideology appeared once again, the doctrine of free trade was expressed in the GATT treaty, and efforts were made to integrate Europe both economically and also politically (e.g. the EEC and EFTA).

In the Second World War, nationalism and racism were losing ideologies. Racist ideas became almost totally discredited and were openly asserted only by extremist groups. Nationalism had been utilized as the driving force in three major European wars, in which Germany had attacked France. A new era was now envisioned, where future wars were made impossible through intensive economic cooperation. The formation of the European Coal and Steel Community was one important step in this direction, which, followed by several other agreements culminating in the treaty of Rome in 1956, led to the establishment of the European Economic Community. Economic cooperation became more and more intense, even if political cooperation lagged behind.

It is true, as has often been said, that the EEC has not had a great effect on the large-scale immigration to Europe. The argument is that both the EEC and this immigration, which came mostly from countries of emigration outside Europe, originated in the same period of international economic cooperation and aid to developing countries. The economic reconstruction of Europe was followed by rapid economic growth, and one of the preconditions for this growth was an international division of labor. Thus, nationalism in Western Europe was replaced by a renewed economic liberalism, and for international migration this meant that recruitment of foreign labor as well as spontaneous immigration of foreign workers was welcomed as a means of sustaining rapid economic growth.

Public opinion in Europe has been far from indifferent to the wave of nationalism that swept over Africa and Asia and other parts of the world as national liberation wars have been fought and new states created in Algeria, Biafra, Vietnam, etc. The Czechoslovakians in 1968 and the

Poles in 1981 also won much sympathy for those who demand the right of self-determination. During this same period, and influenced by this new nationalism in the Third World, there has arisen a new ethnicity or a new appreciation of the values of national origin, language, and "roots". By making members of the majority population more aware of the situation of the immigrant minorities, this new ethnicity may have helped make possible the discussion of multicultural policy alternatives. But large amounts of immigration have at the same time also given rise to strengthened anti-immigrant feelings among indigenous populations.

It is tempting to predict how some of these trends will develop in the immediate future. National states will continue to exist, yet they are already undergoing major changes and this process will continue. A growing international division of labor with the technical innovations that affect it give examples of the increasing interdependence of the world's national states. The population explosion, the shortage of natural resources, the threat of war and other problems will make it increasingly necessary for national states to transfer part of their sovereign rights to international bodies.

Migration pressure from developing countries may increase in the future, but Western Europe will be reluctant to allow large-scale labor immigration again. This does not mean that there will be no immigration from countries outside Europe. On the contrary, such immigration will probably increase, not in order to supply industries with cheap labor, but simply because European states will not be able to stop all immigration.

In the past, from around 1960 to the period 1970–74, labor migration to the six European project countries had assumed large proportions. Afterwards, recruitment of labor was "stopped" and labor immigration was sharply reduced. Economic conditions in both sending and receiving countries during those ten to fifteen years were favorable for heavy migration. Economic growth was slow in the countries around the Mediterranean, and living standards there were considerably lower than in the immigration countries. On the other hand, in France, Germany, the Netherlands, and Britain a period of rapid economic growth began about fifteen years after the end of the Second World War. Sweden and Switzerland had already experienced such economic growth beginning at the end of the war, and in Switzerland immigration began on a large scale in the 1950s.

Other factors also led to a need for immigrant labor. Changes in education and job expectations resulted in an upward movement of native workers from low-paid, low-status, dirty, and dangerous jobs, which were then filled by immigrants. A period of restructuring began in many industries, and those who could not compete successfully for domestic labor were forced to employ immigrant labor in order to survive. Immigrant labor quickly became a necessity for the functioning of many of the European economies.

There was a demand for immigrant labor in the heavy metal and building industries as well as in service and light consumer-goods industries, such as textiles and chemicals. There were opportunities for both skilled and unskilled workers. Firms were able to utilize their full capacity – without making structural changes – by employing more workers during periods of expansion: investment in plant modernization was sometimes postponed in favor of immediate production with more labor-intensive methods. In France new investments were encouraged by profits made thanks to a generous supply of foreign labor. An important factor in the popularity of immigration among business and political leaders was the belief that immigrant labor would serve to cushion the business cycle, i.e. when economic growth slowed down, most foreign workers would return to their home countries. This belief was institutionalized in the "rotation system" in Switzerland and Germany. But the same notion was generally accepted in the other project countries.

Germany and Switzerland had perhaps the strongest attraction for foreign workers. Economic growth has been rapid in these two countries, which enjoy high living standards and strong currencies. Germany established recruitment offices in Italy, Spain, Greece, Yugoslavia, and Turkey in an attempt to obtain the best selection of available applicants. Switzerland relied on spontaneous immigration from neighboring countries, although private recruitment also took place. As already mentioned, France made plans after the Second World War for state-directed recruitment, but the system never functioned as intended. Employers ignored it, either recruiting directly in foreign countries or simply employing the large numbers of "illegal" immigrants that entered France in the hope of finding work. After a time the state accepted this laissez-faire arrangement and control over immigration became progressively weaker. In addition, foreign workers in France were distributed more among smaller enterprises than was the case in the other project countries, and they even made an important contribution to agriculture (seasonal labor in the vineyards, for example).

Neither the Netherlands nor Britain has had as great a need for foreign labor as the other project countries. Britain's economic growth was not as rapid as Germany's or Switzerland's and it was able to rely on a steady stream of colonial or post-colonial immigrants to fill any labor shortages that arose. This may partly explain why Britain has never related immigration as closely to economic interests as other countries have. Not even the employers in Britain's low-wage industries seemed to appreciate fully the valuable contribution they received from New Commonwealth immigration. The Netherlands began its period of growth relatively late and, although organized public recruitment took place, the need for foreign labor never became acute.

Sweden has organized both public and private recruitment of labor abroad, e.g. from Yugoslavia and Greece. But most immigration has come through indirect recruitment of friends and relatives by people already working in Sweden. There is some resemblance to the French situation in that immigrants have sought employment on their own initiative as soon as jobs became available. The difference, of course, is that Sweden has never tolerated illegal immigration; the state has always been able to maintain control over the admission and employment conditions of foreign citizens.

A high standard of living exists in all of the project countries. The equivalent of a year's wages in an emigration country can often be earned in a few months in a project country. But taxes and general living conditions have meant that an immigrant's labor might bring a better return in some immigration countries than in others; moreover, accumulated savings might be worth more in the currencies of some countries, such as Germany or Switzerland. Until the 1970–74 turning point, all the states were able to maintain a relatively high level of employment; at the same time, economic growth was good – even exceptional in Germany. There has been a discussion of whether the "German miracle" would have been possible without large-scale immigration, or the question could be reversed to ask to what degree economic expansion gave rise to immigration. Regardless of the answer there is clearly a connection between growth and migration.

The turning point

Why was labor recruitment terminated and new labor immigration more or less stopped in every country during the period 1970–74? There are several reasons, and we will have to return to this question, as here we can discuss only one of the most important factors, the economic downturn that followed the first oil crisis. The oil embargo and the subsequent great increase in oil prices placed a severe strain on Western Europe's economies. A long period of restructuring began and even ten years later is still in progress. France, in particular, made a strong effort to modernize and make its industry more efficient. Part of that effort implied a reduction of France's dependence on immigrant labor.

In general, the project countries have all undergone a similar economic crisis, although not all to the same degree. Inflation and unemployment struck at the same time and economic growth dropped to almost zero. This economic downturn cannot be characterized as a temporary recession that can be cured by increased government expenditures. It required nothing less than a long-term adaptation to a new world economy, in which the total supply of natural resources is limited. Rapid economic growth could not be allowed to continue as previously, and old technologies had to be replaced by new ones. The automatization and computerization of production further reduced the demand for labor and brought about increased unemployment.

All of this has drastically changed the structure of immigration to the project countries, but it has not put an end to all immigration. Family immigration and the acceptance of refugees has continued. Most important, attempts in France and in Germany to encourage return through financial compensation have not proven successful. Even when a reduction has occurred in the number of immigrants employed, it has been less substantial than what was previously expected, and great numbers of resident foreign workers have not been expelled or otherwise sent back to their countries of origin, even when unemployed. Only in Switzerland did return migration increase. In Germany, there was instead a decrease in returns even though the unemployment rate went up. It is likely that one of the reasons for this was that Germany applied a different system of unemployment compensation to Switzerland. The immigration "stop" in Western Europe should thus be seen primarily as a halt to the recruitment of *new* foreign workers.

The "stagflationary" economy lasted unexpectedly long and hopes for an improvement were not fulfilled. Even if such an improvement should occur, it is doubtful whether immigration of foreign labor would once again resume the proportions of the 1960s. It is true that there is still such a wide gap between the living standards of immigration and emigration countries that large and perhaps growing segments of the world's population may want to emigrate to more industrialized countries. But these countries have important reasons to strictly limit their immigration, besides their poor economies.

In the beginning of the 1970s, the long-term social and cultural costs of immigration were taken seriously for the first time. In countries like Germany and Switzerland where foreign workers were considered temporary guests, the insight that a new immigrant policy was needed came later than in other countries. Immigrants and their families did not leave as a result of the new, weak economic situation. There were great risks that a dual labor market, where immigrants and their children were given the worst jobs, might become permanent, and that immigrants would have to stay in the worst housing areas. The conclusion was that a new large wave of immigration should be avoided as long as the cost of the initial wave of immigration was not yet paid for.

The economic downturn that followed the oil crisis intitiated the changes in immigration policy that we call the turning point. But it is reasonable to conclude that this turning point would probably have occurred anyhow, perhaps a little later and probably at different stages in the immigrant countries. Labor immigration had to be reduced if only because of the socioeconomic conditions that previous large-scale immigration had created. At this time, the interrelationship between regulation of immigration and immigrant policy was discovered. But the results of this realization were very different in each of the project countries.

9

Immigration regulation and aliens control

Immigration regulation is the control that a sovereign state exercises over the entry of foreign citizens and their access to residence and employment. As mentioned previously, most countries in Western Europe developed organized systems of immigration regulation at around the same time in the early 1900s. During periods of severe unemployment in the 1920s and 1930s, immigration control was strictly applied in protection of the national labor market. But we have seen that a new period of economic liberalism followed after the Second World War, once more liberalizing immigration control and opening the way for a great increase in labor migration.

Since aliens laws entrusted administrative bodies with great discretionary powers, it was not necessary in most countries to make amendments to these laws each time a more strict or a more liberal immigration regulation was introduced. What was needed was only a change in the application of existing provisions of the laws. But in Britain new legislation was continuously introduced in order to limit the size of colonial immigration.

In this chapter we shall compare regulation both before and after the turning point in the early 1970s, and discuss what kind of regulation has been used in countries with guestworker systems and in those countries with a system of permanent immigration. We shall also ask why Germany has not been willing to acknowledge a large, de facto permanent immigration, and why Sweden has not applied a guestworker system. As we have seen in the previous chapter, some explanations to this may be found in each country's history and immigration traditions (for instance, Germany's employment of foreign labor before 1914 and during both wars), or in a history of relations between immigration and emigration countries (as for instance Britain's colonial past). In sum, immigration policy has, like anything, been influenced by historical precedents and by traditional patterns of behavior.

At the same time, immigration policy has first of all been influenced by economic considerations, such as the current labor market situation at a particular time, and the profitability in the short and long term of immigrant labor. These economic considerations will, however, as we have observed in the previous discussion, often conflict with nationalistic interests. Too sizeable immigration is considered "over-foreignization" in Switzerland, for instance, and whites in Britain have reacted when immigration from Pakistan, India and the West Indies results in a heavy concentration of non-whites in some housing areas.

Guestworker systems and permanent systems

Germany and Switzerland have often been characterized as having rotation or guestworker systems. Great Britain and Sweden, on the other hand, represent the diametrical opposition, i.e. systems of permanent immigration. France and the Netherlands are said to fall somewhere in between the two poles.

On closer inspection, a number of objections may be raised concerning this placement of each of the project countries. The British and Swedish systems are not permanent in all respects, and the rotation or guestworker systems have not really functioned all the time. Yet it is still possible that the simplified labels partly reflect the true picture.

A rotational system, in the purest sense, would require the replacement of departed "guests" with new workers employed under the same temporal restrictions; the Swiss system of seasonal workers comes very close to this ideal model, although even there workers are allowed to return as often as they can find a job after spending a couple of months outside the country. None of the project countries has ever carried the rotation system to its logical extreme, i.e. the massive use of forced repatriation.

In a rotation or guestworker system, individual immigrants are issued work and residence permits valid for a limited time only and often the work permits are tied to a specific job (sometimes a specific employer). Family reunification is not encouraged, and immigrant policy measures such as good housing or language instruction are given little attention. Education for immigrant children is not directed to preparing them for a prolonged stay in the country of immigration but for the return, e.g. through teaching immigrant students their mother-tongue languages, as has been the case in some *Länder* in Germany, e.g. Bavaria.

The basic idea in a rotation system is that foreign workers will be needed only temporarily. In the host countries, they are offered better working conditions than those they can obtain in their own countries, yet below the average in the host country. The sending countries benefit because they can place part of their surplus manpower and in exchange receive valuable foreign currency from savings sent to relatives who have stayed in the home country. The sending countries also hope that the workers who are temporarily abroad will later bring back technical skills learned in the countries of immigration, though this does not often happen.

This ideal type of rotation has never materialized, however, for many reasons. The period of postwar economic expansion lasted throughout the 1950s and 1960s, and a recession – which many expected – either did not occur or, to the extent that it did, never forced large numbers of foreign workers to return home. In 1966–67, however, quite a number of foreign workers left Germany to return home, but when there was a new downturn in economic development at the beginning of the 1970s, return migration of the same size did not occur. Among other reasons, this was because the average duration of stay in Germany had become much longer, because wage increases in Germany meant that an individual lost much more by returning home, and because the recession also hit the countries of emigration where unemployment and underemployment were already severe.

In the 1970s there were significant reductions in the number of foreign citizens in the labor force in Germany, but they included only a part of the country's immigrant labor. Moreover, large-scale immigration of family members kept the size of the foreign population at roughly the same level as before.

Sweden and Britain provide examples of a policy of permanent immigration. But neither of these two countries view permanent immigration, as is often done, as a means to a long-term increase in population, or for the cultivation of new land or the colonization of new territory. Permanent immigration in Sweden and Britain has been characterized not by a policy of unlimited immigration over open borders, but by the granting of a guarantee to immigrants who have been admitted that they will not be forced to leave the country again. The choice of return is open for them, but it is their choice. It is not the policy of Sweden nor of Britain to presuppose that foreign citizens will actually return. The assumption is the opposite, that they will probably decide to stay, and that immigration policy shall be organized with this in mind.

From first permit to permanent status

The most decisive criterion in judging systems of immigration regulation is whether and under what conditions permanent status is granted. In a guestworker system the basic principle is of course that immigration is temporary and the immigrants shall for this reason not be given any guarantees that they can stay permanently in the country. And if the time period is not always definitely determined from the beginning, a system of periodic permits, which gives the host country an opportunity to decide whether the guests are wanted for still another period, is used.

In a permanent regulation system, on the other hand, it is intended that immigrants settle for an indefinite period, if they so wish. To control the quality of individual immigrants, the state may issue some kind of first permit for a shorter duration. But within a reasonable time, a clear guarantee of a permanent stay in the host country is given. However, the granting of this permanent status does not also imply that naturalization will follow after a number of years. Full citizenship is often easier to acquire in the permanent system than in the guestworker system, but it may be obtained in both. Guarantees for permanent residence are, however, of more immediate concern to immigrants than citizenship.

The longer foreign citizens reside in any country, the more likely it is that their permits will be extended and that they will be granted permanent status, i.e. permanent residence and work permits. In other words there is a certain process through which immigrants establish themselves as permanent residents. Our first concern will be a discussion of this road towards a guaranteed place in the host society.

Temporary status

At the time of the first application for immigration, foreigners must declare whether they intend to stay longer than the specified time that is allowed tourists and other visitors (usually three to six months). If they want to stay longer, they must obtain a residence permit, often before crossing the border. The initial permit, normally valid for one year, may in some countries restrict the holder to residence in certain regions.

Immigrants are usually not granted a residence permit unless they can prove that they have sufficient means of support. To take employment in the host country, they must obtain a work permit, also first issued for one year only. In addition, a work permit is usually valid only for employment within a certain occupation, and it may be restricted to a certain employer (Switzerland) or a certain geographic region (France, Switzerland). New immigrants must wait a further period of time before they can send for their families, and family members are not always automatically given work permits, even when they are admitted as residents.

Thus, a new immigrant has an insecure and restricted position in all of the project countries (though to a varying extent). In this respect their position differs greatly from that of some "privileged" aliens. We refer here to those who are citizens of EEC countries and who are "privileged" in Germany, the Netherlands, France and, since 1973, Britain, as well as to those who are citizens of the Scandinavian countries and who are "privileged" in Sweden. These "privileged" aliens generally either do not need work and residence permits or receive them automatically, thus proceeding immediately to a state of security and freedom that ordinary immigrants do not reach for some years. The same holds true for political refugees, but only for those who are granted political asylum or who are given a corresponding "privileged" status.

When permits expire, they may be renewed for successively longer durations (France, the Netherlands) or for additional intervals of one year (Switzerland, Britain, Germany). Sometimes a renewal implies a relaxation in previous occupational restrictions. But none of the project countries completely guarantees that work and residence permits will be renewed. There are wide variations from country to country, both in legal procedures and in the extent of discretionary power given to individual officials responsible for decisions in regard to these permits.

In France, Switzerland, the Netherlands, and Germany this power lies largely in the hands of local officials. In Britain such arbitrary decisions are made by central civil servants in the Home Office. Decisions on permit renewals in Sweden are not completely free from this arbitrariness, either. But Sweden's permanent immigration policy has meant that renewal of residence and work permits is almost automatic after one year. In Germany and Switzerland the renewal of temporary permits depends heavily on labor market conditions. If, for instance, an immigrant is unemployed for longer than the period for which unemployment benefits are given or for longer than the five months stipulated in the ILO convention of 1974, their permits will not be renewed and they may be expelled from the host country.

Permanent status

A permanent resident and work permit usually entitles an immigrant to reside anywhere in the host country for an unlimited period of time and to work in any occupation. Furthermore, it gives an immigrant the right to bring in his spouse and dependent children, who will themselves receive permanent status, which usually includes the right to work. An immigrant with permanent status has in short most of the rights – and duties – of a citizen in social and civil matters (though not necessarily in political ones). But the granting of permanent status is sometimes arbitrarily made, and it may be limited in duration.

The project countries differ in their minimum requirements for obtaining permanent status. Germany and Switzerland require eight and ten years' residence respectively. In Switzerland seasonal workers do not qualify even if they have stayed in the country for ten years, since only years of residence with a regular work permit are counted. In Britain and France the required time is at least four years, and in the Netherlands three to five, depending on the kind of permit. Sweden, finally, has set the shortest residence requirement, demanding only one year of legal stay in the country.

Each country makes exception for certain groups of immigrants who are granted permanent status earlier or even automatically. These are usually the same groups that have already been mentioned, the so-called "privileged" groups. Immigrants within the EEC system have a right to permanent status if they have an offer of employment in one of the member states; they must first obtain a permanent work permit, but this is usually granted automatically. If they become unemployed, however, they can lose their permanent status. Scandinavian and Finnish immigrants in Sweden are exempt from all permits and enjoy full freedom to take up residence and work. In Britain persons defined as "patrials" may live and work in the country without a permit, and they have a right to permanent status.

Immigrants who are not members of such "privileged" groups are seldom guaranteed permanent status, even when they have fulfilled the prescribed residence requirements. In each country these requirements are necessary but not sufficient for an automatic or legally guaranteed permanent status. Only Sweden has a kind of a legally guaranteed system of permanent status. With the advent of the Mitterrand government in France, the grounds for refusing permanent status have become more clearly defined. In Britain and in the Netherlands the decisions of administrative officials carry considerable weight. But most interesting are the striking differences in this respect between Switzerland and Germany.

As mentioned, Germany requires eight and Switzerland ten years of residence for an unlimited permit to reside and work in the country. And immigrants – other than the "privileged" EEC citizens in Germany – have no right to permanent status even after this long period of time. The final decision rests with the relevant administrative officials, who may use their discretion in judging an application for permanent status. Nevertheless, the results in Germany and Switzerland vary considerably in this regard. In Germany, fewer than 25 percent of foreign citizens had obtained permanent status in 1982, while about 75 percent of foreign citizens in Switzerland had done so. The reason is that the Swiss permits have been given more or less automatically, while a long list of conditions discourage immigrants in Germany from applying or from making appeals against rejections.

Naturalization

It is somewhat easier to become naturalized in Germany than in Switzerland, although naturalization in both countries is more difficult and less common than in the other project countries. The result is that

Germany gives less security than the other countries even to those who have resided and worked for more than ten years in the country. In Switzerland the corresponding immigrant group obtains a permanent status which gives them most of the rights of Swiss citizens, but the great majority do not expect ever to be naturalized.

It is true for all the countries, however, that only a small proportion of the total immigrant population asks for and obtains naturalization. This is because many immigrants, no matter how long they have lived abroad, do not consider their stay permanent enough and hope to return some day to their native country. These immigrants are obviously reluctant to change citizenship. Other immigrants plan to stay permanently but prefer nevertheless to retain their own nationality. Although they do not have the right to vote (except for local elections in some countries, for example Sweden), they are in most other respects guaranteed a secure and equal standing. In fact, when they have finally acquired permanent status, there often remains little incentive to strive for naturalization.

In France and Sweden the rate of naturalization is a little higher than in the other countries, indicating that it is relatively easy to acquire citizenship. Their residence requirement of 5 years is the same as in Britain and the Netherlands. Only Germany (10 years) and Switzerland (12 years) have much longer residence requirements.

Family immigration

In guestworker systems, it is preferred that foreign workers are not accompanied by family members. They should come alone, as this stimulates natural return, which is good for the rotation system, and results in large remittances, which is good for the sending countries. In Germany and Switzerland, family immigration has been limited because immigrants have to wait as long as three years before being allowed to send for their dependents. After the "turning point", Germany ruled that family members who had arrived after a certain date (a so-called *Stichtag*) would not be given work permits.

France has made some attempts to reduce family immigration, which has nevertheless been substantial, and was never stopped by enforcement of strict regulations. After some initial hesitation, the Netherlands also applied relatively liberal rules regarding family immigration for foreign workers from the Mediterranean area. Family immigration was of course never questioned for post-colonial immigrants. Sweden and Britain have in principle favored the admission of whole families, but even here delays have occurred, especially as immigration agencies have had to check that people have not tried to cheat the control system.

Finally, any comparisons between the project countries concerning family immigration are substantiated by sex and age statistics. Permanent immigration systems result in a higher share of married women and dependent children than rotation systems.

Labor immigration: spontaneous and by recruitment

Since business and industry have not always been able or willing to carry out long-term planning and investment, they have often taken recourse to short-term measures to alleviate their problems. Employment of foreign labor is a short-term measure of this kind, and when private firms ask for permission to start recruitment they are often backed by the state, which sees it as fostering economic growth which is in the national interest. Recruitment may then be organized either by the state, as in Germany, or by private companies, as in Switzerland. Sweden and other countries actually used both methods simultaneously.

Germany, and eventually the Netherlands, carried public recruitment further than other countries. Treaties were made with several emigration countries, and a number of recruitment offices for the selection of the most suitable workers were opened. France established a state organization to administer recruitment (ONI), but it was cumbersome and unpopular with employers, who preferred either to recruit their own workers abroad or to hire the many illegal immigrants who had entered the country on their own initiative. The French government condoned this situation by allowing immigrants "without papers" to apply for and receive work and residence permits, sometimes even long after entering the country. This practice of "regularization" became one of France's substitutes for recruitment.

The Netherlands before 1971 and Sweden before the turning point in 1972 also needed manpower, and labor transfer treaties were signed with several countries, among them Yugoslavia and Turkey. In Sweden, individual firms were permitted to recruit foreign workers, who were then granted work permits. State-organized recruitment was not developed to an important extent. Nevertheless, by making it easy to obtain the necessary permits and by offering some assistance to immigrants after arrival, it was made clear that foreign labor was necessary and welcome.

Conclusions are not easily found. The relation that might have been expected between guestworker systems and state organized recruitment of foreign labor is found only in Germany. Switzerland has not used public recruitment, while Sweden, a country of permanent immigration, has.

We might risk the conclusion that a guestworker policy will make use of active public recruitment as long as it cannot otherwise obtain enough foreign labor to meet its manpower demands. But when spontaneous immigration is extensive, as it was during this period in all of the project countries, the role of recruitment is reduced or completely abandoned.

Why guestworker systems?

During the 1950s and 1960s none of the project countries made plans for large-scale, permanent immigration, but everywhere foreign labor was increasingly employed and often directly recruited. Aliens laws from the previous interwar and war periods were used for individual controls of foreign citizens more than for regulation of labor immigration, which was left, in a laissez-faire manner, to the free interplay of economic factors on the international labor market. The six project countries developed different strategies for dealing with this new situation, and we have tried to rank these strategies on a rough scale from a guestworker to a permanent system of immigration.

We have also seen that public recruitment of foreign labor is not clearly related to this scale, and we have noted that the unwillingness to accept family reunification and the reluctance to grant the right to permanent residence are outstanding characteristics of the guestworker systems. We have found that Germany has remained committed to this system, as it has not improved the insecure status of its foreign residents, even for those having more than ten years of residence. In a referendum in June 1982, the Swiss people decided not to change the rules that keep most seasonal workers outside the regular Swiss labor market. These rules hold that only those who for five consecutive years have worked for at least 40 months in Switzerland meet the requirements set for a one year regular work permit. And only those who have held such work permits for ten years qualify for a permanent work permit. Even so, three out of four of Switzerland's non-seasonal foreign population have already obtained such permanent status, which for them means an end to rotation.

Even though France has taken measures after its immigration stop in 1974 to increase return migration, and to limit family reunification, France has never applied a rotation system of the same kind as Germany or Switzerland. Instead France has allowed large spontaneous or even illegal immigration which has been regularized after the immigrants' arrival and employment in France. The French system resembles the German and Swiss, however, not only in the size of labor immigration but also in the insecure status of much of the foreign population. Indeed, both illegal immigrants and many foreign workers with short-term permits have lived for extended periods under the threat of deportation from France. But in contrast to Germany and Switzerland, there is better opportunity for those legally admitted or regularized to obtain permanent status and even French citizenship. Immigration is especially encouraged for those who speak French and who are thought able to adopt French culture. In short, France has not officially adopted a guestworker policy, but the results have been much the same.

An element of guestworker policy might be said to have existed also in the Netherlands as long as the illusion remained that foreign workers from the Mediterranean area would stay only temporarily. The 1974 proposal to give returners a bonus of 5,000 guilders also reflects the thinking of a rotation policy. But this proposal was rejected, and Dutch policy has become more and more directed towards permanent residence and integration of the foreign population.

British immigration, finally, has consisted almost completely of over-seas migration. Though there was in fact a shortage of manpower in British industries in the early 1960s, all efforts from 1962 on were directed towards reducing further migration. Traditional commitments to the Commonwealth made this difficult and precluded the alternative of treat-ing those already admitted in Britain as temporary guestworkers. They obviously had no intention of returning and had to be considered as permanent immigrants.

We cannot point to one or two specific explanations of why the systems of Germany and Switzerland definitely became guestworker systems, why France and the Netherlands during one period followed the same path, and why those of Britain and Sweden are permanent systems. Factors that may have contributed to this development have already been mentioned both in the national chapters and in this comparative section. Some of these factors, which will be summarized in the next few pages, are histori-cal traditions and socioeconomic preconditions. Others are perceptions of these traditions and preconditions. Some of the explanation is geographi-cal and historical, the difference between post-colonial and labor immi-gration. Some is from the experience of previous immigration. We shall also need to consider whether the state of a nation is challenged when large-scale immigration takes place.

Another group of factors that may help us explain the outcome is related to a lack of policy planning, as well as to a lack of deeper under-standing of the long-term effects of large-scale immigration. As we have noted, the interrelation between regulation of immigration and immigrant policy was long neglected. The time frame of politicians is often short and this may explain their illusion that workers will return to their own coun-tries.

Sweden, Germany and Switzerland lack parallels to the colonial and post-colonial immigration of Britain, France and the Netherlands. This implies that the former have not received large numbers of "colored" immigrants as the latter countries have. It further implies that the latter have long maintained, and even made efforts to continue, their old ties to the former colonies. As a consequence, preferential treatment has been given to post-colonial immigrants. And when political disturbances have occurred in former colonies, they have often led to migration to the old mother country; Eurasians and Moluccans to the Netherlands, Indians from Kenya and Uganda to Britain, etc. But in all three countries, with the possible exception of the Netherlands, immigration from colonies or former colonies for the purpose of seeking employment has been of far greater importance than the arrival of refugee groups. The existence of colonial ties has in many cases limited the control of immigration, either because the immigrants held, or claimed the right to, the citizenship of the mother country, or because agreements were reached with their home countries that allowed them to enter with few or no restrictions. This problem has been especially acute for Great Britain, as we have noted previously.

International relations and foreign policy considerations have also affected immigration to Sweden, Germany, and Switzerland. This is apparent from the nationalities of the largest immigrant groups in each country. Italians and Germans have traditionally dominated immigration to Switzerland; Turks, Yugoslavs, and Greeks form the largest groups in Germany and are also significant in Sweden, although the largest immigration there has come from the neighboring Scandinavian countries, especially from Finland.

Immigration from colonies and former colonies has tended to be more permanent than have other kinds of migration. Above all, movements to Britain and the Netherlands have gone markedly in *one* direction only. Those that have arrived have either not planned to return or have not been able to do so (e.g. Moluccans in the Netherlands). Differences in living standards between the colonies and the mother country are usually so great that re-migration seldom seems an attractive option. One exception to this pattern, however, is the case of Algerians in France, many of whom returned after temporary employment. This may reflect the shorter distances involved and the less attractive conditions offered in France, or may follow because this migration resembles labor migration more than post-colonial migration.

Of the three countries without post-colonial immigration, Sweden is the only one which applied a system of permanent immigration at an early date. It is a reasonable assumption that one explanation for this exception is the history of Swedish–Finnish relations. Finland was in the past one part of the kingdom of Sweden and there is an historical Swedish-language minority in Finland as well as an immigrant Finnish-language minority in

Tornedalen in Sweden. The Scandinavian countries are divided on defense issues and an economic union has never been successfully established; nevertheless, since 1954 there has been a free Nordic labor market, and cooperation and communication is close (around 60 percent of foreign residents in Sweden come from one of the Scandinavian countries, with about 45 percent coming from Finland). It was in this situation that Sweden decided that all immigrants should be given the same permanent status that the Scandinavians were entitled to. Sweden's policy was at least partly an outcome of its preferential treatment of the Finns caused by historical reasons and because of good inter-Nordic relations.

The two countries with the most permanent systems, Britain and Sweden, are geographically speaking a little more remote from the migratory movements on the European continent than the other four. It might be easier for them to establish efficient immigration control at their borders, and such a control may be considered a prerequisite of a system that gives permanent status to all once they are admitted to the country. But this point should not be given too much weight, since border controls are never absolutely effective and since immigrants are constantly able to find new ways to evade the controls.

More important in explaining the evolution of permanent or guestworker systems, are perceptions of previous experiences with large-scale immigration. Already at the beginning of this century both France and Switzerland were major immigration countries, and for just as long Germany has made repeated use of temporary labor from abroad. In Germany, the new labor immigration of the 1960s was for this reason perceived as another example of what had occurred several times before, and re-migration was anticipated because it had taken place previously.

We should also recall our previous discussion of the new economic liberalism during this period, which is closely related to an intensive European economic cooperation. Transnational relations have emerged quickly, and outspoken nationalism was not in vogue. The project countries differ strongly, however, in their national identities, in their cultures, languages, and political roles, and large-scale immigration of foreign nationalities may have been a challenge to these determinants of national identity.

Britain, France and Germany are great powers with 50–60 million inhabitants, while Switzerland, Sweden, and the Netherlands are small states with only 6–14 million. More important than this, however, is the fact that English and French are international languages, and together with German, are also traditional languages of culture. Dutch is spoken mainly in the Netherlands, and Swedish only in Sweden and Finland. This difference has implications for immigrants' motivation to learn the host country's language as well as for attitudes in the host country towards what language skills may be expected from the immigrants. Countries with "world languages" – and this includes Switzerland too – tend to expect much more than the countries with little-used languages.

By tradition, Switzerland and the Netherlands are multicultural states, but organized in very different ways. In Switzerland, there are eighteen German-speaking cantons, while four are French-speaking, one is Italian-speaking, two are German and French-speaking, and one, Graubünden, is a specific case where the languages are Rhaeto-Romanic, German and Italian. There is a consensus that this numerical balance, which has been established between the national languages, must not be changed. Immigration must not be allowed to upset the order, but since citizens alone are counted for purposes of this numerical balance, permanent immigrants are allowed.

In Switzerland, however, there are several divisions along religious, class, rural–urban, and regional lines, as well as the language divisions. Cohesion in this system is achieved through numerous criss-crossing ties, combining membership in various subgroups. The Netherlands, on the other hand, has only one national language, although Frisian and several dialects are also spoken, but cultural pluralism has meant a division of the country from the top to the bottom, organizing most human activities within the boundaries of religion and class. This traditional "pillarization", as it is called, has recently broken down, but the tradition may have helped to promote the new minority policy for immigrants in the Netherlands.

A contrast is Sweden with a traditionally homogeneous culture. Only the immigration over the recent decades has resulted in some multicultural traits. It is often said that large-scale immigration is more of a challenge to a society without multicultural traditions (like Sweden), than to a country with such traditions (like the Netherlands), but if the proportions of the ethnic or cultural groups are already defined (like Switzerland) the opposite might be true.

The identity of a nation is related to the status of its language and to its ethnic homogeneity or heterogeneity, but also to its political role. The French conviction of the superiority of the French language and culture has meant that those immigrants who are willing and able to learn French have been accepted, while those who were not expected to succeed in this were not desired. France's mission in the world is seen as primarily cultural rather than political, but it is important to take into account that for several hundred years France has been a well-established nation state with about the same borders as it has today.

Divided since 1945, Germany has remained in a formal state of constitutional insecurity, and West Berlin is still under control of the four allied powers that won the Second World War. The future of the German nation cannot even be openly discussed, both because of the superpowers' conflicting interests and because of the condemnation of German national-socialism. Under these circumstances large-scale labor immigration has caused a situation that has been difficult to handle. Four million foreign citizens living in Germany constitute a challenge to German nationality, and an answer is needed to the question of the nation's future. But such an answer is not available, and a reasonable defense is therefore to play down the question and argue that there is no "real" immigration to Germany, only a temporary guestworker program.

What has been said here is of course only speculation about how policy differences might be explained. We have pointed to historical factors like previous immigration and post-colonial commitments or international ties, and we have emphasized the status of language, homogeneity of the nation, and finally the perception of the role and status of the nation. Other explanations need to be discussed, however, but as they are related to the interrelation between regulation of immigration and immigrant policy, we will postpone this part of our discussion until we have compared immigrant policy.

10

Immigrant policy

Immigrant policy slowly began to develop for several reasons. When the size of the immigrant population increased, especially the number of immigrant families, it placed burdens on the social services and led to demands from social workers for greater resources and pleas from local authorities for national or federal assistance. In some countries this development was hastened by public protests or the fear of public protests and by disorders and sometimes actual riots. When the turning point came in the early 1970s, one of the reasons cited for stopping labor immigration was to avoid exacerbating the social problems of resident immigrants. As a result of the "stop" the immigrant population became more stable. Those who returned home could not remigrate, which meant that most chose to remain; they usually qualified for permanent status and were able to send for their families to join them. Large immigrant groups were becoming potential "immigrant minorities" with special needs and problems. Immigrant policy developed as a response to this new situation.

When large-scale labor migration began, no country had an organized national immigrant policy. Voluntary organizations took care of some immigrant problems and local welfare agencies offered assistance, but in general there was no long-term planning and very little understanding of the possible effects of immigration. In guestworker countries where immigration was officially regarded as being only temporary there was no need for a comprehensive immigrant policy. The feeling was that if special arrangements were made for immigrants, they ought to encompass, for instance, temporary housing or education that prepared immigrant children for transfer to schools in their parents' country when they returned. In other countries, where integration or even assimilation was the dominant policy goal, policymakers assumed that the tools of general social welfare would provide the quickest results. This assumption was even stronger in the case of post-colonial immigrants: since they were usually citizens and since several of these groups could already understand the host country's language, no special help was considered necessary.

In Britain and in Sweden, immigrant policy started relatively early. Each time the British regulation of immigration was made more restrictive, it was combined with new legislation against racial discrimination. The living conditions of immigrants were affected to such an extent by discrimination that an improved application of anti-discrimination laws and an active effort to change public opinion were considered the most urgent policy measures. Sweden made two simultaneous decisions at the end of the 1960s: first, that immigrants should be considered permanent residents, and second, that the aim of immigrant policy was to offer immigrants in Sweden conditions equal to those offered to comparable groups of Swedes. Immigrant policy in the Netherlands was not the same for all national immigrant groups for a long time, and only during the past few years has a new "ethnic minorities policy" been developed. This policy recognizes immigrants as special subjects of government attention and aims at their socioeconomic integration and at pluralism in cultural matters. French immigrant policy also started late, although a housing policy for immigrants came early in response to the *bidonvilles* of the 1960s.

During the 1970s, immigrant policy was gradually extended in all of the project countries, including Switzerland and Germany, even though Switzerland has in principle been content to provide only the social welfare services given to all residents of the country. Special measures to improve the socioeconomic conditions of immigrants have not even been proposed by the different pro-immigrant groups struggling to end discrimination against resident foreigners in Switzerland. These groups are in fact convinced that such special measures would be misinterpreted as "reverse discrimination" by the Swiss public and thus serve only to aggravate the anti-foreigner mood that already exists.

In Germany a slow change started, when labor recruitment was terminated in the autumn of 1974 and family immigration continued and even increased, encouraged by a new regulation in 1975 that gave parents a much higher child allowance for children in Germany than for example in Turkey. The belief in return migration was found to be uncertain and at least for the time being immigrants had to be – as it was paradoxically called – "temporarily integrated".

In sum, guestworker countries have started later and invested less in immigrant policy than countries that aimed at permanent immigration. But the difference also depends on political traditions and ideologies. All of the countries are democracies with multiparty systems, political elections, and freedom of expression. It is hardly likely, however, that variations in political structures or in the ideological orientations of the political parties in power can explain differences in immigrant policy. It is more likely that ideological differences *between* the individual countries rather than *within* them have been most decisive.

All six countries combine high standards of living with well-developed social security systems, and all have labor union traditions, although even here the differences are significant. In the immigration countries, in contrast to the emigration countries, the state bears more responsibility for people that need help when sick, unemployed, aged, and so forth. But this responsibility is carried to a different extent in the different countries. In Sweden, for example, the state's responsibility is greater than in Germany, and much greater than in Switzerland.

There are many examples of this difference. Private individuals may need to take greater or lesser care for their own security through special measures, such as insurance. When unemployment strikes, the number and type of labor market remedies varies. Social services for immigrants may also be organized in different ways. In Sweden, Britain,and to a large extent the Netherlands, state and local authorities take charge of immigrants' needs. In the other project countries, however, this responsibility is assumed by voluntary organizations and religious congregations, particularly in social or cultural matters. Financial support may often come from public funds, but the implementation of social policy is left, at least in part, to voluntary organizations.

Sweden and Switzerland are good examples of how different social philosophies can influence immigration policy. The strong drive for equality in Sweden's general social policy has led to demands for both an active immigrant policy and a limitation on the size of immigration. In the Swedish political climate, where government regulations abound, it is not strange that immigrant policy has become highly organized. In Switzerland, on the other hand, emphasis is placed on the individual's responsibility (and ability) to solve most of his own problems; government regulations and intrusions are avoided if possible. Therefore, demands for equality have not been pushed by the Swiss state as they have been in Sweden. Other issues, especially those concerning the economy and the national culture, have been more decisive in determining the size of immigration.

Direct and indirect immigrant policies

In the following discussion a distinction will be made between direct and indirect immigrant policies. We will use the term "direct" immigrant policy to designate government measures in which the instruments used and the programs developed are intended specifically for immigrants; for example, language training, interpreter and information services, special immigrant housing, special classes or schools for immigrant children, and so on. We will use the term "indirect" immigrant policy to designate government measures that are intended to affect all members of the community, including immigrants.

While indirect immigrant policy reflects a country's general social ideology, direct immigrant policy is also an expression of its overall immigration policy. This policy has been officially and explicitly formulated in only two countries, Sweden (1968 and 1975) and the Netherlands (1981), although there is some kind of policy in the other countries as well. It has gradually developed in response to the realization that immigration is not always temporary, but is in fact usually permanent and creates an imperative need for certain social and educational measures.

As regards economic conditions, immigrant policies can be called inequitable or discriminatory when the resources of the host country are distributed unfairly, leaving immigrants with a smaller share than other inhabitants in the same profession, same age group and so on. When immigrants have few social contacts with the indigenous population, it may be the result of an immigration policy based on segregation rather than integration. The central issue usually is, however, whether direct immigrant policy should aim at the assimilation of immigrants or at giving them the opportunity to retain and develop their native languages and cultures.

Labor market

Labor unions have accepted the large-scale immigration of the past with astonishingly few protests. Like other groups in the immigration countries, unions seem not to have realized just how large immigration would become; not until after the "stop" did they begin to reevaluate their position. Unions in Sweden seem to have exercised a heavier influence over immigration policy than have unions in the other countries. This influence derives both from the unusually high degree of unionization among industrial workers (over 90 percent) and office workers (over 70 percent), and from the unions' close relations with the Social Democratic Party that formed the government until 1976 and again from 1982.

Immigrants have not tried to build their own unions in any of the project countries, although conflicts have occurred, including wildcat strikes, in which immigrants took part. Immigrants have for the most part joined the established unions; in fact, this has often been required by the unions before they would accept the entrance of foreign workers in the first place. Immigrants have formed only a minority of the membership and the unions have continued to concentrate on promoting the interests of domestic workers. For this reason it has taken a relatively long time for the special needs of immigrant membersto be taken into account by the trade unions, and for immigrants themselves to reach positions as union representatives.

Trade unions usually demand that all workers, regardless of citizenship, be offered the same wage and work standards. If these demands were not met, foreign labor would become cheaper than domestic labor and the interests of the unions' members would be directly damaged. In principle this demand has been met in every project country. In some, however, immigration has led to the creation of dual labor markets, in which unskilled workers have been directed to certain occupations and only allowed to compete for those jobs. To a certain extent, this situation has developed in all of the project countries: there is a large proportion of immigrant labor in occupations that are considered undesirable by domestic workers, at least in relation to the wages and work conditions offered.

Some countries have directly limited the access of immigrants to parts of the labor market by issuing work permits that are only valid for certain occupations or employers. Even where this has not occurred, however, the results have often been the same. Immigrants have concentrated in certain occupations because of poor ability to speak the language and lack of vocational education, because of discrimination by employers or trade unions as well as because of chain employment, i.e. that new immigrants were recruited by friends and relatives already employed in the same firm. Equal wages and working conditions are required in principle, but immigrants usually do not have access to the same kinds of jobs. The two labor markets are not isolated from one another, however, and some nationality groups succeed better than others in passing the invisible boundary.

A third labor market, for illegal immigrants, may also exist, on which foreign workers are forced to accept low wages and poor working conditions. They must do without, for example, insurance protection and pension benefits; they lack trade union support and therefore become totally dependent on their employers.

We will return later to a discussion of illegal immigration in general. But here we must take note of the fact that the use of illegal labor has been particularly great in France, where numbers were assumed to be about 300,000 at the time President Mitterrand was elected in 1981. It was promised that this would all be legalized, but the conditions set were such that most never was. Germany and the Netherlands also have significant numbers of illegal foreign workers, a problem that has been especially hard to control in Germany. Britain, Switzerland and Sweden, on the other hand, have had few illegal workers.

The project countries have made a relatively comprehensive attempt to help immigrants achieve greater mobility within the existing "dual" labor market. Most of the countries have provided language instruction, vocational education, and special help in finding employment with this aim in mind. In 1973 Sweden went a step further in this area by requiring employers to pay the wages of their foreign workers during 240 hours of language instruction and by providing attractive and very extensive labor market training. Nevertheless, in every country the general conditions of the labor market, which depend in large part on agreements between business and labor, have determined how immigrants are treated. The kinds of special measures characteristic of direct immigrant policy have seldom been used.

Housing
When employers have gone abroad to recruit workers, they have usually had to bear responsibility for providing housing based on certain minimum standards. If foreign workers in Germany and France, for instance, were only supposed to stay temporarily, their quarters did not need to be anything more than simple and provisionary. In a similar fashion the Netherlands, when it accepted Moluccan refugees, was content to provide simple barracks on the assumption that the Moluccans would soon be leaving again. This also happened in Switzerland, and in Sweden, where young foreign workers were initially offered similar types of company housing.

After a period of time, however, and especially if family members were allowed to enter, immigrants went to the regular housing market and began to compete with natives and with other immigrants who arrived spontaneously and therefore seldom received company housing. Once this occurred, the host country's general housing conditions determined what kind of standards immigrants could expect. Additional factors made their situation even worse than that of a comparable native. For one thing, as new arrivals immigrants ended up at the end of the list for good residences with low rents. They were usually either unable or unwilling to buy a residence since they did not intend to remain permanently. Immigrants in Britain are an exception, however; many of them have bought small houses, in part because they plan to stay permanently and in part because they have had no better option. Finally, immigrants are often subject to discrimination by landlords and thus forced to live where they are tolerated. The result of these factors has been nearly the same in all of the project countries: immigrants live concentrated in particular residential areas where the housing standards are often low and the rooms overcrowded.

Different measures have been planned or implemented to try to correct this situation. Attempts have been made in Germany and the Netherlands, among other places, to prevent immigrants from becoming too concentrated in certain areas. Before 1970 the large slum areas in France, the *bidonvilles*, were successively vacated and the occupants offered alternative housing, sometimes built for them under special programs. Immigrants in Germany have gradually sought better housing on their own, but the concentration of nationalities in the larger cities is still so strong that in some areas special ethnic quarters or districts can be observed. Efforts in Britain have centered on general Community Development projects aimed at improving the housing conditions of all residents in certain "inner city" areas, the hope being that immigrants in particular will benefit from the improvements.

Immigrants' housing conditions, in particular the concentration of certain nationalities in the same residential area, is of utmost importance for the planning of immigrant policy. It has gradually become more obvious that the geographical dispersion of immigrants adversely affects, among other things, the possibilities for communities to arrange language instruction and the education of immigrant children, as well as opportunities to form organizations thatcan promote these cultural activities. In spite of this, however, only France has actually tried, as we have seen, to intervene with special housing measures for immigrants, and these have been insufficient. The Netherlands has assigned different kinds of housing to different immigrant groups on the basis of whether they were expected to integrate or to return home soon. In the other project countries, policymakers have been content to let immigrants fall under general housing policy and have been reluctant to recognize their special difficulties and needs. In other words, policymakers have abstained from applying a direct immigrant policy to housing issues.

Education

One consequence of the immigrant housing situation is that immigrant children become concentrated in particular schools where instruction is strongly affected by the presence of many pupils with another linguistic and cultural background. In some cases this has hindered normal instruction so much that the parents of native children have protested. After one such protest in Britain the authorities decided on a policy of dispersing immigrant children, but could not stick to it. Some parents in Sweden have even demanded that their children attend only classes where all pupils have Swedish as their mother tongue; in support of this position they cite the requests made by Finnish parents that their children be placed in classes where everyone's mother tongue is Finnish. In Germany, on occasion, Turkish has become the dominant mother tongue in some schools at the same time as German remains the official language of instruction.

Schools with a high percentage of immigrant pupils have been forced to change and adapt their instruction to these pupils' special needs. Even in Switzerland, which otherwise lacks an immigrant policy, schools have arranged extra language instruction and special help with homework for immigrant children. Special preparatory classes have been used in the other project countries to channel immigrant children as quickly as possible into the regular school system.

Sweden and the Netherlands have made the greatest efforts to offer immigrant children the opportunity to study their mother tongue. Similar opportunities also exist in France. In the Netherlands instruction in the mother tongue is part of the daily school program; it does not seek to prepare immigrant children to return to their native countries but instead aims to strengthen their self-esteem and support the entire minority group that they belong to. Sweden has gone the furthest towards a multicultural education policy. Not only are immigrant children taught to speak their mother tongue, but it is also used as the language of instruction for other subjects. A growing number of classes have been formed where all instruction takes place inthe pupils' mother tongue, although instruction in Swedish is the most important subject. Perhaps the Netherlands and Sweden have moved in the direction of "active bilingualism" for immigrant children earlier than other countries because their respective national languages are spoken by only relatively few people and thus are not attractive as world languages. In France and Britain, on the other hand, the use of the national languages in the instruction of immigrant pupils has hardly ever been questioned. Only in recent years has a discussion begun on the desirability of including immigrant pupils' cultural backgrounds and languages in the school program.

The implementation of education policy in every country depends on local conditions. This is especially true in the Netherlands, Germany, and Switzerland, where responsibility for education policy lies with the regional or local, and not with the national or Federal Government.The school program for immigrant children can be totally different in different regions or communities of these countries. For instance, education policy in Berlin has stressed the need to integrate immigrant children into German society, while in Bavaria the schools have considered it their duty to prepare immigrant children to return eventually to their native countries. With this goal in mind, Bavarian schools have placed emphasis on teaching immigrant children their mother tongue, even at the cost of their failing to learn adequate German. Schools in Sweden and the Netherlands have set completely opposite aims for their education policies; namely, to prepare immigrant children for a permanent stay. They have still emphasized mother-tongue instruction, but not at the expense of learning the host country's language. Both guestworker and permanent immigration countries have thus occasionally shown the same interest in teaching the mother tongue, although they have differed as regards their interest in preparing immigrants to remain or not to remain in the country of immigration.

As long as labor migration was considered an influx of temporary "guests", little thought was given to the problems of educating immigrant children. While it is true that school attendance for immigrant children in Germany was made obligatory in 1964, the controls to ensure that they really were present in school and were achieving satisfactory results long lacked any effective force. Several hundred thousand immigrant children have not received schooling commensurate with that of German children of the same age. They have not obtained equal opportunities on the labor market or in vocational training or advanced studies. The situation is similar, even if not always that serious, in the other project countries as well.

A second generation, partly born in the host country, has grown up there. But they are ill prepared for both return to their parents' country and competitive life in the host country. They tend to increase their demands of the project countries because they compare themselves with other young people of their age who have grown up perhaps in the same poor neighborhood and not, as the first generation, with people who stayed behind in the country of origin. The second generation has had a bad start, but their parents often have high expectations for their children, and they themselves demand more than the living conditions achieved by their parents.

The second generation is still young, mostly under 20 years of age at the beginning of the 1980s. But in all the project countries they have become the center of concern, policy debate, and speculation. There is no real difference in this respect between guestworker countries and countries with more permanent immigration, although there perhaps exists a difference in timing; that is, it has taken the guestworker countries longer to recognize the need for better educational opportunities. Because of this many immigrant children living in the project countries during the 1970s achieved a limited competence in both their own language and the language of the host country.

Equal opportunity versus negative discrimination

Immigrants are in various ways "handicapped" in comparison with people born in the host country. Difficulties accompany the change in country, language, environment, and often occupation. Immigrant workers and their families need help to overcome these difficulties successfully. One host country might provide such help while another host country instead keeps newly arrived foreigners in an insecure position with limited access to the social welfare system.

One can say that direct immigrant policy is "affirmative action" as long as the measures taken are designed to offer immigrants equal opportunities. Discrimination occurs as soon as immigrants, or for that matter any group, are treated differently than the majority of a country's residents, and most of the time this implies that immigrants are treated worse than the indigenous majority. Direct immigrant policy may also include measures to combat such negative discrimination. In fact, all of the project countries formally forbid negative discrimination in many situations: individuals should not be treated differently on the grounds of, for example, race, religion, or nationality.

Britain has made racial equality the centerpiece of its immigrant policy. A series of Race Relations Acts have prohibited direct discrimination in public places and on the labor and housing markets. The 1976 Act also prohibited indirect discrimination and established the Commission for Racial Equality (CRE), a central agency charged with actively promoting good race relations in the community. New Commonwealth immigrants have full civil and political rights and are subject to the same general social welfare policy as everyone else. Almost everything connected with immigration in Britain is considered "race relations", and there is a tendency to disregard the kinds of comparisons that this book attempts. The CRE has been armed with the authority and resources to combat negative discrimination in individual cases, but it has not been equipped to take on the truly "big" problems usually associated with immigrant policy, such as housing programs or language instruction.

Interrelations between regulation and immigrant policy

Immigration was an established fact before immigration policy came into being in all of the countries; similarly, regulation of immigration occurred before immigrant policy. There is a close and mutual dependence between the regulation of immigration and immigrant policy, but there is no one way cause-and-effect relationship. Instead, two parallel developments have taken place. Both have been affected by the other, but have at the same time also been affected by many other factors. For this reason in particular, we must analyze the interrelationship and ask why it has taken so long to understand the importance of this interplay. The turning point in the beginning of the 1970s can help us to illustrate the relations from the perspectives of both the immigrants and the countries involved.

The analytical distinction made in this project between regulation and immigrant policy corresponds to a functional division that is made in all of the project countries. There are different laws enacted to regulate each policy area. Different administrative agencies are responsible for policy implementation. Immigration regulation and control requires public officials such as lawyers, immigration officers, and police who enforce the legislation; for instance, with respect to work permits, deportations, and naturalizations. Other professional workers are used for the implementation of immigrant policy, including teachers, social workers, doctors, and clergy. As a consequence of this difference in recruitment and training, two very different outlooks dominate each policy area. These policy areas are nevertheless dependent on one another; that is, changes made in one area affect the other and vice versa.

Regulation and immigrant policy have been characterized from the individual immigrant's point of view as presenting two faces: one face is hard, unkind, and full of rejection, the other face is friendly and inviting. The hard face is turned towards those who apply for admittance, and the more friendly towards those who have already been accepted. But the two faces go together. The more generous a country's immigrant policy, the stronger are the efforts made by people outside the country to pass through even the most rigorous immigration control. In other words, if a country of immigration offers reasonable housing, good schools for children, and a low level of social discrimination, this represents an invitation to new immigrants to come and to old immigrants to stay permanently. If conditions are negative instead, they may frighten many off from attempting to enter and prompt others to return.

Correspondingly, we might say that strict regulation of immigration mayalso prove inconvenient for those who have already been admitted as immigrants, and who find that family reunion is hindered, visits of relatives are not allowed, and so on.

However, the attraction of the project countries has been consistently very high, regardless of their immigrant policies. The reason for this is of course that immigrants have compared conditions in the host country with what they would have been offered had they not emigrated but stayed in their country of origin. The gap in living standards is so great that large numbers of potential immigrants have at all times been willing to enter the countries of immigration. There is for the same reason no simple and directly obvious relation between the rate of return and the host country's immigrant policy.

Since most immigrants arrived with the intention of returning after a couple of years, the German or Swiss rotation policy seemed to correspond better to their original ideas than, for instance, the Swedish policy of permanent immigration. Intentions change, however, and a large proportion of those who planned to return eventually stayed in Germany and Switzerland just as in Sweden. Return was an illusion shared by most people, and the policy of rotation has only lately been found to rest on unrealistic assumptions. This was not easy to see at an early date, however. First of all, immigrants themselves said that they would go back. And even if the rotation system was not strictly applied to force people to return, it did not give any guarantees that they would be permitted to stay permanently. This reinforced the belief among immigrants that they would one day remigrate and helps explain why this illusion lasted so long.

Countries of emigration also hoped for return, at least at a later point when their economies had become more developed. They therefore preferred a policy of rotation. Yugoslavs have officially been looked upon as workers temporarily abroad and not as workers who have emigrated for good. When the employment situation improves in Yugoslavia or when the Yugoslav workers abroad create new job opportunities, for instance, through their savings, they are supposed to return to Yugoslavia. The German guestworker policy might seem to correspond exactly to this emigration country view of seeing their workers as temporarily abroad. The Swedish immigrant policy could be seen as binding Yugoslav workers too tightly to the host society by offering improved working and housing conditions or better education for children.

Yugoslavia as well as other countries of emigration continued to take an interest in ensuring that their citizens, while temporarily abroad, received a decent life in the host countries, and not least that their children were given a good education. When the temporary work period was extended year after year and it became obvious that large numbers would remain as permanent immigrants, the countries of emigration began to demand improvements in immigrant policy.

In the beginning of the 1970s, recruitment of foreign workers was "stopped", or at least substantially reduced, and those who had not already obtained work and residence permits before that turning point could hardly hope to be admitted thereafter, unless as family members or for special reasons, such as on political or humanitarian grounds. The result was that few immigrants wanted to return if it meant they would lose their permits or their chances to get such permits in the future. To hold permits with a high probability of prolongation became a valuable thing that people did not want to give up. Many immigrants now realized that they were going to remain in Germany, Switzerland, Sweden, etc. for at least a considerable time. As a consequence, they took more interest in immigrant policy, and as they began to plan a future in the host country their demands for improved living conditions increased.

The recruitment stop was a condition necessary for a new immigrant policy, as it provided much needed time for planning and implementation of policy measures. The anticipated large-scale return of temporary guestworkers did not occur. More and more immigrants began instead to plan to stay. This certainly contradicted the original intentions of employers and governments in the project countries, but awareness grew that this was the best solution. Several million immigrants worked in jobs where they could not easily be replaced by others. Employers wanted as little turnover as possible among their employees, and for this reason actually disliked rotation when it functioned properly. They preferred to keep the same persons in their employment as long as they could because it reduced their costs for recruitment and training and improved their labor relations and perhaps production results. Neither private nor public employers could manage without foreign workers, but they wanted the old immigrants and not new replacements for them.

We have thus far discussed mainly economic causes for the turning point, although we have touched upon other causes as well. One of these was the need for better social services to handle immigrant problems. The foreign population had become so large that the impact on housing, education, and culture could not be disregarded any longer. Sweden, the Netherlands, France, and to a certain extent Britain all declared that immigration had to be limited as a first step in the improvement of the situation of those already living in the country. The concept of "stabilization" was frequently used: if only the number of resident immigrants could be kept at a stable level, improvements in their welfare would be possible.

The recruitment stop in Germany in November 1973 was not immediately followed by a change in immigrant policy. The official doctrine still was that Germany was not a country of immigration. In 1975, however, rotation was rejected and replaced by the goal of consolidating foreign employment combined with temporary integration (*Integration auf Zeit*). A report by Heinz Kühn in 1979 demanded the establishment of a consistent integration policy, and even though this demand was never satisfied, something in that direction followed; that is, a program for the integration of the second generation of immigrants in Germany.

In France immigrant policy already existed before the turning point in 1974, especially in the form of programs for immigrant housing and education. But a change took place that same year when the first deputy minister of immigration was appointed and a new immigrant policy was announced, aimed at improving the social situation of the immigrant population. The close relation between regulation and immigrant policy can also be seen in Sweden, although an immigrant policy was formulated earlier there than in other countries. In 1967 Sweden stopped the spontaneous immigration of labor for the same reasons later given by other countries; namely, that immigrants ought to be given living conditions equal to those of the indigenous population.

Immigrant policy in the Netherlands long consisted of special programs for each nationality group. A general immigrant policy was not formulated until 1981. In Britain tougher restrictions on immigration have been combined with the construction of a system for protection against racial discrimination, although affirmative action in favor of immigrants has not been instituted. It took a long time, as we have seen, before the interrelation between immigration regulation and immigrant policy was clearly understood in France and especially in Germany, and by 1983 the required steps were still not taken.

Generalizing, we might conclude that a need had arisen both for regular social service of all kinds and for what we have here called direct immigrant policy programs. For a considerable time, however, this need was either not recognized or neglected under the pretext that immigration was not to be permanent or that special benefits could not be given to immigrants. For countries like Sweden and Britain programs of immigrant policy were already fully in line with their policy of permanent immigration, while a guestworker country like Germany was, forced to undertake a drastic reexamination of previous policy in light of the reality of permanent immigration. Germans, for this reason, needed time to convince themselves that large-scale return was an illusion, that permanent immigration was already a fact, and that a new immigrant policy was seriously needed.

We have maintained here that a country's immigrant policy is influenced, among other things, by its general social welfare policy and by the strength of its trade unions. The more a society takes collective responsibility for the social security of its members and the more equality is emphasized, the more we would expect to find an immigrant policy that promotes the welfare and security of immigrants and seeks to eliminate discrimination against them. The early start and the extensive growth of Swedish immigrant policy has been considered an example of this and has been contrasted with the late and relatively poor immigrant policy of Switzerland. But if this is true, there is another factor that can give a partial explanation of the policy choiceof these two countries. A guestworker policy was not compatible with the Swedish welfare ideology but was compatible with the Swiss individualistic value system.

11

The policymaking process

This chapter discusses how immigration policy is made. Unlike the previous chapters, here we are interested in the origin and form of policy rather than in its content. Though all six of the project countries are democracies where two or more parties compete in free elections, each is governed in a different fashion and has its own particular kinds of institutions and traditions. The parliamentary system of Britain stands in contrast to the presidential system of France; the centralized French system of decisionmaking stands in contrast to the decentralized Swiss system, with its autonomous cantons and local authority, as well as to the federal system of Germany; the multiparty system of the Netherlands stands in contrast to the traditional two-party system of Britain. Despite these considerable differences in political systems, however, there are significant similarities in how immigration policy is made. This chapter will examine those similarities.

Policy or "non-policy"

German politicians have emphatically declared that their country is *not* a country of immigration. This declaration comes as somewhat of a surprise to foreign observers, who note that approximately four million foreign citizens reside in the Federal Republic. The Germans have answered that these foreign citizens, originally recruited as labor, should be regarded as temporary "guestworkers"; in other words, no plans have ever been made in Germany for permanent immigration. The number of foreign workers has become large only because the economy required extra manpower during a period of transition.

This has long been the official line. It provides an example of how economic interests rather than political decisions can shape a country's immigration policy. Market forces are allowed to operate freely and political decisionmakers do not try to influence the outcome; at most, they establish guidelines and rules. In the German case, the Bundesanstalt für Arbeit (BfA), located in Nuremberg, actively assisted in both the recruitment of workers and their placement on the labor market. This was always considered a matter of short-term labor market adjustments – not a matter of "immigration".

Yet when politicians *refrain* from trying to influence outcomes, they nevertheless establish a policy, even if the matter is never formally decided upon. Policymakers may not even be aware that they might have acted in a different way; in other words, that they have in fact been faced with a choice and have chosen *not* to act. They could have affected the outcome of immigration, but instead let matters develop in their own way. For example, West Germany's immigration policy prior to its turning point (1973) can in large part be characterized as a laissez-faire system. In answer to the question of whether Germany, under these circumstances, had an immigration "policy" at all during this period, it should be noted that even such a "non-policy" is a kind of policy: the economy was allowed to import whatever foreign labor it needed, but at the same time permanent immigration was not allowed or encouraged.

Other countries' immigration policies can in a similar way be characterized as laissez-faire prior to their respective turning points. Swiss immigration policy "was not *made* but *grew* out of a permanent trial and error process", according to a high-level bureaucrat quoted by Hoffmann-Nowotny. The Swiss authorities tried to deal with the problems that large-scale immigration gradually caused, but before the country's turning point (1970) economic interests almost completely dominated the policymaking process. French immigration policy was also laissez-faire until its turning point (which began in 1970 but was not made explicit until 1974). Economic needs and interests were allowed to determine how immigration would develop; political decisions came only later in a gradual attempt to solve the problems that had appeared. When the Swedish Riksdag approved in 1968 the basic principles for immigration policy, politicians emphasized that they hoped to be able to assume a greater measure of responsibility for the future development of immigration. In the years that followed, however, the amount of annual immigration was determined by economic conditions and not by formal political plans. The Netherlands only began to develop a thorough and long-term immigration policy at the end of the 1970s, and even here, as Entzinger points out, the role of experts, scientific advisers and special interest groups has been greater than that of politicians.

Britain may be a possible exception to this laissez-faire pattern. Parliament has through political action successively restricted immigration based on traditional colonial commitments and practices. A comparison may be made here with the United States, where both the size of annual immigration and its origin in different areas of the world have been determined by formal political decisions. It must be added, however, that these decisions have not limited the extensive illegal immigration from Mexico and other Latin American countries. Though strict border controls have been implemented, immigration continues to obey the market forces of supply and demand. In this respect one can see a similarity between immigration to the United States and immigration to the European project countries.

Political versus administrative decisions

When politicians refrain from intervening in a policy area, administrative agencies tend to take over. They apply the regulations of immigration control to constantly changing individual cases, forming decisions based on law, past practice, and "standard operating procedures". Administrative interpretations of laws and ordinances gradually develop into an immigration "policy" that grows through "trial and error", to cite Hoffmann-Nowotny again. Administrative agencies also propose adjustments in prevailing regulations as needed, and they can therefore bring about changes in policy. *Administrative* decisions replace *political* decisions, and this continues as long as no fundamental changes in policy are required or proposed.

Even when such fundamental changes occur, however, experts and bureaucrats often assume a decisive influence over their character. Immigration policy is rarely considered a major social or political issue. Of course, it has played a political role at times, for example in certain British election campaigns. But these are exceptions – one can say that in most cases a country's largest political parties are united on the issue of immigration. When opposition arises, it usually comes from small extremist parties on the fringes of the political scene, e.g. from the National Front in Britain and the two over-foreignization parties in Switzerland. There are several explanations why politicians so often leave the responsibility for immigration policy to administrative agencies. These can be grouped in the following fashion:

1. First of all, there is a tradition in all countries that some political decisions are made through a legal procedure in which courts or other judicial bodies interpret the meaning of the constitution or the law of the country. This tradition is strongly developed in some federal states, and Germany is one of these. But Germany has also given extra power to its constitutional court in Karlsruhe by including in its fundamental law a number of rules that are binding even on parliament. Furthermore, according to the German theory of the *Rechts-*

staat, the state shall not act arbitrarily but only in accordance with the law, and the jurists are supposed to possess a certain specialist knowledge of what is right and good. Their competence therefore tends to be extended to cover what in other countries would be considered purely political evaluations. Finally, in all project countries, with the exception of Britain, civil servants have traditionally received mainly a legal education. The implication for the administration of immigration policies is that legal and administrative decisions have often replaced political decisions.

2. Administrative agencies can often take the upper hand because they have more knowledge and expertise as regards immigration policy, which includes a number of technically complicated issues. This is the case with immigration regulation, which presupposes knowledge of international migration, international law, political conditions that influence asylum decisions, and so forth; it is also the case with immigrant policy, which requires knowledge of ethnicity and minorities, bilingualism, and education. It is natural that those who deal every day with immigration policy acquire knowledge of these matters before politicians do. Bureaucrats must face the problems and attempt to find technical solutions for them.

3. Political parties strive to find solutions for social problems in accordance with their party ideologies and the interests of their voters. Yet immigrants, as long as they remain foreign citizens, are not allowed to vote and are therefore never directly represented by any political party. For this reason the position that parties take on immigration issues is usually based on their evaluation of how immigration will affect the welfare of their ordinary (non-immigrant) constituents – not an easy thing to determine in most cases. In general, political parties assume that a certain amount of anti-immigrant feeling exists among their voters, but that these voters want to have the economic advantages that immigration brings. The immigration question places political parties in unfamiliar waters: the issue is not the usual one of how to divide the economic pie between the voters, but instead how to divide it between citizens and non-citizens.

4. One objection to the preceding point might be that several political parties in the project countries reflect class differences, and since immigrants belong more often than not to the working class it would be natural for working-class parties to reflect and protect their interests, even if they are not voters. In other words, the parties are probably aware that immigrants, if they voted, would vote primarily for working-class parties. The results of the past several Swedish local elections, where immigrants are allowed to vote, offer some support

for this supposition. Immigrants cast more votes for social-democratic and communist candidates than they did for non-socialist candidates. The socialist parties have also claimed that immigrants are a natural part of their constituency. Despite this clear expression of immigrants' political preferences, however, no significant differences of opinion on immigration policy have developed between the parties. They continue to respond to immigrants' interests just as much or just as little as they did before.

5. Taking a political stand on an immigration issue can easily have negative consequences for a party or an individual politician. Those responsible for the imposition of restrictive immigration controls can be criticized for the inhumane treatment of individual aliens; examples of this can be found in the Netherlands and Sweden. On the other hand, those responsible for proposals and programs to improve the welfare of the immigrant population may risk being criticized for reverse discrimination or insensitivity to the interests of native constituents; examples of this can be found in Switzerland and Britain. Since immigration policy is often so sensitive, it can be difficult to satisfy public opinion. There is always the risk that a political party or an individual politician might try to benefit from inflaming public opposition based on latent racial, ethnic, or national prejudices. National unanimity on the immigration issue has often been motivated by a desire to avoid this risk.

6. Finally, we can point out that immigration policy has a great deal in common with other political issues affecting a country's international relations. The attitude that "politics stops at the water's edge" often applies to the immigration question as well, where it is relatively easy for political parties to agree to act in the "national interest". Immigration is permitted if it is good for the country's economy, but not otherwise. On the other hand, immigration controls cannot be so stringent that they disturb relations with other countries. In either case the deciding criterion is the "national interest". When a country's political parties agree that decisions on immigration policy should be based on this criterion, they effectively de-politicize the issue. It is in this way abandoned to the control of administrative agencies, employers' interests, and organized pressure groups.

Political parties and public opinion

The above description and explanation notwithstanding, political parties or individual politicians in some of the project countries have gone to the voters on issues of immigration policy. Two politicians in particular,

Enoch Powell in Britain and James Schwarzenbach in Switzerland, have made a name for themselves with stridently xenophobic speeches and drastic proposals for restricting immigration. Moreover, in Britain, Switzerland, and the Netherlands extremist parties have catered to the voters with negative attitudes about immigrants.

Since it is conceivable that immigration could become a political issue in any country, it is important to ask why this has not happened in the other project countries. It seems that political parties everywhere try to avoid taking advantage of whatever anti-immigrant feelings might exist among their voters. Layton-Henry remarked that on occasion a sort of unspoken agreement to forbid racist arguments and attacks seems to have existed between Britain's political parties. The use of racism in politics is generally condemned on both intellectual and moral grounds. Even though racist attitudes can be found in any population, as demonstrated by a number of surveys, it is nevertheless possible to keep them out of the political debate as long as all parties stick to this attitude. Open conflict among ethnic groups can in this way be avoided.

Party discipline has not been strong enough, however, to stop a politician like Powell from defying the party line and acting on his own beliefs, supported by relatively large groups of voters who sympathize with his hitherto taboo message. Britain has a system of majority elections in single-member constituencies, which tends to concentrate public attention on individual candidates. In constituencies where ethnic and nationality conflicts are strong it may be particularly tempting for a candidate to appeal to racial prejudice. In countries with proportional election systems, on the other hand, where votes are cast for parties and not for individual candidates and where constituencies are much larger, it would be very difficult for a politician to gain anything with such tactics. He would probably only succeed in losing the confidence of his party.

The Swiss referendum system also gives politicians and individual citizens and interest organizations the ability to act independently of the political parties. In fact, that is the whole concept behind such a system: to give voters the power to ensure that their representatives act in accordance with the popular will. This includes ensuring that the political parties are not able to suppress opinions (even racist ones) simply because they consider them improper. In a referendum voters can take direct positions on an issue, which means that the political parties have no way of stopping the expression of anti-immigrant sentiments.

It is certainly conceivable that the electoral systems in Britain and the United States and the referendum system in Switzerland make it easier for politicians to benefit from xenophobic and racist attitudes. Perhaps it is a good thing that such attitudes have an outlet if they are indeed widespread in a country. Perhaps the existence of public prejudice calls forth politicians who take advantage of it, rather than the other way around. Enoch Powell could never have met with such success if he had not been surrounded by voters who were, as Layton-Henry puts it, "deeply racially prejudiced".

Britain is an interesting example in this respect. What is in other countries called "immigrant policy" is in Britain called "race relations". The word "immigrants" is often used to refer to persons with brown or black skin, regardless of whether they were born on the British Isles or not. New Commonwealth immigration has been regulated more restrictively because the British people have felt themselves threatened; the race riots of the past are considered signs of a very unstable situation. Opinion surveys have shown that large sectors of the population, regardless of social class or party affiliation, have racist attitudes.

Racial disturbances have also occurred in other countries and politicians have been quick to respond. Many in France have convinced themselves that too high a concentration of immigrants in one place, e.g. a residential neighborhood or a school, will eventually cause trouble. They speak of a "threshold of tolerance" that must not be passed for fear of awakening negative opinions and causing open opposition. Politicians and administrative agencies in Sweden have placed emphasis on improving the relationship between Swedes and immigrants by giving both groups more information about each other. Immigrants get acquainted with Sweden's social conditions and "rules of living", while Swedes get acquainted with immigrants – their importance for Swedish society and their origins. We must also remember that the number of colored immigrants in Sweden is insignificant. Of course, this information campaign cannot stop all racism and anti-immigrant attitudes, but it may help to soften their effect. Most important, this kind of policy reflects the belief that public opinion is something that can be influenced if the conditions are good and does not simply have to be accepted.

In all countries, perhaps most of all in West Germany, there is a moral repudiation of racism. Yet racist attitudes exist nonetheless. The higher their level of education the less people reveal such attitudes. Even if they may have them, they have learned that racism is taboo and should be avoided. For this reason, education is sometimes considered a means of reducing racism, or at least reducing its open expression.

Public opinion may act as a restraint on political action, but it seldom acts as a catalyst. With the exception of a few extreme parties and politicians, no one is anxious to act as the mouthpiece for whatever racist or anti-immigrant feelings the voters might have. At the same time, however, no one is anxious to take measures that might unnecessarily antagonize these voters. Events in Switzerland provide a good example of this. The over-foreignization initiatives were defeated, but, especially as regards the first one, the majority was very small and the initiatives enjoyed the support of a great many voters. Public opinion was strong and politicians hastened to take measures to ensure that it did not become stronger: the global ceiling was introduced in 1970, and it has been maintained ever since. In this way the danger that another initiative might be successful was avoided.

Who makes immigration policy?

After 1970 four of the project countries (Switzerland, Sweden, France, and West Germany) "stopped" immigration – not just temporarily but rather as a part of a more comprehensive change in policy. If we knew who made these decisions, it would probably give us an insight into how immigration policy is formed and which people are able to influence the process. Unfortunately our knowledge is not at present deep enough to allow such an analysis. We can only sketch the contours of the decision-making process in each country.

In Switzerland the referendum initiatives against over-foreignization acted as the catalyst for a new policy. The Federal Council and the parliament responded to the initiative by introducing in 1970 a global ceiling on the number of foreign citizens in the country. While it is true that no maximum number was set for the size of the foreign population, policymakers nevertheless decided that it would not be allowed to become larger and would be reduced if possible.

In France the "stop" came in July 1974 after Giscard d'Estaing took office and appointed the country's first Deputy Minister of Immigration. This minister stood behind the government's decision to suspend all new labor immigration in order to stabilize the immigrant population at its existing size (somewhat over three million) and to gain the time needed to develop a new immigration policy. President Giscard d'Estaing took a personal interest in the formation of this new policy, which was targeted at the need for modernization in French industry. The National Assembly was excluded from the decisionmaking process, and only a small group of government administrators seems to have participated in the deliberations.

In West Germany, the Federal Government's Minister of Labor notified the Bundesanstalt für Arbeit (BfA) in November 1973 that all recruitment of foreign workers at BfA's overseas offices had to cease at once. The immediate explanation for this decree was that it was thought that unemployment would increase during the energy crisis then in progress.

But it soon became obvious that the decision was motivated by long-term considerations. The Bundestag was never consulted. The government did not even make an executive decision. The decree by the Minister of Labor was the only formal measure ever taken. Nevertheless, the decision does not seem to have been preceded by any differences of opinion, although it was certainly followed by some, mainly because it created recruitment problems in some branches of industry and led to requests for exemptions.

In Sweden the "stop" also occurred without any formal decision by either the Riksdag or the government. In fact, the entire matter was simply a question of making some changes in the application of existing regulations for issuing new work permits. This procedure was altered in 1971 so that it corresponded more closely to the economic situation at the time. The change was based on a letter sent from the Swedish labor unions' central organization, Landsorganisationen (LO), to its affiliated national trade union organization. Labor organizations have always been consulted regarding applications for work permits; if they object to an application it is almost always refused. Thus, when, in 1972, LO advised their member organizations that continued recruitment of foreign workers was undesirable, it was only natural that this decision of the trade union movement was to be reflected in a new application of the regulatory procedures. With this, a new immigration policy began.

The decisions of France, Germany, and Sweden to "stop" immigration have an important feature in common: they were all made *without* the public debate and parliamentary discussion that usually surrounds important changes in government policy. The Swiss decision was made in a different fashion for reasons peculiar to its political system. In Germany the decision was made by a labor minister, and the same is true for France, although the timing of the decision – right after a change of presidents – suggests that a greater degree of political leadership was involved.

The German Ministry of Labor and Social Order has a number of consultative organizations concerned with immigration, some of which are composed of representatives from labor and business and others of which encompass voluntary organizations that work for the welfare of resident immigrants. Esser and Korte write that the majority of conflicts regarding immigration involve these latter groups in opposition to the government and to business and labor. The reason for this opposition can be found in the groups' different perspectives: government, business, and labor are primarily concerned with how immigrants ought to be used on the labor market, while voluntary welfare organizations are concerned with the social and cultural issues raised by the long-term presence of foreigners in the country.

In the Netherlands and Britain the turning point in immigration regulation did not happen in the same way as in the above four countries. Therefore, we must find a different means of characterizing their respective decisionmaking processes in the area of immigration policy. Demands for stricter regulation were made in the Netherlands in 1973, but in 1974 immigration from Surinam was still large and even growing, and it continued without restraint until the colony became independent in 1975. Around the same time a series of terrorist actions, planned and executed by young Moluccans, shook the country and forced the government to consider the minorities problem. Still, the events of the mid-1970s did not result in a new policy until 1980; the formulation of this policy occurred, as Entzinger has shown, in an atmosphere of cooperation and relative unity among the political parties. A number of different ministries were involved and the process lacked coordination much of the time, but in the end the government and its advisory organizations succeeded in preparing a proposal, which will be presented to the Dutch parliament for a decision. Throughout this process, pressure came from groups outside the government, primarily Dutch organizations that supported immigrants' cultural and social interests but also organizations of immigrants themselves.

A large number of laws concerning immigration and racism have passed through the British parliament. Parties have at times taken opposing positions, although in general the tendency has been to try to keep the issue out of politics. The first restrictions on immigration were presented in 1962 by a Conservative government, with opposition from the Labour Party. When Labour took over the government two years later, however, they accepted the 1962 measures and strengthened them in 1965. After the expulsion of Indians from Kenya in 1968, Labour introduced and passed a bill that restricted immigration again, this time with clearly racist provisions. The Immigration Act of 1971 was passed under a Conservative government, and Labour offered only token opposition. Margaret Thatcher later made use of the immigration question in the preliminaries for the 1979 election campaign, a move that has been interpreted as both a concession to Conservative groups and an attempt to undermine the electoral support of the National Front. The result has been, however, that party differences have again become pronounced; supported by the Liberal Party and the new Social Democratic Party, Labour has demanded a new immigration policy with no racist overtones. But continual attempts to de-politicize the immigration issue have been largely unsuccessful.

As mentioned previously, it is a common perception in Britain that the general public holds deep racial prejudices. The parties feel that they must take note of these prejudices, yet at the same time they claim that they have no desire to promote them. Racist concepts are a part of the colonial heritage and these concepts have in the past been used to legitimize Britain's relations with its African and Asian colonies. They later became imbedded implicitly, although not explicitly, in much of post-colonial legislation, forming the basis for domestic race discrimination. Immigration legislation since 1962 has followed this general pattern.

Immigrants and policymaking

The possibilities for immigrants to influence immigration policy have been very few, and sometimes non-existent, in all of the project countries. Yet there are signs that this situation may now be changing; relatively large differences in this area already exist between countries. Even without taking any special measures the possibility for immigrants to exercise influence increases year by year as more people either become citizens or receive permanent resident status. The longer the period of residence, the more secure can immigrants be about their position, which makes it easier for them to advance their own demands. Their knowledge of the host country increases and they begin to realize what sort of expectations they ought to have. They begin to compare themselves with the native population and become more and more interested in participating in trade union and political activity.

All of these developments make it likely that immigrants in the six European project countries will in the future become important participants in the formation of immigration policy. This prediction is even more plausible if one considers how immigrant policy has increased in importance since the mid-1970s. The project countries have become interested in trying to integrate resident immigrants ever since realizing that most of them will probably stay permanently. It has therefore been considered important that immigrant representatives participate in policy formation.

Since the beginning of large-scale immigration foreign workers have been able to join trade unions in the host countries; in fact, the unions have usually encouraged them to join, although there are exceptions to this in the Netherlands and in Switzerland. The unions have in some cases made membership a requirement for accepting immigration in the first place. Immigrants in Germany and Sweden are thus members of trade unions to approximately the same degree as native workers (the general rate of unionization is much higher in Sweden than in Germany). But the unions have not always allowed immigrants to vote on union matters on the same basis as native workers, nor have they especially encouraged immigrants to rise to positions of leadership.

A significant improvement in the situation of immigrants in France followed immediately after the election of Mitterrand in 1981, when they were finally given the right of association. Previously immigrants had been forbidden to form special organizations; only organizations in which more than half the members were French citizens were allowed. Participation in political activity was also forbidden, a point clearly illustrated by the extensive expulsions of foreigners after the May riots of 1968.

The right of association has also been limited for immigrants living in Germany. There was considerable concern in the 1960s that communist propaganda would enter the country with foreign workers. The Law of Association included a very vague provision that made it possible to forbid certain kinds of immigrant organizations, e.g. those in which all or the majority of the members were foreign citizens. Organizations could be banned if the members "through their political activity damaged or threatened the security, public order, or other 'important interests' (*erhebliche Belange*) of the Federal Republic or any of its member-states" (Dohse 1981:281, 14:1). In addition, the agencies in charge of aliens affairs had access to information on the political activities of foreigners. Though it was often impossible to determine why an application for an extended residence permit, for example, was refused, foreigners nevertheless felt that information on their political activities could have negative consequences; therefore, it was best not to be a member of an immigrant organization. In a 1974 interview in Tübingen, 54 percent of the Turks questioned answered that they were afraid of being expelled for some trivial matter.

Of course, an insecure legal position does not necessarily result in passivity. Despite the obstacles, a strong and diverse web of immigrant organizations has developed in Germany, and the Turkish ones are certainly not the least successful. There are also well-organized groups of Yugoslavs, Italians, and several other nationalities. The growth of organizations has accelerated since the end of the 1970s when the legal security of many immigrants increased with their acquisition of permanent status.

Switzerland has in general followed the same direction as France and Germany regarding immigrants and policymaking. In Britain, the Netherlands, and Sweden, however, immigrants have been offered totally different possibilities. Since most New Commonwealth immigrants, once admitted to the country, have roughly the same political rights as native-born British citizens, they have played a direct role in shaping immigrant policy with their election ballots and their strong, influential organizations. Immigrants who have resided legally in Sweden for three years are allowed to vote and run for office in municipal elections. Immigrant organizations are encouraged and supported with public funds in order both to give immigrants the opportunity to maintain their national cultures and to give the Swedish authorities formal bodies with whom they can discuss questions of immigration policy. The Netherlands plans to introduce a system of voting rights for immigrants similar to the Swedish one but has first been obliged to make a change in its constitution. At the same time the Netherlands has gone further than Sweden in giving formal minority status to certain ethnic groups.

Decisionmaking bodies in some municipalities, for example in France and Germany, have formed special "reference groups" composed of representatives chosen by local immigrants, to give advice on immigration issues. Similar reference groups have developed in the Netherlands and Sweden on the national level, attached to the ministries and agencies that administer immigrant affairs. Corresponding groups do not exist in Germany; on the contrary, there is a glaring lack of representation for immigrants in the powerful coordinating agency connected to the ministries in Bonn. On the other hand, voting rights for immigrants in municipal elections has been discussed extensively in Germany, but debate has become stalled on the question of constitutional validity. The Christian Democratic Party (CDU) and the central association of trade unions (DGB) have both opposed the proposal; the Liberal Party (FDP), the Social Democratic Party (SPD), and religious organizations have supported it. In France, as mentioned previously, Mitterrand promised to give immigrants voting rights in local elections, but after the Socialist victory his government declared that the reform would not be introduced for several years.

Some concern has been expressed in all of the immigration countries that immigrants of different nationalities might form associations where they would engage in the party politics of their home countries or perhaps isolate themselves from the political and social life of the host country and concentrate on more internal minority affairs. Some immigrant groups have demanded their own institutional structures, e.g. their own schools, neighborhoods, doctors, and so forth. One could reasonably have expected immigrants to form their own trade unions or perhaps their own political parties; such fears have been particularly strong in Germany, where several strong and politically extreme immigrant organizations exist. Yet no clear signs have emerged in any country to indicate that immigrants plan to form trade unions or political parties parallel to the existing ones. Immigrants have worked within the ordinary trade unions. In Sweden at least, they have voted for existing parties and have not used their legal right to form new parties. In fact, they are gradually moving into positions as union representatives and, in Sweden and Britain, as political representatives. The latter is also true for immigrants in the other project countries as soon as they become naturalized citizens.

The administration of immigration policy

We have discovered one more explanation for the lack of coordination of immigration regulation and immigrant policy; namely, that these two policy areas are usually administered by different agencies and organizations. Since none of these agencies has been qualified or competent to take responsibility for both policy areas, the two areas have been perceived as independent of each other.

Immigration regulation and aliens control are by tradition the tasks of the police and border control, and the responsible ministers are the Minister of Justice and Police, as in Switzerland, or the Minister of the Interior, as in France, or the Secretary of State for Home Affairs, as in Britain. Because recruitment of labor is part of labor market policy in general the Minister of Labor has been made responsible for immigration everywhere but in Britain, where no such recruitment has taken place.

Besides the ministries, however, central labor market authorities, such as BfA in Germany, BIGA in Switzerland, and AMS in Sweden, assess the need for labor immigration in relation to the manpower development of the country. It is interesting to note that these agencies have great power not only in Germany and Switzerland but also in Sweden where no guest-worker policy has been adopted. They are already strong organizations because of the great importance attached to full employment. The Swedish Labor Market Board (AMS) has, for instance, taken responsibility for several decisions of great importance for Swedish immigration policy, even if the effect of this has not always been understood. Labor market perspectives dominated measures taken to integrate political refugees into Swedish society because the central agency responsible for these measures was AMS and, according to AMS, nothing was more important to political refugees than placing them in their first job on the labor market.

When immigrant policy is administered in this way within one sector of society (for instance, within the labor market sector or within the cultural and school sector, as may be the case for immigrant minorities, or perhaps within the housing sector), there is a risk that viewpoints and ideas prominent within this sector will take precedence over other ideas.

As mentioned earlier, agencies for regulation and control often hold other views and opinions than agencies for immigrant policy because their staff is trained differently and their immediate aims are formulated in different terms. In none of the project countries has there existed one *single* immigration authority concerned with all aspects of immigration. Instead, a number of authorities with special functions have developed. Only recently can we observe a trend towards increased cooperation and even coordination between these agencies.

Three of the project countries have appointed special deputy ministers for immigration. France was first in 1974, followed by Sweden in 1975 and the Netherlands in 1981. The task of these ministers is not to take over all government decisions concerning immigration and immigrants, but rather to function as coordinators among the relevant ministries and central state or federal agencies. Only in Sweden, however, is the minister for immigration also responsible for regulation and control. In France this task is assumed by the Minister of the Interior and in the Netherlands by the Minister of Justice. Even though they each have a specialized deputy minister for immigration, France and the Netherlands have decided that the two interrelated policy areas should not be entrusted to the same official. Germany does not have a special minister for immigration, but in 1978 the Federal Chancellor appointed a Commissioner for foreigners (Ausländerbeauftragte), which should evaluate the situation of immigrants and make proposals for future immigration policy.

The Swedish system, integrating all aspects of immigration under one administration, was introduced in 1969 when the Swedish Board on Immigration was first established as an independent agency for both policy areas. This system has now and then been criticized for not functioning well enough, but few have demanded that the two aspects of immigration policy be once again separated. Even if they have never been fully integrated, they exist side by side within the same administrative organization.

This is only one example of a general trend towards coordinating the originally very dispersed administration of immigration policy. When policymakers and administrators became more aware in the 1970s of the close relationship between immigration regulation and immigrant policy, they tried to meet the need for oversight, coherence, and planning through reorganization and a new division of responsibility as well as through various working committees in which representatives for several administrative units were asked to cooperate. This trend towards a more integrated administration of immigration policy is probably only beginning.

12

Towards convergence

We have observed a divergence in immigration policy during the period of large-scale labor immigration. The industrialized states of Western Europe made similar economic gains, but they differed in immigration policy, since their preconditions of immigration were in many respects markedly different, and since some states mainly admitted colonial immigrants, while others relied on recruitment of foreign labor.

In this final chapter, we will argue that policy divergence has come to an end; instead, there is now a trend towards policy convergence. In fact, this trend started when recruitment of foreign labor was terminated at the beginning of the 1970s, at what we have called the turning point. But this does not mean that most differences between the project countries' immigration regulation have disappeared, nor that immigrant policy has assumed one and the same form everywhere. The implication is only that a slow and continuous shift in policies has brought the six project countries closer to one another than before. Discussion of a number of explanations for this convergence will allow us to sum up some of the major conclusions from previous chapters. In a short diversion, the immigration policy of the United States will then be compared to the European experiences, and finally, some recommendations will be offered, based on the comparative analysis.

No long-term planning and no partisan divisions

In the 1960s large-scale labor immigration was an established fact before immigration policy came into being. From the beginning there was no attempt to plan the size and composition of the flow of immigration, with the possible exception of Germany, which actively recruited foreign labor for temporary work. There was even less of an attempt to plan immigrant policy. There were no political controversies or partisan divisions over immigration in any of the project countries, with the exception of Britain, where political parties competed in their efforts to restrict colonial and post-colonial immigration.

Immigration policy has been molded by events: by economic interests profitably recruiting abroad as well as by what was thought to be the rewarding export of surplus labor from the sending countries. During the 1960s, immigration was largely left to the decisions of employers and jobseekers on the labor market, and immigration policy was laissez-faire, offering a framework within which immigration took place. Immigrant policy emerged only when the number of immigrants became so large that there were substantial demands for social services and it finally became obvious that a lack of housing facilities, schools, and so on would create serious problems in the future.

It took a long time in all of the project countries for policy planning to get started and for the relationship between immigration regulation and immigrant policy to be acknowledged. Guestworker countries have taken longer than others to perceive the needs and demands posed by the existence of a large immigrant population. They have clung firmly to the belief that their foreign workers would soon remigrate and have therefore postponed all kinds of immigrant policy initiatives much longer than have countries with permanent immigration.

Guestworker countries have inadvertently admitted permanent immigrants

Countries with large colonial immigration, like Britain, France, and the Netherlands, have tended to regard these immigrants as future permanent residents, because of their claim to citizenship in the mother country. But for the special reasons that we have discussed, the country that has made the most decisive commitment to a permanent policy is Sweden. Countries in which the immigration has primarily been labor-motivated have shown a preference for temporary immigration. The fact that Germany and Switzerland have no colonial immigration may give us one explanation of why Germany and Switzerland have guestworkers while Britain has permanent immigrants. But there are also many other possible explanations.

We have pointed to previous experiences of large-scale immigration and to the need for additional population or for a temporary increase in the labor force. We have mentioned the strength of labor unions and the force of a social democratic welfare ideology. We have also discussed the possible impact of to what extent the nation and national culture are seen as being threatened by the immigration of people with other languages, religions, and cultures. We could say that there has not been a real choice between various policy options. It has instead been more of a journey along traditional routes without much thought or deliberation. Looking for explanations, we most often find that preconditions have constrained the number of available options.

Immigrant policy has been more divergent than immigration regulation

There is not as much difference between the project countries with regard to immigration regulation as there is with regard to immigrant policy. Both guestworker countries and countries with permanent immigration have used the same sorts of instruments to implement regulation and control; but, because of a basic divergence in long-run policy aims, immigrant policies differ considerably.

The variations that we have found in immigration regulation and control cannot be explained simply by the existence of guestworker or nonguestworker policies. Recruitment of labor, for instance, has taken place under both policies. More important, policy development followed the same route: during the 1960s all countries allowed relatively free immigration, and afterwards, during the 1970s, they all introduced tight control. In Switzerland, Sweden, Germany, and France we have talked about a "stop" in labor immigration, even though there has not been a stop in all immigration. In Britain and the Netherlands, immigration was gradually reduced until severe immigration control was finally established there also. This control was not equally efficient in all countries, however. We have noted considerable problems with illegal immigrants in France and Germany. We will return to this at the end of the chapter because it may become an urgent issue in the future.

Guestworker countries are naturally not in favor of family reunion, and they often tend to neglect the education of immigrant children, offer only temporary housing, and so on. This kind of immigrant policy follows directly from their policy that immigration should be only temporary and that foreign workers will remigrate after a short period of time. But as we have seen, the outcome has not always followed the same neat logic. Immigrants are, for instance, unexpectedly well integrated in Switzerland, and if anything, better integrated there than many are in France, where the intention has been to admit at least substantial numbers of immigrants as permanent residents and eventually as naturalized French citizens. The outcome seems to be determined less by policy intentions and more by other important factors, such as the origin of the national groups that immigrated, and the economic situation of the host country.

When permanent resident status is generously given, it indicates the end of a guestworker policy

At one crucial point there has always been a very significant difference between guestworker and permanent countries, and this is a difference in immigration regulation and control. Guestworker countries have not been willing to offer foreign workers and their families any guarantees that their residence and work permits would be renewed for long and indefinite periods, whereas countries open for permanent immigration have granted foreign citizens permanent status after a few years and on relatively generous terms.

We have noted that the implication of this difference is that immigrants in guestworker countries have had to deal with much more risk and insecurity concerning their futures. They have had much less of a chance to plan their lives because they do not know how long they will be allowed to remain in the host country. They have not felt free to work actively to improve their own situation or to raise demands through political or labor organizations.

In this respect, the trend among the project countries is towards convergence. Already, 75 percent of foreign citizens in Switzerland have obtained a permit of permanent residence, and while only fewer than 25 percent in Germany have done so, at least the need to change the insecure position of immigrants has been more and more strongly advocated in the German political debate. The reason for this development is, of course, that the guestworker policy has failed on at least one point: foreign workers have stayed for so many years that they qualify for permanent status as well as for citizenship in both Germany and Switzerland, even though such requirements are rigorous in these two countries compared with the other project countries. However, only a very small number of those who qualify actually apply for permanent status or citizenship.

All of the project countries, regardless of their original policy aims, have admitted a large immigrant population, with several languages and cultures represented, and this population will remain in the future. When this situation is recognized, albeit late and reluctantly, the starting point for an immigrant policy is established. Some kind of integration becomes necessary, at least an "integration for some time", as it has been called in Germany. The second generation is free to voice their demands in a way that the first generation never was, and guestworker countries must listen to them just as attentively as must other countries of immigration.

Integration of large immigrant populations is the future task ahead of all the project countries

In trying to explain the initial variance in immigration policy, we have pointed to the countries' long-term preconditions for immigration and immigration policy rather than to their conscious policymaking. We have argued that the outcome has been decided by their economy, population, geography, history, and so on, and their experience of previous large-scale immigration, and not by policy planning and political divisions.

The large-scale labor immigration that took place in all the project countries during the 1960s was a new and a shared experience. Furthermore, all countries stopped the recruitment of foreign labor in the early 1970s, not only because of the depressed economy but also because of the need to stabilize the situation which had emerged from the large-scale and rapid immigrations of previous years. Finally, all the project countries face the same task in the 1980s; namely, to find ways to integrate the immigrant groups into the various aspects of society. The division regarding this goal between guestworker countries and countries with permanent immigration is not as decisive as it was before. In fact, this division is already becoming merely historical. The convergence in policy that we find today is primarily a result of the fact that all countries are facing similar problems.

The United States: immigration is comparable, but immigration policy is not

European labor migration is often compared to the very large migration that has taken place to the United States during the past decades, especially the immigration of undocumented workers from Mexico and other parts of Latin America and from the Caribbean. Although there are several difficulties involved in making a comparison with the USA, a short attempt will be made here to do so. In many respects the similarities are considerable; in other respects there are major and important differences.

During the 1920s and 1950s the USA introduced a more restrictive immigration regulation, in this respect paralleling the European policy development. But in contrast to Europe, there was no "stop" in labor immigration in the 1970s, although there has been a year-by-year fluctuation caused by the varying demands of the American economy. Annual immigration has amounted in absolute numbers to about one million persons, including both legal and illegal immigrants.

The American control system differs from the European (more particularly from the continental, since the British system has some elements in common with the American system). It is based on visa requirements and border controls, and those who manage to pass these controls can be relatively certain that they can stay on in the vast American continent. Only on very rare occasions are illegal foreigners discovered somewhere inside the USA. Those who are apprehended are mostly found somewhere near the border region, trying to make their illegal entrance. As we have seen, Europe has done away with border controls as much as possible in order to promote trade and tourism. Visas have in most cases been removed and residence permits are required only after a three to six months' stay.

The actual number of undocumented workers is apparently not known even to the American authorities. Estimates given are from four million up to twelve million. There is no doubt that there is in the USA an extremely large, illegal immigrant population on top of the large legal immigration that has always taken place throughout its history. The theoretically tight regulation of immigration has not been enforced. The American situation resembles Europe in that labor market demands have in practice been allowed to influence the size of immigration, and if policymakers have not exactly ignored what was going on, they have at least not made long-term plans for integrating the new immigrant population. In both Europe and America, governments have relied on the vague idea that guestworkers, or in America undocumented workers, would probably one day return home.

The gap between the rich industrial host societies and the poor countries of emigration is so wide in both Europe and America, however, that large-scale return has always been unlikely. There exists instead in both cases a latent migration pressure that the immigration countries must be able to control if they are not willing to accept large-scale immigration. Europe may be said to have been more successful in coping with this migratory threat, or perhaps the USA has simply been less willing to attempt to do so.

One important difference is the lack of effective internal control in the USA. Foreign citizens can rent an apartment, take employment, pay taxes, enroll in the social security system etc., without being asked about their immigration status. The theory is that individuals should not have to undergo inquisitive controls which intrude upon their personal liberty. Employers should not have to act as police, asking their employees about their papers.

Labor unions have never been able to organize large parts of the American labor force and are especially weak in the trades where most of the undocumented workers are found. As there is always some degree of risk for most illegal immigrants, they may often be unwilling to organize in unions and demand fair working conditions, decent housing standards, and civil rights. This means that employers and landlords benefit from illegal immigration, and when this economic interest is combined with the traditional American protection of individual freedom and privacy, it becomes very difficult for policymakers to devise an acceptable system to control illegal immigration.

Europe has only lately discovered that large immigration of a temporary nature has a major and lasting impact on the whole of society. Once this fact was understood, a period of policy reconsideration followed, with an emphasis on immigrant policy, promoted by tight immigration regulation and aliens control. The United States is still undecided, considering a possible limited importation of labor for temporary and controlled employment combined with an amnesty for some of the millions of undocumented aliens. This study of European immigration policy may be read as a warning not to underestimate the socioeconomic impact of such a guestworker program.

Political parties have not foreseen the implications of large-scale immigration

We have repeatedly stated that immigration policy has generally not been the subject of partisan political conflict and parliamentary debate. Economic interests have helped to determine the size of immigration, and the executive power, assisted by civil servants and experts, has shaped immigration regulation and immigrant policy. In explaining this we have discussed the legal and technical nature of the problems and argued that there were few conflicting domestic interests about immigration as long as everyone believed that it was good for the whole nation. We have also referred to the illusion that labor immigration was a short-term phenomenon, subject only to economic fluctuations.

It is nevertheless astonishing that such a dramatic change of policy as the sudden stop of immigration, affecting so many interests and full of future implications, could take place without major debate between political parties and without conflict between domestic interest groups. One might perhaps have expected that politicians more than others would have been ready to suggest new policies. This has not been the case, however, and this lack of political foresight may be seen as an indication of two problems: first, that politicians use short-term perspectives most of the time; second, that immigrants suffer a loss of political rights as foreign citizens in the host countries.

Short-term perspectives in politics

Immigration policy can in one respect be compared to environmental policy: in both areas it took a very long time for politicians to notice what had in fact been going on for decades. Costs of production are of course paid by industrial firms, but it was completely unnoticed for many years that there are huge indirect costs to the environment that companies usually did not pay for. They were free to carelessly dispose of great amounts of waste, dangerous, even poisonous, to the environment, without having to pay for the cost that this created for the rest of society. Politicians were not used to thinking about the environmental costs of industrial production, and they often used much too short a time perspective (usually only one or two election periods).

In a similar way, companies have paid only the direct costs of labor immigration, i.e. the immediate costs to the individual firm. This has been possible because politicians were long unaware of other indirect costs. Only after some time did they discover that immigration placed great demands on public expenditures for things such as housing, education and culture.

This parallel between environmental and immigration policies does have its limitations, however. Immigration has been profitable not only for companies, but also for the national economy, since immigrants have been mostly young people in their productive years with some schooling and perhaps also some vocational training already behind them. Immigration countries have saved money that they would otherwise have had to spend on education. There are thus a number of differences between the two policy areas; still, in both, the fact is that the costs to society have been neglected by politicians, because of too short a time perspective.

A dilemma for democracy: immigrants are excluded from political rights

One important reason why politicians have not considered the long-term effects of immigration is their preoccupation with more immediate problems. But they have also disregarded immigrant interests because foreign citizens have no voting rights. Only citizens are entitled to full political and civil rights, according to well established constitutional law. Foreign citizens are excluded, even if they reside and work in a country, pay taxes and educate their children there. The constitutional doctrine is, of course, that foreigners who establish a more permanent residence in the country of immigration shall become naturalized citizens before obtaining political rights. If naturalization takes ten, fifteen, or twenty years, it means that immigrants are deprived of voting rights for this period, and as long as immigrants cannot vote, the political parties fail to consider immigrant needs.

It can be said that political democracy does not fully function when more than ten million men and women in Europe are deprived of voting rights. Moreover, in Germany and Switzerland, foreigners have very limited chances of naturalization. In countries where the requirements for naturalization have been lessened, many foreigners abstain voluntarily from changing their nationality. They identify themselves as Turks, Greeks, or Spaniards and do not want to change their national identity in order to gain full political rights. In some countries like Sweden, foreign citizens have been granted voting rights in local elections in contradiction to traditional constitutional law. Other countries have begun to accept dual citizenship, and this may be a partial solution to the dilemma that national states are confronted with, when large numbers of their adult residents for years lack political rights. In most countries, however, immigrants remain excluded from political participation, and no attempts are made to find even partial solutions.

Remaining policy divergence: cultural pluralism only in small states

Restrictive immigration regulation and a common insight that most immigrants who already live with their families in the European immigration countries will remain there for the future both give evidence of a trend towards convergence. With stable and large immigrant populations, guestworker countries, or what are now perhaps better called *former* guestworker countries, are also formulating new immigrant policies and thereby perhaps looking at what has already been done in some of the other immigration countries. As regards cultural integration, however, the policies are not converging. The issue is whether immigrants will be assimilated into the culture of the host society or be given an opportunity to preserve and develop their national cultures within a pluralistic society.

As we have seen, large countries like France, Britain, and Germany have put emphasis on the value of their own languages and cultures, while small states like the Netherlands and Sweden are more inclined to accept the cultures of the immigrants. In Switzerland, where French, German, and Italian, and Rhaeto-Romanic are official languages, there is not much freedom of choice, other than possibly the freedom to decide what canton or community one wants to live in, because only one language is usually recognized there. A country's policy of cultural integration is reflected in how it educates immigrant children, especially as regards mother-tongue instruction and instruction where the mother tongue is used by the teacher as the language of instruction. While Bavarian schools have emphasized mother-tongue instruction, they have done so in accordance with Bavaria's special kind of guestworker policy. The instruction represents preparation for emigration and is not an expression of multicultural ambitions. Similar models of education for immigrant children thus serve completely different aims in Bavaria than, for instance, in Sweden, where mother-tongue instruction aims at an active bilingualism: preparing for work in Sweden with a good knowledge of the parents' language and an opportunity to share their culture.

Switzerland and Germany had of course no reasons to integrate guest-workers, who were only temporarily employed, but when these workers stayed on for several years, they were asked to make a choice, whether they wanted to stay and assimilate or return to their country of origin. In an early phase of immigration there was a naive belief in countries with permanent immigration as well that a quick assimilation was possible. In fact, however, assimilation was neither easily achieved nor particularly advantageous. What was happening instead was an encounter of cultures where each was at least somewhat influenced by the others but where the host country's majority culture prevailed. Large investment is necessary if one language, for instance Serbo-Croatian, shall live on in the second or third generation in Germany, the Netherlands, or Sweden. Only the Netherlands and Sweden have seriously considered such attempts, inspired among other things by movements toward a new ethnicity. Notwithstanding their policy of cultural integration, however, all countries agree that immigrants must learn the language of the host country because it is the only way to achieve integration, especially on the labor market.

Race relations

Although France and the Netherlands have had significant immigration from the Third World, and although there is a lot of evidence of racial discrimination in other project countries, the issues of prejudice, discrimination, and race relations are discussed in this study mainly in relation to Britain. In Germany, Switzerland, and Sweden the number of colored immigrants has increased, but it is still relatively unusual in most places to meet people of another color. In this respect the three countries with post-colonial immigration present a major difference. Especially in Great Britain, the colored population has not only become quite visible but is a significant part of the population as well.

Prejudice and discrimination against immigrants exists in all of the project countries. It is directed not only against immigrants but against all kinds of easily distinguishable groups: old people, women, handicapped, foreigners, and others. Immigrants are often quickly recognized, because of their language, clothes, habits, or religion, and prejudice and discrimination is therefore often turned against them. But the most visible immigrants are of course those whose skin has a color that differentiates them from the majority population. They are immediately visible even after a lifelong stay in the country, and their children, native born, may be taken for colored immigrants as were their parents. For this reason alone they will be subject to more discrimination than other immigrants.

Immigration to Britain has not been larger than immigration to Germany or France, but many more immigrants have been colored. This seems to make a difference, even if immigrants to Britain in other respects have often been well prepared in advance for integration into British society. They often speak some English, or at least know that English is the language of the educated in the country that they come from. They are often oriented towards English culture, although large differences exist between the local communities they have left and the great cities they have come to.

The race theories and racial ideologies that played such an important role during the Second World War have since then been completely repudiated by social scientists, condemned by all but a very few political parties, and practically banned from political life. It is well established that no difference shall be made between human beings nor between the value of individual men or women based on race. Nevertheless, racist attitudes endure in many places, although they are not openly expressed. Britain is an exception; it strongly emphasizes the racial aspects of immigration. One can hardly imagine that Germany, Switzerland, or France would in a similar manner use labels like "race politics". This does not imply, of course, that there is less racism at the beginning of the 1980s on the continent, but for historical reasons there is more of a taboo against racism than in Britain.

Racial ideas were respectable at the time of the British Empire, and there was already a suggestion of white superiority in the fundamental belief that it was the mission of Great Britain to extend the benefits of civilization to all parts of the Commonwealth. Immigrants encounter racial attitudes in Britain that they have previously met in their home countries. They might sometimes have been even too willing to accept prejudice and discrimination as something familiar from the past. But they have also come to Great Britain with expectations of being treated as citizens with full and equal rights, and not as second-class inhabitants. The second generation, in particular, born and raised in Britain, has demanded opportunities equal to those given other young people in the country.

As we have seen, immigrants thought to be of British (white) ancestry (patrials) are admitted before other (i.e. colored) immigrants, and this is a procedure unique to Britain; there is no corresponding regulation in the other project countries. Furthermore, British immigrant policy is mainly aimed at preventing racial discrimination and mainly administered by the

Commission on Racial Equality. The conclusion to be drawn is not, however, that British policy is not comparable to that of the other countries. On the contrary, we can state that a comparison shows that Britain, like the other project countries, has made increasing efforts to reduce the flow of immigration and at the same time to further the integration of those already in the country. For historical reasons and because of the large number of colored immigrants in Britain, however, immigration policy is perceived and discussed in terms of race relations. The significance of this is not that there are different policy goals, or that they are necessarily harder to achieve, but that they may require different kinds of instruments.

Policy convergence and illegal immigration

The modern history of international migration to Western Europe can be divided into three periods: 1945–60, 1960–74, and thereafter. During the first of these periods there were relatively small migratory flows and a laissez-faire immigration policy. The "unusual" period is the second one, with high international migration including large-scale recruitment of foreign labor. During this second period, which has received a lot of attention in this study, major differences emerged in the project countries. These differences still exist, with important repercussions during the third and last period. But to the extent that we find a policy trend after 1974, it is in the direction of convergence, and the basic reason for this seems to be that all project countries face a similar situation with a strictly limited control of new immigration and a considerable immigrant population which is increasingly inclined to remain permanently.

During the second period, before the "turning point", it was not obvious that immigration regulation and control is closely interrelated to immigrant policy. Afterwards, during the late 1970s, this close relationship was eventually realized. We have demonstrated in this study that large-scale immigration has created a demand for social services and for a whole social infrastructure in the host societies, and we have seen that immigrant policy is often efficient only when indirect measures are supplemented by direct ones, devised to cope with the special difficulties that immigrants are confronted with. All this required again some control of the size and composition of immigration, a fact that was not understood, however, until a reconsideration of policies began in all the project countries.

If the industrialized countries of Western Europe were to open their doors to foreign labor again, there would be no shortage of jobseekers, especially from countries outside Europe. But it is not at all likely that the project countries will once again allow large-scale labor immigration. Their aim will be instead to limit future immigration and to control the illegal traffic that has increased as a direct consequence of stricter regulations.

Those who want to work in Germany or France, for instance, sometimes try to enter as family members or as political refugees, but many also try to make a living as illegal workers without the required work and residence permits. Some employers and landlords may for a time benefit from this situation, and there may exist economic interests in the employment of such workers, for whom the host society bears no responsibility at all. But the general long-run objective of all the project countries is certainly to prevent illegal immigration without an undue disturbance of normal travelling or personal privacy, not least important for the immigrant minorities with ties to their countries of origin.

At the present time, the task ahead is to provide a decent standard of living for both the first and the second generation of the immigrant minorities: Turks in Germany, Algerians in France, Pakistanis in Britain, Moluccans in the Netherlands, Finns in Sweden, Italians in Switzerland and so on. And this will succeed only if further immigration is limited and illegal entry to the countries is effectively stopped.

Select bibliography

General

Almond, G.L. and Powell, B.G. 1966. *Comparative Politics: A Developmental Approach*. Boston, Little Brown.

Castles, S. and Kosack, G. 1973. *Immigrant Workers and Class Structure in Western Europe*. Oxford University Press.

Dohse, K. 1981. *Ausländische Arbeiter und bürgerlicher Staat. Genese und Funktion von staatlicher Ausländerpolitik und Ausländerrecht. Vom Kaiserrecht bis zur Bundesrepublik Deutschland*. Königstein/Taunus, Verlag Anton Hain.

Esser, H. 1980. *Aspekte der Wanderungssoziologie. Assimilation und Integration von Wanderern, ethnischen Gruppen und Minderheiten*. Darmstadt and Neuwied, Luchterhand.

Esser, H., Neumann, K.H. and Weber, W. (ed.) 1979. *Arbeitsmigration und Integration. Sozialwissenschaftliche Grundlagen*. Kronberg, Hanstein.

Freeman, G. 1979. *Immigrant Labor and Racial Conflict in Industrial Societies*. Princeton University Press.

Hoffmann-Nowotny, H.-J. 1973. *Sociologie des Fremdarbeiterproblems: Eine theoretische und empirische Analyse am Beispiel der Schweiz*. Stuttgart, F. Enke.

Hoffmann-Nowotny, H.-J. and Hondrich, K.O. (eds.). 1982. *Ausländer in der Bundesrepublik Deutschland und in der Schweiz, Segregation und Integration: Eine vergleichende Untersuchung*. Frankfurt/New York, Campus.

Horst, C. 1980. *Arbejdskraft: Vare eller menneske? Migration og vest-europaeisk kapitalisme*. Kultursociologiske Skrifter no. 10. Copenhagen, Akademisk forlag.

Krane, R. 1979. *International Labour Migration in Europe*. New York, Praeger.

Kubat, D. (ed.). 1979. *The Politics of Migration Policies*. New York, Centre for Migration Studies. (German edn, E. Gehmacher, D. Kubat and U. Mehrländer, *Ausländerpolitik im Konflikt*, Bonn, 1978.)

Lijphart, A. 1967. 'Typologies of democratic systems', Paper presented at the Seventh World Congress of the International Political Science Association, Brussels.

Miller, M.J. 1981. *Foreign Workers in Western Europe, An Emerging Political Force*. New York, Praeger.

Thomas, E.-J. (ed.). 1982. *Immigrant Workers in Europe: Their Legal Status. A Comparative Study*. Paris, The Unesco Press.

306   Select bibliography

Withol de Wenden, C. 1978. *Les Immigrés dans la Cité.* Paris, La Documentation Française.

Sweden

Björklund, U. 1981. *North to Another Country: The Formation of a Suryoyo Community in Sweden.* Stockholm, EIFO.
Ekberg, J. 1983. *Inkomsteffekter av invandring.* Dissertation, Växjö, Lund Economic Studies.
Engelbrektsson, U.B. 1978. *The Force of Tradition, Turkish Migrants at Home and Abroad.* Dissertation, Göteborg.
Fred, M. 1983. *Managing Culture Contact: The Organisation of Swedish Immigration Policy.* Stockholm, EIFO.
Hamberg, E. and Hammar, T. (eds.). 1981. *Invandringen och framtiden.* Stockholm, Liber.
Hammar, T. 1964. *Sverige åt svenskarna, Invandringspolitik, utlänningskontroll och asylrätt 1900–1932.* Dissertation, Stockholm.
1979. *Det första invandrarvalet.* Stockholm, Liber.
Hammar, T. and Lindby, K. 1979. *Swedish Immigration Research, Introductory Survey and Annotated Bibliography.* Stockholm, EIFO.
Reinans, S. 1980. *Utlänningar på den svenska arbetsmarknaden.* Stockholm, EIFO.
Sachs, L. 1983. *Evil Eye or Bacteria: Turkish Migrant Women and Swedish Health Care.* Dissertation, Stockholm.
Skutnabb-Kangas, T. 1981. *Tvåspråkighet.* Lund, Liber läromedel.
Tung, R.K.C. 1981. *Exit-Voice Catastrophes, Dilemma between Migration and Participation.* Dissertation, Stockholm.
Wadensjö, E. 1973. *Immigration och samhällsekonomi.* Dissertation, Lund.
Widgren, J. *Svensk invandrarpolitik.* Lund, Liber läromedel.

Government documents
Arbetsmarknadsdepartementet. 1978. *Sverige och flyktingarna,* DSA 1978:1, Stockholm.
1979. *Svensk invandrarpolitik inför 1980-talet,* DSA 1979:6, Stockholm.
Invandrarutredningen 3. 1974. *Invandrarna och minoriteterna, English Summary,* SOU 1974:69, Stockholm.
Invandringspolitiken, delbetänkande av invandrarpolitiska kommitén. 1982. *Bakgrund,* SOU 1982:49, Stockholm.
1983. *Förslag,* SOU 1983:29, Stockholm
Kommunal rösträtt för invandrare, rösträttsutredningen. 1975. SOU 1975:15, Stockholm.
Olika ursprung–gemenskap i Sverige. 1983. *Utbildning för språklig och kulturell mångfald,* SOU 1983:57, Stockholm.

The Netherlands
Aalberts, M. and Kamminga, E. 1983. *Politie en Allochtonen.* The Hague, State Publishers.
ACOM (Adviescommissie Onderzoek Minderheden). 1979. *Advies Onderzoek Minderheden.* The Hague, State Publishers.

Bagley, C. 1973. *The Dutch Plural Society: A Comparative Study in Race Relations*. Oxford University Press.

Bovenkerk, F. (ed.). 1978. *Omdat zij anders zijn: Patronen van rasdiscriminatie in Nederland*. Meppel, Boom.

De Graaf, H. 1979. *Evaluatie Centra voor Beroepsoriëntatie en Beroepsoefening*. The Hague, NIMAWO.

De Vries, M. 1981. *Waar komen zij terecht? De positie van jeugdige allochtonen in het onderwijs en op de arbeidsmarkt*. Report prepared for ACOM. The Hague, State Publishers.

Entzinger, H. 1975. "Nederland Immigratieland? Enkele overwegingen bij het overheidsbeleid inzake allochtone minderheden", *Beleid en Maatschappij* (Meppel, Boom), II, 12: 326–36.

—— 1981. "Immigrant minorities in the Netherlands: research and policy development", *New Community* (London, Commission for Racial Equality), IX, 1: 84–90.

Groenendijk, C.A. 1979. "Van Gastarbeider tot Medeburger", *Beleid en Maatschappij* (Meppel, Boom), VI, 2: 52–63 and VI, 5: 151–2.

Harmonisatieraad Welzijnsbeleid, (G)een goede raad. 1981. The Hague, State Publishers.

Köbben, A.J.F. 1979. "De gijzelingsakties van Zuidmolukkers en hun effekten op de samenleving", *Transaktie* (Groningen, Xeno), VIII, 2: 147–54.

Kool, C. and van Praag, C.S. 1982. *Bevolkingsprognoses Allochtonen in Nederland*, Vol. II: *Surinamers en Antillianen*. Rijswijk, Social and Cultural Planning Office.

Lijphart, A. 1975. *The Politics of Accommodation: Pluralism and Democracy in the Netherlands*. Berkeley, University of California Press.

Molleman, H.A.A. 1978. "Culturele minderheden en overheidsbeleid", *Socialisme en Democratie* (Deventer, Kluwer), XXXV, 7–8: 328–45.

Nijzink, T. 1979. *Gemeentelijke woningtoewijzing aan buitenlanders*. Utrecht, Nederlands Centrum Buitenlanders.

Penninx, R. 1981. *Migration, Minorities and Policy in the Netherlands*. Report for the Continuous Reporting System on Migration (SOPEMI) of the OECD. Rijswijk, Ministry of Cultural Affairs, Recreation and Social Work.

Van den Berg-Eldering, L., Adriaansen, A.C. and Grebel, H.W. 1980. *Turkse en Marokkaanse kinderen in het Nederlandse onderwijs*. Leyden, Centre for the Study of Social Conflict.

Van Dijk, P.J.C. and Penninx, R. 1976. *Migration and Development: The Netherlands REMPLOD Project; An Experimental Venture in the Integration of Field Research and Policy Making*. The Hague, IMWOO/NUFFIC.

Van Donselaar, J. and Nelissen, C. 1982. "De deelname van racistische politieke partijen aan de Kamerverkiezingen van 1981", *Intermediair* (Amsterdam, Intermediair), XVIII.

Van Praag, C.S. and Kool, C. 1982. *Bevolkingsprognose allochtonen in Nederland; Turken en Marokkanen, herziene versie 1982*. Rijswijk, Social and Cultural Planning Office.

Veenman, J. and Vijverberg, C.H.T. (eds.). *De arbeidsmarktproblematiek van Molukkers; Een verkennend onderzoek*. Rotterdam, Erasmus University.

WRR (Wetenschappelijke Raad voor het Regeringsbeleid). 1979. *Ethnic Minorities*. The Hague, State Publishers.

Government documents
Beleidsplan Culturele Minderheden in het Onderwijs. 1981. The Hague, Ministry of Education and Science.
Nota Buitenlandse Werknemers, Memorie van Antwoord. 1974. Second Chamber of the States-General, Session 1973–74, 10.504, no. 9.
Notitie Vreemdelingenbeleid. 1979. Second Chamber of the States-General, Session 1978–79, 15.649, nos. 1 & 2.
Ontwerp-Minderhedennota. 1981. The Hague, Ministry of the Interior.

Great Britain

Anwar, M. 1979. *The Myth of Return: Pakistani Immigrants in Britain.* London, Heinemann.
Ballard, R. 1979. 'Ethnic minorities and the social services', in V.S. Khan (ed.), *Minority Families in Britain.* London, Macmillan.
Beetham, D. 1970. *Transport and Turbans: A Comparative Study of Local Politics.* Oxford University Press.
Britain's Black Population. 1980. London, Runnymede Trust.
Butler, D. and Stokes, D. 1969. *Political Change in Britain.* London, Macmillan.
Carrier, N.H. and Jeffrey, J.R. 1951. *External Migration: A Study of Available Statistics 1815–1910.* London, General Registry Office.
Cheetham, J. 1972. 'Immigration', in A.H. Halsey (ed.), *Trends in British Society since 1900.* London, Macmillan.
Conservative Central Office. 1949. *The Right Road for Britain.* London.
  1979. *Conservative Party Manifesto 1979.* London.
Deakin, N. 1972. 'The immigration issue in British politics 1948–64', unpublished PhD thesis, University of Sussex.
Edwards, J. and Batley, R. 1978. *The Politics of Positive Discrimination.* London, Tavistock.
Freeman, 1979. *See General Section.*
Garrard, J.A. 1971. *The English and Immigration.* Oxford University Press.
Lawrence, D. 1978–79. "Prejudice, politics and race", *New Community*, VII, 1: 44–55.
Layton-Henry, Z. 1978. "Race, electoral strategy and the major parties", *Parliamentary Affairs*, XXXI, 3: 268–81.
  1984. *The Politics of Race in Britain.* London, Allen and Unwin.
Layton-Henry, Z. and Taylor, S. 1979. "Immigration and ethnic relations: political aspects no. 2", *New Community*, VII, 3.
  1980. "Immigration and race relations: political aspects no. 4", *New Community*, VIII, 1–2.
Lusgarten, L. 1980. *Legal Control of Racial Discrimination.* London, Macmillan.
Miles, R. and Phizacklea, A. 1977. *The TUC, Black Workers and New Commonwealth Immigration 1954–1973.* Working Paper no. 6, Research Unit on Ethnic Relations, University of Bristol.
Moore, R. and Wallace, T. 1975. *Slamming the Door: The Administration of Immigration Control.* Oxford, Martin Robertson.
Patterson, S. 1965. *Dark Strangers.* London, Tavistock.
Peach, C. 1968. *West Indian Migration to Britain.* Oxford University Press.
Phizacklea, A. and Miles, R. 1980. *Labour and Racism.* London, Routledge and Kegan-Paul.

Ratcliffe, P. 1981. *Racism and Reaction: A Profile of Handsworth.* London, Routledge and Kegan Paul.
Rex, J. and Tomlinson, S. 1979. *Colonial Immigrants in a British City.* London, Routledge and Kegan Paul.
Rose, E.J. *et al.* 1969. *Colour and Citizenship.* Oxford University Press.
Smith, D. 1977. *Racial Disadvantage in Britain.* Harmondsworth, Penguin Books.
Studlar, D. 1974. "British public opinion, colour issues and Enoch Powell, a longitudinal analysis", *British Journal of Political Science,* 4: 371–81.
Tannahill, J.A. 1958. *European Volunteer Workers in Britain.* Manchester University Press.
Trade Union Congress. 1955. *Annual Report.*
Zubrzycki, J. 1956. *Polish Immigrants in Britain.* The Hague, Nijhoff.

Government documents
Department of the Environment (DOE). 1976. *Census Indicators of Urban Deprivation.* Working Note no. 8.
HMSO. 1918. *Royal Commission on Dominions.* Cd 8642.
1934. *Macdonald Report: Report of the Interdepartmental Committee on Migration Policy,* Cmd 4689.
1949. *Royal Commission on Population,* Cmd 7695.
1977. *Policy for the Inner City,* Cmnd 6845.
1981. *Ethnic Minorities in Britain: A Study of Trends in their Position since 1961.* Home Office Research Study no. 68.
1981. *Immigration into Britain: Notes on the Regulations and Procedures.* Central Office of Information Reference Pamphlet no. 164.
1981. *Racial Disadvantage: Fifth Report from the Home Affairs Committee, 1980-81,* House of Commons 424-1.
1981. *Scarman Report: The Brixton Disorders, 10–12 April 1981: Report of an Inquiry by the Rt. Hon. The Lord Scarman,* Cmnd 8427.
1981. *West Indian Children in our Schools: Interim Report of the Committee of Inquiry into the Education of Children from Minority Groups,* Cmnd 8273.
Home Office, 1981. *Racial Attacks: Report of a Home Office Study.*
Ministry of Labour. 1949. *Report of the Working Party on the Employment in the United Kingdom of Surplus Colonial Labour,* Public Records Office, Documents 26/226.
Secretary of State for the Colonies. 1950. *Coloured People from the British Colonial Territories,* Memorandum to the Cabinet, 18 May 1950, Public Records Office, Cabinet Papers (50) 113.

France
Allard, L., Buffard, M., Regazzola, T. and Marie, M. 1977. *Situations migratoires.* Paris, Editions Galilée.
Benoît, J. 1979. *E comme Esclaves.* Paris, A. Moreau.
Briot, F. and Verbunt, G. 1981. *Immigrés dans la crise.* Paris, Editions Ouvrières.
Calvez, C. 1969. "Orientation pour la politique d'immigration et l'action en faveur des travailleurs migrants", *Hommes et Migrations* (Paris), 768.
Cordeiro, A. and Verhaeren, R.E. 1977. *Les travailleurs immigrés et la Sécurité Sociale.* Presses Universitaires de Grenoble.

Costa-Lascoux, J. and de Wenden-Didier, C. 1981. "Les travailleurs immigrés clandestins en France; approche politique et institutionnelle", *Studi Emigrazione* (Centro Studi Emigrazione Roma), 63: 349–70.

Culture Immigrée, 1977. Revue *Autrement* (Paris).

L'Emploi des Travailleurs Immigrés. 1978. *Feuillets pratiques*. Paris, Editions Francis Lefebvre.

Fontanet, J. 1970. "Les trois impératifs d'une politique d'immigration", *Hommes et Migrations* (Paris).

Gani, L. 1972. *Syndicats et travailleurs immigrés*. Paris, Editions Sociales.

Ginesy-Galano, M. 1980. *Le project de loi d'Ornano sur les foyers-hôtels: rappel des origines et analyse critique*. Paris, CIEM.

GISTI (Group d'Information et de soutien des travailleurs immigrés). 1980a. *La loi Bonnet*. Paris, CIEM.

1980b. *Immigration familiale I et II*. Paris, CIEM.

1980c. *La circulaire Stoleru*. Paris, CIEM.

1981a. *Les jeunes étrangers en France*. Paris, CIEM.

1981b. *Les drois des étrangers face à l'administration*. Paris, CIEM.

1981c. *Santé et Protection Sociale des Etrangers*. Paris, CIEM.

Hervo, M. and Charras, M.-A. 1971. *Bidonvilles*. Paris, François Maspero.

Group Oecuménique. 1979a. *Les immigrés en France. Aujourd'hui?* Paris, CIEM.

1979b. *Les raisons de notre refus. Plaidoyer pour l'homme*. Paris, CIEM.

Lebon, A. 1977. *Immigration et VIIe Plan*. Paris, La Documentation Française.

1981. *La contribution des étrangers à la population de la France entre le 1er janvier 1946 et le 1er janvier 1980*. Paris, Ministère du Travail et de la Participation.

Lepors, A. 1977. *Immigration et développement économique et social*. Paris, La Documentation Française.

Mangin, S. 1982. *Le bilan: travailleurs immigrés*. Paris, CIEM.

Minces, J. 1973. *Les travailleurs étrangers en France*. Paris, Editions du Seuil.

Tapinos, G. 1975. *L'immigration étrangère en France 1946–1973*. Paris, Presses Universitaires de France.

Les travailleurs immigrés. 1976. Special issue of *Revue Droit Social*, Paris, Librairie Sociale et Economique.

Verbunt, G. 1980. *L'intégration par l'autonomie. L'attitude de la CFDT, de l'Eglise catholique et de la FASTI face aux revendications d'autonomie des travailleurs immigrés*. Paris, CIEM.

1981. *La nouvelle politique migratoire en France*. Dossiers Migrations no. 5. Paris, CIEM.

Government documents

Office National d'Immigration. 1981. *La nouvelle politique de l'immigration et le dispositif législatif adopté en octobre 1981*. Paris, ONI/Secrétariat d'Etat aux Immigrés.

Inspection Générale des Affaires Sociales (IGAS). 1982. *Le Fonds d'Action Sociale*. Paris, Ministère de la Solidarité Nationale.

Secrétariat d'Etat aux Travailleurs Immigrés. 1977. "Une politique globale de l'immigration, Les 25 mesures nouvelles", *Hommes et Migration* (Paris), 872.

1977. *La Nouvelle Politique de l'Immigration*. Paris, Secrétariat d'Etat aux Travailleurs Immigrés.

Federal Republic of Germany

Ansay, T. and Gessner, V. (eds.). 1974. Gastarbeiter in Gesellschaft und Recht. Munich.

Armengand, A. 1971. 'Die Bevölkerung Europas von 1700–1914', in C.M. Cipolla and K. Borchardt (eds.), *Bevölkerungsgeschichte Europas.* Munich.

Bartels, G., Delbrück, J. and Wiegel, K. 1976. 'Vorschläge zur Reform des Ausländerrechts', in Konrad-Adenauer-Stiftung (ed.), *Integration ausländischer Arbeitnehmer: Verwaltung, Recht, Partizipation.* Bonn.

Becker, F. and Braasch, D. 1980. *Recht der ausländischen Arbeitnehmer. Eine systematische Darstellung.* Darmstadt/Neuwied.

Bodenbender, W. 1976. *Zwischenbilanz der Ausländerpolitik.* Paper presented to the Conference on Bildungsprobleme und Zukunftserwartungen der Kinder Türkischer Gastarbeiter. Munich, Südosteuropa-Gesellschaft.

Brepohl, W. 1948. *Der Aufbau des Ruhrvolkes im Zuge der Ost-West-Wanderung, Beitrage zur deutschen Sozialgeschichte des 19. und 20. Jarhrunderts.* Recklinghausen.

Dohse 1981. *See General Section.*

Esser, H. 1983a. 'Garstarbeiter', in W. Benz (ed.), *Die Bundesrepublik Deutschland,* vol. II. Frankfurt, Fischer.

1983b. 'Ist das Ausländerproblem in der Bundesrepublik Deutschland ein Türkenproblem', in R. Italiaander (ed.), *Fremde raus? Fremdenangst und Ausländerfeindlichkeit.* Frankfurt, Fischer.

Freund, W.S. 1980. *Gastarbeiter. Integration oder Rückkehr? Grundfragen der Ausländerpolitik.* Neustadt/Weinstrasse.

Franz, F. 1974. 'Die aufenthaltsrechtliche Stellung der ausländischen Arbeiter', in Ansay & Gessner 1974.

Heldmann, H.H. 1974. *Ausländerrecht. Disziplinarordnung für eine Minderheit.* Darmstadt/Neuwied.

Kevenhörster, P. 1974. *Ausländische Arbeitnehmer im politischen System der BRD. Ausländer-Interessenvertretung im politischen Entscheidungsprozess.* Opladen.

Korte, H. 1981. 'Entwicklung und Bedeutung von Arbeitsmigration und Ausländerbeschäftigung in der Bundesrepublik Deutschland zwischen 1950 und 1979', in H. Mommsen and W. Schulze, (eds.), *Vom Elend der Handarbeit. Probleme historischer Unterschichtenforschung.* Stuttgart.

Korte, H. and Schmidt, A. 1983. *Migration und ihre sozialen Folgen.* Göttingen.

Kremer, M. and Spangenberg, H. 1980. *Assimilation ausländischer Arbeitnehmer in der Bundesrepublik Deutschland.* Königstein/Taunus.

Lohrmann, R. 1974. 'Politische Auswirkungen der Arbeitskraftewanderungen auf die Bundesrepublik Deutschland', in R. Lohrmann and K. Manfrass (eds.), *Ausländerbeschäftigung und internationale Politik.* Munich.

Mackenroth, G. 1953. *Bevölkerungslehre.* Berlin/Göttingen/Heidelberg.

Mehrländer, U. 1978. 'Bundesrepublik Deutschland', in E. Gehmacher, D. Kubat, und U. Mehrländer (eds.), *Ausländerpolitik im Konflikt.* Bonn.

Meier-Braun, K.-H. 1980. *"Gastarbeiter" oder Einwanderer? Anmerkungen zur Ausländerpolitik in der Bundesrepublik Deutschland.* Frankfurt/Berlin/Vienna.

Von Philippovich, E. (ed.). 1898. *Auswanderung und Auswanderungspolitik in Deutschland.* Leipzig.

Reimann, H. 1980. 'Garstarbeiterpolitik zwischen Integration und Rotation', in Freund 1980.

Rist, R. 1978. *Guestworkers in Germany. The Prospects for Pluralism.* New York/London/Toronto.

Rittstieg, H. 1974. 'Gesellschaftliche Perspektiven des Ausländerrechts', in Ansay & Gessner 1974.

Schäfers, B. 1979. *Sozialstruktur und Wandel der Bundesrepublik Deutschland. Ein Studienbuch zu ihrer Soziologie und Sozialgeschichte.* Stuttgart.

Unger, K. 1980. *Ausländerpolitik in der Bundesrepublik Deutschland.* Bielefelder Studien zur Entwicklungssoziologie. Saarbrücken.

Wehler, H.-U. 1976. 'Die Polen im Ruhrgebiet bis 1918', in Wehler (ed.), *Moderne Deutsche Sozialgeschichte.* Cologne.

Switzerland

Almond and Powell 1966. *See General Section.*

Bickel, W. 1947. *Bevölkerungsgeschichte der Schweiz seit dem Ausgang des Mittelalters.* Zurich, Büchergilde Gutenberg.

Burckhardt, L.F. 1978 'Industry–labor relations: industrial peace', in Luck 1978, pp. 91–111.

Burckhardt, W. 1913. 'Die Einbürgerung der Ausländer in der Schweiz', *Schweizerisches Politisches Jahrbuch* (Bern, K.J. Wyss), 27: 1–114.

Fehrlin, W. 1952. *Die Rechtsgleichheit der Ausländer in der Schweiz.* Dissertation, University of Bern, Stampfli.

Frenkel, M. 1978. 'Swiss federalism in the twentieth century', in Luck 1978, pp. 323–38.

Frisch, M. 1967. *Oeffentlichkeit als Partner.* Frankfurt/Main, Suhrkamp.

Gruner, E. 1978. 'The political system of Switzerland', in Luck 1978, pp. 323–38.

Hoffmann-Nowotny 1973. *See General Section.*

Hoffmann-Nowotny and Hondrich 1982. *See General Section.*

Ilg, A. 1922. *Die Einbürgerungkraft Geburt auf Schweizerboden (Das Ius soli).* Dissertation, University of Zurich, Vienna, Schöler.

Langhard, J. 1913. *Das Niederlassungsrecht der Ausländer in der Schweiz.* Zurich, Orell Füssli.

Lembruch, G. 1967. *A Noncompetitive Pattern of Conflict Management in Liberal Democracies: The Case of Switzerland, Austria and Lebanon.* Paper presented at the Seventh World Congress of the International Political Science Association, Brussels.

Lijphart 1967. *See General Section.*

Luck, J.M. (ed.). 1978. *Modern Switzerland.* Palo Alto, Cal., The Society for the Promotion of Science and Scholarship.

Ludwig, C. (n.d.). *Die Flüchtlingspolitik in der Schweiz in den Jahren 1933 bis 1955. Bericht an den Bundesrat zuhanden der eidgenössischen Räte.* Bern, Bundeskanzlei.

Moser, H.P. 1967. ''Die Rechtsstellung des Ausländers in der Schweiz'', *Referate und Mitteilungen des schweizerischen Juristenvereins, Zeitschrift für Schweizerisches Recht* (Basel, Helbling & Lichtenhahn), pp. 327–488.

Petitmermet, P. 1923. ''Les principes à la base du droit d'établissement des étrangers en Suisse'', *Zeitschrift für Schweizerisches Recht* (Basel, Helbling & Lichtenhahn), pp. 97a–185a.

Rokkan, S. 1970. Foreword in Jürg Steiner, *Gewaltlose Politik und kulturelle*

Vierfalt, Hypothesen entwickelt am Beispiel der Schweiz. Bern und Stuttgart, Paul Haupt.

Ruth, M. 1934. *Das Fremdenpolizeirecht der Schweiz.* Zurich, Polygraphiser Verlag.

1937. "Das Schweizerbürgerrecht", *Zeitschrift für Schweizerisches Recht* (Basel, Helbling & Lichtenhahn), pp. 1a–156a.

Siegenthaler, H. 1978. "Switzerland in the twentieth century: the economy", in Luck 1978, pp. 91–111.

Schlaepfer, R. 1969. *Die Ausländerfrage in der Schweiz vor dem Ersten Weltkrieg.* Dissertation, University of Zurich, Juris Druck und Verlag.

Die Schweiz, Vom Bau der Alpen bis zur Frage nach der Zukunft, 1975. Zurich, Ex Libris.

Steiner, J. 1970. *Gewaltlose Politik und kulturelle Vielfalt, Hypothesen entwickelt am Beispiel der Schweiz,* Bern and Stuttgart, Paul Haupt.

Von Waldkirch, E. 1923. "Die Grundsätze des Niederlassungsrechts der Fremden in der Schweiz", *Zeitschrift für Schweizerisches Recht* (Basel, Helbling & Lichtenhaln), pp. 56a–95a.

Government documents
Bundesamt für Industrie, Gewerbe und Arbeit (BIGA) (ed.). 1964. *Das Problem der ausländischen Arbeitskräfte.* Bericht der Studienkommission für das Problem der ausländischen Arbeitskräfte. Bern, Eidgenössische Drucksachen- und Materialzentrale.

Index

Lightning Source UK Ltd.
Milton Keynes UK
09 March 2010

151126UK00001B/73/P

9 780521 124379